# Sustainable Tourism in Rural Europe

Rural Europe is a highly developed tourism region, representing advanced tourism experience and supposed modern approaches to this industry. That said, it remains highly sensitive and fragile in terms of environmental, social, economic and cultural impacts. This volume focuses on rural Europe as a fascinating example of how tourism development impacts on the communities and the environment of rural regions, and offers insights into how long-term sustainability could be achieved in this specific region, and, correspondingly, in other rural parts of the world.

*Sustainable Tourism in Rural Europe* contains contributions from leading international scholars that review and analyse the concept and practice of sustainable tourism in this region through a multidisciplinary approach which embodies the view that sustainable tourism warrants a holistic approach in terms of its impacts and development potential. Divided into three parts – Key Themes and Issues; the State and Development; and the Local Community and Development – this book addresses contentious and vital issues through theory, detailed research and case studies, offering real-world approaches to sustainable development, showing problems, including local politics, which challenge abstract models. It introduces cutting-edge research dealing with contemporary developments throughout Europe and offers consequential lessons/implications for other rural parts of the world.

This volume will be of interest to students, researchers and academics in the areas of Tourism, Geography and Environmental Studies.

**Donald V. L. Macleod**, Senior Lecturer, University of Glasgow, has researched in the Caribbean, the Canary Islands and Scotland. His research interests include globalization and cultural change, power, cultural heritage, identity, and sustainable tourism, all with a focus on international comparison and development.

**Steven A. Gillespie** is a Lecturer at the University of Glasgow, lecturing in the fields of Carbon Management and Environmental Stewardship. His research interests include population ecology, non-native species and, more recently, ecological attitudes, agritourism, tourism sustainability and climate change.

**Routledge Advances in Tourism**
Edited by Stephen Page
*London Metropolitan University*

# Sustainable Tourism in Rural Europe

Approaches to development

Edited by
Donald V. L. Macleod and
Steven A. Gillespie

Routledge
Taylor & Francis Group

LONDON AND NEW YORK

First published 2011
by Routledge
2 Park Square, Milton Park, Abingdon, Oxon OX14 4RN

Simultaneously published in the USA and Canada
by Routledge
270 Madison Avenue, New York, NY 10016

*Routledge is an imprint of the Taylor & Francis Group, an informa business*

Typeset in Sabon by
Book Now Ltd, London
Printed and bound in Great Britain by
CPI Antony Rowe, Chippenham, Wiltshire

*British Library Cataloguing in Publication Data*
A catalogue record for this book is available from the British Library

*Library of Congress Cataloguing in Publication Data*
Sustainable tourism in rural Europe/edited by Donald V. L. Macleod and
Steven A. Gillespie.
   p. cm.
Includes bibliographical references and index.
1. Ecotourism–Europe. 2. Sustainable development–Europe. 3. Rural
development–Europe. 4. Europe–Rural conditions. I. Macleod, Donald V. L.
II. Gillespie, Steven A.

G155.E8S89 2010
338.4′79 14-dc22                                            2010011590

ISBN: 978–0–415–54799–4 (hbk)
ISBN: 978–0–203–84421–2 (ebk)

# Contents

# Figures

# Tables

# Contributors

**Ausrine Armaitienė** is Associate Professor and Head of the Recreation and Tourism Department at Klaipeda University, Lithuania. She is co-author of the books *Rural Tourism* and *Tourism* (in Lithuanian) and Chief Editor of *Lithuanian–English Tourism Glossary*.

**Bill Bramwell** is Professor of Tourism at Sheffield Hallam University, UK. He co-edits the *Journal of Sustainable Tourism*, and he has edited books on tourism's relationships with partnerships, sustainability in Europe, rural development, and coastal areas in Southern Europe. His research interests include connections between tourism and environmental politics, governance arrangements, and actor perspectives on political economy.

**Catherine Brooks** is Research and Futures Executive with Yorkshire Futures, the Regional Intelligence Observatory. She was previously a Researcher at the European Regional Business and Economic Development Unit (ERBEDU), Leeds Metropolitan University, and the Centre for Regional Economic Development (CRED), University of Cumbria.

**Lynton J. Bussell** is a Senior Lecturer in Economics at Teesside University Business School, Middlesbrough. Prior to taking up this post he worked as a Research Economist at the Northern Development Company. He is currently carrying out research on environmental aspects of tourism within UK National Parks.

**Richard W. Butler** is Emeritus Professor at Strathclyde University. He has published more than a dozen books on tourism, including *The Tourist Area Life Cycle* (2 vols) (2006) and *Tourism and Indigenous Peoples* (2007) with T. Hinch, and has three books currently in press.

**Carl Cater** is a Lecturer in tourism at Aberystwyth University, Wales, and his research centres on the experiential turn in tourism and the subsequent growth of special interest sectors. He is a Fellow of the Royal Geographical Society, a qualified pilot, diver, mountain and tropical forest leader, and maintains an interest in both the practice and pursuit of sustainable outdoor tourism activity. He is co-author (with Erlet Cater) of *Marine Ecotourism: Between the Devil and the Deep Blue Sea* (CABI, 2007), and is an editorial board member of *Tourism Geographies*, the *Journal of Ecotourism* and *Tourism in Marine Environments*.

**Erlet Cater** is an Adjunct Associate Professor in Tourism at the University of Otago, New Zealand and Honorary Fellow in the Department of Geography, the University of Reading, UK. She is co-author, with Carl Cater, of *Marine Ecotourism: Between the Devil and the Deep Blue Sea* (CABI: 2007). She was also co-editor of *Ecotourism: A Sustainable Option?* (1994), an Advisory Editor for both *The Encyclopaedia of Ecotourism* and the *Encyclopaedia of Marine Ecotourism*.

**Samantha Chaperon** is a Lecturer in Events and Tourism Management at the University of Greenwich, UK. Her recently completed PhD thesis examines responses to the issues that surround tourism development and tourism governance in a core–periphery context, with a case study focus on the Maltese Islands.

**Anniken Førde** is Associate Professor in the Department of Sociology, Political Science and Community Planning at the University of Tromsø, Norway. Her research fields are gender studies, rural development, innovation and tourism. Among her publications are co-edited books on cross-disciplinarity and rural entrepreneurship.

**Steven A. Gillespie** is a Lecturer at the University of Glasgow, Dumfries Campus. He teaches in the fields of Environmental Stewardship and Carbon Management. Past research and interests include population ecology of intertidal bivalves, ecological impacts of invasive non-native species and, more recently, ecological attitudes, tourism sustainability and climate change.

**Stefan Gössling** is a Professor of Tourism Research at Linnaeus University, Kalmar, and Professor of Human Ecology at Lund University, both Sweden. He is also the Research Coordinator of the Research Centre for Sustainable Tourism, Western Norway Research Institute.

**C. Michael Hall** is Professor, Department of Management, University of Canterbury, New Zealand; Docent, Department of Geography, University of Oulu, Finland; and Visiting Professor, Linnaeus University School of Business and Economics, Kalmar, Sweden. Co-editor of *Current Issues in Tourism*, he has published widely on tourism and mobility, gastronomy and environmental history.

**Derek Hall** is a Visiting Professor at HAMK University of Applied Sciences, Finland, and has a number of visiting positions within the UK. He has been Head of Geography and Tourism at Sunderland University, and Head of the Department of Leisure and Tourism Management and both

Professor of Regional Development at the Scottish Agricultural College. His books include *Tourism in the New Europe: The Challenges and Opportunities of EU Enlargement* (lead editor); *Rural Tourism and Sustainable Business* (lead editor); and *Europe Goes East: EU Enlargement, Diversity and Uncertainty* (lead editor).

**Johan Hultman** is Associate Professor at the Department of Service Management, Lund University, Sweden. He writes and teaches on issues of nature and environment in tourism from a cultural analysis perspective. He is particularly interested in how nature is transformed into touristic value; how boundaries between nature and society are ordered through tourism and tourist practices; and how lifestyle entrepreneurship balances market rationales with the stewardship of nature.

**Eleri Jones** is a Professor and Director of Research in Cardiff School of Management at the University of Wales Institute, Cardiff. Her research is focused on small and medium-sized tourism enterprises and the challenges their strategic approach (or lack of it) pose to destination development. She has co-edited a book entitled *Tourism SMEs, Service Quality, and Destination Competitiveness* with her colleague Dr Claire Haven-Tang.

**Stratis Koutsoukos** is Deputy Director of the European Regional Business and Economic Development Unit (ERBEDU) and a Senior Lecturer at Leeds Business School. His expertise is on EU policy evaluation, EU Regional Policy and EU Business Studies. His publications include 'The Czech Republic's Structural Funds 2007–13: Critical Issues for Regional Regeneration', in *Urban Regional Management: International Perspectives* (2010).

**David Leslie** is Reader in Tourism at Glasgow Caledonian University. He has been awarded a Fellowship of the Tourism Society. His ongoing research in tourism has led to many publications. David is recognized for his work on tourism and sustainability, reflected in commissions to research progress in Local Agenda 21 and tourism and environmental performance. His publications include *Tourism Enterprises, Environmental Performance and Sustainable Development: Perspectives on Progress from across the Globe* (2009).

**Rory MacLellan** is currently a Lecturer in Tourism and is Programme Leader for Postgraduate Tourism Programmes in the School of Marketing, Tourism and Languages at Edinburgh Napier University. His teaching and research interests cluster around tourism and the natural environment, including rural tourism, sustainable tourism, ecotourism, wildlife tourism and niche markets in outdoor activities. He has published on aspects of tourism and public policy and tourism in the Scottish natural environment, including articles on wildlife holidays and sustainable tourism, and has co-edited a book entitled *Tourism in Scotland* (1998).

**Donald V. L. Macleod** is a Senior Lecturer at the University of Glasgow. He has researched in the Caribbean, the Canary Islands and Scotland and his publications include the books *Tourism, Power and Culture* (2010, co-editor), *Tourism, Globalisation and Cultural Change* (2004), *Niche Tourism in Question* (2003, editor), and *Tourists and Tourism* (1997, co-editor). His research interests include the anthropology of tourism, sustainable tourism development, globalization and cultural change, power, cultural heritage and identity.

**Breda McCarthy** is a Lecturer in Marketing at James Cook University, Townsville, Queensland. She is interested in the strategy formation process, with a particular focus on small to medium-sized enterprises. She is currently conducting case-based research where the focus is on the origins and the nature of networking practices in the arts-tourism sector.

**Ramunas Povilanskas** is Professor in the Department of Recreation and Tourism, Klaipeda University, Lithuania. His research interests currently focus on sustainability of destination management and application of Actor-Network Theory for seaside tourism analysis. He is author of *Landscape Management on the Curonian Spit: A Cross-border Perspective* (2004) where he analyses different tourism-related conflicts on a coastal territory.

**Tom Selwyn** is Professorial Research Associate in the Department of Anthropology, School of Oriental and African Studies, University of London, where he teaches the Anthropology of Tourism at postgraduate and undergraduate levels. Between 2001 and 2006, he directed two TEMPUS projects for the European Commission in Bosnia-Herzegovina and Palestine.

**William Suthers** has worked at Teesside University for over twenty years, initially as a public sector economist and latterly in the field of leisure, tourism and sport. He has published a number of articles and papers about the impact of local public transport since deregulation in 1986.

**David Watkins** trained as a science policy analyst. He is a Professor at Southampton Solent University. His books include *The Survival of the Small Firm: Entrepreneurship and the Economics of Survival* and *The Working Partnership: SMEs and Biodiversity*. He was founding editor of the *International Small Business Journal*.

# Preface

On the 22nd of May 2008 an international conference entitled 'Rural 2008' was organized by the Centre for Research into Regional Development (CRRED); it was hosted by the University of Glasgow and the University of the West of Scotland at the Crichton Campus in Dumfries, Scotland. The conference brought together experts on aspects of European regional development with a focus on rural issues. The idea for this book was developed from one specific panel at the conference: 'Rural regional development: sustainable tourism'; eight of the eighteen chapters in this book are based upon conference papers. Other contributors to the book were personally invited because of their renowned expertise in relevant subject areas, and as editors we would like to thank all the contributors for their sterling efforts in completing the work.

We must also gratefully acknowledge the European Regional Development Fund who match-funded the CRRED project with guidance provided by the South of Scotland European Partnership, enabling the conference to take place. Additionally, we thank the Dumfries-based staff at the University of Glasgow and the University of the West of Scotland for helping to support CRRED.

Donald V. L. Macleod and Steven A. Gillespie

# Introduction

*Donald V. L. Macleod*

This book deals with sustainable tourism in many ways: it addresses theoretical aspects and gives case studies; it utilizes methods from different academic disciplines; it looks at activities from differing perspectives relative to officialdom; it is a multi-disciplinary collection which embraces holistic analysis, context-driven understandings, conceptual critiques, political complexities as well as practical solutions. The regional focus of the book is Europe, in particular the rural parts, an area of great variety, and one which has often experienced tourism in different forms over many centuries; as an indicator of the region's continuing importance, it accounted for around just over half of all worldwide international tourist arrivals in 2008 (UNWTO 2009).

Certainly the specific sites discussed are unique, yet they all reveal experiences which can be relevant not only to other parts of Europe, but also to many places worldwide. Case studies offer contemporary examinations of key issues, with a critical eye, as well as a practical, realistic assessment. Rural Europe, because of its experience of tourism, and its modern infrastructure, but nevertheless occasionally fragile and sensitive composition, offers an excellent object of analysis from which to contemplate situations elsewhere in the world. For these and other reasons, this book makes a crucial and original new contribution to the literature on sustainable tourism.

The importance of rural destinations in regard to tourism sustainability partly relates to the visible and physical vulnerability of the rural environment, the flora, fauna and landscape of the countryside, together with small communities, often peripheral, which may be cultural enclaves with weak political representation. The countryside, as part of the rural setting, has historically been a popular destination for tourists in Europe, and so not only is there a strong association between many diverse hotspots and rural areas, but there is also a substantial history and experience on which to reflect and draw conclusions. Tourism academics have looked at rural areas (e.g. Gössling and Hultman 2006; Hall *et al.* 2003; Roberts and Hall 2001) and also focused on Europe as a region (e.g. Bramwell 2004; Hall *et al.* 2006; Priestley *et al.* 1996; Thomas and Augustyn 2006; Voase 2001) but no book on sustainable tourism dedicated to rural Europe as a whole has yet been published.

A broad, inclusive approach is taken in this book towards the concept 'rural' which is usually defined in terms of population density and size of settlement; for example, the England and Wales Countryside Agency definition excludes settlements with over 10,000 inhabitants. In Scotland, they define rural locations by population density and exclude local authorities of more than 100 persons per km sq; in Norway and Denmark, they only recognize agglomerations of fewer than 200 inhabitants as rural (Roberts and Hall 2001: 11). Other defining characteristics may include land use and economy, such as agriculture and forestry. Traditional social structures are also often associated with rural areas (Lane 1994; see Roberts and Hall 2001, for a detailed discussion of the term 'rural'). The chapters in this book illustrate the variety of situations that the notion of 'rural' embraces while indirectly disclosing commonalities.

Sustainable tourism has been the subject of much discussion in recent years largely following from the major debates on the concept of sustainable development boosted during the 1980s by the Brundtland Report (*Our Common Future*) produced by the World Commission on Environment and Development (WCED 1987; see France 1997, for discussion). There have since been numerous articles and books, as well as dedicated journals (such as the *Journal of Sustainable Tourism*) dealing with the topic (Bramwell *et al.* 1998; France 1997; Gössling *et al.* 2008; Hind and Mitchell 2004; Ioannides *et al.* 2001; Mowforth and Munt 1998; Weaver 2006). Definitions have largely been in agreement regarding resource protection, varying in emphasis on environment, economy and culture, for example, Weaver gives the following generalizing, embracing definition:

> Sustainable tourism may be regarded most basically as the application of the sustainable development idea to the tourism sector – that is, tourism development that meets the needs of the present without compromising the ability of future generations to meet their own needs, or, in concert with Budowski's (1976) 'symbiosis' scenario, tourism that wisely uses and conserves resources in order to maintain their long-term viability. Essentially, sustainable tourism involves the minimization of negative impacts and the maximization of positive impacts.
>
> (Weaver 2006: 10)

In contrast to the above, the following definition places a stronger emphasis on economic success:

> Sustainable tourism is tourism that is developed and maintained in a manner, and at such a scale, that it remains economically viable over an indefinite period and does not undermine the physical and human environment that sustains and nurtures it. It needs to be economically

sustainable, because if tourism is not profitable then it is a moot question to ask whether it is environmentally sustainable – tourism that is unprofitable and unviable will simply cease to exist.

(Ham and Weiler 2002: 36)

A different view is taken by Hardy, Beeton and Pearson in an article exploring the development of the concept 'sustainable tourism' in historical depth and with regard to the idea of sustainable development. They emphasize the relative lack of focus on the community impacted upon by tourism, and in their conclusion state:

> When sustainable tourism has been applied to the industry, more emphasis has often been given to tourism's effects upon the environment and economy, rather than to factors related to its effect on communities. This is ironic given that the definition in *Our Common Future* (WCED, 1987) defined sustainable development largely in terms of a process whereby local communities' subjective needs should be met. Based upon this, it is proposed here that future conceptualisations of sustainable tourism must address the local community to the same extent as the economy and the environment. This may be achieved through processes such as stakeholder involvement.
>
> (Hardy *et al.* 2002: 491)

Hunter (2003) is prepared to accept a variety of definitions within a paradigm similar to sustainable development; while Telfer and Sharpley (2008) link sustainable tourism development closely to sustainable development. Many scholars argue that sustainable tourism may be an ideal only to be strived for and never achieved (cf. Swarbrooke 1999; Ioannides *et al.* 2001). Nevertheless, the idea of sustainable tourism is crucial and of great importance to the industry as well as to the academic community. There is therefore a problem, both for academics and for those who plan, manage and run tourism destinations, in that sustainable tourism is apparently unachievable, elusive, and subject to a myriad of often unforeseen influences. Furthermore, there are always conflicting interests on site at the destination to deal with, as well as competition over resources, to say nothing of the numerous uncontrollable externalities such as economic disasters and climate change. And so, the academic and manager must struggle with the conceptual model of sustainable tourism, and most importantly, understand or be aware of the practical reality on the ground as it appears at the tourist destination.

While recognizing that the concept of 'development' is itself problematic (cf. Britton 1989; Croll and Parkin 1992; Sharpley and Telfer 2002), this book concentrates on the drive to develop sustainable tourism within a region regarded as part of the 'developed' world (despite having pockets of relative depravation). An abstract definition proposed by Sharpley (2002: 23) describes an appropriate approach: 'In short, development can be thought of as a philosophy, a process, the outcome or product of that process, and a plan guiding the process towards desired objectives.' Understandably, this collection does not claim to offer the solution to all problems related to sustainable tourism development in rural Europe, and by extension the world, but it does offer lessons to be learned from actual destinations as examined and contemplated by world-renowned experts. It gives detailed case studies, cutting edge analyses and well-informed opinions of problems and successes.

## Structure of the book

The book is divided into three parts: Part I: Key themes and issues; Part II: The state and development; and Part III: The local community and development. This division enables the focus to begin with a broad, primarily theoretical overview of central themes and issues, thereby setting the scene for the following two parts which are based on case studies. Parts II and III are divided in such a way as to give emphasis to the differing political influences and arrangements of tourism development, often referred to as 'top-down' and 'bottom-up', thereby locating the different actors and their roles in tourism, illustrating how such processes take place and the relevance of official and unofficial bodies, the local community and other stakeholders such as tourists.

### Part I Key themes and issues

This section is devoted to discussion of major themes and issues within tourism studies and related disciplines and begins with a discussion by Richard Butler in Chapter 1 on sustainable tourism and its relationship with the changing rural scene in Europe. He considers the definitions of 'sustainable tourism' and 'rural', acknowledging their complexity and variety while pointing out that coastal areas form an important part of the rural landscape, especially in terms of tourism activity. He also emphasizes the North–South divide in Europe between the colder and warmer parts of the continent which to a large degree have determined tourist behaviour, ranging from walking to sunbathing, and where the volume of visitors seeking sunshine directly impacts on natural resources, demonstrating the relevance of scale and types of tourism to sustainability.

Second homes have become popular in rural destinations and Butler explores the various positive and negative impacts they have on the local community, particularly in economic terms and regarding the utilization of resources. This issue has similarities with the growing trend for retirement to tourism destinations often by ex-tourists, which also places pressure on resources. Perhaps the most pertinent aspect of rural tourism in recent times for sustainability is the dramatic changes noted by Butler, including the increase in number of tourists due to mobility, wealth, and leisure time available, and the increase in types of activity, often involving machinery and the necessary infrastructural and facility development attending them, for example, ski-mobiles, jet-skiing on water, mountain-biking, and off-road driving. These changes bring a new type of activity and impact to rural locations, which Butler considers are often used as a playground for urbanites, and he sees them as causing a serious challenge to sustainability, including the traditional rural way of life. Butler has drawn our attention to the contemporary reality of tourism in rural areas, its lack of sustainability in many cases, and the growth of such tourism, which leads to the realization that there needs to be a renewed effort to understand and deal with the problems that may arise.

In Chapter 2, Michael Hall, Johan Hultman and Stefan Gössling treat mobility as a central concept and concern when considering tourism, locality and sustainable rural development. They contemplate changes in the rural economy which encourage agricultural diversification to include tourism, noting the importance of countryside capital, and above all they stress how mobility, in terms of access and actual travel methods, is a crucial component when considering development and climate change. The complex relationship between rural regions and urban centres is acknowledged and linkages, as well as aspects of social capital, are noted as highly relevant. They argue that the growing stress on a low carbon economy and the potential of slow mobility means that short-travel tourism in rural regions could be key to successful future developments.

David Leslie, in Chapter 3, examines sustainable tourism policy in rural Europe as implemented by the European Union (EU). He shows how tourism is currently on the EU agenda, whereas it was only marginal in earlier times prior to the 1990s. Tourism is recognized as important for the economy and jobs, and EU policy emphasizes enterprise and ecological efficiency. Tourism development has been heavily influenced by environmental policy, and the EU Sustainable Development Strategy has clear implications for tourism in areas such as transportation, conservation and management. Broadly, tourism is seen as a tool for socio-economic development and the EU Agenda for a Sustainable and Competitive European Tourism (2007) is discussed, as is the emphasis on small-scale locally managed, socially responsible tourism.

The issue of ecotourism in the wider rural context is dealt with by Erlet and Carl Cater in Chapter 4, who argue that a holistic approach should be developed recognizing complexities and interrelationships involving activities in and components of rural areas. They use the concept of spread effects and backwash effects resulting from rural ecotourism, and stress that ecotourism must be set in context regarding other economic activities, as well as global events such as climate change. Local communities should be involved in helping to define problems, where an adaptive management which adjusts to evolving situations is necessary to effect sustainable transition. This major 'meta-problem', they suggest, needs a trans-disciplinary approach.

Rural tourism should not be seen in absolute isolation from urban areas, and in Chapter 5, Derek Hall examines tourism in semi-rural environments, in particular, sustainability issues and experiences in the Baltic States. These marginal areas, Hall suggests, may hold pejorative connotations for both urban and rural residents, and the rural–urban fringe areas are character-ized, paradoxically as zones of interaction and repulsion, of mixed, conflicting, confused and dynamic land use. He gives three examples (near the cities of Riga, Vilnius and Kaunus) and shows how the theme of survival is pertinent to all – in physical and psychological manifestations – in a holo-caust memorial park, a castle and heritage village, and a monastery and nature park. These studies demonstrate conflicting land usage, the need to appreciate linkages between cities and rural areas, especially hinterlands, and the importance of cultural and natural resources therein.

## *Part II The state and development*

This section has a focus on top-down, state-driven official development and begins in Chapter 6 with an examination of the impact of EU funding on coastal tourism in Yorkshire by Stratis Koutsoukos and Catherine Brooks. Tourism is worth £6.3 billion to the Yorkshire and Humber region, providing 11 per cent of jobs, and is set firmly within the Regional Economic Strategy which includes climate change as a theme needing attention. Coastal tourism and resorts, including Whitby, have experienced a decline in recent decades, but are seen as worth regenerating for tourism. The EU Objective 2 Programme, among others, has been used to help lengthen tourism seasons and improve the product offering. As an aspect of these processes, they show how partnerships are seen as important and these are examined as well as the types of financial leverage achieved.

Continuing the themes of coastal destinations and official funding, in Chapter 7, Donald Macleod examines tourism on the Canary Island of La Gomera, and he puts it into the context of sustainable tourism development. He examines the history of tourism on the island, in particular showing how the types of tourist are changing gradually and increasing in variety and broadening their interests. A detailed examination is made of how offi-cialdom and the state use the concept of sustainable tourism in policies and planning strategies. Macleod raises the problem of mega-projects such as the airport and the new harbour at Valle Gran Rey, in terms of being wasteful of resources, environmentally unsuitable and out of tune with tourists and their needs. He argues that development should be 'appropriate scale devel-opment'. These issues are relevant to other similar rural destinations, espe-cially small islands, where tourism may be absolutely crucial to the economy: tourism must be considered holistically in relation to broader social, cultural, environmental and economic development, and in relation to global events.

In Chapter 8, Rory MacLellan considers the role of the Destination Management Organization (DMO), looking at the situation in Scotland and the relevance and appropriateness of the DMO for rural destinations. He notes the need for governance and leadership that the DMO can fulfil, and explores various models for destination management. Scotland has recently undergone political changes with devolution and, pertinently, changes to its tourism organizational structure, detailed by MacLellan. Conflict remains between agencies and within regions regarding the widespread development of the DMO and the allocation of general responsibilities. This is a particularly important development in Scotland where tourism forms a major part of the economy, but there may be losses in efficiencies as well as gains for independent activity as the DMO flourishes. Scotland proves to be a complex and highly relevant example for this type of tourism development.

Tom Selwyn, in Chapter 9, examines a programme funded by the European Commission which helps to build the capacities of institutions in partner countries, enabling them to engage in planning formulation and initiatives for the pilgrimage, tourism and cultural industries. The countries involved are Bosnia-Herzegovina and Palestine, both of which have serious economic, political and social difficulties, as well as possessing natural and cultural heritage assets. Both countries could gain substantially from tourism development. Selwyn outlines the university courses taught to the project participants and reviews some of the dissertations produced which give excellent insights into the current situation on the ground. This chapter draws our attention to the political and cultural construction of Europe, as well as its geographical boundaries and neighbours, and emphasizes the rich religious and ethnic composition of the broad region, which has occasionally led to major conflict and is still volatile.

In Chapter 10, Samantha Chaperon and Bill Bramwell examine views on the scale and types of tourism development in the rural peripheries, using the example of the island of Gozo, near Malta. They argue that the views of local residents can assist policy-makers to make better development and marketing decisions, as well as integrate tourism into broader sustainable development strategies. These 'emic' concerns are seen as helping to establish a more humanistic and critical appreciation of sustainable tourism development and the kind of information elicited is of particular use and relevance to peripheral areas. The specific attractions which Gozo possesses include an archaeological heritage reaching back some 7000 years and a traditional way of life which should be organized to attract a niche market of tourists different from those visiting Malta; thus unique qualities and distinctiveness need to be appreciated and maintained. This focus on local views leads into the next section.

### Part III The local community and development

This section focuses on grass-roots, bottom-up development and begins in Chapter 11 with an examination of recreational fishing as a major source of income by Ausrine Armaitiené, Eleri Jones and Ramunas Povilanskas. They look at approaches to the development of sustainable recreational fishing in the Nemunas Delta, part of the Curonian Lagoon in Lithuania which was previously part of the Soviet Union. They recognize the dilemma of whether to rely on commercial exploitation of declining fishing stocks, or shift to providing recreational fishing services. This is part of the largest coastal lagoon in Europe, a region famous for recreational fishing. There are conflicts between socio-economic development objectives and environmental objectives, and the study reveals obstacles to developing recreational fishing as an economic contributor, including the lack of professional skills and a scarcity of accommodation; but there are also 'excitement' factors attracting visitors including fish-cleaning, cooking and fish-smoking facilities. They conclude that commercial fishermen should be properly trained and funded to deal with stock reduction, a task which conservationists alone will not be successful in achieving. Moreover, they argue that local people need to be encouraged to regard the environment as a resource of sustainable economic development, and that conservation needs both top-down regulation and a grass-roots input from local knowledge.

The theme of fish and commerce in a former communist country is further pursued by David Watkins in Chapter 12, in which he focuses on a small family business in Hungary that is composed largely of a fish farm, and is rapidly turning into a tourist destination as well. Watkins considers the origins and development of the fisheries, the structure of the business operation, its principal activities and prospects for development. He also looks at conservation and ecotourism potential, the diversification into tourism and the evolving strategy of the business. Because of its transition from a communist country into a member of the European Union, businesses in Hungary have had a specifically fascinating and important experience, and the chapter details this, by concentrating on family members, their experiences, and the gradual evolution of the business into one which anticipates tourism as providing 40 per cent of its income by 2015.

Continuing the theme of fish and commerce, in Chapter 13, Anniken Førde considers the speedy transition of a small island community in Northern Norway from one based on commercial fishing to one which embraces recreational fishers and tourism following the collapse of the local fishing industry. Tourism has become a strategy for community development and local tourism enterprises have created a common profile of the island as 'the land of the big fish', with deep-sea trophy fishing becoming a kind of 'fish porn' exploiting and exhibiting the sizeable creatures caught. Førde shows how place image and narrative have been constructed by the community and argues that tourism as a strategy of community development implies a complex process of negotiating social identities. The project development group, forced by the collapse of the industry, had insisted on a community approach to business development and the municipality set up a development company which utilizes local knowledge.

The examination of a rural primary industry is continued in Chapter 14 in which Steven Gillespie makes a detailed exploration of agritourism in south-west Scotland. He defines and delineates this form of tourism and in well-documented research shows how important agritourism is to the region, and how necessary it can be for farmers themselves as a means of economic sustenance and also social support. Issues discussed include the gendered aspects of agritourism, the variety of accommodation involved, sustainability in terms of the economy and environment, and the social dimensions of agritourism. Furthermore, the challenges for operators in this business are made clear. This substantially evidenced research has relevance far beyond the borders of Scotland.

In Chapter 15, Lynton Bussell and William Suthers consider the Moorsbus service operating in the North York Moors in terms of a holistic approach to rural bus services. They point out the increased congestion due to tourism which has led to a search for solutions to alleviate the environmental impacts and overcrowding. The subsidized Moorsbus service was introduced to persuade private car drivers to switch to public transport and there were four objectives: to improve social inclusion; to reduce environmental impacts; to maintain links between rural communities; and to help stimulate the rural economy. There is discussion of the merits of a carrot or a stick approach regarding changing people from car travel to public transport usage, and it is argued that here may be the necessity for a 'stick' approach, to force change. However, they recognize that a deeper understanding of visitor typology and motivation is essential. The Moorsbus is seen as successful in reducing carbon emissions, providing access, reducing exclusion, and being of economic benefit to the community. The Park Authority has also realized that a more holistic approach towards operating the Moorsbus is needed which includes all stakeholders in order to reduce conflicts that threaten its viability.

Breda McCarthy, in Chapter 16, examines cultural tourism clusters with a focus on music in south-west Ireland, showing opportunities and problems encountered by small communities. Factors leading to successful clustering are pinpointed and the cultural tourism cluster is noted as consisting of a rather confused and eclectic range of organizations, activities and people. The cluster here is based on seasons, and is small, local and community-driven, but nevertheless it has links with global musical networks. This example gives key features including government involvement, a sophisticated demand pool, and is characterized by entrepreneurship with regional branding being a key outcome.

Finally, the Conclusion summarizes and comments on the following: general themes that have emerged throughout the chapters; the fundamental binary division of approaches to development in the book; the rural dimension of the examples given; broader issues relevant to the discussion, and the cultural context of sustainable tourism development.

## References

Bramwell, B. (ed.) (2004) *Coastal Mass Tourism: Diversification and Sustainable Development in Southern Europe.* Clevedon: Channel View.

Bramwell, B., Henry, I., Jackson, G., Goytia Prat, A., Richards, G. and Van der Straaten, J. (eds) (1998) *Sustainable Tourism Management: Principles and Practice.* Tilburg: Tilburg University Press.

Britton, S. (1989) 'Tourism, dependency and development: a mode of analysis', in T. V. Singh, H. L. Theuns and F. M. Go (eds) *Towards Appropriate Tourism: The Case of Developing Countries.* Frankfurt: Verlag Peter Lang GmbH, pp. 93–116.

Budowski, G. (1976) 'Tourism and environmental conservation: conflict, coexistence, or symbiosis?' *Environmental Conservation,* 3: 27–31.

Coccossis, H. (1996) 'Tourism and sustainability: perspectives and implications', in G. K. Priestley, J. A. Edwards, and H. Coccossis (eds) *Sustainable Tourism? European Experiences.* Wallingford: CABI.

Croll, E. and Parkin, D. (eds) (1992) *Bush Base Forest Farm: Culture, Environment and Development.* London: Routledge.

France, L. (ed.) (1997) *The Earthscan Reader in Sustainable Tourism.* London: Earthscan Publications.

Gössling, S. and Hultman, J. (eds) (2006) *Ecotourism in Scandinavia: Lessons in Theory and Practice.* Wallingford: CABI.

Gössling, S., Hall, C. M. and Weaver, D. (eds) (2008) *Sustainable Tourism Futures.* London: Routledge.

Hall, D., Roberts, L. and Mitchell, M. (eds) (2003) *New Directions in Rural Tourism.* Aldershot: Ashgate.

Hall, D., Smith, M. and Marciszweska, B. (eds) (2006) *Tourism in the New Europe: The Challenges and Opportunities of EU Enlargement.* Wallingford: CABI.

Ham, S. H. and Weiler, E. (2002) 'Interpretation as the centrepiece of sustainable wildlife tourism', in R. Harris, T. Griffin and P. Williams (eds) *Sustainable Tourism: A Global Perspective.* Oxford: Elsevier.

Hardy, A., Beeton, J. S. and Pearson, L. (2002) 'Sustainable tourism: an overview of the concept and its position in relation to conceptualisations of tourism', *Journal of Sustainable Tourism* 10(6): 475–96.

Hind, D. and Mitchell, J. (eds) (2004) *Sustainable Tourism in the Lake District.* Oxford: Business Education Publishers.

Hunter, C. (2003) 'Aspects of the sustainable tourism debate from a natural resource perspective', in R. Harris, T. Griffin and P. Williams (eds) *Sustainable Tourism: A Global Perspective.* Oxford: Elsevier.

Ioannides, D., Apostolopoulos, Y. and Sonmez, S. (eds) (2001) *Mediterranean Islands and Sustainable Tourism Development.* London: Continuum.

Lane, B. (1994) 'What is rural?' *Journal of Sustainable Tourism* 2(1–2): 7–21.

Mowforth, M. and Munt, I. (1998) *Tourism and Sustainability: New Tourism in the Third World.* London: Routledge.

Priestley, G. K., Edwards, J. A. and Coccossis, H. (eds) (1996) *Sustainable Tourism? European Experiences.* Wallingford: CABI.

Roberts, L. and Hall, D. (2001) *Rural Tourism and Recreation: Principles to Practice.* Wallingford: CABI.

Sharpley, R. (2002) 'Tourism: a vehicle for development?', in R. Sharpley and D. J. Telfer (eds) *Tourism and Development: Concepts and Issues.* Clevedon: Channel View, pp. 11–34.

Sharpley, R. and Telfer, D. J. (eds) (2002) *Tourism and Development: Concepts and Issues.* Clevedon: Channel View.

Swarbrooke, J. (1999) *Sustainable Tourism Management.* Wallingford: CABI.

Telfer, D. J. and Sharpley, R. (2008) *Tourism and Development in the Developing World.* London: Routledge.

Thomas, R. and Augustyn, M. (eds) (2006) *Tourism in the New Europe: Perspectives on SME Policies and Practices.* Oxford: Elsevier Science.

UNWTO (2009) *Tourism Highlights: 2009 Edition.* Madrid: UNWTO.

Voase, R. (ed.) (2001) *Tourism in Western Europe: A Collection of Case Histories.* Wallingford: CABI.

WCED (World Commission on Environment and Development) (1987) *Our Common Future.* Melbourne: Oxford University Press.

Weaver, D. (2006) *Sustainable Tourism: Theory and Practice.* Oxford: Elsevier.

# Part I
# Key themes and issues

# 1 Sustainable tourism and the changing rural scene in Europe

*Richard W. Butler*

## Introduction

Sustainable tourism in its many forms might be thought of as a highly appropriate land use to be integrated into the rural landscape of Europe, and indeed, in some respects this is true. In a number of situations, however, what might pass for sustainable tourism can be seen to be incompatible in varying degrees with the modern forms of rural land use that now pervade Europe (Sharpley 2001). Tourism in rural areas goes under a variety of names, rural tourism, agritourism and farm tourism, for example, and has changed significantly over recent decades (Butler 1998), as have views of the 'appropriate' form and function of rural areas (Halfacree 1997). Legislation and policies have resulted in different priorities and economic values for land and land use in rural areas, some of which have been beneficial to tourism, and some of which have tended to be contrary to the goals of sustainable tourism (Cloke 1999).

The chapter explores the patterns and roles of tourism, both sustainable and conventional forms of the activity, in the dynamic landscape of rural Europe and its competing land uses. Much tourist activity takes place out of doors and traditionally there has been an argument for an important relationship between environmental quality and tourist satisfaction. It would be reasonable, therefore, to assume that tourism in rural areas, in Europe, as elsewhere in the world, would be an activity that was welcomed and encouraged by those making a living in rural areas and by tourists themselves (ETC 2001). Such is not always the case, and it would be unwise to assume that tourists and rural residents automatically have a positive relationship, or that tourism and other economic activities in rural areas are always compatible. Similarly, it would be incorrect to imagine that tourism in rural areas of Europe can be generalized as to nature and extent across the continent. Tourism, in sustainable or unsustainable form, is often seen as a disturbance and an unwelcome intrusion into rural areas, and its success or failure depends greatly on the form of tourism being practised and the nature of the rural area in which it is taking place (Briedenhann 2007). Compounding this situation is the fact that both tourism and the rural areas of Europe have undergone massive and numerous changes in the past half century (Halfacree 2006; Hall *et al.* 2003), and to some degree the casual observer of tourism in rural areas often has a perception that is decades behind the current reality (Bunce 2003; Cloke 2003). This chapter introduces some of the major issues and changes that face tourism in rural areas in Europe and speculates briefly on implications for future patterns and possible areas of potential conflict.

## Key issues

There are a number of issues and concerns that are common throughout Europe in the context of tourism in rural areas (Anastasiadou 2008). In most cases, there is little difference between sustainable and non-sustainable tourism in terms of the nature of the relationship with agriculture and other rural pursuits (Butler and Hall 1998). First among these is the issue of definitions.

### Definitions

At the root of any discussion on sustainable tourism in rural areas are the definitions of sustainable tourism and rural area (Bell 2006). Since the introduction of the term 'sustainable development' into common usage (WCED 1987) and its application to tourism, there has been considerable discussion, uncertainty and confusion over what is meant by 'sustainable tourism'. It is unresolved whether it means a form of tourism that is sustainable (viable) or a form of tourism that is symbiotically related to all other forms of human activity and the environment in which it is practised (Butler 1993). This chapter is not the place to attempt to resolve this discussion, if it is capable of being resolved at all, but suffice it to say that in this context sustainable tourism is taken to mean tourism that operates and is operated in line with the principles of sustainable development (which include inter and intra generational equity, a long-term view, operating within limits and with a triple bottom line in terms of priorities). 'Rural area' is similarly difficult to define without disagreement, in part because of its traditional links in many people's perceptions with agriculture, and in part because if it is taken as the opposite of urban, there remains the problem of 'suburban' areas and wilderness areas. In this chapter, rural areas are taken to be those parts of Europe beyond urban areas but which are settled, i.e. they have a human presence on a permanent basis. They may or may not be under agricultural production (Clemmons 2004). The human presence is important, as it is this which distinguishes these areas from wilderness and which also at least partly explains why conflicts and disagreements arise when tourism takes place in these areas (Hallikainen 2001).

One further issue related to definitions exists. There is often an inappropriate perception that rural areas are inland, a view that tends to be reinforced by image and advertisement, as pictures of rural areas rarely show coastal locations (Häyrynen 2004). As noted below, coastal rural areas are highly popular tourist destinations, probably more so than inland rural locations, and thus any focus on tourism in rural areas should include tourism to coastal destinations also, not just valleys, mountains and market towns in the interior of Europe. As well, while rural areas are attractive to tourists, it must be remembered most tourists are by definition international visitors (see the United Nations World Tourism Organisation 2008 definition; (UNWTO-UNEP-WMO 2008) and that in most European countries they visit urban centres in far larger numbers than they visit rural destinations. The great European cities such as London, Paris, Madrid, Rome, are the key destinations for tourists when they travel abroad, along with resorts such as Benidorm, Palma, Blackpool, Malaga, and Nice. Much leisure visitation to the rural areas of Europe is by domestic 'tourists' or recreationists (Butler *et al.* 1998a) rather than their foreign counterparts. As most people spend only a few weeks away on holiday, frequently only one or two weeks, the level of visitation to rural areas is necessarily limited. The fact that visitors can access most sites in large urban centres or large resorts on foot or by public transport but need a car to access most rural areas, particularly those that are 'deeply' rural, means that foreign visitors using public transport (rail, air, ship) would need to hire a car to visit rural areas, which can be a deterrent or at least a financial constraint. Thus if strict definitions are held to, numbers of visitors engaged in sustainable tourism to rural areas would be small compared to all tourism visitors to rural areas and tiny when measured against all tourists across Europe. A somewhat less circumscribed scenario will be used in the discussions below.

In summary, it can be argued that when considering sustainable tourism in rural areas we should be considering those forms of tourism that are compatible with other rural activities and the rural environment in its many forms, from the northern tundra to the Mediterranean semi-desert landscape (Sharpley 2004). The forms of tourism that can be regarded as sustainable should also be of such a form and at such a scale that they do not negatively affect the environments (economic, physical and social) in which they are practised to such a degree that they cause irreparable and undesirable change (Butler 1993).

## The North–South divide

It was noted above that there is great diversity in the environment of Europe and this is mirrored by activities and attitudes of tourists in rural areas in Europe (Roberts and Hall 2001). Many of the differences in behaviour of sustainable or other tourists across Europe can be related to differences in climate, in physical geography and in culture. That may appear a rather reactionary deterministic viewpoint and so some specific examples may be necessary to justify such a view. The great variation in climate between northern Europe (Scandinavia, the UK, Ireland) and Mediterranean/Adriatic Europe (Greece, Italy, Malta, Cyprus, the Balkans) has meant that much of the tourism practised in rural and coastal areas in the south is 'sun' tourism, what is often termed 'mass tourism' (Butler and Stiakaki 2001; Farsari *et al.* 2007). Such tourism, often quite unfairly, is regarded as unsustainable, undesirable and unsupportive in its destinations, although rarely by those making a living from tourism in such areas.

Tourism in southern Europe is primarily based on the marine coastline and climate, and to a lesser degree cultural and historical heritage, and popularized greatly by northern Europeans (UNEP *et al.* 2000), and in recent years also by locals in increasing numbers as the southern countries have benefitted from the economic regional development policies of the European Union (Clemmons 2004; Fleischer and Felenstein 2000). Tourism in Northern Europe, on the other hand, has relatively few sun-seeking elements, and much more emphasis is put upon active pursuits such as hiking, and nature observation, with the appeal lying in the landscape, and the cultural and natural heritage of the region (Hallikainen 1998). Those engaging in tourism in northern Europe tend also to be more active, more 'green', more affluent, and more educated on average than those heading to the southern beaches (Lehtinen 2006). The much desired 'upmarket sustainable tourist' (Ioannides and Holcomb 2003) compared to the 'golden hordes' in these comments are highly generalized in order to support the argument, and there are certainly tourists who visit southern Europe and avoid beach resorts, but relatively few of them visit or stay in rural areas, most concentrating on the cultural and historic centres such as Florence, or Athens (Ioannides *et al.* 2001). Some certainly find their way to the vineyards of the Rhone, the monasteries of Greece, the Trudos Mountains in Cyprus and coastal villages in Istria, but they are small in number in both relative and absolute terms.

In northern Europe, much of the rural visitation is to cultural and historic sites, or to impressive natural landscapes, including places such as the national parks in the United Kingdom or in the Tatra of central Europe, coastal settlements and the high plateau in Scandinavia, and of course the Alpine valleys in Germany, Austria and Switzerland in particular. In the offshore islands of Europe, this North–South divide is equally, if not more evident than on the mainland. The southern islands of the Mediterranean (the Balearics, Malta, Cyprus), the Canaries (Bianchi 2004), the Azores and to a lesser extent Madeira, all rely heavily on 'mass tourism', and efforts to develop sustainable tourism, for example, in Calvia in Mallorca, have generally had limited success at best (Dodds 2007; Ioannides *et al.* 2001). Tourism to northern and western isles such as the Hebrides, Orkney, Shetland, the Faroes, Iceland and the Lofotens is almost all related to the natural and cultural heritage of those locations, with fewer family groups with children and more elderly couples represented in the tourist market (Butler 2006).

*Second homes*

A feature of tourism in rural areas for many years has been the presence of second homes (also known as holiday homes, cottages, weekend retreats, and country estates). Second homes, often increasingly 'purpose built for an inessential purpose' as Wolfe (1977) succinctly described them, have been a source of concern in many rural areas in Europe for a long time, and this 'problem' has increased rather than decreased over the years (Brougham and Butler 1981) reflecting increased affluence, mobility, and time, on the one hand, and dissatisfaction with the quality of life in urban areas, on the other. The result has been an unequal financial competition for rural properties, on the one side, by rural residents or would-be residents in specific locations, and, on the other, by generally more affluent urbanites seeking access to rural 'idyllity' (Bunce 2003; Coppock 1977). While the properties involved in this competition may be seen as being 'taken away' in the view of rural-based individuals who desire them for permanent homes, in many cases they are properties no longer desired by their rural owners, no longer serving their original purpose as rural labourers' homes or homes for extended family members. Thus to the sellers they are often a form of retirement income or pension pot, and while they may share their neighbours' concerns over the effects increasing absentee landlords may have on community viability and social intercourse, the chance of well-deserved financial support to match often low levels of financial return from agricultural practices often takes precedence (Gannon 1994).

It is appropriate to speculate about the sustainability of such phenomena as second homes in rural settings. Tourism based on these premises inevitably involves travel, most frequently by car (especially in the UK, and in Scandinavia), and increasingly in the case of property owners in rural France, Spain, and Ireland, by air as well as car, and thus can be viewed as highly unsustainable, as well as having some undesirable ecological impacts (Hiltunen 2007). On the other hand, the almost universal upgrading of such properties by new owners can be important in maintaining the viability of local suppliers of skilled work, and hence the sustainability of local communities, and in some cases certainly, increasing the market for locally supplied produce, from food to crafts (Countryside Commission 1995). Thus much depends on the activities engaged in while utilizing the second homes. In Northern Europe, particularly Scandinavia, activities such as walking, cross-country skiing in winter, fishing, observing nature, collecting berries and other native food stuffs are particularly important and can generally be regarded as sustainable (Müller 2007; Sandell 2006). In Southern Europe, especially the Mediterranean littoral, second homes are much more likely to be associated with sun and sea-related activities which may be seen as less sustainable.

Another factor enters the discussion here, and that is the fact that it would appear that many of the second homes in northern Europe are properties which already belonged to the family using them and have been inherited by the current generation (Pitkänen 2008). Many of these properties will have been traditional family homes or properties, now no longer used by past family members who were inhabitants of the rural areas. Thus such properties are maintained and often 'improved' in the sense of being made more sustainable in terms of lower energy consumption. On the other hand, many of the properties in southern Europe match Wolfe's description (see above) and have been built specifically as second homes for the tourist market, thus representing a net loss of rural land and overall sustainability rather than a possible net gain in sustainability as in the case of their northern counterparts (Ilbery 1998). There is no easy solution to the issue of second homes and tourism in rural areas. In some situations they represent the continuation of family links with a region and in such situations are generally found much less objectionable than properties bought for tourism purposes by people who have no links with the community (Brougham and Butler 1981; McIntyre *et al.* 2006). They may be a form of economic sustainability, representing wealth transference from urban to rural areas and provide an increased market for rural produce and labour. Alternatively they can represent 'unfair' competition for rural housing, loss of rural agricultural land and production, increased demands on power and water supplies, and unsustainable consumption of energy to reach them, as well as a source of undesirable activities that disturb local permanent residents. The continuum is a long one and has been met by both positive support for holiday villages and also by threats and actions in the form of arson and damage (Coppock 1977). It is an issue that is likely to remain a bone of contention in rural areas as long as these parts of Europe are seen as desirable playgrounds by urban residents, a viewpoint that is long established and unlikely to change in the foreseeable future (Bell 2006; Hall *et al.* 2003).

Related to the second home issue discussed above is that of retirement to the countryside on amenity and leisure grounds, which often has its origins in earlier tourist visitation to rural areas. Rural areas of Europe are increasingly seen by many as eminently preferable environments to the urban settings in which most people live (Hopkins 1998; Horton 2008). Like those who can afford to purchase or rent a second home in a rural area, those able to live in rural areas and work in an urban settlement often choose to resettle in rural environs, a practice made easier by efficient rail and road connections in many European countries (Cloke 1999). For those not able to live in rural areas but work in cities, there is still the possibility of retiring to amenity locations once their working life is completed. Popular tourist destinations often become popular retirement locations, a trend long existing in the United Kingdom, for example, where the south coast of England has been a retirement focus for close to a century, a fact noted by Gilbert (1939). In more recent decades, this pattern has been repeated in Spain in particular (Barke 2004) where the various Costas and their interiors have become converted into settlements for retirees from northern Europe, many of whom first visited the regions as conventional tourists. European legislation prohibiting the prevention of foreigners buying property in other European Union member states has enabled this practice, often at the expense of rural residents, who, as in the case of second homes, cannot compete with more affluent retirees. As well, there is little evidence that retirement in rural areas by non-residents is in any way a sustainable practice, placing as it does increasing demands for power, water, and other utilities and services on rural communities. Thus even if the initial visits were for sustainable tourism, subsequent commuting or retirement does not continue this form of visitation.

### Changes in rural tourism

Tourism (of all types) that involves agriculture directly does not have a long history, although tourist visitation to agricultural areas does, particularly in the United Kingdom and the north central countries of Europe such as France, Switzerland, Germany, the Low Countries and to a lesser degree Italy (Butler *et al.* 1998b). In early days, people visited rural areas mostly to view the landscape and in smaller numbers to hunt and fish. Only the very rich could afford to stay in rural areas on holiday, and then it was normally in the form of their own estates (such as Balmoral or Sandringham of the Royal estates in the United Kingdom) or second homes (see below). It is perhaps appropriate to note, however, that while hunting and fishing are resource-extractive activities, they are almost always managed on a sustained yield (or sustainable) basis as the value of the resources is dependent on their continuing reproduction at satisfactory levels year after year.

One of the few exceptions to this pattern of use is found in some Mediterranean areas, for example, Malta, where shooting of wild birds, generally on migration to and from northern Europe, has traditionally been uncoordinated, uncontrolled and illegal. Only in recent years following Malta's membership in the European Union and pressure from various NGOs, has some element of sustainability appeared, although much of the shooting activity is still technically illegal. Mass visitation to rural areas was impossible for the vast majority of people before the advent of mass transportation, and thus did not precede the railway and particularly the motor car. The great popularization of rural areas for tourism in Europe is essentially post-Second World War, although rural areas were used for short-term recreation and leisure pursuits by local residents and those living close to the countryside for many centuries (Hall *et al.* 2003; Sharpley 2004). Much of this tourism was essentially viewing rural areas and rural pursuits, rather than active engagement in rural-related activities (Busby and Rendle 2000; Saarinen 2004). Rural resident involvement in tourism was mostly in terms of the provision of produce and of accommodation, particularly in inns and following the advent of car-borne tourism, in private residences in the form of bed and breakfast provision. Little of this was related specifically to rural activities or to sustainable tourism, although the tourism was perhaps sustainable in the sense that it was at such a low level in terms of numbers that there were few negative impacts and little exceeding of limits, a situation improved by more appropriate management intervention (Romeiro and Costa 2010).

Over the past few decades, however, tourism in rural areas in Europe has seen the emergence of several different variations, including farm tourism, agritourism, wine tourism, gastronomic tourism and festival tourism, all of which have involved close links between tourism and rural communities (McGehee 2007; Roberts and Hall 2001). In many cases across Europe these forms of tourism have been actively promoted by levels of government from commune/parish/village level up to and including the European Union, with financial and technical support becoming available in increasing amounts as these forms of tourism were seen as both sustainable in a general sense and also capable of increasing employment and hence the economic viability of rural communities and regions. The European Union LEADER (*Liaison Entre Actions de Développement de l'Economie Rurale*) projects, engaged in enthusiastically in Portugal (Kastenholz 2000) and several Mediterranean countries in particular have seen considerable investment in rural festivals, wine routes, and agritourism. The appearance of 'slow food' in Italy has similarly provided a stimulus to rural gourmet tourism, and wine tourism, popular in France and Germany for many years, has seen considerable growth in Italy, Portugal and Spain as well. Europe has seen much less in the way of development of farm tourism, however, than has occurred in other parts of the world. There are very few equivalents of the 'dude ranches' of the United States, popularized in the movies *City Slickers* (I and II), and farm holidays have not been as popular in Europe as, for example, in New Zealand.

Thus tourism use of rural areas has been and remains essentially a spectator pastime, with relatively little participation in rural activities: visits to a farm, perhaps, rather than participation on a farm. Most tourist activities have been reasonably sustainable, or at least not unsustainable. However, increasingly in recent years, the nature of many tourist activities in rural areas has changed to become less sustainable because these activities have become more technologically dependent. Improved or at least increased technology has given rise to increased mobility within the rural environment as well as easier access to the rural environment, thus allowing more people to visit those areas and to visit more parts of those areas than before. This phenomenon was experienced dramatically in North America from the 1970s onwards with the appearance of the snowmobile (Butler 1974) with subsequent impacts (safety, trespass, damage, environmental, criminal, noise and disturbance) on rural residents. Thus rural areas in Europe now are exposed not only to far greater numbers of tourists than before, but to many visitors who are not engaged in what might be regarded as sustainable tourism activities (Cavaco 1995; Kastenholz 2000; Roberts and Hall 2001).

Many visitors now require specific facilities to engage in their chosen activities, whether this be trails for skiing, for walking, for mountain biking or off-road vehicles from cars to motor bikes and quad bikes, or slipways to provide access to water bodies for swimming, sailing, wind-surfing, power boating, and water and jet-skiing (the last a spin-off from snowmobiling with similar effects). Whereas what might have been regarded as 'traditional' forms of tourism in rural areas (e.g. sight-seeing, walking, nature study, bird-watching, art, picnics, photography, heritage resource visitation) were generally compatible with each other and with agricultural activities in general, or in many ways 'sustainable', the newer activities such as mountain biking, off-roading, power-boating, jet-skiing, water-skiing, even 'twitching' (near-competitive bird watching) are not only less compatible, if not incompatible with each other and the older forms of tourism, as well as other rural activities, they are much less sustainable by any definition of the term. Thus the potential for conflict and disagreement over level and type of tourism in rural areas is inevitable. Cross-country skiers encountering snowmobilers in northern Europe face similar problems to those observing birds in the Camargue being disturbed by motorized visitors, or walkers in the United Kingdom meeting off-road users using cars and motor-bikes. It is not simply a case of motorized versus non-motorized users or sustainable versus less sustainable users, but a deeper problem of the increasing inability of rural areas, even protected ones, to accommodate a significantly increased number and variety of tourist visitors (Bowler *et al.* 1992; Sandell 2006).

## Conclusion

This chapter has not presented a very positive picture of sustainable tourism in rural areas in Europe, but it can be argued that despite the considerable rhetoric and good intentions to the contrary, much of the increased tourism to rural areas has not been of the sustainable variety. In the promotion of agritourism and the other forms of sustainable tourism (Fleischer and Felenstein 2000; *The Times* 2009; Williams and Balaz 2010), it is often forgotten that much of the mass conventional tourism in coastal regions of Europe has taken place in what were originally rural areas, and it is tourism itself which has converted those erstwhile rural communities into urban tourism centres. Whether that process is 'good' or 'bad' is not for discussion here, neither can it be resolved here whether traditional mass tourism is actually less environmentally impactful on a per capita basis than the more upmarket so-called sustainable tourism or not. What is important is to note that tourism, sustainable and unsustainable, is an ever increasing presence in rural areas throughout Europe, partly as a result of population increase and movement, and partly because increased tourism reflects increased mobility, affluence and leisure time, as well as a well-established and continuing perception that rural areas are playgrounds for urban residents.

Such a situation inevitably results in areas of potential conflict or at least disagreement. The issue of alienation of property from traditional rural residents and activities for leisure purposes has already been discussed. Different attitudes about development and 'modernization', including the development of transportation facilities and similar infrastructural issues abound in rural areas as in all communities, with incomers and long-term residents often holding opposing views. Such scenarios are likely to increase if current trends of movement from urban to rural areas for amenity and leisure purposes continue in the future. Making the countryside more attractive as a destination for tourists and recreationists (Sharpley 2007), while possibly assisting rural regional redevelopment, also makes such areas more attractive and accessible for all urban residents, even if not everyone wants to visit or live in the countryside (Williams 2009). While compensation may be provided to farmers for allowing increased access to land (*The Times* 2009) and for taking land out of agricultural production (Williams and Balaz 2010), such steps are not always seen as beneficial to traditional rural ways of life (Horton 2008). Indeed, many of the steps taken to ensure a more sustainable future often meet opposition from traditional and entrenched viewpoints (Gössling *et al.* 2009). The fact that many such policies are created by politicians in urban centres and do not originate in rural communities also helps explain some of the resentment to the changing priorities being 'imposed' on rural areas, and the fact that at least some rural residents feel the countryside is seen as little more than a playground and a setting for urban-based tourism and recreation. Whether these activities are sustainable or unsustainable is of relatively little importance compared to the effects on traditional rural life that they are perceived to have.

Efforts to improve the lot of farmers and other rural residents therefore, may in fact be accentuating this pattern of use. As Frost and Jay (1967: 69) wrote many years ago in relation to the countryside, 'As long as it is defended for what it is not by those who do not know it, and exploited for what it is by those who do, it is likely to go on suffering for a very long time to come.'

## References

Anastasiadou, C. (2008) 'Tourism interest groups in the EU policy arena: characteristics, relationships and challenges', *Current Issues in Tourism* 11(1): 24–62.

Barke, M. (2004 'Rural tourism in Spain', *International Journal of Tourism Research* 6(3): 137–49.

Bell, D. (2006) 'Variations on the rural idyll', in P. Cloke, T. Marsden and P. H. Mooney (eds) *Handbook of Rural Studies*. London: Sage, pp. 147–60.

Bianchi, R. (2004) 'Tourism restructuring and the politics of sustainability: a critical view from the European periphery (the Canary Islands)', *Journal of Sustainable Tourism* 12(6): 495–529.

Bowler, I. R., Bryant, C. R. and Nellis, M. D. (1992) *Contemporary Rural Systems in Transition:* Vol. 2, *Economy and Society*. Wallingford: CABI.

Briedenhann, J. (2007) 'The role of the public sector in rural tourism: respondents' views', *Current Issues in Tourism* 10(6): 584–607.

Brougham, J. E. and Butler, R. W. (1981) 'The application of segmentation analysis to explain resident attitudes to social impacts of tourism', *Annals of Tourism Research* 8(4): 569–90.

Bunce, M. (2003) 'Reproducing rural idylls', in P. Cloke (ed.) *Country Visions.* Harlow: Pearson, pp. 14–30.

Busby, G. and Rendle, S. (2000) 'The transition from tourism on farms to farm tourism', *Tourism Management* 21(6): 635–42.

Butler, R. W. (1974) 'The impact of off road vehicles on travel', *Journal of Travel Research* XIII(1): 1–7.

—— (1993) 'Tourism: an evolutionary perspective', in J. G. Nelson, R. W. Butler and G. Wall (eds) *Tourism and Sustainable Development: Monitoring, Planning, Managing.* Waterloo: Heritage Resources Centre, pp. 27–44.

—— (1998) 'Rural recreation and tourism', in B. Ibery (ed.) *The Geography of Rural Change.* Harlow: Longman, pp. 211–32.

—— (2006) 'Contrasting coldwater and warmwater island tourist destinations', in G. Balcacchino (ed.) *Advances in Tourism Research, Extreme Tourism: Lessons from the World's Cold Water Islands.* London: Macmillan.

Butler, R. W. and Hall, C. M. (1998) 'The sustainability of tourism and recreation in rural areas', in R. W. Butler, C. M. Hall and J. Jenkins (eds) *Tourism and Recreation in Rural Areas.* London: Routledge, pp. 249–58.

Butler, R. W. and Stiakaki, E. (2001) 'Tourism and sustainability in the Mediterranean: issues and implications from Hydra', in D. Ioannides, Y. Apostolopoulos and S. Sonmez (eds) *Mediterranean Islands and Sustainable Tourism Development: Practices, Management and Policies.* London: Continuum, pp. 282–300.

Butler, R. W., Hall, C. M. and Jenkins, J. M. (1998a) 'Introduction', in R. W. Butler, C. M. Hall and J. M. Jenkins (eds) *Tourism and Recreation in Rural Areas.* London: Routledge, pp. 3–16.

—— (1998b) *Tourism and Recreation in Rural Areas.* London: Routledge.

Cavaco, C. (1995) 'Rural tourism: the creation of new tourist spaces', in A. Montonari and A. Williams (eds) *European Tourism: Regions, Spaces and Restructuring.* Chichester: John Wiley & Sons, Ltd, pp. 129–49.

Clemmons, R. (2004) 'Keeping farmers on the land: agritourism in the European Union', *Iowa Agricultural Review* 10(3): 8–9.

Cloke, P. (1997) 'Country backwater to virtual village? Rural studies and "the cultural turn"', *Journal of Rural Studies* 13(4): 367–75.

—— (1999) 'The country', in P. Cloke, P. Crang and M. Goodwin (eds) *Introducing Human Geographies.* London: Arnold, pp. 256–67.

—— (2003) 'Knowing ruralities?' In P. Cloke (ed.) *Country Visions.* Harlow: Pearson, pp. 1–13.

Coppock, T. (1977) *Second Homes: Curse or Blessing?* Oxford: Pergamon Press.

Countryside Commission (1995) 'Sustainable rural tourism: opportunities for local action, CCP483', Cheltenham: Countryside Commission.

Dodds, R. (2007) 'Sustainable tourism and policy implementation: lessons from the case of Calvia, Spain', *Current Issues in Tourism* 10(1): 296–322.

ETC (2001) *Working for the Countryside: A Strategy for Rural Tourism.* London: English Tourist Council/Countryside Agency.

Farsari, Y., Butler, R. W. and Prastacos, P. (2007) 'Sustainable tourism policy in Mediterranean destinations: issues and interrelationships', *International Journal of Tourism Policy* 1(1): 58–78.

Fleischer, A. and Felenstein, D. (2000) 'Support for rural tourism: does it make a difference?', *Annals of Tourism Research* 27(4): 1007–24.

Frost, D. and Jay, A. (1967) *To England with Love*. London: Hodder.

Gannon, A. (1994) 'Rural tourism as a factor in rural community economic development for economies in transition', *Journal of Sustainable Tourism* 2(1–2): 51–60.

Gilbert, E. W. (939) 'The growth of inland and coastal resorts in England and Wales', *Scottish Geographical Magazine* 55(1): 16–35.

Gössling, S., Hall, C. M. and Weaver, D. B. (2009) *Sustainable Tourism Futures: Perspectives on Systems, Restructuring and Innovations*. London: Routledge.

Halfacree, K. (1997) 'Contrasting roles for the post-productivist countryside: a postmodern perspective on counterurbanisation', in P. Cloke and J. Little (eds) *Contested Countryside Cultures: Otherness, Marginalisation and Rurality*. London: Routledge, pp. 70–93.

—— (2006) 'From dropping out to leaning on? British counter-cultural back-to-the-land in a changing rurality', *Progress in Human Geography* 30(3): 309–36.

Hall, D., Mitchell, M. and Roberts, L. (2003) 'Tourism and the countryside: dynamic relationships', in D. Hall, M. Mitchell, and L. Roberts (eds) *New Directions in Rural Tourism*. Aldershot: Ashgate, pp. 3–15.

Hallikainen, V. (1998) *The Finnish Wilderness Experience*. Research Papers 711. Rovaniemi Research Station. Vantaa: Finnish Forest Research Institute.

—— (2001) 'Erämaat Suomessa [The wilderness in Finland]', in J. Kangas and A. Kokko (eds) *Mesän eri käyttömuotojen arvottaminen ja yhteensovittaminen* [The valuation and reconciliation of different forest uses]. Research Papers 800. Kannus Research Station. Vantaa: Finnish Forest Research Institute, pp. 111–19.

Häyrynen, M. (2004) 'Countryside imagery in Finnish national discourse', in H. Palang, H. Sooväli, M. Antrop and G. Setten (eds) *European Rural Landscapes: Persistence and Change in a Globalising Environment*. Dordrecht: Kluwer Academic Publishers, pp. 114–22.

Hiltunen, M. J. (2007) 'Environmental impacts of rural second home tourism: Case Lake District in Finland', *Scandinavian Journal of Hospitality and Tourism* 7(3): 243–65.

Hopkins, J. (1998) 'Signs of the post-rural: marketing myths of a symbolic countryside', *Geografiska Annaler* 80B: 65–81.

Horton, J. (2008) 'Producing Postman Pat: the popular cultural construction of idyllic rurality', *Journal of Rural Studies* 24: 389–98.

Ilbery, B. (1998) 'Dimensions of rural change', in B. Ibery (ed.) *The Geography of Rural Change*. Harlow: Longman, pp. 1–10.

Ioannides, D. and Holcomb, B. (2003) 'Misguided policy initiatives in small-island destinations: why do up-market tourism policies fail?', *Tourism Geographies* 5(1): 38–48.

Ioannides, D., Apostolopoulos, Y. and Sonmez, S. (2001) *Mediterranean Islands and Sustainable Tourism Development*. London: Continuum.

Kastenholz, E. (2000) 'The market for rural tourism in north and central Portugal: a benefit segmentation approach', in G. Richards and D. Hall (eds) *Tourism and Sustainable Community Development*. London: Routledge, pp. 268–84.

Lehtinen, A. (2006) *Postcolonialism, Multitude, and the Politics of Nature: On the*

*Changing Geographies of the European North.* Lanham, MD: University Press of America.

McGehee, N. G.(2007) 'An agritourism model: a Weberian perspective', *Journal of Sustainable Tourism* 15(2): 111–24.

McIntyre, N., Williams, D. and McHugh, K. (2006) *Multiple Dwelling and Tourism: Negotiating Place, Home and Identity.* Wallingford: CABI, pp. 278–94.

Müller, D. K. (2007) 'Second homes in the Nordic countries: between common heritage and exclusive commodity', *Scandinavian Journal of Hospitality and Tourism* 7(3): 193–201.

Pitkänen, K. (2008) 'Second home landscape: the meaning(s) of landscape for second home tourism in Finland', *Tourism Geographies* 10(2): 169–92.

Roberts, L. and Hall, D. (2001) *Rural Tourism and Recreation: Principles to Practice.* Wallingford: CABI.

Romeiro, P. P. and Costa, C. (2010) 'The potential of management networks in the innovation and competitiveness of rural tourism: a case study on the Valle del Jerte (Spain)', *Current Issues in Tourism* 13(1): 75–91.

Saarinen, J. (2004) 'Tourism and touristic representations of nature', in A. A. Dew, C. M. Hall and A. M. Williams (eds) *A Companion to Tourism.* Oxford: Blackwell, pp. 438–49.

Sandell, K. (2006) 'Access under stress: the right of public access tradition in Sweden', in N. McIntyre, D. Williams and K. McHugh (eds) *Multiple Dwelling and Tourism: Negotiating Place, Home and Identity.* Wallingford: CABI, pp. 278–94.

Sharpley, R. (2001) 'Sustainable rural tourism: ideal or idyll?', in L. Roberts and D. Hall (eds) *Rural Tourism and Recreation: Principles to Practice.* Wallingford: CABI, pp. 57–8.

—— (2004) 'Tourism and the countryside in Lew', in A. A. Dew, C. M. Hall and A. Williams (eds) *A Companion to Tourism.* Oxford: Blackwell, pp. 374–86.

—— (2007) 'Flagship attractions and sustainable rural tourism development: the case of the Alnwick Garden, England', *Journal of Sustainable Tourism* 15(2): 125–43.

*The Times* (2009) 'Grants to farmers for not obstructing footpaths', 7 October, p. 67.

UNEP, WTO and Plan Blue (2000) *Final Report: International Seminar on Sustainable Tourism and Competitiveness in the Islands of the Mediterranean.* Capri.

UNWTO-UNEP-WMO (United Nations World Tourism Organization, United Nations Environment Programme, World Meteorological Organisation) (2008) 'Climate change and tourism: responding to global challenges', Madrid: UNWTO.

WCED (World Commission on Environment and Development) (1987) *Our Common Future.* Oxford: Blackwell.

Williams, A. M. and Balaz, M. (2010) 'The European Union: between the global and the national and between neo-liberalism and interventionism', in W. Sunitkul and R. W. Butler (eds) *Tourism and Political Change.* Oxford: Goodfellow.

Williams, S. (2009) 'Preferences or barriers: why do some people not visit the countryside?', *Countryside Recreation Journal* 17(1): 17–19.

Wolfe, R. I. (1977) 'Second homes: purpose built for an inessential purpose', in T. Coppock (ed.) *Second Homes: Curse or Blessing.* Oxford: Pergamon, pp. 184–211.

# 2 Tourism mobility, locality and sustainable rural development

*C. Michael Hall, Johan Hultman and Stefan Gössling*

## Introduction

Although often portrayed in nostalgic and romantic terms in tourism and place marketing, European agriculture has been undergoing significant change since the onset of the industrial urbanizing population. This has been evidenced not only by changes in the technology of agriculture but also the regulation of agricultural and rural space, and changes to rural economy and employment. There is consensus that trends in European agriculture over the past few hundred years – including the movement from small-scale to large-scale farms, from organic to industrial production, and from poly-culture to monoculture – have had a wide range of implications for sustainability. This has included such diverse issues as land conversion and the associated loss of biodiversity and ecosystems, changes in nutrient cycles, problems associated with water use for irrigation and associated down-stream water quality, use of chemicals, ethical questions such as those relating to animal welfare and genetically modified organisms, infectious diseases, biosecurity, food safety, emissions of greenhouse gases, as well as socioeconomic aspects related to regional development, loss of employment, and declining incomes of farmers (e.g. Bhalli *et al.* 2009; Chapagain and Hoekstra 2008; Lawton and May 1995; Vitousek *et al.* 1997; Zollitsch *et al.* 2007). Given these unsustainable developments in agriculture, described by Marsden (2003: 3) as 'the race to the bottom', there have been attempts to restructure rural production systems and to move towards multifunc-tional agriculture and more diversified rural economies (e.g. Labarthe 2009; Pfeifer *et al.* 2009; Renting *et al.* 2009). Often, this has involved calls to move from traditional agriculture, i.e. the production of 'food and fibre', to new agriculture, including the 'production of nature and new spaces for leisure' (Wilson 2009: 269), i.e. economic diversification based on the devel-opment of services.

Changes to rural areas have been inextricably linked to developments in global and local economies, and tourism has emerged as one of the central means by which rural areas adjust themselves economically, socially, and politically to the new global environment. The regional restructuring associated with globalization has usually involved attempts by regions to widen their economic base to include tourism as part of a 'natural' progression towards a tertiary economy, as employment in traditional Western agriculture declines and farm sizes reduce, a process which is sometimes referred to as the development of a 'post-productivist' countryside (Ward 1993; see Hall and Müller 2004; Williams and Hall 2000, 2002;) or 'rural dilution' (Smailes 2002). However, such changes, which also include second home development, lifestyle migration and other forms of exurbanization, have a range of consequences for the sustainability of rural locations (Cocklin and Dibden 2005; Tonts and Black 2002) as well as implications for the economic and social constructions of rurality, personal and collective identity and rural activities (e.g. Brandth and Haugen 2005; Gibson *et al.* 2005).

Rural areas have a wide range of resources attractive to tourists, which Garrod *et al.* (2006) describe as the 'countryside capital'. These include natural resources such as the landscape, wildlife, air quality, waterways, forests, agricultural buildings, as well as cultural resources including local customs, languages, foods, crafts, ways of life, and festivals. Arguably the growing urbanization of many countries has made 'countryside capital' even more important with respect to the considerable potential to address growing demand in the consumption of emotions and immateriality. But the challenges are manifold, and many of them concern processes where traditionally non-economic values are reinterpreted, translated and commoditized into economic exchange value. Tourism is not alone in this process as it is closely related to broader issues of place marketing and imaging. Nevertheless, tourism is intimately connected to the place marketing process because of the way in which it is often used as a focus for regional redevelopment, revitalization and promotion strategies that place a strong emphasis on the social construction of place, including rural places, for the purposes of consumption and the attraction of mobile firms, capital and people. Indeed, it has been argued that the commodification of rurality through place marketing and real estate promotion, although contributing to the policies of governments to accumulate capital in rural areas, is also contributing to a simultaneous 'creative destruction' of the countryside ideal (Walmsley 2003). This is not a new issue in tourism studies and practice but the relation between urban and rural, rather than, for example, northern and southern, areas calls for specific analytical foci.

Of particular interest given the role of tourism and rural place marketing in attracting mobile people is a perspective on flows, accessibility and temporality. Such a perspective can, in turn, be dealt with in several different ways. For example, in a case study-based analysis, George, Mair and Reid (2009) presented a comprehensive outcome-focused contribution on rural change. These authors addressed questions of identity, social relations, conflict and participation in the face of gentrification, rural place branding and public–private development schemes revolving around tourism. This chapter addresses these issues as well, but arrives there through a discussion of changing rurality in relation to tourism mobility. Inherent in rural change and development in association with tourism is changing patterns and ratio- nales for mobility and accessibility and new temporal rhythms of movement between urban, exurban and rural areas. From a perspective focusing on sustainable rural practices associated with tourism, these new mobility regimes and the ways in which they affect the social and physical construc- tion of place and place-meaning are of crucial interest. This chapter traces aspects of rural development in relation to changing conditions and modes of mobility in order to outline critical issues for future exurban and rural change.

## Tourism mobility and everyday accessibility: rural development revisited

Mobility carries an enormous amount of social and cultural power and its consequences for ordering social relations have only recently begun to be analyzed in a systematic manner (Haldrup and Larsen 2006). The general issue raised in this chapter is in what ways tourism mobility is presently ordering and constructing rural development in economic and social terms. Arguably, this is critical for rural sustainability in at least two ways. First, rural and ex-urban areas in late capitalist societies are subject to forces of change at various spatial scales, which affect modes and principles of economic output, social relations and accessibility (Table 2.1). Second, there is increased recognition of the environmental impacts of mobility, and tourism mobility in particular. Nevertheless, it must be recognized that the effects of such change processes are contextual. Along with the emergence of a discursive hegemony for an economy based on experience production – working in tandem with development, planning and service provision dereg- ulation in some late industrial European rural areas and strong interventionist policies in others (Potter 2006) – tourism policies and strate- gies appear in many different manifestations.

In the case of the effects of social and economic change many near- or peri-urban areas are being shaped by the more or less explicit development of tourist servicescapes where themed and sometimes highly regulated spaces (golf courses, shopping villages, horse riding, themed visitor centres; see Ek and Hultman, 2008; Hultman and Andersson Cederholm 2008; Weaver, 2005) become defining features in the attraction of tourists and day-trippers and the commodification of the imagined rurality of the peri- urban fringe for the consumption of urbanites. In more rural areas, change might centre on urban demand for leisure and tradition in the form of the transformation of thre rural infrastructure into second homes, farm shops, bed-and-breakfast businesses and the commercialization of cultural heritage (cf. the 'urban playgrounds' discussed in George et al. 2009: 154). While in even more peripheral areas tourism-related change may focus on activities

*Table 2.1* Characteristics of tourism consumption and production in rural areas

| Dimension | Rural destination category | | |
| --- | --- | --- | --- |
| | *Peri-urban* | *Resort periphery* | *Non-resort periphery* |
| Accessibility | Easy car accessibility from major urban centre (up to 3 hours drive one way in some locations, though usually up to one to 1.5 hours one way). | Highly accessible via direct flights as well as good excellent road or rail access. | No direct flights. Relatively poor road and rail access. |
| Tourism activities | Primarily daytrips. Limited overnight stays. | Integrated resort developments in high amenity areas such as coast, lakes or mountain locations. | Sometimes transit stops, secondary destinations or location for nature-based activities, such as fishing, hunting and foraging. |
| Second home characteristics | Weekend homes. Easy access from primary residence. Many second homes are purpose built often as an investment with a long term view towards retirement housing. Second homes represent a significant addition to housing stock. Some reuse of existing housing stock for second homes. | Vacation homes. Often concentrated in real estate developments. Many purpose built but also some adaptive reuse from existing housing stock. Competition from second home purchaser with local people for available housing stock. Some second homes may be used for retirement housing although availability of health facilities will be a limiting factor. | Dispersed vacation homes. Second homes often connected to family roots. Second home development places no pressure on housing stock as usually adaptive reuse. Development usually welcomed as it helps to support government and health service provision as well as retail services. |

*Continued overleaf*

Table 2.1 Continued

| Dimension | Rural destination category | | |
| --- | --- | --- | --- |
| | *Peri-urban* | *Resort periphery* | *Non-resort periphery* |
| Accommodation characteristics | Homestays and bed and breakfasts developed primarily by lifestyle entrepreneurs, often as part of a larger tourism or agricultural business. A small number of boutique resorts and hotels catering to the urban centre leisure and meetings market. | Large resort developments with a range of accommodation options (e.g. mountain resorts). Resorts highly corporatised. Some secondary providers seeking to take advantage of 'overflow' from main resort with some developments by a mixture of lifestyle businesses (who had previously visited as tourists) and local people. | Camping, homestays, bed and breakfasts, some small hotels and motels in small towns. Accommodation developments by lifestyle entrepreneurs (often return migrants) as well as local people seeking to use existing spare accommodation, e.g. farm stays. |
| Labour force | Primarily local people, many from same urban centre as daytrippers. Workforce does not place extra pressure on housing supply beyond that of 'normal' peri-urbanisation processes. | Some local people but substantial amount of outside labour attracted. Often highly seasonal. Places substantial seasonal pressures on housing supply. | Primarily local people. Limited numbers of external employees, some of which may be extended family. Often highly seasonal. Though little pressure on housing supply. |
| Direct contribution to environmental change | Substantial affects in terms of land use but dispersed through peri-urban area. | High effects in resort areas as a result of intensive accommodation, infrastructure and leisure resource development. | Relatively low direct contribution to environmental change; often considerable contribution to conservation. |

Source: After Hall 2010.

such as hunting and fishing, ecotourism and other forms of nature-based tourism as well as seasonal second homes and the provision of home stays. Importantly, in a number or rural areas, tourism is significant for rural change not only because of its direct effects but also because of its contribution to exurbanization – the migration of urban residents to rural environments – usually for lifestyle reasons.

Tourism is deeply embedded in exurban processes. There is considerable evidence that in absolute terms more people in Western industrialized nations, are visiting and appreciating rural areas as part of broader shifts in lifestyle and increased personal mobility (e.g. Butler *et al.* 1998; Hall 2005; Walmsley 2003), and that many more people are seeking to use rural areas for leisure if they are accessible. Therefore, increasing negative economic, physical, and social impacts on rural environments desired by multiple and often conflicting interests, including housing, may be inevitable in some locations. For example, day-tripping and holidaymaking have long been recognized as being forms of environmental scanning by which lifestyle migration and second home opportunities are identified in high amenity environments (e.g. Hall and Müller 2004). Second home development itself may also be a part of a broader lifestyle strategy that utilizes purchase as a precursor to more permanent retirement or lifestyle migration – an increasingly regular occurrence in many locations that further blurs the boundaries between migration, tourism and permanent residence (Coles *et al.* 2005). Furthermore, tourism is also a significant employment mechanism as well as landscape use which has its own effects on rural environments, with resort and second-home development being particularly significant (Gallent *et al.* 2005; Hall and Müller 2004; Müller and Jansson 2007).

The second primary dimension of rural change and sustainability is that of mobility. However, what is increasingly clear is that tourism mobility has a critical environmental impact. Following the Inter-governmental Panel on Climate Change (IPCC 2007), the assertion that climate change is now unequivocal, the Davos Declaration (UNWTO 2007) has prioritized the need for the tourism sector to respond to the climate change challenge. It is calculated that 5 per cent of global $CO_2$ emissions are a result of tourism, most of this (75 per cent) being a result of travel (UNWTO 2007). At the national level, this share is higher. For instance, one recent publication calculates that 11 per cent of Swedish emissions are derived from tourism (Gössling and Hall 2008), while the Swedish government has set its target of emission reductions at 40 per cent less by 2020 compared to 1990. Clearly, then, tourism mobility is a critical issue to address when planning for a low carbon future, but this should be seen in relation to economic and social change in rural areas. This last point is critical as the role of tourism as a desired element of the rural economy presents a clear policy paradox for rural locations with respect to the growth of concern as to the carbon contribution of tourism mobility (Table 2.2).

As Table 2.2 shows, emissions associated with various lifestyle/holiday

*Table 2.2*  Individual carbon footprints associated with exurban migration, regional and international tourism

| Transition/activity | Calculation | Emissions |
|---|---|---|
| Migration from city centre to peri-urban area, commuting to city for work (20 km one way, 200 trips per year) | 20km × 200 × 2 = 8,000 km per year | 2.1 t $CO_2$ (at 0.266 kg $CO_2$ per km)[1] |
| Second home, 150 km (one way, 20 trips per year by car) | 150 km × 2 × 20 = 6,000 km per year | 0.8 t $CO_2$ (at 0.133 kg $CO_2$ per km)[2] |
| Second home, 150 km (one way, 20 trips per year by train) | 150 km × 2 × 20 = 6,000 km per year | 0.16 t $CO_2$ (at 0.027 kg $CO_2$ per km)[3] |
| International holidays, 7,000 km (once a year) | 7,000 km × 2 = 14,000 pkm | 1.55 t $CO_2$ (at 0.111 kg $CO_2$ per km)[4] |
| Sustainable emissions per capita per year (world average) | | 3.5 t $CO_2$[5] |

Sources: UNWTO-UNEP-WMO (2008).

Notes:
[1] Based on the UNWTO-UNEP-WMO estimate of 0.266 g per km for leisure car travel at one passenger per car.
[2] UNWTO-UNEP-WMO value for leisure car travel, based on an occupancy rate of 50 per cent.
[3] UNWTO-UNEP-WMO (2008), average emission factor for train travel in Europe at 60 per cent occupancy rate.
[4] UNWTO-UNEP-WMO value for long-haul flights, note that non-$CO_2$ radiative forcing is not considered.
[5] Current emissions are in the order of 4.3 t $CO_2$ per capita per year, which the IPCC (2007) suggests is too high. Sustainable emissions up to 2020 are here assumed to be roughly 20 per cent lower – notably in a situation of global population growth.

choices can be significant and vary considerably. Notably, values are illustrative, as changing any input parameter changes the overall outcome considerably. First of all, it is important to note that sustainable per capita emissions on a worldwide basis are in the order of just 3.5 t $CO_2$ per year (IPCC 2007). As recent studies in, for instance, Germany have shown, the public sector may already account for 1.25 t $CO_2$, a value that might be representative of the European Union more generally (Umweltbundesamt 2007). This would leave a sustainable emissions budget of less than 2.5 t $CO_2$ per capita per year. Each of the lifestyle choices in Table 2.2 would reduce this budget considerably, with commuting to work from the countryside accounting for 2.1 t $CO_2$ per year (or more than 4 t $CO_2$ if the distance is 40 km one way); a second home 150 km from the place of permanent residence leads to emissions of 0.8 t $CO_2$ if visited 20 times per year, and a typical long-haul holiday over a distance of 7,000 km leads to emission of more than 1.5 t $CO_2$. Clearly, living in the countryside and commuting to the city is the least sustainable choice, particularly when such lifestyles are backed up with SUVs and long-haul holidays. Vice versa, if regional holidays are a standard choice, as are, for instance, second homes visited over longer summer periods in Sweden (e.g. Hall and Müller 2004), emissions can be comparably low, in particular if public transport is used to reach the second home. As an example, 20 visits to a second home or regional attractions over a distance of 150 km one way, will, if based on the train, lead to emissions of just 160 kg $CO_2$, i.e. 20 per cent of those caused by car travel (at 0.027 kg $CO_2$ per pkm; UNWTO-UNEP-WMO 2008). Overall, this data shows that even if associated with frequent visits, regional holidays cause comparably low emissions.

As the discussion on the role of tourism within rural social and economic change suggests, accessibility is critical to the development of tourism in rural areas and, indeed, to the broader rural economy. In fact, there is a substantial legacy of the problems of rural areas being understood in terms of the problem of accessibility, which Moseley's seminal work identified as a concept

> [B]asically relating to people's ability to reach the things which are important to them. And if rural areas are in essence those parts of the country where people and activities are widely spaced, then it should come as no surprise to learn that problems of inaccessibility are particularly serious there. Indeed they are linked with a number of more visible ills such as the inadequacy of employment opportunities, selective depopulation and repopulation, the isolation and loneliness of certain vulnerable groups and the disproportionately high cost of providing services.
>
> (Moseley 1979: 1)

Much contemporary rural development planning is geared towards trying to overcome problems of inaccessibility of rural locations given that transport availability determines access to markets for both goods and services as well as connectivity to economic and social networks. Moreover, the relative accessibility of a location will influence its capacity to capture mobile capital, firms and people – including tourists. As Hall (2005) argued, in the nineteenth century, places sought to attract the railway line, in the twentieth century the motorway and road, and in the twenty-first century airports. The development or attraction of transport infrastructure reflects a concern of rural areas to expand the opportunities for mobility especially when the rationalization and corporatization of public transport infrastructure as a result of neoliberal policy settings in Europe since the early 1980s have often served to constrain rural transport supply. Therefore, the promotion of rural tourism and the development of tourism attractions and resorts are often undertaken via public–private partnerships and networks in which local and regional governments undertake to develop transport infrastructure in order to encourage tourism mobility. This is done not only because of the potential employment and economic generation that tourism may bring but also because encouraging tourism mobility provides justification for transport infrastructure as a result of an increased number of consumers of transport as well as the potential increase in the tax base as a result of shifts in overall consumption and economic activity.

The transport infrastructure which enables rural tourism usually serves the inbound tourist market as well as the local population and businesses. Any understanding of tourism's contribution to rural sustainability therefore needs to be able to account for both the environmental effects of tourism mobility as well as the potential social and economic impacts of any loss of that mobility in terms of infrastructure use and economic contribution. As Moseley (2003: 21) noted:

> This is important in the context of local development . . . since it raises questions about policies that may seem 'green' – for example the development of eco-tourism based on the sustainable use of local environmental and manufactured capital, only for that tourism to rely on tourists making extravagant demands on fossil fuels by travelling hundreds or thousands of miles for the experience.

Unfortunately, the complexity of such policy conundrums has not usually been explored in the specific context of rural development programmes financed by national governments or the European Union, with attention to carbon reduction or at least environmental impacts usually only understood at the level of the destination rather than the wider context of the trip.

One influential institution in this regard is the funding of rural development projects by the European Union as LEADER programs (an acronym for the French *Liaison Entre de Développement de l'Economie Rurale*, i.e. cooperative action to develop rural economies, with a 2007–13 budget amounting to over €13 billion, see Dargan and Shucksmith 2008; European Commission 2008). The single most important aspect of LEADER programs is that funding is conditional upon cooperation between private, public and non-profit stakeholders in local action groups. Development initiatives must originate from local actors, and local action groups define the exact geographical area encompassed by each LEADER project (for empirical studies of LEADER and tourism, see Holloway *et al.* 2006; Koutsouris 2008). Local social capital, cultural values and natures are in this way embedded from the beginning in development schemes. This has consequences when we begin to consider rural and tourism development together through the concept of countryside capital. Specifically, it becomes evident that the issue of locality in relation to commodity circulation/outlet and tourist mobility is of interest, both from a producer and a consumer point of view.

The definition of rural sustainability has become tied to urban economies in ways that suggest that the analytical focus should be on, for example, linkages, traceability, knowledge contents and production processes when it comes to food and food production, and sociability between hosts and guests, the social construction of markets, value transformations and the commoditization of nature, traditions and knowledge where tourism is concerned (Andersson Cederholm and Hultman 2010; Hultman and Andersson Cederholm 2008). Central, then, to an understanding of how rural tourism and rural development are difficult to separate in a sustainability context, is the formation of a mobility regime where rural economic development is reliant upon the inflow and circulation of urban consumers.

## Regimes of mobility and immobility in rural development

Tourism mobility orders social relations, and tourism and leisure travel concerns social value creation through mobility. By being mobile, the individual reproduces a value system based upon experiences, sensuality and sociability. At the same time, tourism is very clearly a value-creating process for rural actors involved in its production such as destination networks and hospitality providers (LRF 2009). The value created by mobility is thus reproduced by use across boundaries of production and consumption. Historically, there have been no significant social limits to tourism mobility – if anything, mobility has been encouraged as socially desirable (Larsen *et al.* 2007).

This is, of course, problematic considering the persuasive cognitive bond between distance and expectations for extraordinary experiences that much tourism marketing relies on. Exoticism, difference, authenticity and origin have traditionally been powerful drivers of tourism mobility, and the tourist's quest for worthwhile experiences has long been framed by long-distance travel. But at the same time, the large majority of all tourism mobility is domestic (UNWTO-UNEP-WMO 2008). There is a substantial demand for short trips and near-experiences. Presently, this coincides with a long-standing process of rural restructuring where diversification at the firm level has been a central issue for small farm businesses. The institutional encouragement for this kind of diversification is massive – from the UNWTO, to supra-national bodies such as the EU, to national programs such as the Swedish Landscape Program, and to regions and individual municipalities where the incentives for rural agricultural firms to join tourism schemes can be written into strategic policy declarations and plans. The diversification taking place in farm businesses is – contrary to many other economic activities – a profitable proposition even under conditions of economic decline. In Sweden, the LRF (the Federation of Swedish Farmers) reports that rural businesses diversifying into small-scale food production, commercial but small-scale horse-related activities and tourism showed unchanged or increased profitability during 2008–9, despite global economic decline. In addition, 90 per cent of the studied farm businesses expected unchanged or increased profitability during 2009–10, and the optimism – as well as new investments in infrastructure and land management practices – is greatest in those businesses focusing on small-scale food production and tourism (LRF 2009). In terms of future rural change, tourism offers great potential for a sustainability turn within experience-based destination economies. There are signals that such a development will have short-distance visitors as a core target group. In an evaluation of a LEADER project in Southern Sweden, it was found that 80 per cent of the 4,500 visits to a one-week event revolving around literary heritage originated from points less than 50 kilometres from the hosting municipality (Hultman and Andersson Cederholm 2009). Following this, the management of mobility and the reinforcement of short-distance travel trends with rural destinations as target areas may well become critical challenges in order to mitigate climate change with tourism as a strategic tool.

## Slow/low carbon mobility and experience production

In the intersection between mobility and climate change, economic decline and tourism interest in issues of authenticity and locality, concepts and products associated with staycation and slow travel have emerged. This typically implies tourism products where the mode of mobility is a defining feature, but with short-distance and low-carbon modes of mobility respectively. In slow travel products, marketing is geared towards the inclusion of the actual phase of transportation as a crucial part of the experience product (e.g. Fritidsresor 2009). This is of particular interest in rural destination economies for two reasons. The first is that rural tourism and hospitality businesses are often small-scale and lifestyle-oriented. In addition, such businesses are often organized around ideals of stewardship, cultural heritage and values associated with nature. The second is that governmental and supra-national incitements for the economic development in rural areas in Europe frequently take form around locally embedded social relations. Sometimes, as in the case of EU-funded LEADER programs, this kind of cooperation between local public, commercial and non-commercial actors is an absolute condition for funding. One of the consequences is that local social capital become part of the experience products offered to rural tourists.

Considering the importance of local embeddedness, rural tourism offers development opportunities where slow/low carbon modes of travel can be utilized as a marketing tool. The slow movement has been discussed in relation to food and practices of eating (Leith 2003; Miele and Murdoch 2002; Pietrykowski 2004), but the cultural economy of slow/low carbon tourism mobility has not been an issue to the same degree. As in analyses of other kinds of mobilities and immobilites within a general mobility paradigm taking shape in the social sciences (Baerenholdt *et al.* 2004; Büscher and Urry 2009; Sheller and Urry 2004, 2006), the strategic use of slow modes of tourism mobility calls for new ways of linking mobility with social aspects of place not only for tourists but also for those who live in rural communities.

Tourism is undoubtedly going to remain important for the economic base of many rural locations especially as urbanization processes continue around the world. However, the use of tourism mobility as a policy solution to the problems facing many rural areas does need to be placed in a wider context beyond that of contemporary neoliberal agendas and narrow understandings of environmental impact. Central to this is an improved comprehension of how to expand the effective personal space (space–time prism) of people suffering economic and social accessibility deprivation so that they can more easily reach desired 'things' and how to bring within their personal space more of what it is that they desire (Moseley 2003): the former is an issue of transport policy, the latter is an issue of service delivery and the geographical distribution of those services. In the development of a post-carbon or low-emissions future for rural areas, it therefore becomes essential to understand that the use of tourism as a development tool is embedded within broader issues of service provision and the role of the state. There is clearly potential for win–win scenarios with the development of more public bus and train transport infrastructure, which can be used by both rural inhabitants and tourists. However, the focus of many rural development agencies on car and aircraft access, while perhaps initially appealing with respect to network connectivity, clearly creates a major issue with respect to journey emissions and the overall contribution that tourism makes to sustainability.

# References

Andersson Cederholm, E. and Hultman, J. (2010) 'The value of intimacy: negotiating commercial relationships in lifestyle entrepreneurship', *Scandinavian Journal of Tourism and Hospitality* 10(1): 16–32.

Baerenholdt, J-O., Haldrup, M., Larsen, J. and Urry, J. (2004) *Performing Tourist Places*. Aldershot: Ashgate.

Bhalli, J. A., Ali, T., Asi, M. R., Khalid, Z. M., Ceppi, M. and Khan, Q. M. (2009) 'DNA damage in Pakistani agricultural workers exposed to mixture of pesticides', *Environmental and Molecular Mutagenesis* 50(1): 37–45.

Brandth, B. and Haugen, M. S. (2005) 'Doing rural masculinity: from logging to outfield tourism', *Journal of Gender Studies* 14(1): 13–22.

Büscher, M. and Urry, J. (2009) 'Mobile methods and the empirical', *European Journal of Social Theory* 12(1): 99–116.

Butler, R. W., Hall, C. M. and Jenkins, J. (eds) (1998) *Tourism and Recreation in Rural Areas*. Chichester: John Wiley & Sons, Ltd.

Chapagain, A. K. and Hoekstra, A. Y. (2008) 'The global component of freshwater demand and supply: an assessment of virtual water flows between nations as a result of trade in agricultural and industrial products', *Water International* 33(1): 19–32.

Cocklin, C. and Dibden, J. (2005) *Sustainability and Change in Rural Australia.* Sydney: Academy of the Social Sciences in Australia, University of New South Wales Press.

Coles, T., Hall, C. M. and Duval, D. (2005) 'Mobilising tourism: a post-disciplinary critique', *Tourism Recreation Research* 30(2): 31–41.

Dargan, L. and Shucksmith, M. (2008) 'LEADER and innovation', *Sociologia Ruralis* 48(3): 274–91.

Ek, R. and Hultman, J. (2008) 'Sticky landscapes and smooth experiences: the biopower of tourism mobilities in the Öresund region', *Mobilities* 3(2): 223–42.

European Commission (2008) 'Report', available at: http://ec.europa.eu/agriculture/rurdev (accessed 20 November 2009).

Fritidsresor (2009) 'Train travel', available at: www.fritidsresor.se/resor/Resa-med-tag (accessed 2 December 2009).

Gallent, N., Mace, A. and Tewdwr-Jones, M. (eds) (2005) *Second Homes: European Perspectives and UK Policies.* Aldershot: Ashgate.

Garrod, B., Wornell, R. and Youell, R. (2006) 'Re-conceptualising rural resources as countryside capital: the case of rural tourism', *Journal of Rural Studies* 22: 117–28.

George, E. W., Mair, H. and Reid, D. G. (2009) *Rural Tourism Developmen: Localism and Cultural Change.* Clevedon: Channel View.

Gibson, L., Lynch, P. A. and Morrison, A. (2005) 'The Local Destination Tourism Network: development issues', *Tourism and Hospitality: Planning & Development* 2(2): 87–99.

Gössling, S. and Hall, C. M. (2008) 'Swedish tourism and climate change mitigation: an emerging conflict?', *Scandinavian Journal of Hospitality and Tourism* 8(2): 141–58.

Haldrup, M. and Larsen, J, (2006) 'Material cultures of tourism', *Leisure Studies* 25(3): 275–89.

Hall, C. M. (2005) *Tourism: Rethinking the Social Science of Mobility.* Harlow: Prentice-Hall.

—— (2010) 'Housing tourists: accommodating short-term visitors', in D. Marcouliier, M. Lapping and O. Furuseth (eds) *Rural Housing and the Exurbanization Process*, Aldershot: Ashgate.

Hall, C. M. and Müller, D. (eds) (2004) *Tourism, Mobility and Second Homes: Between Elite Landscape and Common Ground.* Clevedon: Channel View.

Holloway, L., Cox, R., Venn, L., Kneafsey, M., Dowler, E. and Tuomainen, H. (2006) 'Managing sustainable farmed landscape through "alternative" food networks: a case study from Italy', *Geographical Journal* 172(3): 219–29.

Hultman, J. and Andersson Cederholm, E. (2008) 'Experiences of ecology: (dis) ordering nature as a visitor attraction', *Tourism and Hospitality: Planning & Development* 5(2): 81–95.

—— (2009) 'A processual assessment of the Leader project Nässelfrossa', unpublished report, Department of Service Management, Lund University (in Swedish).

IPCC (2007) *Intergovernmental Panel on Climate Change Fourth Assessment Report – Climate Change 2007: Synthesis Report.* Available at: www.ipcc.ch/ipccreports/ar4-syr.htm.

Koutsouris, A. (2008) 'The battlefield for (sustainable) rural development: the case of Lake Plastiras, Central Greece', *Sociologia Ruralis* 48(3): 241–56.

Labarthe, P. (2009) 'Extension services and multifunctional agriculture: lessons learnt from the French and Dutch contexts and approaches', *Journal of Environmental Management* 90: 193–202.

Larsen, J., Urry, J. and Axhausen, K. W. (2007) 'Networks and tourism: mobile social life', *Annals of Tourism Research* 34(1): 244–62.

Lawton, J. H. and May, R. M. (1995) *Extinction Rates*. Oxford: Oxford University Press.

Leith, A. (2003) 'Slow food and the politics of pork fat: Italian food and European identity', *Ethnos* 68(4): 437–62.

LRF (2009) *Outlook 2009 for Contract Work, Horse Business, Rental, Tourism and Small-Scale Tourism Business*. Stockholm: LRF (in Swedish).

Marsden, T. (2003) *The Condition of Rural Sustainability*. Assen: Van Gorcum.

Miele, M. and Murdoch, J. (2002) 'The practical aesthetics of traditional cuisines: slow food in Tuscany', *Sociologia Ruralis* 42(4): 312–28.

Moseley, M. J. (1979) *Accessibility: The Rural Challenge*. London: Methuen.

—— (2003) *Rural Development: Principles and Practice*. London: Sage.

Müller, D. and Jansson, B. (eds) (2007) *Tourism in Peripheries: Perspectives from the Far North and South*. Wallingford: CABI.

Pfeifer, C., Jongeneel, R. A., Sonneveld, M. P. W. and Stoorvogel, J. J. (2009) 'Landscape properties as drivers for farm diversification: a Dutch case study', *Land Use Policy* 26: 1106–15.

Pietrykowski, B. (2004) 'You are what you eat: the social economy of the slow food movement', *Review of Social Economy* LXII(3): 307–21.

Potter, C. (2006) 'Competing narratives for the future of European agriculture: the agri-environmental consequences of neoliberalization in the context of the Doha Round', *The Geographical Journal* 172(3): 190–6.

Renting, H., Rossing, W. A. H., Groot, J. C. J., Van der Ploeg, J. D., Laurent, C., Perraud, D., Stobbelaar, D. J. and Van Ittersum, M. K. (2009) 'Exploring multifunctional agriculture: a review of conceptual approaches and prospects for an integrative transitional framework', *Journal of Environmental Management* 90: 112–23.

Sheller, M. and Urry, J. (eds) (2004) *Tourism Mobilities: Places to Play, Places in Play*. London: Routledge.

—— (2006) 'The new mobilities paradigm', *Environment and Planning A* 38(2): 207–26.

Smailes, P. J. (2002) 'From rural dilution to multifunctional countryside: some pointers to the future for South Australia', *Australian Geographer* 33(1): 79–95.

Tonts, M. and Black, A. (2002) 'Changing farm business structures and the sustainability of rural communities and regions: issues for research', *Sustaining Regions* 1, 17–23.

Umweltbundesamt (2007) 'CO$_2$ calculator' (in German). Available at: www.umweltbundesamt.de/energy/index.htm (accessed 2 December 2009).

UNWTO (2007) *Davos Declaration: Climate Change and Tourism Responding to Global Challenges*. Davos, Switzerland, 3 October.

UNWTO-UNEP-WMO (United Nations World Tourism Organisation, United Nations Environment Programme, World Meteorological Organisation) (2008) 'Climate change and tourism: responding to global challenges', Madrid: UNWTO.

Vitousek, P. M., Aber, J. D., Howarth, R. W., Likens, G. E., Matson, P. A., Schindler, D. W., Schlesinger, W. H. and Tilman, D. G. (1997) 'Human alteration of the global nitrogen cycle: sources and consequences', *Ecological Applications* 7(3): 737–50.

Walmsley, D. J. (2003) 'Rural tourism: a case of lifestyle-led opportunities', *Australian Geographer* 34(1): 61–72.

Ward, N. (1993) 'The agricultural treadmill and the rural environment in the post-productivist era', *Sociologica Ruralis* 33: 348–64.

Weaver, D. (2005) 'The distinctive dynamics of ex-urban tourism', *International Journal of Tourism Research* 7(1): 23–33.

Williams, A. M. and Hall, C. M. (2000) 'Tourism and migration: new relationships between production and consumption', *Tourism Geographies* 2(1): 5–27.

—— (2002) 'Tourism, migration, circulation and mobility: the contingencies of time and place', in C. M. Hall and A. M. Williams (eds) *Tourism and Migration: New Relationships Between Consumption and Production.* Dordrecht: Kluwer.

Wilson, G. A. (2009) 'The spatiality of multifunctional agriculture: a human geography perspective', *Geoforum* 40: 269–80.

Zollitsch, W., Winkler, C., Waiblinger, S. and Haslberger, A. (2007) *Sustainable Food Production and Ethics.* Wageningen: Wageningen Academic Publishers.

# 3 The European Union, sustainable tourism policy and rural Europe

*David Leslie*

## Introduction

Rural areas in Europe are estimated to account for 91 per cent of the European Union (EU) territory and for 56 per cent of the population (EC 2005a). These rural areas across Europe have been shaped and managed, to a greater or lesser degree, by agricultural and forestry practices for centuries. But agriculture as the main bulwark of rural economies has been in decline while tourism has grown, generating substantial visitor spending. It is now the biggest sector of the economy in many rural areas, overtaking such established land uses as farming, forestry, fishing and field sports, both in terms of employment and Gross Domestic Product (GDP) (Leslie 2007). However, tourism during the early decades of the European Union received little attention (see Robinson 1993); essentially it was seen as the responsibility of the Member States.

Indeed, there was no legal basis for EU support, i.e. it was not defined as a competence under the Treaty of Rome. However, the attention it did gain was within the context of Directorate DGXXIII, which had responsibility for small and medium-sized enterprises (SMEs) and Services. By the 1980s, it was the case (and very much still is) that it is more EU policy in other areas which has had the greatest impact on tourism (see Thomas 1996), in particular, for example, consumer information and protection (Leslie 1996), and programmes aimed at regional and social development (see Montanari and Williams 1995). Thus development of tourism in rural areas in one way or another has gained substantially from EU measures, of which there are over 250 which impact on tourism (Hall 2008; also see EC 2004a and www.europa.eu.int/comm/enterprises). These measures are diverse thus, and albeit briefly, the following discussion on the EU, tourism policy and rural tourism first draws attention to a number of initiatives which are indirectly important to tourism development (see Table 3.1). Attention then turns to EU environmental initiatives, which have certainly aided rural tourism development opportunities through, for example, conservation but more recently hold greater significance in the increasing attention given to energy consumption and waste management. In combination, these two areas serve

*Table 3.1* Selected EU developments impacting on tourism

| | |
|---|---|
| 1987 | Single European Act |
| 1993 | Maastricht Treaty of European Union |
| | Enterprise DG established |
| 1997 | Amsterdam Treaty |
| 1998 | Working Time Directive |
| 1999 | The Euro introduced |
| 2000 | Lisbon Treaty – aims to improve welfare and living conditions in a sustainable way but accent on 'Economic Growth and Jobs' |
| 2000 | Agenda 2000 – expansion of EU – recognition of potential of tourism as a tool for regeneration, particularly in context of expansion and needs of 'eastern' states |
| 2005 | Implementing the Community Lisbon Programme: Modern SME Policy for Growth and Employment |
| 2005 | Competitiveness and Innovation Framework programme |
| 2007 | Small and medium-sized enterprises – key for delivering growth and jobs. A mid-term review of Modern SME policy |
| 2008 | 'Think Small First': A 'Small Business Act' for Europe |

to demonstrate the EU's commitment to both economic development and the environment; as exemplified by the Treaty of Amsterdam (1997) (see below). This provides the wider context within which to consider the ensuing discussion on the EU's progress towards the development of policy for sustainable tourism development and supporting measures that increasingly encompass those wider directives and policy instruments.

## The wider context

Today, tourism is very much on the EU's agenda, recognized arguably far more so for its economic aspects and job creation potential than for any other consideration (see EU 2008). As Ianniello (Head of Tourism Unit, Enterprise and Industry DG) recently stated:

> Tourism is one of the biggest and fastest expanding sectors of the European economy. When considered together with its related activities, tourism can be seen to impact on almost every other sector, from transport to construction and from culture to agriculture.
>
> (2008: 4)

This shift belatedly coincides with the decline of major traditional and manufacturing industries across Europe, which has catalyzed a substantial increase in focus on the contribution and impact of SMEs (see Hall 2005). Witness the statement that: 'The EU has thus placed the needs of SMEs at the heart of the Lisbon Growth and Jobs strategy, notably since 2005 with the use of the partnership approach, which has achieved tangible results' (EC 2008: 2). Prior to the ascension of the recent new members, SMEs in the

EU accounted for 23m enterprises, 75m jobs (80 per cent of overall employment) and 99 per cent of all enterprises (EC 2005b). Tourism when considered in terms of the overall tourism economy accounts for 11 per cent of GDP and 12 per cent of employment (Ianniello 2008). As regards tourism enterprises, very few (approx. 1 per cent) are not SMEs; the majority in fact are actually micro-enterprises (i.e. employ less than 10 persons) and are predominantly in the hospitality sector. The significance of these SMEs is that they are now very much a major focus of the EU, recognized for their diversity (EC 2008) and with regard to their impact on the environment (Leslie 2007).

There is a clear emphasis in EU policy on enterprises and the promotion of eco-efficiency – reducing ecological impacts and resource use towards more sustainable levels. Significantly, the creation of the Enterprise Directorate General (DG) with its orientation to SMEs (see Table 3.1) means that tourism enterprises are now very much a focus within the more general area of the Enterprise Directorate. Thus, they are subject to the influence of EU policy instruments promoting the 'greening' of enterprise, as well as those instruments aimed at the promotion and development of SMEs (see EC 2007a) and the promotion of entrepreneurship. This is explicitly manifest in the EU's initiative 'Think Small First' principle, which includes aims to simplify the burden of regulations and place an accent on competitiveness. Essentially this reinforces the value of SMEs within the EU and the need to promote and support but also further encourages: 'increased energy efficiency, partly through the implementation of environmental management systems in SMEs' (EC 2008: 16). This was furthered through the first 'European SME Week' in June 2009, which aimed to promote the role of EU policy by advocating SME support measures, share best practice, and so forth.

## The influence of environmental policy initiatives

There is no question that EU environmental policy in the last quarter of the twentieth century (see Baker 2002, for a comprehensive review) has influenced tourism development and enterprises, particularly with regard to the impacts of tourism (see Murphy 2001). A key theme of many programmes pertinent to the tourism arena is the EU's commitment to the promotion of economic activities while seeking to maintain and improve the quality of the environment. Witness the Treaty of Amsterdam, which aimed to promote 'a harmonious, balanced and sustainable development of economic activities' and 'a high level of protection and improvement of the quality of the environment' (Connelly and Smith 2003: 261). This is well illustrated, for example, by the European Landscape Convention. Steps taken to further this approach include the integration of the objectives of sustainable development (SD) into structural funds projects and other support initiatives; for example, the principles of the LEADER programme include issues of concern regarding the impacts of rural tourism (see EC 2000; Leslie 2007). These programmes, such as LEADER, in rural areas are now subject to requirements brought in under the EU's 'Rural Development Policy' (EC 2005a), which combines three central themes:

- improving the competitiveness of the agricultural and forestry sector;
- improving the environment and countryside;
- improving the quality of life in rural areas and encouraging diversification of the rural economy.

This heralds a greater emphasis on a coherent strategy across the EU with every Member State required to produce a rural development programme specifying funding and measures. The overall aim of EU strategy is to ensure consistency and identify where EU assistance can be most effective (Table 3.2). Evidence of the LEADER approach to development and supporting funding is manifest in encouraging the bottom-up approach in the planning and management of developments. The LEADER I and II programmes are also particularly notable in the context of rural tourism for the recognition of the potential of interrelationships between different economic activities in local economies, for example, the promotion of handicrafts and rural tourism services, and the need for rural diversification (Leslie 2007). However, arguably the most substantive evidence of explicit recognition of tourism in the context of EU environmental policy prior to 2000 is that of the 5th Environmental Action Plan (EAP) – 'Towards Sustainability'. This EAP has a strong focus on the consumption of resources and the need to reduce wasteful consumption, which is seen as a responsibility of all organizations and all persons. It promotes the 'polluter pays' principle. Tourism is also one of the five sectors identified and includes the objective of reconciling potential negative impacts of tourism with development. This plan also catalyzed an extensive number of eco-label schemes relating to tourism (Leslie 2007). While tourism was explicitly noted for negative impacts, the 5th EAP also held benefits for rural tourism, for example, through promoting conservation of habitats such as nature tourism. As Metsahallitus, the Finnish Forest and Park Service stated: 'The economic utilization of protected areas for ecotourism, for example, is permissible where it does not endanger achievement of conservation aims' (cited in Hall 2008: 112).

This theme of promoting the objectives of SD has continued to grow in significance, heralded in the sixth EAP (2001–10) 'Our Future, Our Choice', which promotes the integration of environmental policies and SD objectives in all EU policies, including the objective of 'greening' production methods and consumption (EC 2004b). This heralded a shift from a focus on 'end-of-pipe' solutions to issues and themes (Connelly and Smith 2003); all of which is applicable to tourism: for example, the promotion of information to consumers (such as eco-labels) and enterprises about the environmental

*Table 3.2* Selected major environmental policy initiatives and measures

| 1973 | First Environmental Action Plan |
| 1979 | Conservation of European Wildlife and Natural Habitats |
| 1990 | European Environmental Authority (EEA) |
| 1992 | Biological Diversity Convention: an outcome of the UNEP World Congress 1992 (The Earth Summit) supported<br>UNESCO's World Heritage Site Programme: supported |
| 1992 | Integrated Product Policy (IPP) – analyze product in terms of whole life cycle which is influential to eco-labeling schemes |
| 1992 | Protection of the Architectural Heritage |
| 1992 | Habitat Directive |
| 1993 | Community Eco-Management Audit Scheme introduced |
| 1993 | Fifth Environmental Action Programme introduced |
| 1994 | Packaging and Packaging Waste Directive |
| 1996 | Integrated pollution prevention and control (IPPC) |
| 1997 | Treaty of Amsterdam |
| 2000 | Sixth Environment Action Programme |
| 2000 | European Landscape Convention |
| 2000 | Natura 2000 |
| 2002 | Corporate Social Responsibility (CSR): a business contribution to sustainable development |
| 2002 | European SMEs and social and environment responsibility |
| 2004 | Strategy for Integrating the Environment into Industry |
| 2005 | Rural Development Policy |
| 2006 | Making Europe a pole of excellence on CSR |
| 2006 | EU Sustainable Development Strategy |

impacts of products and processes to encourage them to be more 'environmentally friendly' in their choices. This is reinforced in the 'Strategy for Integrating the Environment into Industry', which states the need to 'encourage changes in the behaviour of consumers' (EC 2004c: 4). This applies not only to consumers but also the personal values of the owners/ managers of enterprises (see EC 2002a). The sixth EAP called specifically for enterprises to 'go green' by way of becoming more efficient in the use of resources and reducing waste (EC 2001). These aims have been furthered promulgated through the EU's initiative 'responsible entrepreneurship', more widely known as Corporate Social Responsibility (CSR), which is seen as a way towards balancing the three pillars of sustainability which itself is considered by the EU to be societal responsibility (EC 2002b). Nicolau (2008) makes the point that CSR activities have social benefits as well as a positive influence on perceptions of the enterprise and argues that tourists respond well to clear messages relating to such activity, a point well exemplified by Ballantyre *et al.* (2009). Overall, there is no doubt that the quality of the environment has been gaining more explicit attention in EU policy, which has subsequently become more manifest in tourism since the turn of the century (see below); for example, encouraging rural tourism enterprises to adopt 'responsible behaviour' and to address their environmental performance (see EC 2000).

More widely, the incorporation of SD objectives in all EU policy areas in regional development programmes is seen to be a potentially fruitful approach as Bodorkos and Pataki argue: 'The potential for EU subsidies proved to be a good "instrumental" argument to initiate discussions with and open communication spaces on local values, assets and development directions' (2009: 1126). For example, this generates the need for a rural development plan involving the establishment of a local level organization to lead the planning and management development process involved; well illustrated by the European Charter for Sustainable Tourism in Protected Areas, 'EUROPARCS'. This is a good example of the 'bottom-up approach', i.e. resource-based, local community-led tourism planning and development within which the emphasis on rural development 'based on local resources and capabilities contributes to a more ecologically benign process than development for serving distant markets' (ibid.: 1129). This approach is being aided by a shift in emphasis in agricultural policy to adopt a more holistic approach – taking into consideration the wider economy and environment (TSG 2007).

The final policy identified in Table 3.2 is the launch of the EU's Sustainable Development Strategy (EC 2006b), which highlights as key challenges: sustainable transport, sustainable consumption and production and the conservation and management of natural resources. Further to this, the commitment of the EU to addressing climate change manifest in the accent on energy usage and targets, i.e. to reduce greenhouse gas emissions by 20 per cent; increase renewable energy sources by 20 per cent and improve energy efficiency by 20 per cent by 2020 (EC 2009) holds implications for rural tourism. The thrust on reducing greenhouse gas emissions will impact on transportation costs and thus tourists; especially given the possibility of instruments (e.g. see the Directive on Energy Performance and the Emission Trading Scheme proposals) being introduced to reduce air and car-based travel. The potential for which appears all the more likely in the wake of a report on the progress of EU's sustainable development strategy, which notes substantive challenges of achieving sustainable transport and that there are few signs of a shift towards more sustainable production and consumption (ECORYS 2008). Conversely, some progress was identified in the areas of biodiversity and natural resource management, which is a positive for rural tourism. This brings into focus tensions between economic growth and consumer /environmental protection, recognized as a source of friction within the EU but considered to be contrived conflict; as the EU's Vice-president for Enterprise and Industry argued: 'whatever may be ecologically wrong cannot be economically right' (Verheugen 2006: 1), a stance that supports the introduction of policy instruments to further the EU's sustainability objectives.

Overall, not only is the EU continuing to further policy and directives aimed at progress towards SD with an accent on resource management, in particular, waste (see EEA 2005), but also the steps they are taking are becoming more focused, notably in this context manifest in tourism policy initiatives (see below). However, the quality of the environment and the development of tourism within that environment are not uncontested and thus these initiatives will almost certainly result in added costs to the operations of rural tourism (see Bingham *et al.* 2003). Even so, as the OECD (2009) argue, it is the responsibility of the tourism business to ensure that the products offered have as little impact on the environment as possible. The EU's European Destinations of Excellence (EDEN) policy, introduced in 2007, supports this approach. It applies to tourism in protected areas, e.g. Natura 2000 or other protected area status, where visitor demand must be comparatively low and development evidence sustainability criteria. EDEN therefore is a way of promoting rural tourism in less popular locations, potentially drawing tourists from 'honey pots'. However, while the EC has introduced many substantive measures to address the quality of the environment, implementation of EU policy is difficult due to sector differences, problems arising due to the different agencies involved and various people dealing with different aspects of policy. As Beuner *et al.* (2009) argue, the attention in Member States is often more on compliance with Directives resulting in a loss of focus on the environmental objectives.

### Rise in attention to tourism

As noted earlier, tourism attracted little attention prior to the 1990s (see Table 3.3). The 'Community Action' was rather more a comment of intent encompassing vaguely defined aims across a broad spectrum of activity. Even so, rural tourism, especially in disadvantaged or 'less favoured' areas, attracted attention and ultimately support through EU structural programmes and related funding, especially from the European Regional Development Fund (ERDF) (Leslie *et al.* 1989). However, during the 1980s, while ERDF funding was substantial (approx. 7 per cent of the EU's budget in 1984), only a small percentage of that funded tourism projects – even so, at the project level this was substantial (Pearce 1988). This situation changed little in rural areas in the 1990s (see Cavaco 1995). The ERDF continues and, subject to key criteria relating to sustainability, is funding sustainable tourism-related projects; so too is the European Social Fund for employment, i.e. education and training. More recently, there is the new European Agricultural Fund for Regional Development, which is supporting diversification into tourism activities as well as giving consideration to projects relating to the countryside, environment and cultural heritage (see EC 2005c).

Certainly in terms of EU rhetoric, if not in actual effect, this *laissez-faire* approach started to change in the 1990s. One factor which certainly contributed to the increased attention witnessed during this period is the ascension of Greece (1981), Spain and Portugal (1986): countries with comparatively very high tourism activity. Key 'stepping stones' during this period in the development of the EU's approach to and policy for tourism

*Table 3.3*  Key stepping stones in the development of the EU's approach to tourism, 1982–99

| | |
|---|---|
| 1982 | Initial guidelines on a Community Policy for Tourism: only guidelines; three priority areas identified: seasonality, promote other forms of tourism; social tourism |
| 1984 | Council confirmed support for Community involvement in tourism |
| 1986 | Community Action in the Field of Tourism |
| 1986 | Advisory Committee on tourism established |
| 1990 | European Year of Tourism – opportunity for lobbying |
| 1990 | Community Action Plan to promote rural tourism |
| 1991 | Community Action Plan to Assist Tourism: This was the first time tourism was recognized explicitly as a concern for European Policy. Aims: improve knowledge of industry and greater consistency in community measures; staggering of holidays, transnational measures to support cooperation; three main areas: tourist consumer rights; cultural tourism; tourism's physical impacts. Also of note, attention to tourism information and marketing; and in wider context/other area: transportation; competition rules; attention to structural funds and tourism as a tool for regeneration |
| 1994 | Environment Council of EU – recognized promotion of tourism in long term requires protection of vulnerable areas, e.g. coastlines, historic town centres |
| 1995 | Green Paper on Tourism: consultation, to stimulate thought on future direction of policy<br>The consensus was that there should be an EU policy and plan for tourism |
| 1996 | Tourism and EU: focus on 'Tourism Means Jobs' |
| 1996 | First Multiannual Programme to Assist European Tourism: Philoxenia 1997–2000 (did not gain the support of all member states); clear focus on employment<br>Similar aims to earlier action plans, e.g. knowledge and information, improve cooperation between states, industry, stakeholders, etc., improve quality and competitiveness, remove obstacles to development<br>Also to promote environmental protection and sustainable development in tourism |
| 1998 | High level group on Tourism and Employment established |
| 1999 | For the first time, tourism not specifically mentioned in the portfolio of any Commissioner |

are presented in Table 3.3. Overall, the thrust of these measures and interventions is that tourism is seen as an economic activity and a creator of jobs. This emphasis on employment and the potential of tourism developments to generate jobs gained further impetus arising from the Lisbon Strategy, manifest in subsequent tourism policy initiatives (see EC 2006a, 2007b). These are particularly directed at socio-economic development and aim to combine competitiveness and employment with European territorial objectives. In parallel with this, attention to the impacts of tourism development on the environment continued.

## Progress towards a sustainable tourism policy

The opening decade of this century witnessed a further increase in the focus on tourism with a stream of policy initiatives (see Table 3.4). At the outset, there was a thrust towards promoting quality tourism that is competitive, responsive to social needs and attentive to the preservation of cultural and natural environments with an emphasis on SD objectives. This approach was to be supported by structural funds through the integration of SD objectives in projects funded by the EU. Furthermore, a key point was that tourism development must be integrative in planning and management processes and thus involve all stakeholders; for example, as illustrated in LEADER I and II programmes. This accent on quality was reinforced in 2001 in the communication 'Improving the quality of tourist products' and 'Working together for the future of European Tourism', adopted in late 2001. Shortly following this came the 'Measurement methods and tools necessary for monitoring the quality of tourist destinations and services – indicators and benchmarking' which included sustainability concerns. Subsequently, in 2004, the 'Manual for evaluating the quality performance of tourist destinations and services' was produced (see EU 2008) and the European Parliament issued a 'Resolution on new prospects and new challenges for sustainable European Tourism'. Reinforcement of this, and the presence of SD on the political agenda of Europe, in terms of tourism are not difficult to identify, for example, witness the EU's aim to 'promote sustainable development of tourism activities in Europe by defining and

*Table 3.4*  Major EU tourism policy initiatives post 1999

| | |
|---|---|
| 2000 | Tourism now a 'unit' within the newly created DG Enterprise and Information Society [known as Enterprise DG] created from DGIII, XIII and most of XXIII |
| 2000 | European Parliament: tourism policy considered to come under the Committee of Regional Affairs, Transport and Tourism |
| 2000 | Tourism Summit |
| 2000 | Report on Community measure affecting tourism |
| 2000 | Towards Quality Rural Tourism: Integrative Quality Management of Rural Destinations |
| 2001 | Working together for the future of Europe tourism |
| 2001 | Improving the quality of tourist products |
| 2002 | Agenda 21 – Sustainability in the European Tourism Sector |
| 2003 | Basic orientations for the sustainability of European tourism |
| 2003 | Structure, performance and competitiveness of European tourism and its enterprises |
| 2003 | Using Natural and Cultural Heritage to Develop Sustainable Tourism |
| 2004 | Tourism Sustainability Group established |
| 2004 | Manual for evaluating the quality performance of tourist destinations and services |
| 2005 | Council conclusions on the sustainability of European tourism |
| 2006 | Making Tourism More Sustainable – a guide for policy-makers |
| 2006 | Renewed tourism EU policy: towards a stronger partnership for European Tourism |
| 2007 | An Agenda for a sustainable and competitive European Tourism |
| 2008 | Network for the competitiveness and sustainability of European Tourism – aims to support small and micro enterprises |

implementing an Agenda 21' (EC 2003a: 4). This affirmed the role of local Agenda 21 planning and local governance (see EC 2002c). Indeed, a major outcome of the EU's Tourism Sustainability Group (TSG), established in 2004, was projected to be an 'Agenda 21 for European Tourism by 2007', which was expected to include some form of business impact assessment (Leslie 2007).

As noted, the EU's requirement for Member States to produce a 'Rural Development Policy' is especially important to rural tourism. The aims of such a policy are to promote economic activity and diversification in rural areas while at the same time seeking to protect and manage rural resources in a comprehensive way with due regard for SD objectives. Thus, tourism enterprises are not to be considered solely in terms of their products/services but in the wider context of their external environment; a continuation of earlier approaches to tourism (EC 2000, 2003b). Recognition of the role tourism can play in contributing to diversification in rural environments is further evident in support by the European Agricultural Fund for Rural Development. A key requirement of these rural development policies is for an integrative approach. This is applicable to tourism policy and reinforces Cawley and Gillmor's (2008) point on the need to integrate all stakeholders in rural development tourism policy and planning, in the process to achieve agreement between potentially diametrically opposed factions, e.g. tourism entrepreneurs and local residents not involved in tourism. Essentially, this places control in the hands of stakeholders at the local level, which demands working together and thus cooperation and networking with the key objective of achieving some form of sustainability in tourism. Overall, rural development policies and integrative tourism policy and planning can generate creative outcomes, especially through the promotion of networks/clusters. For example, promoting tourism to a region through a thematic approach based on related elements of an area's cultural heritage (see EC 2003c; Leslie 2005). Furthermore, while networking is invariably driven by economic factors, as Erkus-Ozturk and Eraydin (2010) argue, this can encourage attention to environmental quality at the local level through the involvement of environmental groups.

Essentially, the EU's approach is based on reinforcing the existing framework and maximizing the initiatives involved, more specifically, better 'monitoring and reporting of the sustainability of tourism, activities that further tourism consumption patterns by European citizens, and promoting sustainability in the tourism value chain and destinations' (EC 2003b: 3). Subsequent iterations may be seen as little more than furthering these objectives but with more explicit attention to aspects of SD. To illustrate: in 2006, the Commission produced *A Renewed EU Tourism Policy: Towards a Stronger Partnership for European Tourism*, the overall aim of which was 'to improve the competitiveness of the European tourism industry and create more and better jobs through the sustainable growth of tourism in Europe and globally'(EC 2006a: 4), in effect, the promotion of 'sustainable tourism', which essentially is but best practice in the development and management of tourism within destination localities (see Leslie 2009). As Ioannides encapsulates: 'The EU's approach is that "sustainable tourism" is development of tourism in such a way as not to degrade the environment or inhibit the successful development and well being of other activities and processes' (2009: 56). In terms of rural tourism, this mirrors the view of Priestley *et al.* of a decade earlier that essentially the approach may best be described as 'ecologically sustainable tourism' (1996: 9) with the priority on natural resources and ecosystems. However, the orientation to economic growth was further supported by the finding that tourism was showing a comparatively higher growth rate in employment than the average for the economy as a whole (EC 2006a). A number of other key factors, which support the development of rural tourism are as follows:

- the diversity in provision and the importance of maintaining this diversity (also acknowledged in the renewed Lisbon Treaty);
- that uncontrolled development generates negative impacts on the environment;
- the ageing demographic profile across Europe's population; an outcome of this is suggested to be the growing demand for rural tourism, i.e. away from coastal resorts and 'sand, sun and sea'.

Attention was also given to the development of performance criteria, e.g. ecolabels and promotion of the new Europe Flower Label, and that sustainability issues should be included in all certification programmes, thus linking quality tourism with environmental performance and reinforcing the view that there is a need to be more environmentally aware *and* environmentally friendly in practice. To this end, there was evident consideration given to Codes of Conduct and the introduction of a tourist tax in some form or other to fund conservation. While the latest policy contains little more than a reiteration of what has already been expressed, there is greater emphasis on the environmental performance of tourism enterprises and perhaps the first indicative step towards the introduction of instruments to further the objectives of sustainability and conserving/preserving the natural and cultural heritage.

In 2007, the TSG produced the 'Action for More Sustainable European Tourism'; a detailed framework, which included designating specific activities to specific stakeholder groups and, notably, a timetable for implementation. It also included a general note for specific supporting actions as well as proposals for promoting Europe as a tourist destination. However, given the preceding comments relating to the establishment of the TSG it is noteworthy that the anticipated policy proposal title of a 'European Agenda 21 for Tourism' (arguably thus seen as informed by Agenda 21 (see Leslie and Hughes 1997)) was changed to an 'Agenda for Sustainability of European Tourism' prior to the final title. These titular changes reinforce the perception that essentially the EU primarily considers tourism even more so now as a tool for economic development. However, major points of note are:

- the orientation to tourism development which is high quality, small-scale, high in revenue retention in local economy and with an accent on diversification;
- recognition that nature- and culture-related tourism demand is increasing;
- tourism enterprises and tourists need to be more pro-environment; thus promotes adoption of environmental management systems.

Overall, as the objectives and aims demonstrate (see Table 3.5), this Report encompasses everything already covered by the EU in relation to tourism since the Community Action Plan, with the added incorporation of initiatives relating to enterprises in general and also environment policy.

Following the TSG's report, the EU produced the *Agenda for a Sustainable and Competitive European Tourism* (EC 2007b), which is seen as the 'New' tourism policy. This Agenda primarily aims to sustain tourism promotion and development and rather downplays dimensions of sustainability. It confirms the view that tourism is seen as a major tool for regional and local development throughout the EU. Verheugen stated recently: 'Tourism is a strategically important sector for the European economy and can play an important role in reaching the goals of the Growth and Jobs Strategy' (2008: 2). This 'Agenda' is clearly based on the TSG's Report, as the following objectives evidence:

- Promote competitiveness and sustainability; as such enterprises should address 'sustainability concerns in a socially responsible manner' (EC 2007b: 13) while integrating sustainability is seen to enhance competitive advantage.
- Improve the regulatory environment e.g. facilitate new starts.
- Enhance the understanding and visibility of tourism.
- Promotion of European destinations, i.e. European Destination Tourism Portal (see www.visiteurope.com).

The principles articulated for achieving a competitive and sustainable tourism throughout the EU are as follows (EC 2007b: 6):

- Take a holistic and integrated approach.
- Plan for the long term.
- Achieve an appropriate pace and rhythm of development.
- Involve all stakeholders.
- Utilize best available knowledge.
- Minimize and manage risk (precautionary approach).
- Promote negative impacts, e.g. externalities should be included in costs (polluter pays principle).

*Table 3.5* Action for More Sustainable European Tourism: objectives and aims

---

OBJECTIVES

1  Economic prosperity

- to ensure the long-term competitiveness, viability and prosperity of tourism enterprises and destinations
- to provide quality employment opportunities, offering fair pay and conditions for all employees and avoiding all forms of discrimination.

2  Social equity and cohesion

- to enhance the quality of life of local communities through tourism, and engage them in its planning and management
- to provide a safe, satisfying and fulfilling experience for visitors, available to all without discrimination by gender, race, religion, disability or in other ways.

3  Environmental and cultural protection

- to minimize pollution and degradation of the global and local environment and the use of scarce resources by tourism activities
- to maintain and strengthen cultural richness and biodiversity and contribute to their appreciation and conservation.
  [p.3]

AIMS include:

Reducing the seasonality of demand.

Addressing the impact of tourism transport: reducing emissions from transport – increasing alternatives to popular transport – e.g. away from the plane and the car.

Increase carbon offsetting schemes.

Adoption of polluter pays, e.g. through adjusting taxation and pricing.

Improving the quality of tourism jobs.

Maintaining and enhancing community prosperity and quality of life, in face of change.

Minimizing resources use and production of waste.

Conserving and giving value to natural and cultural heritage.

Making holidays available to all.

Using tourism as a tool in global sustainable development.

---

Source: TSG (2007)

- Set and respect limits, where appropriate, e.g. apply carrying capacity models.
- Undertake continuous monitoring.

In effect, this is a policy agenda for tourism development which reinforces the overall approach of the EU since the 1990s with an increasing accent on the development of enterprise but with an emphasis on small-scale, locally managed and controlled tourism which is socially responsible. In this, the EC recognizes the dominance of small and micro enterprises in supply, in support of which it recently announced the establishment of 'Networks for the competitiveness and sustainability of European Tourism' specifically to support these tourism enterprises. Overall, this 'Agenda' recognizes previous and ongoing policy initiatives and measures and as such reflects the view of Ianniello (2008: 6) that tourism increasingly is seen as needing integration in all policy areas and that all policies should give considered attention to their potential or actual impact on tourism.

## Conclusion

Throughout the early decades of the EU, attention to tourism was fragmented and piecemeal with no strategic direction or underpinning in terms of 'competence'. However, tourism did benefit as a result of general measures taken by the EC which aimed to address industry in general, for example, consumer protection, and particularly in the area of addressing environmental issues, which benefited the development of tourism in rural areas. Additionally, tourism development opportunities have gained through measures designed to aid regional development in 'less advantaged areas'. However, throughout the 1990s, there was an emergent shift in attention to tourism. In part, this change in emphasis arose as a result of its recognition as a 'competence' within the scope of services but also as a result of the decline of major sectors in the economy due to globalization and increasing competition outside of the European bloc. Thus, as more traditional sectors of the economy across the EU declined (e.g. large enterprises involved in manufacturing), more attention was given to SMEs which hitherto had largely been excluded from many general measures and policy instruments.

As evident from the discussion, the first decade of the twenty-first century has witnessed a growing emphasis on tourism with the accent on its potential to generate economic growth and jobs. Over the same period the EC has continued to address environmental issues and promote the objectives of sustainable development, in the process integrating environmental and sustainability criteria into funding measures to further such objectives. This process reinforces the current approach of the EC to attaining policy objectives, which is orientated to using policy instruments rather than regulation. However, whether instruments in themselves will achieve the targeted outcomes, for instance, regarding energy and waste management and reductions in greenhouse gas emissions, is a matter of debate. Furthermore, there is no doubt that the EC's agenda on sustainability is increasingly being translated into actions which directly or indirectly impact on tourism development and those enterprises which seek to meet the needs of tourists; for example, Directives and Council Regulations relating to waste management and energy consumption. Indeed, tourism is now seen as needing integration in all related EC policies and that there should be better consideration and coordination between policies which may impact on tourism (see Ianniello 2008).

This attention to the objectives of SD, coupled with a plethora of non-sectoral specific policies and Directives germaine to sustainability, not only reinforces the advocacy of social responsibility but also attention to the promotion of tourism development attuned both to social and community needs and with regard to reducing potential negative impacts on the environment, and is now well established. Furthermore, policy also now encompasses the need to attend to the wider aspects involved in maximizing the role of rural tourism in contributing to aiding local economies, generating new markets and encouraging diversification: in particular, to encourage tourism in currently less popular tourist destinations, which is partly seen as a way of reducing seasonality and congestion elsewhere. Thus, attention to and consideration for the sustainability of tourism in Europe are well established, with a clear accent on conserving the natural and cultural heritage and in so doing promoting the distinctiveness of European tourism. However, the overarching view of the EC is that the environment is important but not at the cost of economic development and generation of jobs. As such, the success of the latest policy development, particularly given the EC's accent on partnerships, is very dependent on the actions of all the stakeholders involved. This is especially evident in rural tourism, which is recognized as a tool for development and diversification and, as such, supported by a range of other policy initiatives such as Rural Development Planning.

The priority of policy, as established in *An Agenda for a Sustainable and Competitive European Tourism*, albeit with its emphasis on economic growth and jobs, is on natural resources and ecosystems and thus an accent on soft forms of tourism activity, e.g. nature, ecotourism and adventure tourism. In other words, rural resource-based tourism development with attention to community needs and diversification within the local/regional economy. This approach could lead to both conservation and economic activity which promotes resource management and addresses environmental degradation as well as contributing to drawing attention to, and potentially mitigating, rural problems whether of patterns of land use, local community or the local economy.

## References

Baker, S. (2002) 'The evolution of European Union environmental policy: from growth to sustainable development?', in S. Baker, M. Kousis, D. Richardson and S. Young (eds) *The Politics of Sustainable Development: Theory, Policy and Practice within the European Union*. London, Routledge, pp. 91–106.

Ballantyre, R., Packer, J. and Hughes, K. (2009) 'Tourists' support for conservation messages and sustainable management practices in wildlife tourism experiences', *Tourism Management* 30(5): 658–64.

Beuner, R., ven der Knapp, W. G. M. and Biesbroek, G. R. (2009) 'Implementation and integration of EU Environmental Directives: experiences from The Netherlands', *Environmental Policy and Governance* 19: 57–69.

Bingham, N., Blowers, A. and Belshaw, C. (eds) (2003) *Contested Environments*. Chichester: John Wiley & Sons.

Bodorkos, B. and Pataki, G. (2009) 'Linking academic and local knowledge: community based research and service learning for sustainable development in Hungary', *Journal of Cleaner Production* 17: 1123–31.

Cavaco, C. (1995) 'Rural tourism: the creation of new tourist spaces', in A. Montanari and A. M. Williams (eds) *European Tourism: Regions, Spaces and Restructuring*. Chichester: John Wiley & Sons, pp. 127–50.

Cawley, M and Gillmor, D. A. (2008) 'Integrated rural tourism: concepts and practices', *Annals of Tourism* 35(2): 316–37.

Connelly, J. and Smith, G. (2003) *Politics and the Environment: From Theory to Practice*. London: Routledge.

EC (2000) *Towards Quality Rural Tourism: Integrated Quality Management [IQM] of Rural Destinations*. Brussels: DG XXIII Tourism Directorate. Commission of the European Communities.

—— (2001) *Executive Summary from E.C. Environment 2010: Our Future, Our Choice*. 6th A.P COM (2001) 31 Final. Brussels: Commission of the European Communities.

—— (2002a) *European SMEs and Social and Environment Responsibility*. Observatory of European SMES 2002/No. 4. Brussels: Commission of the European Communities.

—— (2002b) *Corporate Social Responsibility: A Business Contribution to Sustainable Development*. COM (2002) 347 Final. Luxembourg: Commission of the European Communities, 2 July.

—— (2002c) *Agenda 21: Sustainability in the European Tourism Sector*. COM (2002) 347 Final. Brussels: Commission of the European Communities, 2 June.

—— (2003a) *Structure, Performance and Competitiveness of European Tourism and its Enterprises*. Brussels: Commission of the European Communities.

—— (2003b) *Basic orientations for the Sustainability of European Tourism*. COM (2003) 716 Enterprise Directorate-General, Brussels: European Commission, 21 November.

—— (2003c) *Using Natural and Cultural Heritage to Develop Sustainable Tourism*. Directorate-General Enterprise – Tourism Unit. Brussels: Commission of the European Communities.

—— (2004a) *EU Support for Tourism Enterprises and Tourist Destinations: An Internet Guide*. Directorate D – Unit D3. Brussels: Commission of the European Communities.

—— (2004b) *The European Union 6th Environmental Action Programme – TowardsaA Thematic Strategy on the Sustainable Use of Natural Resources: 'Pathways Through Society'* – Working Group 2 – Use of Natural Resources. Final Report COM (2003) 572. Brussels: Commission of the European Communities, 15 October.

—— (2004c) *Strategy for Integrating the Environment into Industry*. Brussels: Commission of the European Communities.

—— (2005a) *'Rural Development Policy' 2007–2013*. Council Regulation (EC) No.1698. Brussels: Commission of the European Communities.

—— (2005b) *Implementing the Community Lisbon Programme Modern SME Policy for Growth and Employment.* Communication from the Commission of the European Communities COM (2005) 551 final. Brussels: Commission of the European Communities, 10 November.

—— (2005c) *Competitiveness and Innovation Framework Programme.* COM (2005) 121 Final. Brussels: Commission of the European Communities, 6 April.

—— (2006a) *Renewed Tourism EU policy: towards a stronger partnership for European Tourism.* COM (2006) 134 Final. Brussels: Commission of the European Communities. 17 March.

—— (2006b) *Sustainable Development Strategy.* Luxembourg: Commission of the European Communities.

—— (2007a) *Small and Medium Sized Enterprises: Key for Delivering Growth and Jobs: A Mid Term Review of Modern SME Policy.* COM (2007) 592 Final. Brussels: Commission of the European Communities, 4 October.

—— (2007b) *An Agenda for a Sustainable and Competitive European Tourism.* COM (2007) 621 Final. Brussels: Commission of the European Communities, 19 October.

—— (2008) *'Think Small First' A 'Small Business Act' for Europe.* COM (2008) 394 Final. Brussels: Commission of the European Communities, 25 June.

—— (2009) www._ec.europa.eu/enterprise/environment (accessed 20 May 2009).

ECORYS (2008) *Progress on EU Sustainable Development Strategy: Final Report.* Rotterdam: ECORYS Nederland, BV, February.

EEA (2005) *Environmental Policy Integration in Europe: Technical Report 2.* Copenhagen: European Environment Agency, May.

Erkus-Ozturk, H. and Eraydin, A. (2010) 'Environmental governance for sustainable tourism development: Collaborative networks and organisation building in the Antalya tourism region', *Tourism Management* 31(1): 113–24.

EU (2008) *Quality in Tourism Product.* Available at www.europa.eu.int/comm/ enterprises/services/tourism (accessed 15 May 2009).

Hall, C. M. (2005) *Tourism: Rethinking the Social Science of Mobility.* Harlow: Pearson.

—— (2008) *Tourism Planning: Policies, Processes and Relationships.* Harlow: Pearson. Available at: http://europa.eu.int/comm/enterprises/services/tourism/ policy-areas/measures.htm.

Ianniello, F. (2008) *EU Tourism Policy.* Research EU Focus. Number 1, September, pp. 4–7.

Ioannides, D. (2009) 'Hypothesizing the shifting mosaic of attitudes through time: a dynamic framework for sustainable tourism development in a "Mediterranean Isle"', in S.F. McCool and R.N. Moisey (eds) *Tourism, Recreation and Sustainability: Linking Culture and the Environment.* London: CABI, pp. 51–75.

Leslie, D. (1996) 'Consumer policy', in R. Thomas (ed.) *The Hospitality Industry, Tourism and Europe: Perspectives on Policies.* London: Cassell, pp. 182–99.

—— (2005) 'Sustainability and Environmental Management in Sigala', in M. Leslie and D. Leslie (eds) *International Cultural Tourism: Management, Implications and Cases.* Oxford: Elsevier, pp. 111–21.

—— (2007) 'Scottish rural tourism enterprises and the sustainability of their communities: a local Agenda 21 approach', in R. Thomas and M. Augustyn (eds) *Tourism in the New Europe: Perspectives on SME Policies and Practices.* Oxford: Elsevier, pp. 89–108.

—— (ed.) (2009) *Tourism Enterprises and Sustainable Development: International Perspectives on Responses to the Sustainability Agenda*. New York: Routledge.

Leslie, D. and Hughes, G. (1997) 'Agenda 21, local authorities and tourism in the UK', *International Journal of Managing Leisure* 2(3): 143–54.

Leslie, D., McDowell, D. A. and McGurran, F. (1989) 'European Regional Development Fund and Northern Ireland: the additionality issue', *Public Policy and Administration* 4(3): 32–41.

Montanari, A. and Williams, A. M. (eds) (1995) *European Tourism: Regions, Spaces and Restructuring*. Chichester: John Wiley & Sons.

Murphy, J. (2001) 'From production to consumption: environmental policy in the European Union', in M. J. Cohen and J. Murphy (eds) *Exploring Sustainable Consumption: Environmental Policy and the Social Sciences*. Amsterdam: Pergamon, pp. 39–58.

Nicolau, J. L. (2008) 'Corporate social responsibility: worth-creating activities', *Annals of Tourism Research* 35(4): 990–1006.

OECD (2009) *The Impact of Culture on Tourism*. Paris: OECD.

Pearce, D. G. (1988) 'Tourism and regional development in the European Community', *Tourism Management* 9(1): 13–23.

Priestley, G. K., Edwards, J. A. and Coccosis, H. (eds) (1996) *Sustainable Tourism? European Experiences*. Wallingford: CABI.

Robinson, G. (1993) 'Tourism and tourism policy in the European Community: an overview', *International Journal of Hospitality Management* 12(1): 7–20.

Thomas, R. (ed.) (1996) *The Hospitality Industry, Tourism and Europe: Perspectives on Policies*. London: Cassell.

TSG (2007) *Action for More Sustainable European Tourism: Report of the Tourism Sustainability Group*. Brussels, February.

Verheugen, G. (2006) 'Sustainability and Competitiveness', address by Vice President of EC for Enterprise and Industry at the meeting of the ENVI Committee, Strasbourg, 12 June 2006, available at: www.ec.europa.eu/enterprise/environment/ (accessed 10 May, 2009).

—— (2008) 'Welcome Message. Vice-President of the EC and Commissioner for Enterprise and Industry', *Research EU Focus*. Number 1, September, p. 2.

# 4 Ecotourism in the wider rural context

*Carl Cater and Erlet Cater*

## Introduction

Faced with the scenario of declining agricultural incomes over recent decades in Europe, rural tourism has been viewed as something of a silver bullet: as Hall and Page (1999: 195) describe, 'a panacea for solving all the economic and social ills of the countryside', and has consequently been widely inserted into rural development strategies. The significance of tourism to rural development in Europe was recognized, for example, by successive LEADER local rural development programmes. European Union (EU) LEADER programmes [I] 1991–94; [II] 1995–99; and [+] 2000–2006 all emphasized rural tourism as a means of economic diversification, for example, in LEADER I over one-third of European projects were tourism-related (Sharpley 2002), and 44 per cent of LEADER I funded projects in Ireland were associated with rural tourism, accounting for 50 per cent of the LEADER funds directed to Ireland at that time (Hall and Page 1999). Widespread support for rural tourism throughout Europe was reflected by structural funding programmes 'as a means of addressing the socioeconomic challenges facing industries in peripheral rural regions' (Sharpley and Craven 2001: 528).

It is of interest that, in this way, rural tourism was thought to satisfy two fundamental criteria of sustainable tourism development called for by Hunter (1995): not only to be largely sustainable in itself but also, importantly, to contribute towards sustainable development in rural areas. Until relatively recently, as Sharpley (2004: 374) points out, rural tourist activities were usually closely allied to 'the "traditional" countryside, characterised by a politically, economically, and socially dominant agricultural sector and associated settlement patterns' and were thus largely viewed as 'passive, relaxing, and traditional'. Rural tourism was therefore seen to be synonymous with sustainable tourism development, 'with all that is implied for the nature, scale, character and ownership of tourism development' (Sharpley and Roberts 2004: 121). Page and Getz (1997: 15) also declare that 'Tourism in a rural context displays many of the features of the symbiotic relationship which exists between tourism and the environment.' Two major developments have, however, served to shatter this illusion: the fragmentation of rural systems in general (Sharpley 2004: 374) and that of rural tourism itself.

It is, therefore, into this post-productionist scenario that rural ecotourism is inserted. It follows that, despite its intrinsic key attributes being succinctly summarized as nature-based, environmentally educated and sustainably managed (Blamey 2001), its success, or even its very existence, as a sustainable rural development strategy may be compromised.

In the same way that Sharpley (2004: 375) suggests that much rural tourism research in the past was essentially 'tourism-centric', so, too, is there the danger of ecotourism centricity. If rural ecotourism is to deliver its promise, regard must be paid to the overall context in which it is to be situated. There are, unfortunately, all too many examples across the globe where ecotourism has been regarded as an automatic panacea and inserted into contexts where there is much going on to militate against its sustainability and its potential to contribute towards sustainable development. This is hardly surprising given the fragmented, sectoral approach to planning of rural areas in the past which had such a poor record of success. It is imperative, therefore, that a holistic approach is adopted, recognizing the complexities of interrelationships within and between activities and components of rural areas, and appreciating the myriad of co-dependencies and interdependencies at work which condition the prospects for rural ecotourism in any one locality.

A useful framework for beginning to appreciate these interrelationships is Gunnar Myrdal's theory of Circular and Cumulative Causation which outlines essentially what are positive, 'spread', effects and negative, 'backwash', effects operating at different scalar levels (Myrdal 1957). Myrdal, as a Swedish economist, was examining these processes with regard to the prospects for the economic development of underdeveloped regions, but it can be adapted to illustrate how the prospects for rural ecotourism are conditioned by the overall context in which it is nested. The positive, economic, socio-cultural and environmental spread effects of rural ecotourism can serve to widen the economic base, generate employment, reverse rural out-migration and disseminate awareness of sound environmental practice. The countervailing, negative, backwash effects, however, may work together to militate against the success and even the very existence of rural ecotourism as suggested above.

The positive, spread, effects include: economic growth and diversification through employment creation; the creation of new markets for agricultural products (Butler, for example, describes the widespread growth in the market for farm produce and how 'excursions into rural hinterlands for purchasing of rural produce . . . [are] now a major form of tourism and recreation' (2001: 436)); the broadening of a region's economic base; socio-cultural development including repopulation of rural areas; maintenance and improvement of public services; revitalization of local crafts, customs and cultural identities; protection and improvement of the natural and built environment; and increased opportunities for social contact and exchange (Sharpley 2002).

Set against these spread effects, however, countervailing, negative, back-wash effects may work together to prejudice sustainable outcomes for rural ecotourism. Backwash effects hinge around the fact that other, often competing, activities, are frequently detrimental to rural ecotourism. Unfortunately, due to structural inequalities, whereby powerful interests enmeshed in the global political economy dominate, backwash effects are often stronger than the positive, spread effects. This is particularly evident in rural locations in many parts of Europe where, as Butler (2001: 436) points out, 'distances from metropolitan centres to rural areas are small' and 'land no longer viable for agricultural production is often highly desired for residential or commercial use' and has a much higher value attached to it than under agriculture or 'low intensity tourism'.

## Rural ecotourism in context

There are various scale levels to consider when we examine the impact of other economic activities on rural ecotourism: First, it is necessary to view rural ecotourism in the context of nature tourism at large in the rural environment. What is crucial to recognize here is that while nature tourism may be ecologically based, it is far from certain that it will be ecologically sound. Increasing engagement in active pursuits in the countryside has led to the observation that 'The rural may indeed have become another playground' (Sharpley and Roberts 2004: 120). As Butler (2001: 436) suggests, 'many of the newer forms of leisure activities which are being pursued in the rural landscape are at the opposite end of the spectrum to ecotourism' and he goes on to observe that many such activities are characterized by being mechanized and dependent on high technology, placing 'little value on the innate naturalness of the environment in which they are practised'. A glaring example of this ilk is in Norway where

> a growing number of Norwegians are not raised according to these [traditional approaches to nature] and during the past decades new groups of nature users have entered the scene: people using motorized vehicles in the countryside such as snowmobiles and quad bikes
>
> (Viken 2006: 40)

Similarly, in Austria, Hummelbrunner and Miglbauer describe how:

> New trend sports are becoming a more and more familiar feature, even in remote rural areas, which offer the necessary terrain and ample natural resources for the practice of sports such as: mountain biking, rafting, hydro-speed, para-gliding, bungee-jumping, free climbing. They

bring with them a series [of] ecological, social and ethical conflicts and increasing tension between 'conserving' and 'utilising' natural resources.

(1994: 49)

Second, echoing the observation of the fragmented nature of rural tourism made above, we need to view rural ecotourism in the context of other rural tourism market segments which are dependent upon, and consequently impact upon, the natural environment. Lane (1994: 9) draws attention to the complexity of rural tourism as a 'multi-faceted activity', not only consisting of special interest nature holidays and ecotourism, but also including activities such as walking, riding, adventure, sport, hunting and angling. Page and Getz (1997: 6) argue that 'rural areas are places to be consumed and where production is based on establishing new places for tourism' and they describe 'the insatiable tourism appetite for rural environments' stimulated by, among other factors, the designation of environments as special places to visit (ibid.: 14). National Parks are a case in point. Such is their popularity in the UK, for example, in particular at weekends and National Holidays, that the most popular 'honeypot' locations become seriously congested. The Peak District National Park, for example, receives an estimated 30 million visitors a year, and locations such as Speedwell Cavern are characterized by nose-to-tail traffic jams.

While peripheral rural coastlines, by and large, have been spared the onslaught of mass visitation, with areas such as the Shannon Estuary actually benefitting from the introduction of new forms of tourism such as dolphin watching (Garrod and Wilson 2004), other remote peripheral rural coastlines have not been spared and have come within the reach of international tourism. An example is the knock-on effects of cruise ship visitation to the remote rural coastlines of Svalbard. While local cruise tour operators roughly balance visitation between the capital, Longyearbyen and outlying areas (in 2005, 6,183 and 8,782 respectively), external tour operators and overseas cruise lines disembarked only 4,894 around Longyearbyen but over ten times as many (49,832) outside – leading to the situation where 'there will soon be no places left unvisited along the coast of Svalbard' (Viken 2006: 51). The prospects for ecotourism must therefore be viewed in the light of such pressures, as Milne (1998) suggests, it is pointless to create a dichotomy between alternative and mass tourism when the reality is that all types of tourism development are interlinked. The fragmentation of rural tourism discussed above undeniably offers rural locations new opportunities for diversification and differentiation; the point to be made, however, is that prospects for sustainable ecotourism must be assessed in the light of other tourist activities present in the area.

Third, it is essential that we set rural ecotourism in the context of other economic activities. It seems ironic that tourism is promoted as a tool of economic diversification away from agriculture in rural areas but that policy-makers fail to acknowledge its significance through appropriate measures. This was poignantly illustrated in the Foot and Mouth epidemic of 2001 in the UK. Blake *et al.* (2001: 3) described how 'The closure of foot-paths and inland waterways to the public, as well as the inaccessibility of businesses within exclusion zones around infected areas . . . had a devastating effect on rural tourism activities'. Indeed, it has been suggested that the epidemic had much greater adverse effects on tourism than on agriculture. The cost of the epidemic to UK tourism from 2001–2 was estimated to be between £2.7 and £3.2 billion, with a further £1.8–2.2 billion to industries and services supported by tourism. Compensation to farmers amounted to approximately £1.15 billion (Franks *et al.* 2003), whereas tourism businesses saw precious little concrete measures other than for rate relief and tax deferment. Sharpley and Craven (2001: 533) describe how local rural tourism businesses were not only expected 'to seek advice and financial assistance from a variety of sources' but also any support was short term and 'principally on a deferral or loan basis', the latter at an interest rate of as high as 8.5 per cent which would considerably inhibit repayment prospects.

Another example of a potentially conflicting activity is that of fish farming which brings an obvious visual impact in rural coastal environments; considerable marine pollution, despite claims to the contrary; the potential for escapees disrupting the natural ecology including contamination of wild stocks; and conflict with local seal populations (in 2005, sixty seals were slaughtered by a fish farm company in the European Special Area for Conservation at Oban in Scotland (Carter 2005)). All these adverse impacts have obvious ramifications for environmental integrity and, hence, for ecotourism.

In the same way that it is inappropriate to divorce ecotourism from all other forms of tourism, so too do we ignore other economic activities *vis-à-vis* rural ecotourism at our peril when weighing up prospects for sustainability. As Butler (1998: 28) puts it: it is 'inconceivable to discuss sustainable tourism any more than we might discuss any other single activity . . . we cannot hope to achieve sustainability in one sector alone, when each is linked to and dependent on the others'. It is clear that rural ecotourism should not be regarded as an isolated alternative, disassociating it from all other forms of economic activity, reflecting Sharpley's (2004: 375) call for rural tourism management and development to be 'located within the frameworks of both overall tourism activity within a region or nation-state and also regional/national policy formulation for an integrated, multi-purpose countryside'.

The fourth and final context is that of the global. George *et al.* (2009) describe how the various processes of environmental, political, social and cultural change are acting to redefine rural spaces around the world. Global environmental change, as Gössling and Hall (2006: 1) point out, threatens 'the very foundations of tourism through climate change, modifications of global biogeochemical cycles, land alteration, the loss of non-renewable resources, unsustainable use of renewable resources and gross reductions in biodiversity'. Climate change is probably the most important consideration as it both produces and is a production of the manifestations of global environmental change suggested by Gössling and Hall. There has been a considerable impact of climate change on species distribution over the past two decades and, consequently, on the prospects for viewing wildlife by ecotourists (Cater and Cater 2007). This is particularly evident in rural coastal locations where the northward shift in cold water plankton, attributable to a 2°C rise in water temperatures in the North Sea (Wardlow 2004), has caused a corresponding decline in populations of sandeels which depend on the cold water plankton. The sandeel constitutes an important part of the diet for over 100 species of marine wildlife, including 40 species of birds, 12 species of marine mammals, 45 species of fishes and some invertebrates (Robards *et al.* 1999). Many of these, such as puffins, skuas, tern, minke whales, fin whales, humpback whales, white-beaked dolphins, grey seals and Harp seals, are popular viewing for ecotourists. It was postulated that the low sightings of minke whales off the west coast of Scotland in 2005 were down to the low stocks of sandeels. Over recent years there has been a catastrophic decline in the numbers of certain species of seabirds, for which sandeels constitute the staple diet. In the south Shetlands, where there were over 1,200 guillemot nests, all were empty in the Spring of 2004, and elsewhere on the Shetlands 24,000 arctic tern nests were almost entirely empty (Schulman 2005). In the summer of 2004, guillemots produced almost no young in Orkney and Shetland, yet more than 172,000 breeding pairs were recorded in the last national census: Seabird 2000. More than 6,800 pairs of great skuas were recorded in Shetland in the same census and yet only a handful of chicks were produced in 2004 (McCarthy 2004). The spectacular seabirds of the Northern Isles are doubly important. As well as their scientific value, they are of enormous significance to Orkney and Shetland tourism, being the principal draw for many visitors. Birdwatching in general is appealing to more and more people, evidenced by the fact that membership of the Royal Society for the Protection of Birds (RSPB) in the UK doubled between 1987 and 1997, with the current figure at over one million.

Other ways in which the global-local nexus is manifest in dictating prospects for rural ecotourism are through the influence of international governance (the EU LEADER programmes and the push for Integrated Rural Development being a case in point); and through the all-pervasive influence of the processes of globalization whereby prospects of and for ecotourism in rural areas are linked to multiscale politico-economic processes. Zimmerer and Bassett (2003: 288) point to the need to go 'beyond single geographical scale factors influencing land and resource use (e.g. the village) to consider the many regional, national and international dimensions'.

## Implications for rural development

So, what are the implications of all these inter-relationships for rural development? The wider context in which ecotourism is set as a process and as a principle is important, because that context has a vital role to play in prospects for sustainable outcomes for rural development. Gordon and Goodall (2000: 292) state that the aim must be 'to understand, in a theoretically informed way how the processes of interaction between tourism and sets of place characteristics operate, and develop over time, in different contexts'.

Linking in with rural development policies, we can see in Europe that LEADER programmes marked a fundamental shift in EU support policies from a sectoral approach (agriculture) to one that is territorial (rural). The emphasis is on an integrated approach to rural development which 'must be local and community driven within a coherent European framework' (Shortall and Shucksmith 1998). Ray describes how:

> The announcement of the LEADER initiative was a signal that EU rural development policy was to include a further local targeting of Structural Fund Policy. The organisations that were to instigate the design and implementation of LEADER were to be local in their membership (with a strong presence for the private sector) and to encourage 'bottom-up' development at the very local level. Thus, LEADER was not only about spatial scale, it was also to be based on a strong ethos of local participation in the design and implementation phases.
>
> (1998: 80)

As he points out, rural tourism (raising standards of quality, area-level booking agencies, etc.) was one of the local proposals that would be seen to conform to certain categories of measure compatible with the reform of EU Structural Funds at the time.

So, from these requirements, it can be inferred that space is the integrative key, with different scalar levels providing the context in terms of the physical, technological, ecological, economic, cultural, social, political and institutional contexts which both shape and are shaped by tourism. It is therefore essential that the ramifications of changes to more ecologically sustainable forms of production, such as rural ecotourism, are considered in relation to social conditions and implications for economic and social sustainability (Hudson, cited in Williams and Shaw 1998). Sustainable development 'must be viewed as an evolving complex system' in which 'the alteration or disturbance of one component from within or without, may affect a hundred others' (Farrell and Twining-Ward 2005: 110). The essential dilemma is to reconcile different, sometimes polarized, often conflicting, viewpoints and values while recognizing that nothing is fixed or static: 'sustainability concepts are themselves forever evolving, adapting to site and regionally specific conditions, and they can never be cast as universal' (ibid.: 110). How do we begin to appreciate, and respond to, the vast complexity of interactions and interchanges involved in rural ecotourism? It is obvious that the viewpoint of any one stakeholder, researcher or facilitator will constitute only a partial insight, so the central message is that of a concerted, collective approach, conceptually and practically.

It is also clear that the approach needs to be problem-focused and that the local community needs to be involved from the very outset by defining the problem. All these features point towards a transdisciplinary approach, necessarily also trans-sectoral.

## The need for transdisciplinarity

The context for planning for sustainable rural ecotourism may be regarded as a prime example of a meta-problem, as described by Hall (2000) who examines how both tourism and the environment constitute meta-problems as they are characterized by highly interconnected planning and policy issues. For a multitude of reasons, rural tourism policy and, in turn, the context for planning for sustainable rural ecotourism, can be regarded as a prime example of a meta-problem. This is hardly surprising, given the fact that each of its components: sustainability, the rural environment and tourism are, in themselves, meta-problems. Policy and planning issues for rural ecotourism are far from simple as they 'cut across fields of expertise and administrative boundaries and, seemingly, become connected with almost everything else' (Ackoff, cited in Hall 2000: 145). Despite, or indeed perhaps because of, increasing and intensive multiple use of the countryside, policy-making has tended to be dominated by a sectoral approach which is primarily reactive and formulated on a piecemeal basis without interagency consultation, resulting in policies which often have conflicting objectives, resulting in environmental damage or ineffective implementation. Decision-making is thus highly fragmented and characterized by internal duplication and overlap, reflecting competition within and between sectors (Vallejo 1994). Given the almost unparalleled complexities involved, it is obvious that it is necessary to draw on a range of disciplines in order to better understand the multiple contexts, issues and viewpoints implicated in rural ecotourism. The essential challenge, however, is to move towards a holistic, integrated approach, rather than the piecemeal, disjointed, approaches which have characterized rural tourism to date.

A wide range of disciplines can be drawn upon to throw light on the complexities of the interlinkages and interchanges that exist within and between the diversity of processes which operate in the countryside, and, in turn, dictate the variability, viability, and vulnerability, as well as the validity and value of rural ecotourism. However, while varying disciplinary perspectives are invaluable, for example, in embracing different scale levels as in political ecology, or throwing light on tourist motivation and experience through humanistic psychology, they are only part of the whole. Furthermore, 'monodisciplinary analyses of environmental decisions are unable to reflect the nature of decision making adequately, leading to "thin" explanations' (Adger *et al*. 2003: 1097).

It could be argued that a multidisciplinary approach is a step in the right direction insofar as it involves a number of disciplines coming together with specialists working alongside one another. However, while it enables issues and problems to be examined from different perspectives, each disciplinary group will be working within its own field on a specific aspect of the same issue, and the end product of this exercise will only be a juxtaposition of disciplinary outputs. Visser (2004) suggests that this outcome must be avoided as there will be no systematic attempt at integration. Farrell and Twining-Ward (2004: 286) reiterate Norgaard's call for a 'transformation from disciplinary to interdisciplinary or even transdisciplinary thinking'.

Visser (2004: 29) recognizes that interdisciplinarity 'has been on the policy agenda for almost two decades, as the public awareness and the recognition of the intricate relationships between natural and social phenomena have become widespread'. It involves specialists working inter-actively on a problem, contributing their experience and disciplinary knowl-edge by transferring concepts and methods from one discipline to another. Adger *et al*. (2003) advocate an interdisciplinary approach to environmental decision-making because it enables a more holistic or 'thick' understanding of environmental decisions, accommodating plural methodologies and methods. While interdisciplinarity provides cross-fertilization of ideas between disciplines, however, merely to appreciate the interlinkages and interchanges is not enough: a move towards greater coherence (Laffoley *et al*. 2004) is necessary.

Recognizing that the confines of interdisciplinarity mean that 'there is still an enormous gap between recognition of complex interfaces and the implementation of an integrative approach to the kind, size and contents of these interelationships', Visser advocates a transdisciplinary approach for coastal zone research (2004: 29) which is equally applicable to inland areas. The main assumption of transdisciplinarity is that it transcends disciplinary divisions and boundaries, recognizing that the real world and its problems are not neatly ordered into confined disciplines. Consequently, transdiscipli-narity is problem-focused: starting from real-world problems and drawing from many disciplines to build knowledge around these. Visser (ibid.: 27–9) outlines what she considers to be four distinguishing, advantageous, features of transdisciplinarity. First, she identifies an essential paradox: because transdisciplinary research challenges existing assumptions and concepts, it forces reflexivity within individual disciplines, with members questioning their own premises and theories. Second, it is transparent insofar as it identifies conflicts and complementarities between disciplines. Third, it is realistic as it accommodates disjunctures, recognizing that diverse disciplines will attach differing values to certain concepts. Finally, transdisciplinarity aims at advancing the research agenda by identifying 'new research questions and concepts that move beyond the partner disciplines' (2004: 29). Farrell and Twining-Ward also advocate transdisciplinarity, arguing that 'the wider, more versatile, research oriented transdisciplinary approach allows for better understanding of the integration of natural and social systems' (2004: 286). Visser reasons that:

> The relevance of a transdisciplinary, and thus necessarily a transsectoral, approach is that it tries to move beyond the boundaries, knowledge, and assumptions of government institutions. Such an approach necessarily involves other segments and groups of society, with different and not sectorally determined bodies of knowledge, ranging from coastal communities . . . to NGOs together with central and decentralized government institutions and international organisations.
>
> (2004: 30)

Perhaps two of the most fundamental requirements of a transdisciplinary approach are that it is problem-focused, and that the knowledge of local rural communities is of paramount importance in problem definition. An example of a transdisciplinary approach arriving at a combined strategy for rural revitalization which includes rural ecotourism comes from the Piedmont Alps in Italy, north of Lake Maggiore, where local communities were faced with the consequences of progressive land abandonment (Höchtl *et al.* 2006: 323) as abandoned farmland had become transformed into '"wild areas" covered by dense shrub and woodland' through a process of natural reforestation. This had resulted in a concomitant decline in biodiversity, along with a loss of rural landscape and traditional land use practices. The central problem was how to ensure sustainable future landscape development. A six-year research project started with local perceptions which defined the problems perceived by the local community. Subsequent identification of core questions to be answered resulted in methodologies derived from disciplines not necessarily interrelated being combined and developed freely. 'They were transferred to new fields of application, which go beyond the traditional use: i.e. they were used in a transdisciplinary manner' (ibid.: 325). Flexible methodological practices were derived stemming from dialogue about problems by academics, policy decision-makers and lay-people. For the first time, the 'everyday activities' of the latter, their traditional land-use practices, were regarded as useful and were acknowledged by 'experts'. The resultant strategy recommended supporting existing agriculture and forestry practices as much as establishing new agricultural businesses and the development of ecotourism. This was implemented by the National Park administration in the Alpe Straolgio in the region in 2003 (ibid.: 327).

# Conclusion and lessons to be learned

Essentially this type of 'real-level' research (Höchtl *et al*. 2006) yields a great amount of practical and theoretical knowledge for researchers and stakeholders alike which 'grounds' rural ecotourism into the overall, place-specific, context. As Hall (2001: 613) suggests, there is 'no universal "best way": each region needs to select the appropriate policy mix for its own development requirements'. It is also essential to pay regard to the changing nature of both tourism and the countryside, so it becomes evident that the situation is far from fixed or static. Farrell and Twining-Ward (2004: 288) describe how 'Understanding of sustainability has shifted from the notion of a stable achievable goal, to the concept of transition based on multiple spatial and temporal scales in a dynamic landscape of human values.' As they later go on to argue:

> Varying temporal and spatial scales involved in the interaction of subsystems within tourism systems, and the evolving aspirations and values of local people and their representative stakeholders involved in co-management, together with the probability of surprise from within or outside the system, will always prevent the uniform achievement of permanence.
>
> (Ibid.: 111)

There is a need to recognize the above wherever and whenever 'continual change and evolution prevents the attainment of simultaneous sustainability' (ibid.: 119).

Awareness of this inescapable reality led to the emergence during the 1990s of the concept of the sustainability transition, which, as Farrell and Twining-Ward describe, incorporates a 'place-based' understanding of the interactions between environment and society, and it adopts a systems approach using adaptive management and social learning, indicating that there is no one management endpoint but 'continual development towards biophysical and human well-being' (ibid.: 118).

The challenge of a multiplicity of spatial and temporal scales, as well as changing human activity, inevitably demands flexibility, striking an appropriate balance across social, economic and environmental boundaries (see Laffoley *et al*. 2004: 58). As Farrell and Twining-Ward argue, there is a need for tourism researchers to venture outside the core tourism system:

> To explore the other connections and interactions that extend as far as tourism significantly affects the ways of life, the economic wellbeing of the system, and the people involved, either directly or indirectly. This comprehensive tourism system encompasses multiple system levels from the core, to the global or Earth system, all inter-related, open and hierarchical.
>
> (2004: 280)

Adding in the question of environmental integrity, it is obvious that two-way relationships are implicit, with rural ecotourism being not only instrumental in shaping but also being shaped by multiple system components and levels. Farrell and Twining-Ward go on to identify the existence of complex adaptive tourism systems (CATS), which require adaptive management concepts such as adaptive carrying capacity that factor in 'new scientific knowledge, locality, seasonality, tourist behaviour and local preferences' (ibid.: 284). Such adaptive management would adjust to the diverse, different, and continually evolving situations in rural environments in order to effect a sustainability transition. This is likely to involve compromises which will be site-specific. Outcomes may well prove to be suboptimal from the viewpoints of some or all concerned but, in the circumstances, more acceptable, feasible and practicable than hitherto unrealistic, unattainable end goals, thus resulting in more sustainable rural ecotourism than previously.

## References

Adger, W. N., Brown, K., Fairbrass, J., Jordan, A., Paavola,J., Rosendo, S. and Seyfang, G. (2003) 'Governance for sustainability: towards a "thick" analysis of environmental decisionmaking', *Environment and Planning A* 35: 1095–110.

Blake, A., Sinclair, T. and Sugiyarto, G. (2001) 'The economy-wide effects of Foot and Mouth Disease in the UK economy', paper given at the 3rd Annual Conference of the European Trade Study Group 2001. Available at: www.nottingham. ac.uk/ttri/pdf/2001_3.pdf.

Blamey, R. K. (2001) 'Principles of ecotourism', in D. B. Weaver (ed.) *The Encyclopedia of Ecotourism*. Wallingford: CABI, pp. 5–22.

Butler, R. (1998) 'Sustainable tourism-looking backwards to progress?' in C. M. Hall, and A. A. Lew (eds) *Sustainable Tourism: A Geographical Perspective*. Harlow: Longman, pp. 25–34.

—— (2001) 'Rural development', in D. B. Weaver (ed.) *The Encyclopedia of Ecotourism*. Wallingford: CABI, pp. 433–46.

Carter, M. (2005) 'The illegal killing of Scotland's seals: further eyewitness accounts'. Available at: www.salmonfarmmonitor.org/guest.html (accessed 30 January 2006).

Cater, C. and Cater, E. (2007) *Marine Ecotourism: Between the Devil and the Deep Blue Sea*. Wallingford: CABI.

Farrell, B. H. and Twining-Ward, L. (2004) 'Reconceptualizing tourism', *Annals of Tourism Research* 31(2): 274–95.

—— (2005) 'Seven steps towards sustainability: tourism in the context of new knowledge', *Journal of Sustainable Tourism* 13(2): 109–22.

Franks, J., Lowe, P., Phillipson, J. and Scott, C. (2003) 'The impact of foot and mouth disease on farm businesses in Cumbria', *Land Use Policy* 20(2): 159–68.

Garrod, B. and Wilson, J. C. (2004) 'Nature on the edge? Marine ecotourism in peripheral coastal areas', *Journal of Sustainable Tourism* 12(2): 95–128.

George, E. W., Mair, H. and Reid, D. G. (2009) *Rural Tourism Development: Localism and Cultural Change*. Clevedon: Channel View.

Gordon, I. and Goodall, B. (2000) 'Localities and tourism', *Tourism Geographies* 2(3): 290–311.

Gössling, S. and Hall, C. M. (eds) (2006) *Tourism and Global Environmental Change: Ecological, Economic, Social and Political Interrelationships.* London: Routledge.

Hall, C. M. (2000) 'Rethinking collaboration and partnership: a public policy perspective', in B. Bramwell and B. Lane, *Tourism Collaboration and Partnerships: Politics, Practice and Sustainability.* Clevedon: Channel View, pp. 143–58.

—— (2001) 'Trends in ocean and coastal tourism: the end of the last frontier?' *Ocean & Coastal Management* 44: 601–18.

Hall, C. M. and Page, S. J. (1999) *The Geography of Tourism and Recreation.* London: Routledge.

Hall, D., Roberts, L. and Mitchell, M. (2004) *New Directions in Rural Tourism.* Aldershot: Ashgate.

Höchtl, F., Lehringer, S. and Konold, W. (2006) 'Pure theory or useful tool: experiences with transdisciplinarity in the Piedmont Alps', *Environmental Science and Policy* 9(4): 322–9.

Hummelbrunner, R. and Miglbauer, E. (1994) 'Tourism promotion and the potential in peripheral areas: the Austrian case', *Journal of Sustainable Tourism* 2(1&2): 41–50.

Hunter, C. J. (1995) 'On the need to re-conceptualise sustainable tourism development', *Journal of Sustainable Tourism* 3(3): 155–65.

Laffoley, D. d'A, Maltby, E., Vincent, M. A., Mee, L., Dunn, E., Gilliland, P., Hamer, J. P., Mortimer, D. and Pound, D. (2004) *The Ecosystem Approach: Coherent Actions for Marine and Coastal Environments: A Report to the UK Government.* Peterborough: English Nature.

Lane, B. (1994) 'What is rural tourism?' *Journal of Sustainable Tourism*, 2: 7–21.

McCarthy, M. (2004) 'Disaster at sea: global warming hits UK birds', *The Independent.* 30 July 30.

Milne, S. S. (1998) 'Tourism and sustainable development: the global-local nexus', in C. M. Hall and A. A. Lew (eds) *Sustainable Tourism.* London: Addison-Wesley, pp. 35–48.

Myrdal, G. (1957) *Economic Theory and Underdeveloped Regions.* London: Methuen.

Page, S. J. and Getz, D. (1997) 'The business of rural tourism: international perspectives', in S. J. Page and D. Getz (eds) *The Business of Rural Tourism: International Perspectives.* London: International Thomson Business Press, pp. 3–37.

Ray, C. (1998) 'Territory, structures and interpretation: two case studies of the European Union's LEADER I Programme', *Journal of Rural Studies* 14(1): 79–87.

Robards, M. D., Willson, M. F., Armstrong, R. H. and Piatt, J. F. (1999) 'Sand lance: a review of biology and predator relations and annotated bibliography', *Research Paper PNW-RP 521.* Portland, OR: United States Department of Agriculture Forest Service, Pacific Northwest Research Station.

Roberts, L. and Hall, D. (2001) *Rural Tourism and Recreation: Principles to Practice.* Wallingford: CABI.

Schulman, A. (2005) 'A warm unwelcome', available at: www.grist.org/news/maindish/2005/01/25/schulman-seabirds (accessed 25 January 2006).

Sharpley, R. (2002) 'Rural tourism and the challenge of tourism diversification: the case of Cyprus', *Tourism Management* 23(3): 233–44.

—— (2004) 'Tourism and the countryside', in A. A. Lew, C. M. Hall and A. M. Williams (eds) *A Companion to Tourism*. Oxford: Blackwell, pp. 374–86.

Sharpley, R. and Craven, B. (2001) 'The 2001 foot and mouth crisis: rural economy and tourism policy implications: a comment', *Current Issues in Tourism* 4(6): 527–37.

Sharpley, R. and Roberts, L. (2004) 'Rural tourism: 10 years on', *International Journal of Tourism Research* 6: 119–24.

Shortall, S. and Shucksmith, M. (1998) 'Integrated rural development: issues arising from the Scottish experience' *European Planning Studies* 6(1): 73–88.

Vallejo, S. M. (1994) 'New structures for decision making in integrated ocean policy: introduction', in P. B. Payoyo (ed.) *Ocean Governance: Sustainable Development of the Seas*. Tokyo: UN University Press. Available at: www.unu.edu/unupress/unupbooks/uu15oe/uu15oe0b.htm (accessed 6 May 2004).

Viken, A. (2006) 'Ecotourism in Norway: non-existence or co-existence?' in S. Gössling and J. Hultman (eds) *Ecotourism in Scandinavia: Lessons in Theory and Practice*. Wallingford: CABI.

Visser, L. E. (2004) 'Reflections on transdisciplinarity, integrated coastal development, and governance', in L. E. Visser (ed.) *Challenging Coasts: Transdisciplinary Excursions into Integrated Coastal Zone Development*. Amsterdam: Amsterdam University Press, pp. 23–47.

Wardlow, J. (2004) *Will Puffins Disappear?* Available at: www.ch4.org.uk/edu article.php/Will+Puffins+Disappear per cent3F (accessed 25 January 2006).

Williams, A. M. and Shaw, G. (1998) 'Tourism and the environment: sustainability and economic restructuring', in C. M. Hall and A. A. Lew (eds) *Sustainable Tourism: A Geographical Perspective*. Harlow: Longman, pp. 49–59.

Zimmerer, K. S. and Bassett, T. J. (2003) 'Future directions in political ecology: nature-society fusions and scales of interaction', in K. S. Zimmerer and T.J. Bassett, *Political Ecology: An Integrative Approach to Geography and Environment-Development Studies*. New York: The Guilford Press, pp. 275–95.

# 5   Tourism in semi-rural environments

## Sustainability issues and experience from the Baltic States

*Derek Hall*

## Introduction

This chapter aims briefly to draw together three under-represented themes in the tourism literature:

- the conceptualization of tourism in semi-rural environments, beyond, yet strongly influenced by, the urban periphery;
- sustainability issues relating to tourism within the urban-rural continuum;
- emerging tourism experiences in the Baltic States (Estonia, Latvia, Lithuania) under conditions of transition.

It concludes, unsurprisingly, that there is a rich seam of potential research issues to be mined at this interface.

The literature on tourism in peripheral areas is now substantial (e.g. Brown and Hall 2000b; Hall and Boyd 2005). The appeal of peripheries is based on their power to signify to the visitor the unspoilt, pristine, and traditional – in contrast to the symbolic associations of the centre with the inauthentic, jaded, and modern (Scott 2000: 59; Urry 1995). But if we conceptualize the urban-rural fringe neither as a periphery nor a centre, but as a margin, even a vacuum, between the two, we are suggesting that it can draw selectively on the positive and negative elements of both periphery and centre. If perceptions of peripheries raise paradoxes (Brown and Hall 2000a), then conceptions of such 'inner' marginal areas suggest further contradictions of space and imagery. In post-Soviet societies, this is especially true.

Just as the English language literature on the consequences of post-communist restructuring for the old Stalinist mono-technic cities and regions of Central and Eastern Europe (CEE) is limited (Lintz *et al.* 2007), so the spaces between dynamic cities and their often impoverished rural hinterlands have been neglected in the wider literature in general, and in the tourism literature in particular.

## Tourism and marginality in the Baltic States

For travellers and analysts from a number of other countries, the Baltic States themselves will be perceived as peripheral – on the northern margin of continental Europe and part of the northern or Baltic rim (e.g. Porter 2001). For many in the 'West', these countries' absorption by the Soviet Union from 1944 until the fragmentation of the latter in 1990–91 substantially reinforced their psychological as well as geographical peripherality.

Since the early 1990s, however, these countries' post-Soviet transitions have witnessed the role of tourism playing an important part in:

- consolidating relations with the rest of Europe, contributing to positive national imagery and assisting the pathway to EU accession in 2004 (Clottey and Lennon 2003; Druva-Druvaskalne *et al.* 2006; Endzina and Luneva 2004; Jaakson 2000; Jarvis and Kallas 2006, 2008; Vihalemm 2007);
- facilitating foreign direct investment, labour mobility, and domestic entrepreneurial development as important elements in the restructuring of these countries' national economies (Aun 1996; Burinskiene and Rudzkiene 2005; Jaakson 1996a, 1996b; Worthington 2001);
- rebuilding, rejuvenating and re-imaging a wide range of urban areas, including pre-existing resort areas, many with considerable heritage appeal (Müristaja 2003; Peil 2005; Saarinen and Kask 2008; Upchurch and Teivane 2000; Worthington 2003, 2004);
- introducing the concepts of sustainability, rural- and eco-tourism (to assist a revival and diversification of rural economies), of integrated rural development and enhancement of environmental conservation policies (Armatienė *et al.* 2006; Granberg 2004; Hall 2005; Herslund 2007; Jaakson 1998; Pilāts 2004; Unwin 1996, 1997).

Writing in mid-2009, at a time of economic recession and when the Kremlin appeared to be seeking to rewrite or even recapture its history in the Baltic States (e.g. Walker 2009), the interrelated issues of sustainability, heritage and development paths were very much alive in Lithuania, Latvia and Estonia. Tourism is a significant element in such debates.

## The semi-rural margin

Increasing population density in and adjacent to major urban areas has led to greater competition for space between housing, industry, transport, agriculture, forestry, nature conservation, recreation and tourism, with simultaneous demands to meet a large number of societal needs on scarce 'peri-urban' land (Vandermeulen *et al.* 2009). 'Semi-rural', 'peri-urban', 'urban periphery', 'rural-urban fringe', 'rural-urban continuum', all are terms used to describe the area just beyond, or interlacing with, major urban built-up areas. As the focus of this chapter, these marginal 'transition' zones may have a number of (often common) characteristics (Table 5.1).

Given some of these characteristics, such marginal areas may hold or represent pejorative connotations for both urban and rural residents – isolation hospitals, prisons, noxious activity, and dereliction. Further, the enforcement of restrictive green belt policies may appear to be negatively restrictive for land developers. Land scarcity, and the appropriate management of land uses, have long been reported as a problem for farmers in peri-urban regions in a number of countries (e.g. Vesterby and Heimlich 1991).

*Table 5.1* Potential characteristics of semi-rural fringe areas

- Temporal transition, in terms of their internal functional characteristics (e.g. the decline of market gardening or the growth of retail parks).
- Spatial transition, in relation to the actual areas concerned (spatially shifting outwards in advance of urban growth).
- A combination of both transitions (e.g. agricultural land left fallow in speculative anticipation of urban land use development).
- As a consequence of the above, physical definition may be poor, ever-shifting or non-existent in terms of obvious boundaries.
- Or, by contrast, the presence of major physical barriers such as a transport artery or a major natural feature, perhaps in combination with planning restrictions, may impose explicit physical boundaries and a static, relatively permanent areal extent.
- A less stringent application of planning regulations may prevail.
- But paradoxically, the establishment of, for example, statutory green belts, may represent proscriptive physical planning policies that specifically exclude particular land uses and activities.
- In such circumstances, they may provide green lungs adjacent to or even penetrating the urban built-up area to provide perhaps much-needed open space, access to nature, and corridors for outdoor leisure pursuits.
- Extensive space-using activities may be present that are particularly related to:
  - transport functions: highway interchanges, urban by-passes, rows of car showrooms, park-and-ride parking areas, railway marshalling yards, airports, landing strips;
  - leisure activities: 'out of town' shopping malls and 'megastores' with associated extensive parking provision, leisure complexes – multi-screen cinemas, theme parks, arenas/sports stadiums, zoos, farm parks;
  - institutions: schools, university campuses, hospitals, nursing homes, prisons and detention centres;
  - new business activity: business parks/estates.
- Natural or artificial environmental constraints or opportunities, such as:
  - water bodies (reservoirs and lakes for leisure activity, floodplains inhibiting development and/or high quality agriculture);
  - ancient forests (sites of leisure hunting, 'dark' activities, conservation);
  - difficult topography encouraging 'extreme' leisure pursuits, inhibiting formal development, except for sporadic high status residential locations, which may or may not have been authorized: ironically, in poor developing societies these areas might be those colonized by informally developed 'shanty towns'.
- Noxious and potentially health-threatening land uses: municipal rubbish dumps, incinerators, power stations, quarries.

These factors can often result in a land use vacuum: land left fallow because it is unworkable, unprofitable or awaiting development.

Daugstad (2008) has referred to a reorientation in landscape perception in rural tourism from 'spectacularization' to 'multi-sensing', and marginal fringe areas would not at first sight appear to fit easily into her frame of reference. They usually lack any spectacular features, natural or otherwise, but the opportunities for multiple activities and the sense-challenging sights and sounds of such areas might suggest a possible accommodation in such a conceptualization, if only for pejorative reasons. Such areas may also well articulate the tension between local residents seeking economic development to enhance their employment opportunities and property values, and visitors seeking to preserve valued leisure amenities (Kianicka *et al.* 2006).

Such areas may be considered as zones confronting potential conflict and conflicting interests:

- planning versus development
- environment versus economic activity
- use versus disuse
- residents versus visitors
- rural versus urban values.

In the latter case, we may recognize the existence of conflicting or competing conceptualizations that to some extent mirror real-world perceptions:

- urban studies and urban development idealizations of such areas regarding them as 'peri-urban': peripheral to yet inexorably part of urbanization processes (e.g. Hoggart 2005); while
- rural studies and rural development conceptualizations view such zones as a particular type of rural area that is most influenced by urban demands, land values and accessibility, such as the EU LEADER Programme's typology of rural 'situations', type 8 'in a peri-urban location' (Roberts and Hall 2001: 12).

In practical terms, such fragmentation may result in a lack of coherence, and significantly for their use (or misuse), these areas may thus be psychologically marginalized for both urban and rural dwellers, and as such, may be subconsciously or unconsciously devalued or shunned. Recurring issues for sustainability that arise from these characteristics include: access, transience, imagery and the potential for conflicting land uses.

Thus rural-urban fringe areas may be characterized, paradoxically, as zones of interaction and repulsion, of mixed, integrated, conflicting, confused, transient and dynamic land uses.

# Sustainable tourism development in the Baltic States in transition processes

## *Sustainable development policy framework for tourism in the Baltic States*

The Lithuanian sustainable development strategy (SDS), approved in 2003, is the country's main policy document (Lithuanian Ministry of Environment 2003). Policy monitoring takes place through a task force of representatives from relevant ministries that prepare a biennial report on the strategy's implementation. This is submitted to the country's sustainable development commission, established in 2000, chaired by the prime minister. The goals of the SDS are expressed in terms of four sets of indicators: economic, environmental, social and those relating to regional development. As in the other two Baltic States, harmonization with EU law and practice, for example, in environmental impact assessment (Kruopienė *et al.* 2009), dominated much of the decade prior to accession in 2004.

The Latvian SDS was approved in 2002. The country's environment agency is responsible for the preparation of the *National Report of the Indicators of Sustainable Development* on an annual basis. Since 2003, the Ministry of Environmental Protection and Regional Development has been responsible for collating annual reports concerning the achievement of goals within this strategy. These are scrutinized and assessed by the country's Sustainable Development Commission.

Estonia's national strategy on sustainable development, *Sustainable Estonia 21*, was approved in 2005. It provides a long-term development framework to 2030. A general development principle of the country is 'to integrate the requirement to be successful in global competition with a sustainable development model and preservation of the traditional values of Estonia'. The SDS defines Estonian long-term development goals as taking into consideration interaction between environmental and development factors, and most particularly the sustainability of the Estonian nation and culture and an improvement in 'welfare' and ecological balance (Streimikiene *et al.* 2009).

# Contrasting case study examples of heritage tourism attractions and sustainability issues in semi-rural environments

The following three brief case study examples are taken from Latvia and Lithuania. They are based on a combination of the author's empirical experience and literature searches. The reasons for not including a case study from Estonia largely relate to: (1) the fact that tourism in Estonia is generally better known in the 'West', not least because of its long associations with the Finnish market, given the two countries' cultural and geographical affinities (e.g. see Komppula *et al.* 2006;), and (2) the author's briefer experience in this most northernly of the three Baltic States. Nonetheless, Estonia does share with Latvia and Lithuania similar issues of development sustainability, in an environment of marked economic recession, a recent history of Soviet domination, a significant ethnic Russian minority population, contested cultural histories and a post-Soviet transition trajectory to EU accession in 2004.

Of the three case studies, two are located in the semi-rural margins of capital cities (Riga, Vilnius) and the other is in a peri-urban fringe adjacent to a second city (Kaunas). In all three cases, these cities have shown substantial economic dynamism in recent years (until the very recent downturn), while peripheral smaller centres have fared less well. Indeed, the town of Salaspils, adjacent to the first case study and the scene of much energy-rich industrial development and in-migration during the Soviet period, has suffered as a 'single-industry' centre (Lintz et al. 2007). But being adjacent to a capital city, it has not endured the issues of isolation and peripherality experienced by the 'cathedrals in the desert' recognized by Grabher (1997) in East Germany and elsewhere in CEE.

While one of the case studies is characterized by 'dark tourism' (Lennon and Foley 2000; Stone and Sharpley 2008), the other two combine elements of social and built cultural heritage within distinctive environmental settings. Yet a theme that runs through all the examples and articulates at least one underpinning principle of sustainability is that of survival, both in its physical and psychological manifestations: of the memory of genocide in Salaspils, of the culture of the Karaite ethnic group in Trakai, and of the Catholic order of St Casimir's Sisters in Pažaislis.

### Salaspils Holocaust Memorial Park, south-east of Riga, Latvia

Salaspils Memorial Park is just beyond the outer fingers of Riga's built-up area, 15km south-east from the capital's city centre. First mentioned as a settlement in 1186, Salaspils has long been associated with war, death and destruction. In 1206, a Liv chieftain organized the first revolt against German Crusaders here, while in 1605, the main battle of the Polish-Swedish war and one of the largest in seventeenth-century Europe was fought here, when 10,000 were killed. Later in the nineteenth century, military summer camps were organized here, while during World War I, a front line remained here for two years, destroying many of the area's buildings and farmsteads.

During the late 1950s and early 1960s, a number of industrial enterprises and governmental institutions were established around the town, including a nuclear reactor plant and four branches of the Academy of Sciences. The reactor was operational from 1969 to 1998. It is now demolished. Salaspils is also the site of the Soviet-built Riga HES hydro-electric power scheme and the Riga TEC-2 thermal power station. The hydropower dam created a massive reservoir that flooded many monuments of Salaspils' ancient history. Many of the incoming workers for these schemes were ethnic Russians. By the twenty-first century the population of Salaspils had reached 21,000, of whom 42 per cent were Latvian and the same proportion were Russian. The town has now become a commuter dormitory, although there is no visitor accommodation in Salaspils itself (Salaspils Region Council 2009).

Outside of the town is the Nazi concentration camp, Kurtenhof, the largest civilian concentration camp in the Baltics. Built in 1941, the 40ha camp operated for three years. In 1944, as the Red Army approached, inmates were forced to exhume and burn the thousands of bodies buried at the camp, which was then razed to the ground by the retreating Nazis. Although the figures are disputed, an estimated 45,000 Jews from Riga and a further 55,000 other people (Austrians, Belgians, Czechs, Dutch, French, Latvian, Polish and Soviet citizens), from other Nazi-occupied countries were murdered here.

The Salaspils Memorial, which now dominates the site of the former camp, was erected in 1967 to honour those who died there. In 'this befouled meadow' (Robinson 2002), a huge concrete wall in the shape of a long beam – which has become little more than a rotting concrete shell – marks the position of the former entrance. Representing the dividing line between life and death, it bears the line from a poem by the Latvian writer Eižēns Vēveris (a prisoner at Salaspils): '*Aiz šiem vārtiem vaid zeme*' ('Beyond these gates the earth moans'). There is a door at each end, and a series of steps takes the visitor through a number of gloomy, damp rooms, giving the impression of a dank mausoleum. There is also a small, poorly kept, exhibition with badly preserved photographs of the camp. The seven monumental Soviet sculptures which stand in the grounds beyond the wall are intended to represent suffering and the spirit of defiance and resistance of those imprisoned and killed. They dominate the landscape of the site – itself surrounded by pine and birch forest – in their brutalist Soviet style (see Leong 2002), and like many constructions from the period, are not ageing well. A narrow path leads through the woods to the place where prisoners were executed. The stillness of the site is broken by the amplified ticking of an underground metronome located by the main entry point (Baister and Patrick 2002: 142–3; Taylor *et al.* 2006: 120), and by barking dogs from a nearby farmhouse.

As Wight and Lennon (2007: 528) point out in the case of Lithuania, the 'dark' heritage landscape of the Baltic States is beset with moral complexities that surround the commemoration of the region's nations' tragic past. They highlight the reticence of some destinations and cultural groups to confront 'dissonant' heritage (Tunbridge and Ashworth 1996), a factor which may help to explain the neglected air of the Salaspils Memorial area. Although the Salaspils Region Council set up a donation fund for the memorial (see www.salaspils.lv/en/i.php?id = 60), the physical fabric of the site requires substantial attention. There is no visitor infrastructure to disturb the solemnity of the place, apart from the parking area about 500m from the nearest entry point. A total absence of commercialization or commodification is matched by the lack of obvious personnel; only the occasional cleaner/gardener appears to be on site.

Visitor numbers appear to be small, although no records exist as there are several potential entry areas – the site is relatively open – and no admission is charged. The site lends itself to visits by organized groups, and this appears to have been the accepted mode of visitation.

### Trakai Castle and heritage village, west of Vilnius, Lithuania

Located 18km west of Vilnius city centre, just beyond the outstretched fingers of the capital's built-up area, the old peninsula settlement of Trakai, itself a former Lithuanian capital, with its castles and surrounding lakes, acts as a popular day trip for Vilnius residents, and a prime half-day excursion destination for all the capital's tour companies. Most of the linear settlement extends along a 2km-long tombolo strung out between three lakes.

The ruins of the fourteenth-century peninsula castle, destroyed in the seventeenth century, stand in stark contrast to the island castle, the largest of its type in Lithuania, which originates from around 1400, and has been comprehensively restored in Gothic red brick. Serial destruction and reconstruction of this imposing monument persisted throughout Trakai's subsequent history. In recent times, a round of reconstruction commenced in the 1950s only to be halted following the Soviet First Secretary Nikita Khrushchev's speech of December 1960 declaring that to continue such a reconstruction would only serve to glorify Lithuania's feudal past. Work eventually recommenced in the 1980s and was completed in the following decade. Today, the castle's 'iconic' image is familiar to most Lithuanians and visitors to the country as it is employed ubiquitously in tourism marketing material. It has been lauded, rather whimsically, as 'a truly magical sight filled with enchanting medieval atmosphere' (Taylor *et al.* 2006: 173). Situated on an island in Lake Galvė, it is linked to the shore by wooden footbridges.

The castle's medieval character acts as the setting for re-enactments, and various knights' clubs regularly organize tournaments here. Concerts, operas and plays are staged in the castle grounds in summer. It also houses the Trakai History Museum, established in 1962.

Trakai Municipality (Malūkas 2009) claims that the district is visited by approximately two million tourists annually. Visitors can undertake yacht trips, rent their own paddle or rowing boat, hire bicycles, horse ride or paraglide here. A range of pension-type accommodation is available for overnight stays.

Historically, communities of Tatars, Russians, Poles, Jews and Lithuanians have lived here, and still 21 per cent of Trakai's population is Polish.

The village's cultural distinctiveness, however, derives from the presence of a small minority, the Karaites (Karaimai) – a Judaist sect originating in Baghdad, which adheres to the law of Moses. The Karaite form of Judaism follows only the Tanach, the Jewish Bible, rejecting rabbinic interpretations. When Grand Duke Witold of Lithuania defeated the Tatars in the Crimea in 1392, among prisoners brought back to Lithuania were 330 Karaite families who settled in Trakai. They speak a Turkic language and were regarded by both Russians and Nazis as non-Jews, thereby escaping the worst excesses of the pogroms and the Holocaust. Around one hundred remain.

The Karaites' colourful wooden houses represent one of their most notable cultural characteristics, with three-windowed gable ends facing the main street. Among these are the sect's museum – a small but well-kept collection of old photographs, documents, costume, jewellery and weapons – and an eighteenth-century *kenesa* (prayer house) (see CJA 2006). Both were restored in the 1990s. Visitor consumption of Karaim culture is most explicit in their two lakeside restaurants in the village. These offer '*kibinai*', pasty-shaped pastries filled with juicy meat, as well as other fare.

What is claimed to be Europe's only historical national park (see www. seniejitrakai.lt) was established here in 1991 to preserve Trakai as a centre of historical, cultural and environmental distinctiveness. In the latter case, two hundred glacial lakes interweave a morainic landscape to provide a distinctive and valuable series of diverse ecosystems.

## *Pažaislis Monastery and Nature Park, east of Kaunas, Lithuania*

Kaunas is Lithuania's second city, about 100km away – about two hours' drive west – from Vilnius. It has a population of more than 400,000, over 90 per cent of which is ethnically Lithuanian, rendering the city far more homogeneous than the country's capital. Visitor access to Kaunas from Western Europe was enhanced following the country's EU accession, when low-cost airlines began using the city's small airport, and, notably, Ryanair adopted it as the company's base in Lithuania.

Founded in the eleventh century, the city has suffered from being a focus of conflict on innumerable occasions: it is claimed to have been reduced to ashes thirteen times before World War II. Today it is an important economic and cultural centre. Pažaislis is a wooded promontory around 9km to the east of the city centre with explicit boundaries: a looping elevated railway line separating it from the fringes of Kaunas city to the west and north, and Kaunas Sea (Kauno marios) – a large artificial lake created by damming (for hydro-electricity) the Nemunas river – to the east, south, south-west and north-east. Fringed by beaches, two small harbours and the blankness of the embanked railway, Pažaislis comprises a forest park and an 'architectural reserve', within which Pažaislis Monastery stands (KMRPA n.d.; State Department of Tourism 2007). It is the area of the Kauno Marios regional park closest to the city, and although with a restricted number of landward access points, is nonetheless quickly accessible from the city centre as a popular day trip destination for a range of leisure activities.

Pažaislis Monastery, the largest complex of its kind in Lithuania, is a fine example of seventeenth-century baroque architecture. The monastery church has a 50m high cupola and a sumptuous interior modelled on a Venetian design, with pink and black marble brought from Krakow, and more than 140 frescoes on the walls and ceilings (Šinkūnaitė n.d.). It is surrounded by both formal and productive gardens maintained by resident nuns within the walled compound. The monastery's history has seen it pass from Catholic to Orthodox control in the nineteenth century, then, with national independence, restored in 1920 by the Sisters of St Casimir. The Soviets converted the buildings into an archive, a 'psychiatric hospital', and, from 1966, an art gallery, for which purpose it underwent restoration.

A nationally important summer music festival held annually since 1996 encompasses classical and chamber music, jazz and popular music alongside open air pageants and drama performances. The 2009 season was inaugurated at the Monastery with Leonard Bernstein's *Mass* performed by the Lithuanian State Symphony Orchestra and the Kaunas State Choir.

### Discussions from the case studies: tourism and sustainabiilty in semi-rural heritage margins

In all three cases, access by public transport is poor, and requires, at best, additional walking of a kilometre or more. For example, in the case of the Salaspils Memorial site, a 25-minute train journey from central Riga drops the visitor at an unmanned forest halt (Dārziņa) where a poorly signposted, unmade forest path should be followed for about 15 minutes to the memorial (*piemineklis*). The Riga tourist office advises that visitors should not walk this footpath alone (Taylor *et al.* 2006: 120). The nearest bus route from the city centre circuitously arrives at its terminus in a forest village, on the wrong side of the fast four-lane highway (which cannot be seen at this point), where no signposting for the site can be found. On eventually crossing the highway, the memorial site's granite sign ('Salaspils 1941–44') is found to be accompanied by gaggles of ladies of the night (and day) congregating on the forest turn-off from the main highway to accommodate unofficial truck stops. This is an unfortunate juxtaposing.

In societies with rapidly growing car ownership and more sedentary lifestyles, such poor public transport provision and accompanying lack of signposting inevitably encourage car use for direct access. While traffic congestion is not a likely problem at Salaspils, it is already evident at Trakai, with substantial parking and congestion at busy weekends along a relatively narrow single road through the village, and at Pažaislis, where there are severely limited legitimate parking opportunities within the forest park.

Conflicting land uses are notable at all three locations, although in the case of both Trakai and Pažaislis, the conflicts are mostly between different types of leisure activities. In the former, active waterborne sports conflict with ecotourism; cultural and heritage appreciation (of the Karaite) may be swamped by mass day trip visitation, generating commodification, litter, and the temporary destruction of 'atmosphere'. But there are also underlying conflicts with wider implications. In the case of Salaspils, these are ideological, as perhaps reflected in the poor maintenance of the physical fabric of the site, and for Trakai and Pažaislis they are exemplified in creeping urban development pressures attempting to undermine officially declared protected areas and the increasing motorization of Baltic leisure society. Strengthened integrated planning and management will be needed in both cases.

As noted earlier, 'survival' is an underlying theme for sustainability in all three examples: survival of the memory of the Holocaust, of Karaim culture, and of the Order of the Sisters of St Casimir. Each of these can be enhanced through well-managed and planned tourism and leisure – being protected from degradation and commodification while benefiting from visitor income and support. But to the current observer, while Pažaislis can flourish so long as its competing leisure activities are not overwhelming, Trakai requires stronger cultural and environmental management (as set out in its strategic development plan for 2008–15: Municipality of the Region of Trakai 2009), if the quality of its cultural heritage is to be sustained. Salaspils Memorial requires substantial additional commitment. The fact that prostitutes can gather to pursue their employment during the daytime at the memorial's roadside sign is an indictment of local administration and management, and a clear indication of underlying cultural tensions and attitudes.

## Conclusion: lessons to be learned

Semi-rural marginal areas, by their very nature, are diverse, both within and between cultures. The three case studies employed in this chapter may not necessarily be typical of such areas in general, nor of peri-urban areas in their specific countries. Nonetheless, a number of key themes have emerged:

- Being located close to major urban areas, such margins are likely to experience heightened land use conflicts.
- Any uniqueness attached to specific semi-rural areas, as, for example, in the case of the Karaim culture in Trakai, will be placed under increasing pressure from mass short-term visitation from the nearby city.
- These factors therefore require strong integrated planning and management.
- But peri-urban areas with, unlike the case studies, few distinguishing characteristics, may suffer from weak planning and management, disaffection, neglect and a range of consequential environmental and social problems.

- By contrast, well-managed leisure/tourism development can help integrate, give meaning to, and enhance identity for an area.
- But poorly managed or unplanned tourism/leisure can exacerbate problems of fragmentation, environmental degradation (congestion, visual pollution of haphazard car parking), and commodification.
- Although the Baltic States are experiencing a period of severe economic downturn and political uncertainty, there is a need to appreciate the regional and national importance of explicit linkages between capital/ major cities and rural areas, particularly their hinterlands, and the cultural and natural resources that may reside within them.
- Such linkages can be exemplified by good practice in tourism and leisure management.
- This role can be particularly important in relatively small and compact countries, as the Baltic States are.

## References

Armatienė, A., Povilanskas, R. and Jones, E. (2006) 'Lithuania: sustainable rural tourism development in the Baltic coastal region', in D. Hall, M. Smith and B. Marciszewska (eds) *Tourism in the New Europe: The Challenges and Opportunities of EU Enlargement.* Wallingford: CABI Publishing, pp. 183–95.

Aun, C. (1996) 'Economic developments and tourism opportunities in Estonia', *Journal of Baltic Studies* 27(2): 95–132.

Baister, S. and Patrick, C. (2002) *Latvia.* 3rd edn. Chalfont St Peter: Bradt.

Brown, F. and Hall, D. (2000a) 'Introduction', in F. Brown and D. Hall (eds) *Tourism in Peripheral Areas.* Clevedon: Channel View, pp. 1–6.

—— (eds) (2000b) *Tourism in Peripheral Areas.* Clevedon: Channel View.

Burinskiene, M. and Rudzkiene, V. (2005) 'Modelling and forecasting of country tourism development in Lithuania', *Journal of Environmental Engineering and Landscape Management* 13(3): 116–20.

CJA (Center for Jewish Art) (2006) *Preserved Wooden Synagogues in Lithuania.* Vilnius: CJA. Available at: http://cja.huji.ac.il[sic]/Architecture/Wooden-syna gogues-Lithuania.htm.

Clottey, B. and Lennon, R. (2003) 'Transitional economy tourism: Lithuanian travel consumers' perceptions of Lithuania', *International Journal of Travel Research* 5: 295–303.

Daugstad, K. (2008) 'Negotiating landscape in rural tourism', *Annals of Tourism Research* 35(2): 402–26.

Druva-Druvaskalne, I., Ābols, I. and Šļara, A. (2006) 'Latvia tourism: decisive factors and tourism development', in D. Hall, M. Smith and B. Marciszewska (eds) *Tourism in the New Europe: The Challenges and Opportunities of EU Enlargement.* Wallingford: CABI Publishing, pp. 170–82.

Endzina, I. and Luneva, L. (2004) 'Development of a national branding strategy: the case of Latvia', *Place Branding* 1(1): 94–105.

Grabher, G. (1997) 'Adaptation at the cost of adaptability? Restructuring the Eastern German regional economy', in G. Grabher and D. Stark (eds) *Restructuring Networks in Post-socialism: Legacies, Linkages and Localities.* Oxford: Oxford University Press, pp. 107–34.

Granberg, L. (2004) 'From agriculture to tourism: constructing new relations between rural nature and culture in Lithuania and Finland', in I. Alanen (ed.) *Mapping the Rural Problem in the Baltic Countryside: Transition Processes in the Rural Areas of Estonia, Latvia and Lithuania*. Aldershot: Ashgate, pp. 159–78.

Hall, C. M. and Boyd, S. (2005) *Nature-based Tourism in Peripheral Areas*. Clevedon: Channel View.

Hall, D. (2005) 'Sustainable rural tourism and rural change', in D. Schmied (ed.) *Winning and Losing: The Changing Geography of Europe's Rural Areas*. Aldershot: Ashgate, pp. 72–89.

Herslund, L. (2007) 'Rural diversification in the Baltic countryside: a local perspective', *GeoJournal* 70(1): 47–59.

Hoggart, K. (2005) *The City's Hinterland: Dynamism and Divergence in Europe's Peri-Urban Territories*. Aldershot: Ashgate.

Jaakson, R. (1996a) 'Planning the future and the future of planning in the Baltics', *Journal of Baltic Studies* 27(1): 3–20.

—— (1996b) 'Tourism in transition in post-Soviet Estonia', *Annals of Tourism Research* 23(3): 617–34.

—— (1998) 'Tourism development in peripheral regions of post-Soviet states: a case study of strategic planning on Hiiumaa, Estonia', *International Planning Studies* 3(2): 249–72.

—— (2000) 'Supra-national spatial planning of the Baltic Sea region and competing narratives for tourism', *European Planning Studies* 8(5): 565–79.

Jarvis, J. and Kallas, P. (2006) 'Estonia – switching unions: impacts of EU membership on tourism development', in D. Hall, M. Smith and B. Marciszewska (eds) *Tourism in the New Europe: The Challenges and Opportunities of EU Enlargement*. Wallingford: CABI Publishing, pp. 154–69.

—— (2008) 'Estonian tourism and the accession effect: the impact of European Union membership on the contemporary patterns of the Estonian tourist industry', *Tourism Geographies* 10(4): 474–94.

Kianicka, S., Buchecker, M., Hunziker, M. and Müller-Böker, U. (2006) 'Locals' and tourists' sense of place', *Mountain Research and Development* 26: 55–63.

KMRPA (Kauno Marios Regional Park Administration) (n.d.) *Kauno Marios Regional Park*. Kaunas: Kauno Marios Regional Park Administration.

Komppula, R., Peltonen, A., Ylkänen, T. and Kokkila, T. (2006) 'The Baltics' accession: Finnish perspectives', in D. Hall, M. Smith and B. Marciszewska (eds) *Tourism in the New Europe: The Challenges and Opportunities of EU Enlargement*. CABI Publishing, pp. 139–53.

Kruopienė, J., Židonienė, S. and Dvarionenė, J. (2009) 'Current practice and shortcomings of EIA in Lithuania', *Environmental Impact Assessment Review* 29: 305–9.

Lennon, J. and Foley, M. (2000) *Dark Tourism: The Attraction of Death and Disaster*. London: Thomson.

Leong, A. (2002) *Centaur: The Life and Work of Ernst Neizvestny*. Lanham, MD: Rowman and Littlefield.

Lintz, G., Müller, B. and Schmude, K. (2007) 'The future of industrial cities and regions in central and eastern Europe', *Geoforum* 38, 512–19.

Lithuanian Ministry of Environment (2003) *National Sustainable Development Strategy*. Vilnius: Lithuanian Ministry of Environment.

Malūkas, E. (2009) 'General information about Trakai. Trakai, Lithuania: Trakai Municipality', available at: www.trakai.lt/index.php?-1426392344.

Municipality of the Region of Trakai (2009) *Strategic Plan for Development of Trakai District 2008–15*. Trakai, Lithuania: Municipality of the Region of Trakai. Available at: www.trakai.lt/index.php?-1587808609.

Müristaja, H. (2003) 'Development trends and the association of stakeholders in tourism development process in the case of Pärnu County (Estonia)', paper presented at European Regional Studies Association Congress, Vienna. Available at: www-sre.wu-wien.ac.at/ersa/ersaconfs/ersa03/cdrom/papers/504.pdf.

Peil, T. (2005) 'Estonian heritage connections – people, past and place: the Pakri peninsula', *International Journal of Heritage Studies* 11(1): 53–65.

Pilāts, V. (2004) *Nature and Ecotourism in Latvia*. Riga: Latvian Institute.

Porter, M. E. (2001) *The Baltic Rim Regional Agenda*. Stockholm: Baltic Development Forum, Institute of International Business, Stockholm School of Economics.

Roberts, L. and Hall, D. (2001) *Rural Tourism and Recreation: Principles to Practice*. Wallingford: CABI.

Robinson, H. (2002) 'The view from Khrushchev's head', *The New York Times* 25 August.

Saarinen, J. and Kask, T. (2008) 'Transforming tourism spaces in changing socio-political contexts: the case of Pärnu, Estonia, as a tourist destination', *Tourism Geographies* 10(4): 452–73.

Salaspils Region Council (2009) 'Salaspils', available at: www.salaspils.lv.

Scott, J. (2000) 'Peripheries, artificial peripheries, and centres', in F. Brown, F. and D. Hall (eds) *Tourism in Peripheral Areas*. Clevedon: Channel View, pp. 58–73.

Šinkūnaitė, L. (n.d.) *The Pažaislis Monastery Ensemble*. Kaunas: St Casimir Sister's Congregation.

State Department of Tourism (2007) *Nemunas Water Route Map*. Vilnius: State Department of Tourism, Lithuania Ministry of the Economy.

Stone, P. and Sharpley, R. (2008) 'Consuming dark tourism: a thanalogical perspective', *Annals of Tourism Research* 35(2): 574–95.

Streimikiene, D., Simanaviciene, Z. and Kovaliov, R. (2009) 'Corporate social responsibility for implementation of sustainable energy development in Baltic States', *Renewable and Sustainable Energy Reviews* 13: 813–24.

Taylor, N., Baister, S., Jarvis, H. and Patrick, C. (2006) *Baltic Capitals*, 3rd edn. Chalfont St Peter: Bradt.

Tunbridge, J. E. and Ashworth, G. J. (1996) *Dissonant Heritage: The Management of the Past as a Resource in Conflict*. Chichester: John Wiley & Sons.

Unwin, T. (1996) 'Tourist development in Estonia: images, sustainability, and integrated rural development', *Tourism Management* 17(4): 265–76.

—— (1997) 'Agricultural restructuring and integrated rural development in Estonia', *Journal of Rural Studies* 13(1): 93–112.

Upchurch, R. S. and Teivane, U. (2000) 'Residents' perceptions of tourism development in Riga, Latvia', *Tourism Management* 21: 499–507.

Urry, J. (1995) *Consuming Places*. London: Routledge.

Vandermeulen, V., Gellynck, X., Van Huylenbroeck, G., Van Orshoven, J. and Bomans, K. (2009) 'Farmland for tomorrow in densely populated areas', *Land Use Policy* 26: 859–68.

Vesterby, M. and Heimlich, R. E. (1991) 'Land-use and demographic change – results from fast-growth counties', *Land Economics* 67: 279–91.

Vihalemm, P. (2007) 'Changing spatial relations in the Baltic region and the role of the media', *European Societies* 9(5): 777–96.

Walker, S. (2009) 'Alarm in Baltic as Kremlin seizes control of Soviet past', *The Independent* 11 June, p. 28.

Wight, A. C. and Lennon, J. J. (2007) 'Selective interpretation and eclectic human heritage in Lithuania', *Tourism Management* 28: 519–29.

Worthington, B. (2001) 'Riding the "J" curve – tourism and successful transition in Estonia', *Post Communist Economies* 13(3): 389–400.

——— (2003) 'Change in an Estonian resort: contrasting development contexts', *Annals of Tourism Research* 30(2): 369–85.

——— (2004) 'Estonian national heritage, tourism, and paradoxes of transformation', in D. Hall (ed.) *Tourism and Transition: Governance, Transformation and Development*. Wallingford: CABI, pp. 83–94.

# Part II
# The state and development

# 6 The impact of European Union funding on coastal tourism in Yorkshire

## Stratis Koutsoukos and Catherine Brooks

## Introduction

The Yorkshire and Humber region covers 15,413 sq km and has a population of around 5 million people. It contains some of England's most scenic landscapes, including the North York Moors National Park and parts of the Yorkshire Dales and Peak District National Parks. Tourism is important economically for the region, particularly the rural areas. It is estimated that tourism is now worth £6.3 billion to the regional economy (Yorkshire Forward 2008). Tourism supports almost 245,000 jobs, around 11 per cent of the total workforce, in over 23,000 businesses, mostly small. Most of the tourism is domestic, from within the UK, although there are 1.2 million overseas visitors annually. The region accounts for 10 per cent of England's domestic tourist trips and 9 per cent of total spend (Yorkshire Tourist Board 2008).

Tourism can be divided into three broad spatial sectors: the coast, the countryside, and the cities and historic towns; these are often interlinked, however. The top destination is York, which attracts around four million visitors a year, and many of these also visit other parts of Yorkshire. Visitors to the coast also frequently make day trips to destinations such as York. Leisure tourism is largely seasonal, peaking in August each year. Business tourism and city breaks are sectors of growing importance, particularly for cities such as Leeds.

Regional tourism is promoted by the tourist board (Welcome to Yorkshire), supported by a number of other sub-regional tourism partnerships and local marketing groups (and Lincolnshire Tourism in northern Lincolnshire). Strategic responsibility for regional tourism support lies with the regional development agency, Yorkshire Forward, which aims to achieve a 5 per cent annual growth in visitor spend over the next five years, increasing the value of tourism through quality and sustainable growth, and using tourism to modernize the region's image (Yorkshire Forward 2008). Yorkshire Forward, which has recently decided to invest £30 million in tourism over the next three years, has set the tourism sector firmly within the context of the Regional Economic Strategy (RES):

Tourism is already a significant contributor to the regional economy but has the potential to be much more so . . . Strategic priorities for tourism include quality, sustainability, good intelligence and innovation. A far-sighted approach will be adopted that takes account of how issues like climate change will affect tourism.

(Yorkshire Forward 2006: 55)

The Regional Spatial Strategy (RSS), which overlaps with the RES in providing overall strategic direction for the region (GOYH 2008),[1] identifies tourism as one of the key sectors that should be supported in strategies and investment decisions, with a particular emphasis on sustainable tourism. The RSS recognizes that with climate change, the region will get warmer, with winters becoming wetter and summers drier, leading to opportunities for greater tourism potential, although extreme events such as floods will become more frequent and coastal erosion is likely to increase. It identifies improving 'the public realm and quality of the built environment of coastal resorts and the coast's natural environment as the basis for economic diversification and regeneration', and highlights the importance of 'upgrading tourism facilities in ways which promote higher value activity, reduce seasonality and support urban regeneration' (ibid.: 78, 153).

## Coastal tourism

The region's seaside resorts developed largely in the nineteenth century, when the railways opened up mass tourism to the working classes from industrial areas in the hinterland (Beckerson and Walton 2005; Walton 2000). Coastal tourism in Yorkshire has traditionally been characterized by long-stay, low-spend visits by domestic tourists in lower socio-economic groups, with a high volume of repeat business.

Social and economic changes in the twentieth century have had considerable impact on traditional coastal tourism, however. Low cost flights and package holidays abroad and the decline of British seaside resorts have deeply affected and changed the nature of competition in the sector. There are complex issues facing all coastal towns, such as changes in tourism trends, seasonality of the seaside economy, frequent high levels of deprivation, physical isolation inhibiting economic growth, and in-migration of older people and out-migration of younger people placing pressure on community services (House of Commons CLG Committee 2007).

Yorkshire's coastal towns have seen the decline of two key economic sectors: tourism and fishing. The cumulative effect has been a profound loss of employment with resulting social and economic deprivation. Some parts of coastal towns exhibit similar social problems to the worst inner-city areas, with pockets of acute deprivation and high unemployment, low wages, and low levels of educational attainment. Bridlington and Whitby, for example, feature among the most deprived in a recent study, which found that a majority of seaside towns have above-average levels of deprivation (Beatty *et al.* 2008).

However, tourism is still seen as a viable economic sector of activity for many coastal towns (Beatty and Fothergill 2003; Deloitte 2008). Regeneration programmes have taken place in many resorts in recent years (English Heritage 2007), and some have adopted strategies of diversification and product differentiation to increase sustainability, targeting higher-value niche markets and the demand for shorter, more frequent breaks through the year. In Yorkshire, resorts such as Scarborough and Whitby are now competing by attempting to broaden and improve their tourism offer, linking to the rural hinterland and cultural/heritage themes, to attract visitors from a higher socio-economic background and wider catchment areas rather than their traditional regional working-class markets.

## EU regional policy and Structural Funds

European Union (EU) regional policy, delivered through the Structural Funds and the Cohesion Fund, aims to reduce disparities in the levels of development between regions in the EU, and to create economic and social cohesion. Regional policy expenditure now represents over one-third of the EU budget. In the current programming period (2007–13), two financial instruments are particularly important: the European Regional Development Fund (ERDF), which provides support for the creation of infrastructure and productive job-creating investment, mainly for businesses; and the European Social Fund (ESF), which assists the unemployed and disadvantaged, mainly by funding training measures.

The situation was more complex in the programming period 2000–6, with Structural Funds administered through a far greater diversity of financial instruments: ERDF, ESF, the European Agricultural Guidance and Guarantee Fund (EAGGF), and the Financial Instrument for Fisheries Guidance (FIFG). The ERDF and the ESF provided the majority of the funds in the UK. Additionally, smaller amounts of aid were also granted by four Community Initiatives to encourage cross-border, transnational and interregional cooperation (INTERREG III), the regeneration of cities and neighbourhoods in crisis (URBAN II), equality in the labour market (EQUAL), and the development of rural areas (LEADER+).

## Structural Funds in Yorkshire and the Humber, 2000–6

Structural Funds were deployed in Europe under two main Objectives: Objective 1, to promote the development and structural adjustment of lagging regions; and Objective 2, socio-economic conversion of industrial, urban or rural zones through economic regeneration leading to creation of jobs. South Yorkshire was eligible for Objective 1 funding to counteract the loss of its traditional industrial base, but is not considered further here as it has no coastline. Much of Yorkshire and Humber was eligible for Objective 2 funding, and within this area the coastal zones are the focus here.

The Government Office for Yorkshire and the Humber (GOYH) was the Managing Authority for the regional Objective 2 Programme. The overall aims and Priorities of the Programme were set out in the *Single Programming Document* (SPD) (GOYH 2004). The SPD was based on the six objectives of the RES, ensuring a good strategic fit with Yorkshire Forward's priorities. The Priorities were broken down into more detail, describing their component Measures, in the *Programme Complement* (GOYH 2005).

The Objective 2 programme was an investment programme to support business growth and entrepreneurship, connect people to opportunities, and fund physical infrastructure developments that promote economic development, with a contribution of almost £350 million of European Structural Funds, mainly ERDF and ESF, alongside UK public and private sector sources. The programme had two business support priorities (Priority 1 and Priority 2), a community-led economic and social renewal priority (Priority 3), a capital investment priority (Priority 4), and a venture capital fund priority (Priority 5). Priorities were further subdivided into Measure-level objectives.

### The Objective 2 programme and tourism

Tourism was not a stand-alone priority within the Objective 2 programme, although a number of Measures were relevant directly or indirectly to the support of tourism activity, and one of the opportunities identified in the SPD was lengthening the tourism season and improving the cultural and tourism product as a whole. The most direct assistance was within Priority 4, which was targeted also to a number of coastal areas. Measure 4.4, 'Supporting the development of the region's locational assets', which aimed to maximize the benefits of major investments in the Humber Trade Zone and other key locations, was of particular relevance. Eligible activities under this measure included design competitions, establishing and developing business associations, and assistance for marketing and long-term visitor strategies to increase spend and lengthen the tourism season.

Some Measures within the business support priorities, while not directly targeted at tourism and coastal areas, were also available and relevant to supporting tourism activity development, for example, Measure 2.1, 'The development of new customers and new markets', and Measure 2.2, 'Helping businesses adapt to the demands of new product and process innovation'.

There were a number of tourism-related projects financed mostly through the ERDF in the course of the programme, but as tourism was not identified either as a Priority or within the Government Office database, it was not always easy to extract data for this study. Few ESF-funded projects appear to have dealt directly with training for the tourism sector. Interviews were carried out with key civil servants, and the Compendium of ERDF Projects database was interrogated to identify individual projects with a tourism character. Results were then compiled in an attempt to separate coastal from non-coastal projects. Additionally, a number of interviews were carried out in relation to key tourism projects. The resulting data are discussed briefly in relation to three factors:

1   Partnerships, or the degree to which programme and project delivery was enhanced or hindered through the influence and structures of the Structural Funds.
2   Financial leverage achieved, or the degree to which Structural Funds helped unlock significant additional financial resources from the public and private sectors.
3   The local and regional economic, social and environmental impact of the Structural Funds.

### Partnerships

Partnership structures reflected to a large degree the Priorities and Measures architecture of the Objective 2 programme, and policies and strategies at regional and sub-regional level that do not focus specifically on coastal tourism, but rather on the whole tourism offer (e.g. the *Moors and Coast Tourism Strategy*, Moors and Coast Area Tourism Partnership 2006).

Local authorities usually played the greatest part in coastal tourism partnerships; and due to significant market failure, regeneration, including in tourism destinations, was mostly funded by the public sector. Frequently local stakeholders formed partnerships to complement the work of local authorities. For large-scale local Master Plan projects, the best approach was found to be to consult local communities at an early stage and throughout the conceptual development of the project. Conversely, failure to respond to local community aspirations could result in problems later; for example, in Whitby, local residents rejected part of the concept for the proposed ERDF-funded marina and environs redevelopment as put forward by Scarborough Borough Council, on the basis that this would alter the appearance of the area significantly and did not match local aspirations.

A number of challenges were identified in developing and sustaining partnerships. Partnership working is resource-intensive, and requires strong public sector support, in particular from local authorities, and especially in areas of high deprivation, low connectivity and localities experiencing market failure and low levels of collective aspiration. It was often very difficult to engage the private sector in partnerships and investment, with differences in approaches and ultimate goals being the main causes. The best examples of successful collaboration relied on clear and shared visions, well-prepared and thought-through plans, and focused public sector investment for a decisive delivery. Often partnerships were too focused on drawing down the funds, and did not employ sufficient resources to track delivery, performance and outcomes.

*Financial leverage*

In total, 55 projects in the Objective 2 programme were deemed to be in the tourism sector within Yorkshire and The Humber (Table 6.1), accounting for approximately 8 per cent of the programme and representing a total value exceeding £92.6 million invested. Of those, 26 were on the coast, representing around 68 per cent of the total ERDF contribution towards tourism projects, with a total value of funds invested exceeding £65 million (Table 6.2). The average rate of ERDF contributions to coastal tourism projects was approximately 28 per cent, while private sector funds represented 23 per cent, and other public sector funds amounted to 50 per cent of the total value (Table 6.3).

Private sector co-financing contributions were concentrated particularly in Measure 4.2 in support of Hull's city centre Integrated Development Plan, giving Hull the highest rate of private sector financial leverage on the region's coast, 38 per cent (Table 6.3). The majority of those contributions (over £8 million) were for the Hull 'East River Bank Tourism Catalyst' project, which aimed to develop the necessary infrastructure to support tourism growth by improving the public realm. Most of the private sector contributions were associated with a new three-star hotel. ERDF funding was used to support the abnormal costs of developing a derelict waterfront site.

The second highest rate of private sector financial leverage was at Cleethorpes, North East Lincolnshire, a traditional seaside resort in decline. Over half of the ERDF funding went towards the Meridian Lakeside Arena project, to improve the connectivity of the various accommodation facilities and tourist attractions, and to extend the leisure tourist season by enabling events earlier and later in the year. Other large ERDF-funded projects included initiatives marketing Cleethorpes as a premier tourist destination and event provider.

Attracting private sector funding for tourism projects was difficult for many localities in the Objective 2 area that had suffered neglect and deprivation. Hull's success has been due to targeting intervention on the marina and waterfront areas, that were highly visible (central) and neglected, underused and in parts derelict (i.e. where change would be most visible). Public confidence associated with the density of the investment, and high-visibility and high-profile projects such as The Deep (anecdotal evidence indicates that the number of overnight stays in Hull doubled following the opening of The Deep in 2002), made it easier to attract private investors. Rural coastal areas have in comparison not had the same concentration of public resources, and unlike urban coastal centres they have not been as successful in attracting private finance (Table 6.3).

Table 6.1 Objective 2 (2000–6) ERDF projects related to tourism

| Objective 2 | ERDF grant offer (£) | Private (£) | Other public (£) | Voluntary (£) | Income (£) | Original forecast | |
|---|---|---|---|---|---|---|---|
| | | | | | | Gross jobs accommodated | Gross new jobs create |
| Priority 1: A new entrepreneurship agenda | | | | | | | |
| Measure 1.2 | 10,322 | 1,475 | 17,694 | 0 | 0 | 0 | 5 |
| Priority 2: Bringing down barriers to competitiveness | | | | | | | |
| Measure 2.1 | 51,613 | 7,374 | 88,473 | 0 | 0 | 0 | 25 |
| Measure 2.2 | 303,651 | 211,687 | 510,222 | 25,500 | 0 | 0 | 100 |
| Priority 4: Capturing the employment benefits of diversity | | | | | | | |
| Measure 4.2 | 23,528,718 | 14,938,656 | 43,237,473 | 88,669 | 0 | 310 | 832 |
| Measure 4.3 | 1,244,745 | 115,000 | 2,043,102 | 0 | 0 | 20 | 30 |
| Measure 4.4 | 2,069,495 | 1,131,748 | 2,912,774 | 116,861 | 0 | 0 | 359 |
| Total | 27,208,544 | 16,405,940 | 48,809,738 | 231,030 | 0 | 330 | 1,351 |

Source: GOYH Compendium of Objective 2 (2000–2006) ERDF Projects in Yorkshire and The Humber.

Note:
Total number of projects = 55.

Table 6.2  Objective 2 (2000–6) ERDF projects related to coastal tourism

| Objective 2 | ERDF Grant Offer (£) | Private (£) | Other Public (£) | Voluntary (£) | Income (£) | Original forecast | |
|---|---|---|---|---|---|---|---|
| | | | | | | Gross jobs accommodated | Gross new jobs created |
| Priority 4: Capturing the employment benefits of diversity | | | | | | | |
| Measure 4.2 | 16,880,260 | 14,227,925 | 30,918,298 | 0 | 0 | 252 | 586 |
| Measure 4.4 | 1,512,215 | 889,418 | 2,097,392 | 0 | 0 | 0 | 316 |
| Total | 18,392,475 | 13,673,748 | 33,005,690 | 0 | 0 | 252 | 902 |

Source: GOYH Compendium of Objective 2 (2000–6) ERDF Projects in Yorkshire and The Humber.

Note:
Total number of projects = 26.

Table 6.3  Coastal tourism projects by town: ERDF (2000–6) and other funding sources

| Town/city | ERDF | | Other public | | Private sector | | Voluntary sector | |
|---|---|---|---|---|---|---|---|---|
| | £ | % of total for town | £ | % of total for town | £ | % of total for town | £ | % of total for town |
| Hull | 7,106,295 | 22.6 | 12,426,605 | 39.6 | 11,864,952 | 37.8 | | |
| Bridlington | 4,705,166 | 33.9 | 8,614,023 | 62.0 | 577,800 | 4.2 | | |
| Cleethorpes | 3,097,094 | 34.7 | 3,915,671 | 43.9 | 1,916,709 | 21.5 | | |
| Whitby | 1,946,203 | 33.1 | 3,564,610 | 60.6 | 158,750 | 2.7 | 209,313 | 3.6 |
| Scarborough | 1,509,748 | 23.0 | 4,458,091 | 68.0 | 591,226 | 9.0 | | |
| Staithes | 27,789 | 44.5 | 26,690 | 42.8 | 7,906 | 12.7 | | |
| Average % | | 27.6 | | 49.5 | | 22.7 | | 0.3 |

Source: GOYH Compendium of Objective 2 (2000–6) ERDF Projects in Yorkshire and The Humber.

*The economic and social impact*

It is very difficult to assess the direct impact that Structural Funds have had in coastal areas, as a complex set of interrelated factors are at work, and studies on the issue and labour market data collected locally tend to be limited. The ERDF-funded tourism-related projects were forecast to accommodate over 250 jobs and create 902 new ones (Table 6.2). Some areas were (prior to the recession) showing improvement in employment statistics as part of a longer-term trend. As the tourism product in Hull is improving, for example, so is job creation. However, a proportion of these new jobs are filled by migrant workers, although the City Council is trying to encourage training schemes to help Hull residents take advantage of these job opportunities. A combination of approaches has in some instances led to successful 'place-making'[2] and 'place-shaping'[3] approaches being adopted, often encouraged by the independent and more flexible nature afforded by the application of EU Structural Funds, as opposed to national funding streams which are often tied to specific elements of delivery.

The joint impact of ERDF and other public sector investment is most noteworthy in the context of evolving labour markets in seaside towns. It was recognized, for example, that coastal locations needed to diversify economic activity by investing in new sectors. Key areas of investment required included public sector pump-priming in business park developments, and the provision of sites and premises appropriate for local businesses. Office development was seen to facilitate growth in the commercial and financial services sectors and within market towns. It is in these areas where the ERDF has had a strong impact.

Results are mixed; on the one hand, some localities where traditional industries like fishing are still declining are struggling to re-invent themselves and to identify key growth sectors, and public policy is failing or at best succeeding in slowing down the decline. By contrast, sustained and long-term public intervention in some areas is showing promise in developing new sectors and identities. Scarborough's encouragement of creative industries and entrepreneurship through the Scarborough Renaissance Partnership, leading to its winning the prestigious Enterprising Britain 2008 and Enterprising Europe 2008/09 awards, is a prime example, and the creative and tourism sectors continue to benefit each other. The successful use of the heritage approach to regeneration focusing on historic buildings, as seen in Whitby, Scarborough, Bridlington and Hull, is also notable. Hull's past, for example, was rooted deeply in a strong maritime tradition and historic legacy, which led to a clustering of tourism projects linked to celebrating its heritage, such as the refurbishment, with ERDF funding, of Oriel Chambers and Wilberforce House in the Museums Quarter as a lasting legacy of the bicentenary of the abolition of the slave trade. The ERDF-funded restoration of historic spa buildings at Scarborough and Bridlington has also served to raise the profile of these towns, leverage private sector investment in nearby hotels, and increase visitor numbers and spend.

## Conclusion

Although tourism is not the highest priority for EU regional policy, and in quantitative terms the proportion of Structural Funds expenditure on tourism programmes and projects across the EU is relatively small, the impact in qualitative terms on regional development has been found to be substantial, especially in those coastal regions that are highly dependent on the tourism sector (European Parliament, 2008).

The Yorkshire and Humber Objective 2 Programme is still being wound up, so the full picture of the impact of the Structural Funds is not yet available. The programme focused particularly on assisting small businesses and building capacity in deprived communities; the final figures for increasing numbers of jobs and employability are not yet known, nor whether the direct effects are long-lasting and sustainable. The indirect effects are even harder to define, for example, in terms of community pride and self-confidence within a regenerated area, and may continue to be apparent long after the programme's end.

The programme's ultimate impact on intra-regional disparities is also unclear; however, in areas of deprivation, the causes of social exclusion are so multi-stranded, deep-rooted and complex that there can be no 'quick fix', and reducing disparities may take many years to achieve. A good example is a locality such as Whitby, which illustrates 20–25 years of sustained commitment to transformation. Some of the difficulties faced in permanently reducing social exclusion in particular areas were shown in the Mid-Term Evaluation, which found no discernible improvement in disadvantaged urban areas (ERBEDU *et al.* 2003). What is certain, however, is that most of the Objective 2 projects would not have happened as they did without the Structural Funds, and disadvantaged communities in the Objective 2 areas would have been the poorer for their absence.

In terms of partnerships, a combination of strong local authority roles, public sector investment and the use of masterplanning and special delivery partnership vehicles have proved to be the most effective delivery mechanism for ERDF-funded tourism projects, particularly in larger coastal urban conurbations, and often also generated a greater confidence in the private sector.

EU Structural Funds have had a varied impact on the coastal tourism offer in Yorkshire and the Humber. Strong targeted and grouped sets of themed projects, as for example in Scarborough and Hull, have provided a 'critical mass' of tourism and cultural heritage activity which has been put in place with the aid of EU Structural Funds and other public money, and are likely to be sustainable in the longer term and encourage future development and investor confidence. However, the nature and length of decline suffered by some coastal localities mean that regeneration investment in infrastructure through 'place-making' initiatives is insufficient on its own. Hull, Scarborough and Whitby have rebranded themselves and changed the way they are perceived, reflecting a need for a 'place-shaping' approach.

Notwithstanding the future possibilities of global warming increasing the potential for traditional 'sun, sea and sand' tourism in the region, the best hope for the coastal tourism sector is to continue differentiating the coastal tourism offer to target niche and high-value markets, stressing cultural and natural heritage and distinctiveness, and where possible investing in innovative, high-quality 'flagship' projects.

In the current programming period (2007–13), with less EU funding available, the priorities for expenditure are narrower and more focused, with greater emphasis on the renewed Lisbon objectives on developing the knowledge economy and competitiveness; tourism is not likely to benefit from the Structural Funds in this round. This will place greater pressure on national and regional mainstream programmes to continue to regenerate coastal areas and the development of their tourism-based local economies. Tourism remains a fragmented sector in the UK, however, and there are still few signs of concerted action to fill the gaps.

## Lessons to be learned

1   In the UK, there is a need for a new national coastal policy input and review of the support for tourism activity in coastal areas. Coastal towns where traditional sectors have declined often face more severe problems than inland towns in terms of multiple deprivation, unemployment, poor educational attainment and population imbalance. Tourism, however, even when in decline because of wider market competitive forces, remains an important employment sector, with potential that needs unlocking.

2   EU Structural Funds have had a varied impact on the tourism offer of coastal towns in Yorkshire, but have been most effective in targeted initiatives with a clear transformational plan. Objective 2 funding was limited in scale, and its impact is spread across a wide geographical area. The 'thinning' of European public policy means a limited ability to affect change in seaside locations. On the other hand, as, for example, in Scarborough and Hull, strong targeted and grouped sets of themed projects have provided a 'critical mass' of tourist and heritage activity which has been put in place in the hope that it can be sustained and encourage future development.

3   There is a need to change from place-making to place-shaping. The nature and length of decline suffered by some coastal localities mean that investment in infrastructure and place-making initiatives is insufficient on its own. Hull, Scarborough and Whitby have had to rebrand themselves and change the way they are perceived, reflecting a need for a place-shaping approach. Skills training is to be considered alongside physical investment, as well as marketing and clustering, and 'critical mass development' of new activities. At the same time, investment in architectural distinctiveness and higher quality design to achieve

place-shaping and to change perceptions can be achieved with coastal tourism flagship projects.

4   The potential in partnership delivery is influenced by the nature of the seaside town and the scale of ERDF and matched public sector resource investment from other mainstream programmes. In larger coastal urban conurbations, a combination of a stronger local authority role, public sector investment from a wide range of programmes, and the use of masterplanning and special delivery partnership vehicles (e.g. in Hull and its urban regeneration company), have proved to be an effective delivery mechanism for ERDF-funded tourism projects, often generating a greater confidence from the private sector.

5   Due to the scale of the Yorkshire and Humber Objective 2 Programme investment, reverse leverage of Structural Funds appears to have occurred. National mainstream public sector programmes. e.g. Single Regeneration Budget, Neighbourhood Renewal Fund, Lottery and Millennium funds were instrumental in matching and levering ERDF programme funding. This is particularly the case in smaller settlements and localities.

6   Investing in a tourism heritage-based approach as a tool for renewing distinctiveness, character and identity in coastal areas, and differentiating the tourism offer from coastal resorts to heritage seaside towns, needs to be further developed. Whitby is a good example of such an approach, but consideration needs to be given to timescales, as it often takes longer than seven years of investment to achieve this change.

7   Investment in cultural themed tourism as a way of differentiating the tourism offer in towns and settlements that have historically performed an industrial function is required. Making use of the historic fabric and creatively linking it to the creative and cultural industries and business service industries is an approach used in Scarborough, for example, which promises success.

## Notes

1   Following the Government's Subnational Review of Economic Development and Regeneration, after 2010 the RSS and RES will be replaced by a single Integrated Regional Strategy.

2   'Place-making' is an integrated approach to spatial development to create more 'liveable' towns and cities, and an integral part of the Sustainable Communities approach and the Bristol Accord, where it is described as 'an integrated approach to territorial cohesion' (Office of the Deputy Prime Minister 2006: 33).

3   This concept first appeared in the Lyons Inquiry (Lyons 2007), which considers the role of local government in wider participative decision-making beyond the traditional models of service provider and vehicle for investment in public infrastructure. Place-making through 'place-shaping' underlines the importance of communities taking responsibility for their own economic fortunes, and for striking the right balance between economic, environmental and social objectives and concerns.

# References

Beatty, C. and Fothergill, S. (2003) *The Seaside Economy: The Final Report of the Seaside Towns Research Project*. Sheffield: Centre for Regional Economic and Social Research, Sheffield Hallam University.

Beatty, C., Fothergill, S. and Wilson, I. (2008) *England's Seaside Towns: A Benchmarking Study*. London: Department for Communities and Local Government.

Beckerson, J. and Walton, J. K. (2005) 'Selling air: marketing the intangible at British resorts', in J. K. Walton (ed.) *Histories of Tourism: Representation, Identity and Conflict*. Clevedon: Channel View, pp. 55–68.

Deloitte (2008) *The Economic Case for the Visitor Economy*. Report for VisitBritain and the Tourism Alliance as part of the British Tourism Framework Review, London: Deloitte.

English Heritage (2007) *An Asset and a Challenge: Heritage and Regeneration in Coastal Towns in England*. London: English Heritage.

ERBEDU, CUDEM and Centre for City and Regional Studies (CCRS), University of Hull (2003) *Mid-term Evaluation of the Yorkshire and Humber 2000–2006 Objective 2 Programme*. Report for Government Office for Yorkshire and the Humber, the Office of the Deputy Prime Minister and the European Commission, Leeds: Leeds Metropolitan University.

European Parliament (2008) *The Impact of Tourism on Coastal Areas: Regional Development Aspects*. Report prepared by CSIL and ERBEDU, Brussels: Directorate General for Internal Policies of the Union, Policy Department B: Structural and Cohesion Policies.

GOYH (2004) *Yorkshire and The Humber Objective 2 Programme 2000–2006: Single Programming Document*, revised December 2004. Leeds: Government Office for Yorkshire and The Humber.

—— (2005) *Yorkshire and The Humber Objective 2 Programme 2000–2006: Programme Complement*, revised April 2005. Leeds: Government Office for Yorkshire and The Humber.

—— (2008) *The Yorkshire and Humber Plan: Regional Spatial Strategy to 2026*. Leeds: Government Office for Yorkshire and The Humber.

House of Commons CLG Committee (2007) *Coastal Towns: Second Report of Session 2006–07*. Norwich: The Stationery Office.

Lyons, Sir M. (2007) *Place-Shaping: A Shared Ambition for the Future of Local Government*. London: The Stationery Office.

Moors and Coast Area Tourism Partnership (2006) *Moors and Coast Tourism Strategy 2006–2009*. Thirsk: Moors and Coast Area Tourism Partnership.

Office of the Deputy Prime Minister (2006) *UK Presidency: EU Ministerial Informal Summit on Sustainable Communities, European Evidence Review Papers*. London: Office of the Deputy Prime Minister.

Walton, J. K. (2000) *The British Seaside: Holidays and Resorts in the Twentieth Century*. Manchester: Manchester University Press.

Yorkshire Forward (2006) *The Regional Economic Strategy for Yorkshire and Humber, 2006–2015*. Leeds: Yorkshire Forward.

—— (2008) *Visitor Economy Strategy*. Leeds: Yorkshire Forward.

Yorkshire Tourist Board (2008) *Tourism Information Pack 2008*. Leeds: Yorkshire Tourist Board.

# 7 A Canary Island in the context of sustainable tourism development

*Donald V. L. Macleod*

## Introduction

La Gomera is one of the Canary Islands, an archipelago off the northwest coast of Africa. It is an autonomous region of Spain with an island government subject to the national government in specific areas of activity. La Gomera has a population of around 23,000 (2006) and is circular in shape covering 378 square kilometres. Since the inclusion of Spain in the European Community in 1986, La Gomera has received funding for development projects, focused on infrastructural work related to transport and access. This chapter considers the ways in which tourism has developed on the island of La Gomera; in particular, the most popular destination, Valle Gran Rey (VGR) with its fishing port of Vueltas, which has been responsible for attracting most tourists to the island. It places the development of tourism into the context of sustainability and looks at the way that tourism in its many forms and parts has changed and evolved and is influenced by strategic official plans.

The organization of the chapter gives priority to discussion of the destination in terms of tourism development; there follows a detailed look at the port of Vueltas, giving a rich picture of actual changes. Thereafter a look at various authorized plans gives the official approach to development projects, some of which have been implemented, while some are in process, or are to be enacted. These plans set up a framework within which the authorities hope to contain tourism development. There follows a discussion on the concept of sustainable tourism development and its relevance to the plans. The concluding section draws attention to lessons learned.

## The development of tourism on La Gomera

Tourists began arriving on La Gomera in the late 1960s; they were the more adventurous types who were prepared to brave the relatively harsh transportation, topography and lack of accommodation in comparison to the experience on the larger islands such as Tenerife. By 1975, a ferry link had been established between the south of Tenerife (Los Cristianos) and the capital and port of San Sebastian on La Gomera. This link enabled quicker access and helped the growth of tourism which was composed largely of German backpackers. The main market for these tourists was during the winter months, when the north of Europe was experiencing cold weather. Gradually a flow of summer visitors from Tenerife and mainland Spain began, most being friends and relatives of the indigenous population, the Gomeros. This broad trend remained a slowly growing stream of arrivals through the 1980s and 1990s, with the Germans being joined to a lesser extent by Dutch and British visitors. There were also regular arrivals of day-trippers travelling by coach from Tenerife via the ferry, to tour the island – visiting San Sebastian, a Visitors Centre in the north of the island, and occasionally VGR. In this period the tourists, those who stay for at least one night, were predominantly German 'alternative' tourists carrying backpacks and obtaining a room on their arrival. They have been described as aged between 20 and 45, well educated, interested in the local culture and environment and seeking relaxation (see Duysens 1989; Macleod 2004).

During the 1990s, patterns of tourism began to diversify. There were already a few hotels on the islands, at San Sebastian and Santiago, and one was built in VGR (Hotel Gran Rey) in 1996. This added to the apartment complexes which were run by business consortia, as opposed to the small apartments and rooms offered by local families which have provided the bulk of accommodation. With the increasing marketing of the destination overseas through the businesses and agencies growing to promote the hotel and large apartment complexes, boosted dramatically by the internet, it became easier to access different markets including the package tourist. Infrastructural changes such as new and bigger roads, tunnelling and new harbour facilities have meant that the destination is more easily reached and with comfort. As a consequence, different types of tourist have begun to arrive: the mature, retired, 60-years of age plus group (Third Age); young families; and package tourists who prefer pre-arranged accommodation. Activity tourism has also grown, especially walking tours, dolphin-watching, diving and mountain-biking. More recently canoeing, snorkelling and bird-watching have been promoted, and for the culturally oriented there are dancing lessons, meditation classes and Spanish language lessons. These activities attract a particular type of tourist, some interested in spending the week walking or learning Spanish, others buying a week-long package including diverse activities. Foreign settlers have largely been responsible for this new activity-tourism growth, through offering the product and reacting to trends.

While tourism has grown in volume and diversity, the primary product industries of agriculture and fishing, on which the indigenous population had hitherto depended, have experienced quick declines. This has had major repercussions on the tourism industry and generally for the local population in terms of their attitudes towards and relationship with the tourism industry and tourists. Tourism has therefore, within a generation, grown from a minor and occasional source of income to the major industry in VGR and a critical element in the economy of La Gomera. Writing about the Garajonay National Park, a World Heritage Site on the island, Fernandez states: 'The only sign of hope for the future would appear to be some form of combination of agriculture through the development of rural tourism' (2002: 99). Regarding the Canary Islands as a whole, Pascual notes: 'Tourism and related economic activities have been the economic motor of the archipelago since the 1970s' (2004: 61).

The sustainability of tourism development is of major importance to La Gomera and the other Canary Islands. This is recognized in official documents and the tourism industry has received due respect, although it is debatable as to the appropriateness of certain projects sponsored by officialdom. In the following section a detailed examination is made of tourism-related development in VGR, especially Vueltas, showing actual changes illustrating how the character and profile of the settlement have been transformed.

## Specific changes relating to tourism

Valle Gran Rey is a municipality of La Gomera, with its own locally elected council. It is the most popular destination by a long way on the island, having three beaches, a beautiful valley surrounded by massive mountains and cliffs (700m high) enabling walking and swimming (limited by lack of sand and a dangerous sea in winter). VGR has a resident population of 5,166 (2009) and currently some 128 separate apartment businesses offering 943 apartments (mostly with two beds) officially recorded by the local council. There are additionally numerous unofficial accommodation outlets. A look at actual changes recorded mainly in the popular port area of Vueltas, especially since 1991, will give a distinct picture of what has been going on.

Vueltas began as a fishing settlement and the port for Valle Gran Rey. It was established in the early 1900s by fishermen who hunted tuna, and it grew to have a population over 300 by the 1930s. Fishing remained the dominant economic activity until the 1990s during which time activity fluctuated and was reduced by the global scenario including competition from large foreign vessels in nearby waters, other producers, European Union accession which meant new regulations on activities, and the displacement of workers from fishing into other sectors, especially tourism (see Macleod 2004; Mesa-Moreno 1982; Pascual 2004). Many fishermen began to let rooms in their own homes, or even build apartments for tourists during the mid-1980s, and Vueltas became the main centre for backpacker accommodation in the valley, as well as the focus for bars, restaurants and the nightlife. The number of professional registered fishermen has dropped from 85 in 1980 (Mesa-Moreno 1982) to 53 in 2002, and down to 19 in 2009 (figures from fishing cooperative, Vueltas). Fishermen themselves say there are only a handful of full-time fishermen left; others operate part-time, and retired fishermen continue to fish regularly.

The large loss in recent years has been partly due to two big boats (Faluas) ceasing operations from Vueltas. Other factors accounting for the reduction include the attraction of different work for the sons of fishermen, stimulated by educational opportunities, work in tourism and a realization that fishing has too many risks (see Macleod 2004). Moreover, experienced fishermen talk of the degradation of the coastal fishing zone through overfishing, especially the use of traps, meaning that in 2009 catches are estimated to be only 20 per cent of the annual catches during the 1980s.

In contrast to the fishing sector, the tourism and the related sector have grown substantially. Beginning in the early 1980s when a fisherman extended his house to accommodate tourists, by 1991 there were approximately 36 separate family apartment businesses in Vueltas, growing to 44 in 2009. These apartments remain owned by local families and range from rooms in private homes to separate blocks of up to 12 different apartments: self-contained with cooking and washing facilities (cf. Bianchi and Santana Talavera 2004 on household resource usage).

While the accommodation sector in Vueltas remains largely in the hands of indigenous inhabitants, often families of fishermen, the service outlets such as shops, cafes and tourism-related businesses are dominated by foreign settlers who might be regarded as 'cultural brokers' between the resident population and visiting tourists. The following review of changes since 1991 illustrates this pattern.

There were 33 recorded businesses in 1991 (excluding the accommodation sector); by March 2009 the number of businesses in Vueltas was approximately 62, which included an increase in bars/restaurants from 13 to 20, and boutiques up from 1 to 7, whereas supermarket numbers had decreased from 6 to 3. The situation with the supermarkets (small family-run stores) is highly relevant as they represented one of the few types of business that Gomeros were confident and dominant in operating (see Macleod 2004). One reason for this reduction is the opening nearby of a SPAR supermarket (a multinational company) giving huge competition through low prices and a wider selection of goods, applauded by local people.

New developments since 2002 include a Gomeran traditional food and wine outlet, an ice-cream shop, a bakery (German style), a German-style butchers, a large internet outlet, and most relevant to the diversifying tourism product, a walking-tour office, a mountain-bike hire and tour shop, a Kayak-tour office, a scuba-dive office, and a dolphin-tour office. These latter outlets represent a new form of tourism which now attracts people from northern Europe: activity tourism (cf. Roberts and Hall 2001: 167; Novelli 2005: 143). All these activity outlets are run by foreign settlers.

Along with the increase in service outlets and accommodation businesses the demand for property has grown, a demand exacerbated by the opening up of markets to a global audience with the advent of the internet, preceded by an official property agent mediating between sellers and buyers. In 1991, a one-bedroomed flat could be bought in the district for £39,000: by 2002, prices had risen to £70,000 and by 2009, the minimum price in Vueltas was £90,000. There have been approximately 50 new residential flats built in Vueltas since the year 2000.

Changes seen in Vueltas related to tourism in terms of service outlets and accommodation have been replicated to varying extents throughout the entire valley coastal area, especially the small districts of Playa Calera and Borbalan. The building of residential homes and shops aimed at the local population has been extensive in Borbalan which now joins on to Vueltas in a ribbon development. Elsewhere two hotels have been built on the beach-front at Puntilla (Gran Rey, a three-star hotel) and Playa Calera (an 'Aparthotel' with apartments). The entire coastal settlement has seen rapid growth and continues to be experiencing more construction of residential housing, tourist apartments and outlets.

Most significantly for Vueltas, a massive harbour extension creating a second harbour side by side with the original, with the intention of enabling a car-ferry to dock, is under construction. It was completed as a harbour in its first phase of construction, costing almost 13 million euros. This project began in December 2002 and is still to be completed, as the second phase has not yet been initiated. In 2009, the harbour was out of use and off limits to the public. The construction period was a time of serious disruption and loss of income to the tourism trade in Vueltas: noise, construction traffic, fumes and the general mayhem caused by quarrying of the nearby cliffs and massive building work turned people away. This is one of numerous EU-funded projects on the island; others include the extension of roads and the creation of new roads which link Vueltas to the main beach area and to the central road exiting the valley. A passenger-only ferry has also operated intermittently enabling people to arrive direct from Tenerife, rather than having to catch a bus or taxi from San Sebastian.

These infrastructural transformations improving access have had corresponding influences on the type of tourist visiting VGR as have certain global trends – the growth in the mature or 'Third Age' (post-retirement) sector has led very recently to many package tourists arriving who have retired. This market has been well developed on other Canary Islands such as Tenerife, but was hitherto negligible on La Gomera. At the other end of the spectrum young families have increased in numbers as visitors, for similar reasons related to accessibility, accommodation and the relative ease of booking a secure package tour. At one time in the early 1990s, VGR was notorious for single mothers and their young children staying in winter. These continue to arrive and are joined by other, more conventional families.

Another group that has increased in numbers is the 'activity tourist' who spend much of their time walking in the uplands: there is a World Heritage Site sub-tropical cloud forest covering 10 per cent of the island (national park Garajonay), numerous ravines (max. height is around 1500m), forest walks and coastal hikes which have been fully explored, mapped and described in books. Mountain-biking has increased, following trails and traditional road routes. A dolphin-watching tour company 'Club de Mar' was created in the early 1990s by a German settler, and its popularity led to the development of a research group (specialist scientists) and a centre for studying cetaceans. The original company has been replaced by a new company 'Oceano' which offers a small boat tour (capacity 10 passengers) with expert advice: their office also hosts information media and a cetacean research centre (Marine Education Environment Research). Two larger tour boats also took advantage of this market in the 1990s, but by 2009 there was only one such boat (capacity 60) offering dolphin tours.

Activity tourism products on offer include kayaking tours which explore the coast of the VGR estuary, based at the port; this is a small new business operating a few days a week. There is also a German who offers bird-watching tours and photography tours; another offers snorkel tours (3-hour sessions): these are both private individuals doing tours on demand.

These nature-based activities demonstrate a major feature of tourism, in particular as it is developing in VGR: a change in the relationship between people and the natural environment. Whereas, prior to the development of tourism, people had wrested a mode of livelihood through agriculture and fishing, seeing the natural environment as a means of direct production, it is now consumed in a different manner, more passively, aesthetically, educationally, in a way that excludes immediate survival necessity, but magnifies passive appreciation or active leisure engagement. The environment becomes a means of entertainment, albeit occasionally with a serious-minded appreciation. This is most notable with dolphin tours, where such creatures would at one time have been seen as competition in the hunt for fish by professional fishers.

Other activity tourism offerings include culture-based experiences such as Spanish language lessons, flamenco dancing, yoga, and meditation classes. These, together with the outdoor physical activities, represent a gradual and profound change in the way tourists in VGR have behaved and interacted with their physical surroundings over the past 20 years. In 1989, there were no organized tours from VGR; people hired cars, hitched, took public buses or simply walked in to the mountains. No dolphin tours existed. By 1991, bikes could be hired. The vast majority of tourists relaxed on the beaches and took occasional walks; to see a morning jogger was almost impossible whereas in 2009 they are numerous. The 'tourist gaze' (Urry 2002) has diversified on the island through product growth, becoming more scientific, pro-actively searching, appreciating and engaging with the natural and cultural heritage.

Changes in the tourist behaviour include a reduction in the period of stay, with many remaining for shorter periods of time, one week rather than two. There are more nationalities arriving, especially from The Netherlands and Scandinavia. Unfortunately the tourism authorities do not maintain adequate statistics on tourists visiting La Gomera, rather, numbers arriving are lumped indiscriminately with those of the much more popular destination Tenerife; and ferry passengers are recorded with no useful distinction between islanders and international travellers. However, the changes detailed above tell their own story in terms of demand for services and patterns of behaviour, and we might ask, what do they say about the development of tourism and its sustainability for the future?

One answer regarding the development of tourism in VGR is that its growing diversity may enhance future sustainability. From a resort attracting predominantly German alternative tourists in the winter and Spanish '*veranistas*' in the summer it has transformed into one which attracts a rich variety including alternative, activity, family, third age, backpackers, and package tourists; and from various countries including Germany, the UK, Ireland, Scandinavia, Spain, Switzerland.

## Official plans for tourism and the development of the region

In the previous section we looked at the private businesses involved in the growth of tourism which had been forming independently of any fixed, regulated and structured plan, apart from their response to circumstances and personal views of the future. We now turn to officially authorized plans relating to tourism and its development: plans and projects which are driven by elected representatives and the state bureaucracies, sometimes influenced by larger, more powerful political or international groupings including the European Union. The different levels of authority relevant to this exploration of developments in VGR are as follows: (1) the local municipal council (*Ayuntamiento*) of Valle Gran Rey; (2) the Island Council of La Gomera (*Cabildo*); (3) the Canary Islands government; (4) the national government of Spain; and (5) the European Union.

The following quote from the head of the Inter-Island Council of La Gomera illustrates the approach taken towards tourism and elements that are being prioritized:

> Our aim is to preserve the balance between conserving the island's unique landscape while at the same time improving the quality of life of its inhabitants and responding to the demands of a high-quality tourist industry. Well aware that the charms of La Gomera lies mainly in the conservation of its rich historical heritage and its stunning natural landscape, the inter-island council has opted to promote two types of tourist activity, both considered compatible with the protection of our local environment and the maintenance of our high-quality services and facilities. These two activities are rural or green tourism and controlled development of conventional tourism. In short, the island is preparing to launch itself on the tourist market, with the aim of modernising its economy and improving the quality of life of its inhabitants, while at

the same time preserving its natural heritage and individual identity for future generations.

(Curbelo Curbelo 2002: 6)

Maintaining the natural heritage and cultural heritage is high on the agenda for tourism development, and tourism is perceived as being very important to the island economy. It is worth examining some of the specific individual projects that have been established, or are being designed, that deal directly with tourism development in VGR and the island as a whole.

## The POI

The POI (*Programma Operative Intergrado de la Isla de La Gomera*) had received funding from the European Union (EU) (up to £30 million) as well as the Spanish government, and was intended to develop the entire island, helping it to integrate with the other six islands, and it was responsible for funding the construction of infrastructure such as roads, tunnels and the island airport. The plan became operational in 1991 and sought to create employment, reduce income disparities between Gomeros and other islanders, correct disparities in wealth on the islands, control strategic resources (water, energy and environment) and improve the quality of life (POI 1990, Madrid). These objectives reflected the EU goals of reducing regional inequalities, and the plan's introduction was a major repercussion of Spain joining the European Community in 1986. Road improvements and road construction followed in VGR, built in accordance with EU planning requirements together with tunnels which made access to VGR quicker.

However, the POI led to an ill-fated plan to transform the seafront of VGR. The VGR Municipal Council had created a proposal: 'Project for the regeneration of the coast of VGR' which included creating artificial bays, halting the natural removal of sand in winter from the main coastal beach using groynes, building a coastal pathway containing kiosks and bars, and artificially reconstructing two natural bathing locations. This was seen by many as ruining the natural attractiveness of the coast, as well as upsetting the marine ecology and impacting on the fishery. For the first time in its recorded history the people of VGR challenged the local council in what turned from an underground petition into an open public protest – they were supported by others from the island and beyond, with environmental and political motives (see Macleod 2004: 147). The protestors won their argument and the project was shelved (cf. Boissevain 2004: 255, on the protest).

## The PTE

In 2002, a plan for tourism development on the island was approved, and it was published in 2003: *Plan Territorial Especial de Desarrollo Turistico de la Isla de la Gomera* (PTE). This had as its aim to identify and delimit zones, to consider provisions for development, define characteristics and delimit land use in different environments. It is considered a basis for the sustainable development of the island (Boletín Oficial de Canarias 2003: 10799). Article 9 'Objectives of the Order' seeks to achieve the following:

> The PTE has an objective to give order to tourism activity, to contribute to the rationalisation and stabilisation of sustainable development regarding the natural environment and resource use. It will do this by regulating touristic activity – accommodation and services, according to the category of zone, delimit zones and help protect and recuperate historic heritage, agriculture, and recognising different ways of developing specialist tourism and conventional tourism. It will establish a maximum level of growth and speed of growth in tourism construction.
>
> (BOC 2003: 10802)

The plan outlines in great detail the specific types of tourism it seeks to control and the actual limitations (especially spatial) on the development of dedicated, named sites. It is an official guideline and regulation template for any development and it gives insight into the goals of the authors in terms of types of tourism planned for, and the methods of maintaining tourism as well as the island's current assets.

In the plan 'PTE' there was recognition of the massive redevelopment of the port harbour in Vueltas among others on the island. This redevelopment went ahead in 2002: the project, known as 'Preparation of the Port at Vueltas', was due to be completed by June 2005. But in 2009, it remains incomplete and out of use. The old port remains, and has been joined by a massive new harbour with a huge protective dyke wall capable of allowing a car ferry to dock. The new harbour is not in use; many years of construction, cliff quarrying, harbour dredging and heavy traffic made Vueltas unattractive to visitors. The finalization of the project will take many more years, involving more heavy construction in the second phase of development.

### *The* Plan General

The harbour preparation plan is recognised and detailed in another plan which is undergoing final stage preparation for possible approval in late 2010, known as '*Plan General de Valle Gran Rey*'. This plan deals with the district's physical environment, taking into account its cultural and natural heritage; it details zoning for different types of building programmes and road building with illustrations of outcomes. One section addresses the new harbour and its related transport support infrastructure, especially roads. Another section shows the design for the creation of a promenade along the seafront and a new road running parallel to it. A member of the tourism office staff in VGR suggested that the plan will definitely provide for car ferries and that together with the occasional berthing of huge cruise ships, the port development will increase visitor numbers and spend, as well as simplify access to Tenerife and other islands for local people and reduce the transport costs of goods to VGR. They anticipated that VGR would attract a similar profile of tourist in the future as it currently does: those people seeking a quiet place for relaxation and those who enjoy outdoor activities such as walking.

### The problem with mega-projects

The '*Plan General*' will involve massive road building programmes along the entire coastal plain of VGR, imposing a network running parallel to the coast, involving passing through what is currently agricultural land (terraces and banana plantations); it will also incorporate the Phase Two harbour preparation. There is a risk that this will impact on the charm of the destination, part of which is its relatively unspoilt and natural coastline, as mentioned above when defended by many locals. Added to the loss of charm will be the loss of its unique quality, perhaps its unique selling point in terms of competition with larger more urbanized and standardized resorts such as Los Cristianos, Tenerife, one hour away by ferry across the sea.

This risk involving the loss of charm and consequently demand from tourists illustrates the danger of what may be termed a 'mega-project': a massive civil engineering programme that potentially dramatically changes a destination, costing huge sums of money. These mega-projects may not always take into account the opportunity costs of construction in terms of lost income to the resort during construction, the final result on the destination in terms of changing its character from an unspoilt village to a huge harbour port, and the future impact on tourists with a likely reduction in number of those who seek a quiet rural setting.

La Gomera currently has an airport which was built partly through funding from the POI programme during the 1990s. In March 2009, it dealt with just two flights in and out per day (to North Tenerife). This is an example of a mega-project which is probably a waste of money. Together with the huge harbour at Vueltas, it represents spending on tourism-related projects which was not realistically and sensitively thought through. Such developments suggest a number of problems including a lack of serious thought about the island's tourism, especially the types of visitors, their motivation, and the island's unique qualities. There needs to be more flexibility and cultural awareness in the funding and preparation procedure. Projects should be better tailored to circumstances and more appropriate development needs to be undertaken.

In a paper examining policy and sustainable tourism development in the Canary Islands, Bianchi makes a concluding point regarding official plans and regulations which resonates with the above findings:

The exemption of luxury accommodation, marinas and rural tourism, etc. from the new restrictions opens up new territories and 'products' in the name of 'quality' tourism development. This reinforces the control of resources by an 'alliance' of external capital and tour operators, powerful consortiums of regional capital, landowners and a range of entrenched political cliques, at the expense of labour, civil society, small investors, and, of course, the region's ecology.

(Bianchi 2004: 522)

Perhaps a new plan currently in preparation for the island will be more sensitive to the natural environment and to the needs and motivations of visitors. The '*Estrategia de Turismo Sostenible de La Gomera*', derived from the '*Carta Europea*' will be executed between 2008 and 2012 and has its focus on the World Heritage Site National Park Garajonay, and also looks at key tourism locations on the island. It gives guidelines to businesses and public entities and will track the progress of specified organizations.

## Sustainable tourism development and the official plans

Sustainable development is mentioned in the plan (PTE) to develop tourism on the island and the importance of resources, both natural and cultural, is recognized along with other traditional industries such as agriculture as they relate to the economy. However, the concept of sustainable development as it relates to tourism was not sufficiently explained in the PTE. Encouragingly, the '*Estrategia de turismo Sostenible de La Gomera*' has a detailed description and proposals relating to sustainable tourism, including sections on protecting natural, cultural and historical heritage, maintaining the quality of local life, improving the quality of tourism offerings and the satisfaction of tourists, with detailed actions to be taken such as 'improve the tourism equipment in VGR'. However, this programme is yet to be implemented and the concept of sustainable tourism development is not as straightforward as some plans would lead the reader to believe. This section analyses the meanings and practices along with commentaries on the concept and specific problems which islands experience.

Swarbrooke (1999: 3) gives an overarching definition:

By sustainable we generally mean development which meets our needs today without compromising the ability of people in the future to meet their needs. It is thus about taking a longer-term perspective than is usual in human decision-making and implies a need for intervention and planning. The concept of sustainability clearly embraces the environment, people and economic systems.

Sustainable tourism therefore is an ideal to strive for, but something which needs independent objective analysis; in practice, it is strongly related to the context of power at the locality and with relevant stakeholders. Ioannides *et al.* (2001) share some of Swarbrooke's opinions and state that 'the implementation of sustainable tourism is elusive', and while there is no consensus on the definition, ' Even so, sustainable development can be a guiding fiction' (ibid.: 3).

As an island, La Gomera shares problems with other insular communities, especially those arising from peripheral isolation and small scale. These problems include a limited resource base, a small domestic market, diseconomies of scale, poor accessibility, an infrastructural limitation and a dependency on external powers (ibid.: 5). Manifestations of these generic problems where tourism becomes a major part of the island experience include: pollution of the environment, aesthetic destruction such as ribbon developments of buildings, loss of biodiversity in flora and fauna, loss of open space. In economic terms there might be inflation of land, property and goods prices, the displacement of labour with tourism services, a shortage of labour supply (ibid.). More specifically, Pascual (2004) observed that tourism and related activities have been the economic motor for the Canary Islands and that most of the expansion has been in the coastal zones, directly impacting on communities of fishers among others. Regarding displacement, he notes that the workforce in fishing diminished by 35 per cent between 1991 and 1996. Figures from VGR suggest this trend is continuing.

It is important to consider tourism development in the broader context of general economic and social development as emphasized by Tom Selwyn (mentioned in Ioannides *et al.* 2001: 13) who stresses the need to recognize the role of democratic control as well as the historically achieved social and economic patterns at the destination. It is also noted that: 'Policy-makers need to pursue tourism development in a manner that achieves overall balance in growth while also seeking to expand the opportunities for economic diversification' and that: 'Tourism must operate within a region's capacity limits' (ibid.: 18–19).

## Conclusion

La Gomera has experienced a steady growth in tourism since the 1970s, especially in Valle Gran Rey, by far the most popular destination on the small island. From its beginning as the relaxing resort for alternative backpackers, it has emerged into a centre for nature-based activities and beach-based relaxation for a wide spectrum of tourist types in terms of age, social status and interests. Nationalities visiting the island have also diversified, although German and Spanish remain dominant according to the season. Recently, since the mid-1990s, the product offering has broadened, especially in relation to activity tourism, and the destination offers a diverse portfolio, reliant on small-scale entrepreneurs, mostly foreign settlers.

## Lessons to be learned

The recognition of a destination's complex mix of tourism types has repercussions for the understanding of sustainable tourism development, in the sense that some types may remain 'sustainable' and others not. Of course there may be a general, all-embracing trend, but this will mask specific individual trajectories, and it is absolutely vital to recognize and understand these if we are to ensure successful and acceptable tourism development.

It is apparent that sustainable tourism development is an ideal scenario which is worthwhile striving for, but that a destination must be considered in terms of its specific qualities, such as natural and cultural resources, political, economic and social character. Furthermore, the views of the indigenous population should be considered in any plan to promote or control development. There is a need to concentrate on the destination in a holistic and long-term manner. There is also a need to be aware of the larger global picture: the external factors over which management and others will not have any control, such as the world economy, climate change, political upheavals, international competition and the ever-changing demographics and desires of the international tourism market.

As a concept, sustainable tourism development is rightly criticized for being difficult, if impossible to achieve, essentially contestable: it is most usefully to be considered as an ideal objective. While it should be regarded as a holistic goal, it is in reality composed of interrelated but usually separate parts wherein the economic dimension is prioritized for businesses. Different stakeholders champion different aspects, for example, the economy, the environment, but rarely culture.

To an extent, the concept of sustainable tourism development remains a weak means of dealing with actual situations, where a strong grasp of local conditions as well as global circumstances is needed. Management for development needs to be flexible, well informed, sensitive and long-term. There should be an approach which might be called 'appropriate scale development' (ASD) in which subtle, tailored projects are designed in a bespoke manner for different scenarios.

The large state-driven and authorized plans we have considered impacting on La Gomera, and specifically VGR are clumsy and inappropriate in places. They develop over decades and may eventually become obsolete, wasteful and potentially destructive. These produce expensive ornaments (the airport) or white elephants (the harbour) which may possibly become useful, but at immense expense. A more appropriate scale development project should be sensitive to the type of tourist visiting the destination regarding motivations, demography, needs, and so on, as well as looking at the successful small business products, like activity tourism which is flourishing, learning from this and giving support where needed, while considering resource controls for the long term. Not only would such projects be directed at the successful types of tourism, but they should help maintain the destination's unique characteristics, the selling point, a matter which is of increasing relevance in a standardized and regularized global market where competition is ferocious. When a destination is almost completely dependent economically on tourism, those who plan, manage and spend public money on projects must adopt an approach that is thoughtful and knowledgeable about the qualities, socio-cultural composition, history and environment of the destination and the relevant wider global scenario.

## Acknowledgements

I am grateful to The Carnegie Trust which funded the fieldwork in 2009 that forms the bulk of the research material for this chapter.

## References

Bianchi, R. (2004) 'Tourism restructuring and the politics of sustainability: a critical view from the European periphery (The Canary Islands)', *Journal of Sustainable Tourism* 12(6): 495–529.

Bianchi, R. and Santana Talavera, A. (2004) 'Between the sea and the land: exploring the social organisation of tourism development in a Gran Canaria fishing village', in J. Boissevain and T. Selwyn (eds) *Contesting the Foreshore: Tourism, Society and Politics on the Coast*. Amsterdam: Amsterdam University Press.

BOC (2003) *Boletín Oficial de Canarias*, 120, 5/6/2003. Tenerife: Ayuntamiento de Santiago del Teide.

Boissevain, J. (2004) 'Hotels, tuna pens, and civil society: contesting the foreshore in Malta', in J. Boissevain and T. Selwyn (eds) *Contesting the Foreshore: Tourism, Society and Politics on the Coast*. Amsterdam: Amsterdam University Press, pp. 233–60.

Boissevain, J. and Selwyn T. (eds) (2004) *Contesting the Foreshore: Tourism, Society and Politics on the Coast*. Amsterdam: Amsterdam University Press.

Curbelo Curbelo, C. (2002) *Tourist Guide La Gomera: Tenerife (Statement from the President of the La Gomera Inter-Island Council)*. Tenerife: Graficas Tenerife.

Duysens, B. (1989) 'Turismo, ocio y cultura juvenile: el caso del turismo de mochila en La Gomera', *ERES (Antropología)* 1(2): 115–26.

Fernandez, A. (2002) *National Park Garajonay La Gomera*. San Sebastian, La Gomera: Ministerio de Medio Ambiente.

Ioannides, D., Apostolopoulos, Y. and Sonmez, S. (2001) 'Searching for sustainable tourism development in the insular Mediterranean', in D. Ioannides, Y. Apostolopoulos and S. Sonmez (eds) *Mediterranean Islands and Sustainable Tourism Development: Practices, Management and Policies*. London: Continuum, pp. 3–22.

Macleod, D. V. L. (2004) *Tourism, Globalisation and Cultural Change: An Island Community Perspective*. Clevedon: Channel View.

Mesa-Morena, C. (1982) 'Antropologica social de las communidades pesqueras en Valle Gran Rey', in C. Mesa-Moreno, J. Pascual-Fernandez and A. J. Perez-Soza (eds) *La Pesca en Canarias*. Tenerife: CCPC, pp. 73–115.

Novelli, M. (2005) *Niche Tourism: Contemporary Issues, Trends and Cases*. Oxford: Elsevier.

Pascual, J. (2004) 'Littoral fishermen, aquaculture, and tourism in the Canary Islands: attitudes and economic strategies', in J. Boissevain and T. Selwyn (eds) *Contesting the Foreshore: Tourism, Society and Politics on the Coast*. Amsterdam: Amsterdam University Press.

Roberts, L. and Hall, D. (2001) *Rural Tourism and Recreation: Principles to Practice*. Wallingford: CABI.

Swarbrooke, J. (1999) *Sustainable Tourism Management*. Wallingford: CABI.

Urry, J. (2002) *The Tourist Gaze*, 2nd edn. London: Sage.

# 8 The role of destination management organizations

## Models for sustainable rural destinations in Scotland?

*Rory MacLellan*

## Introduction

Scotland has experienced a number of organizational structures, models, programmes and initiatives in an attempt to promote and 'manage' tourism at a variety of spatial scales. These have utilized a range of interpretations of the destination and incorporated a variety of objectives depending on prevailing political priorities at the time: emphasis has changed on a number of policies such as prominence of public or private sector leadership; rural or urban focus; and economic, social or environmental imperatives. It has been argued that in reality disorganization characterizes tourism destinations (Ritchie and Crouch 2003) whereby a loose association of tourism-related businesses, organizations and interest groups work together with the local community in a semi-organized, partly cooperative fashion. The term 'community approach' has been used to describe this, especially in rural contexts. But like many communities, these frequently lack cohesion and continuity and are often driven in opposing directions depending on the interests of partners involved.

The one objective normally agreed on epitomizes the role of tourism destination organizations: promotion, in particular the creation of image and positioning of the destination under a united vision. The modern concept of the Destination Management Organization (DMO) is to transform the 'M' to stand for management rather than simply marketing. In theory, the DMO should be responsible for the well-being of all aspects of the destination, thus neatly complying with the holistic purposes of sustainable destinations in an ecological, economic and socio-cultural sense; but the key to achieving the elusive sustainable destination, it seems, is governance. Although governance has always been the key challenge, new communication technologies, namely Destination Management Systems (DMS), claim to provide complete and up-to-date information on a particular destination, thereby offering some solutions to complex decision-making.

In the past two decades, innovations in destination management have been sought to improve tourism planning and policies and it is in this context that current DMO models are examined. This chapter seeks to critique past attempts, such as the Tourism Management Programmes of the 1990s, but mainly focuses on the current structures, in particular, the recent rash of rural DMOs. The definitions, locations chosen and drive behind their inception are reviewed. A key question is the extent to which they have been initiated with a top-down (national tourism agency-led) or bottom-up community perspective. By placing these embryonic destination groups within the historical organizational context and comparing these with international examples, the chapter hopes to make some observations on their adherence to or divergence from current theory of best practice in destination management.

In doing so, reference is made to destination models including: development cycles; business models; sense of place, space and image formation; destination typologies, TALC resort (product) life cycles; Force Field Analysis; and destination competitiveness models. The literature indicates that the majority of the research is qualitative, typically in case study format (Brey *et al.* 2007). This suggests a lack of systematic measurement of destination management achievements and a failure to learn from past mistakes. The chapter attempts to explore the extent to which the above has been the case through an examination of recently established tourism destination management organizations in rural Scotland. These should illustrate the complex and contested nature of tourism destinations and the pitfalls in assuming there is a quick technological or organizational fix.

## Destination management models

Academics have sought to define and understand tourism destinations for several decades using a variety of perspectives and definitions. Tourism destinations tend to be defined with a mix of demand and supply perspectives: from defining a destination in planning terms as a zone or 'a geographic area containing a critical mass of development that satisfies traveller objectives' (Gunn 1994: 27); or 'A tourism destination, in its simplest terms, is a particular geographical region within which the visitor enjoys various types of travel experiences' (Ritchie and Crouch 2003), to a greater emphasis on the marketing and organization of a destination: 'A destination is a defined geographical region which is understood by its visitors as a unique entity, with a political and legislative framework for tourism marketing and planning' (Buhalis 2000: 98). The differences between the physical, geographical definition with boundaries and administrations and the perceptual one, based on consumer perspectives, images and branding illustrates the core tension at the heart of establishing and promoting destinations. Added to this confusion is use of terms such as resorts, places or tourism regions, often as synonyms for destination.

## Destination models

To aid understanding, tourism academics provide numerous case studies that attempt to explain the tourism destination: stage development cycles, business models, sense of place and image, specific destination types – urban, peripheral, resort, coastal, mountain. It has been noted that in spite of the volume of destination resort literature, the majority of research is qualitative, typically in case study format (Brey *et al.* 2007): their systematic review of articles reveals that consumers, industry overviews and resort management issues have been of greatest interest to academic researchers. However, the influence of tourism on surrounding local communities and their role in overall tourism success have been less well researched. For example, opportunities to augment tourism destination research include examination of private and public partnerships; succession planning; further understanding of environmental impacts in rural locations; and impacts of local and regional government legislation.

Many of the earlier studies of tourism destinations examined how they evolved over time, notably Butler's Tourism Area Life Cycle or TALC (Butler 2005). It is now 30 years since the original model first appeared in the academic literature (Butler 1980), and contrary to the normally restricted life of most academic models, it is still applied, cited in tourism text books, and used in research studies (Baum 2005; Prideaux 2000). A review of the literature on the TALC model and its application (Lagiewski 2006) demonstrated this fact clearly, with over fifty examples of published research papers relating to the TALC model being included. Some authors have been critical of the model, others have suggested it is inapplicable in specific settings (Choy 1992). Others have proposed valid modifications of the model (e.g. Agarwal 2002), suggested alternative arguments for the patterns of development examined (Ioannides 1992), and argued for the application of other theories, sometimes in conjunction with the TALC (Gale and Botterill 2005).

One form of analysis which addresses the importance of including the private sector, and has particular relevance to the TALC, is Force Field Analysis (FFA). Similar to the original product life cycle model, this is adopted from the business literature. Johnson and Scholes (2002) used Force Field Analysis when studying organizational culture in the context of local governments in the United Kingdom and the forces affecting productivity and finding opportunities to change an existing culture and way of thinking. The approach allows organizations and corporations, and by implication, also communities, to explore some key questions when they are considering development strategies and changing approaches, for example, the need to anticipate market changes and be proactive in terms of development. The IPA (importance performance analysis) model is another which emphasizes business and destination competitiveness through the application of tourism and generic business factors (Enright and Newton 2004).

The issue of complexity is addressed in the dynamic destination management model (DDMM) (Sainaghi 2006). Sainaghi links established destination managers to the formulation of good destination strategy by introducing a dynamic element to his dynamic destination management model. The research is based on longitudinal case studies that involved real-world analysis of six European DMOs, three Alpine and three seaside resorts. The author points out the advantages of managing a destination through the DDMM, for example, pinpointing areas where the DMO should intervene in terms of resources and processes, identifying stakeholder responsibilities and clarification of complex connections that tie DMO actions with those of local firms and the public sector.

Another comparative study of European destinations focuses on the need for an integrated quality management system to maintain competitiveness for tourist destinations (Go and Govers 2000). The study presents the results of eight best practice case studies of different destinations in four European countries, which were part of a European Commission (DG XXIII) project. The aim of the study was to determine whether selected European destinations apply integrated quality management as a means of improving their competitiveness. The authors report that integrated quality management in tourist destinations is rather underdeveloped and that destinations tend to be strong in one element, such as policy and strategy or human resources management, as opposed to showing a balanced and integrated approach to quality management.

There are also approaches to destination analysis that focus on image, branding, place and space rather than administrative or organizational matters. These include academic articles from the fields of marketing (Blain *et al.* 2005; Caldwell and Freire 2004) and sociology (the seminal 'Tourist Gaze', Urry 2002) but also commercial consultancy reports, notably *The Power of Destinations* from the Communications Group plc (2005) which has been influential in current destination marketing approaches in the UK. The core difference is in the conception of destination as a brand rather than a geographical entity. Destination branding is about how consumers perceive the destination and goes beyond creating a logo or a slogan. From a marketing communications standpoint, it is about capturing the distinct elements of the destination and communicating these elements through the brand's components such as identity, essence, personality, image, character and culture. Destination positioning is managing these components to create a unique position of the destination brand in the consumer's mind. There is now a considerable body of research on destination image from general conceptual framework for the Tourism Destination Image (TDI) (Gallarza *et al.* 2002; see also Baloglu and McCleary 1999) to more specialized studies on place categories, for example, heritage, urban, rural or resort destination branding. The trick is not to expect brand positioning for one category to work for all. The TDI model attempts an overarching framework by including four features, each of which underlines a useful dimension of the concept of image for strategic management of destinations: 'complexity' which underlines an analytical dimension; 'multiplicity' provides an action dimension; 'relativistic' character translates TDI as a strategic tool; and 'dynamic' character allows for tactical decisions based on TDI. However interesting this model may be to academics, it has yet to capture the hearts and minds of destination managers.

A key reason for this may lie in issues of ownership and stakeholder involvement in destinations. The complexity of ownership does not lend itself to common branding or management. The concerns of multiple ownership in tourism destinations are addressed by Mottiar and Tucker (2007) where they look at tourism destination clusters and networks. They focus on one specific form of practice which occurs when more than one small or micro business within a specific destination is owned by the same entrepreneur. This again reinforces the need for a variety of approaches drawing on a number of disciplines.

However, a constant consideration identified by commentators remains the importance of governance or leadership in managing and promoting destinations. Ritchie and Crouch (2003) note that disorganization characterizes most tourism destinations where the norm is for a loose collection of enterprises, organizations and groups to work together in a semi-organized, partly cooperative fashion, but which are ultimately driven by their own self-interest. Stakeholders typically have differing priorities and establishing frameworks within which these might be agreed have become more sophisticated in recent decades. The prevailing philosophy of sustainability has brought us four categories of objectives for destinations to balance: ecological; economic; socio-cultural; and political (the key one, governance) (ibid.: 44–7) although the importance of maintaining competitiveness is included in the complex and perhaps unworkable competitive destination model developed by Ritchie and Crouch. Clearly, achieving balance takes time and requires both awareness raising and compromise. The foundation and constitution of any destination organization must be strong enough to work with pre-existing power structures and multiple stakeholders in a spirit of cooperation and competition rather than conflict.

Throughout this brief review of the literature on destination analysis has been the nagging question of the appropriate spatial scale for an effective destination. Many models include this factor but few provide definitive judgements on geographical area or population size. Establishing an optimal size for a tourism destination is an unresolved issue as currently a destination can range from a country or even a continent (Africa) all the way down to an individual attraction or tourism business. Although not administratively convenient for the land use planner or government organization, this diversity reflects the perception of destination in the eyes of the consumer and thus has validity, at least from a marketing perspective. This factor is recognized in the literature on DMOs where, it seems, size does not always matter.

*Destination management organizations (DMOs)*

The term DMO has come to describe any destination organization that attempts to manage and develop tourism. The World Tourism Organization attempted a classification of DMOs, recognizing the variety of scales included: from the long-established National Tourism Authorities (NTAs) or Organizations (NTOs), responsible for management and marketing of tourism at a national level; through regional, provincial or state DMOs (RTOs), responsible for the management and/or marketing of tourism in a geographic region defined for that purpose, sometimes a local government region such as a county, state or province; and then local DMOs, responsible for the management and/or marketing of tourism based on a smaller geographic area or city/town (World Tourism Organization 2004). This emphasizes the difficulty in establishing a common set of criteria and guidelines for the management and operation of DMOs as, clearly, the resources and diversity apparent at the national level will be quite different from that of the local level, as might the strategic priorities. Within the UK, the term is more commonly used with reference to City Marketing Organizations but more recently regions or even relatively small rural areas. Definitions that suggest commonality of purpose tend to be characterized by broad generalizations. Buhalis (2000) talks of DMOs based in local, regional or national government and having political and legislative power as well as the financial means to manage resources rationally and to ensure that all stakeholders can benefit in the long term. This implication that DMOs are normally part of government is not reflected in the public, private, community partnerships characterizing many DMO constitutions. He goes on to note that destination management and marketing should act as tools and facilitators to achieve a complex range of strategic objectives, which should ultimately need to satisfy the needs and wants of all stakeholders. A DMO can in reality be either a public sector agency or a private sector-driven organization. The most effective form is often a mixture; however, a critical element seems to be the importance of providing leadership in tourism management and marketing for the benefit of all involved in the defined area.

There is still some debate regarding the breadth of DMO objectives with some satisfied with marketing while others prefer to broaden this to management of the destination. In reality, the majority of DMOs, at least below the national scale, concern themselves primarily with marketing, if not an even narrower focus on promotions. However, the ideal for DMOs still remains the broader sustainable management of destinations which becomes a highly complex task. Some advocate a technological fix and look to ICT to solve their problems; hence the arrival of the destination management system or DMS.

A universally accepted definition of a DMS does not exist, and this is reflected in the number of synonyms by which such systems are commonly known: Destination Databases, Destination Marketing Systems, Visitor

Information Systems (Frew and O'Connor 1999). Larger destinations recognize ICT as an essential instrument for the development and management of destinations and DMOs today increasingly use technology in order to improve their organizational function and performance (Buhalis 2000). As a result, several destinations are trying to develop DMSs, which will enable them to coordinate their operations and promote their products. Many of these offer highly sophisticated tools at considerable cost, however, in most cases, the DMS remains a marketing communications conduit between consumers and the destination products and services. Few are even close to using the DMS to control and coordinate their many stakeholders by offering products and services to visitors to the destination as envisaged in the theory.

## Historical perspective on the organization of tourism in Scotland

Although Scotland has had a long history of developing tourism, it is only in recent, post-devolution times that the organizational structures have been shaped as a result of in-depth strategic reviews (Scottish Executive 2006). Even after this process, tensions remain between national (Scotland) and regional and local identities and organizations. The continual ebb and flow of tourism organization in Scotland, from consolidation to disintegration, amalgamation to fragmentation, perhaps reflects the tension between national and local identities, public and private sector leadership, rural and urban mind sets. In fact, Scotland's identity has been created, shaped and branded in conjunction with the development of tourism. Scottish tourism marketing has been described as capturing the essence of its brand from its history (Yeoman *et al.* 2005); history has created the sense of place (Durie *et al.* 2005) and is critical to promoting Scotland. A conscious effort has been made to create a national image, 'a collective and united way of describing Scotland to the world' (McCrone *et al.* 1995).

The problematic issue of where tourism fits into the political process has been identified by several authors (Hall 2000) and this has vexed tourism policy-makers in Scotland for decades. The need for a central organization for tourism, such as a National Tourism Organization (NTO) has now been accepted throughout the world and destinations with national aspirations such as Scotland have embraced the NTO model in spite of there being a British Tourist Authority representing the nation state (MacLellan and Smith 1998). The debate has become more refined in the past decade as the simple existence of an NTO is not sufficient to ensure that destinations can compete effectively in the international market place. The evolution of public policy and effective support organizations have moved on to consideration of the most appropriate geographical unit for a tourism organization and the key function of a DMO, whether the 'M' stands for Marketing or the more comprehensive Management. This is relevant to Scotland in that the division of the promotional and development function has long been separated (though still admittedly linked) between government agencies.

The leading tourism agency, VisitScotland, formerly the Scottish Tourist Board, has responsibility for the overall visitor promotion of Scotland and as part of this, has the task of marketing and co-ordinating Area Tourist Board (ATB) activities. Long before 2000, it was clear that for a small country, operating a network of 34 ATBs was not an efficient use of public money, especially as tourists pay little attention to local authority boundaries. An earlier move towards rationalization came in the 1994 Act, which not only required that ATBs be set up across the whole of Scotland, but it also reduced the number of ATBs to 14. Eventually, with the reorganization of VisitScotland (VS) in 2005, quasi-independent ATBs disappeared altogether and their activities and staff were transferred to VS (Hay 2007). The Tourist Boards (Scotland) Act 2006 created an integrated network in which the Area Tourist Boards became part of VisitScotland.

At government agency level, VisitScotland operates in conjunction with the economic development agencies, Scottish Enterprise and Highlands and Islands Enterprise, which have interests in product development, training and development, investment and quality assurance schemes. VisitScotland (VS) is responsible for national marketing, quality, information and, latterly, developing interests in investments and product development. This is not be confused with VisitScotland.com, which until the first half of 2009 was a joint public-private body with responsibilities for marketing and information provision, chiefly through its website, www.visitscotland.com: although it was finally taken over by VS. VisitBritain, the UK's national tourist board is responsible to the UK government but also promotes Scotland internationally in countries where VisitScotland has no or little representation.

Local government also plays a key role in product development, marketing initiatives, orientation and signage, training and events. The major cities have separate marketing bureaux such as Glasgow City Marketing Bureau, which carry out their own national and international activities, for example, the organization of events, meetings and conferences, accommodation bookings, development and implementation of the city branding campaigns. The private sector is represented primarily by the Scottish Tourist Forum (STF), but there are numerous other trade bodies such as the Association of Scottish Visitor Attractions, Tourism Innovation Group, Association of Scotland's Self-Caterers, Historic Houses Association, or the Scottish Tourist Guides Association.

Some tourism interests feel the demise of independent ATBs have left a vacuum at the local level and independent local initiatives have sprung up under different guises. In a sense, there is nothing new in this as experimental regional or local tourism entities have existed for decades. For example, Tourism Management Programmes (TMPs) were set up in a number of primarily rural areas as part of the Tourism and the Environment Task Force which was an early attempt to create sustainable tourism destinations (Go and Govers 2000). These TMPs operated, in some cases, for over a decade and the remnants of some still appear, albeit under new banners. However, the issue of small scale in terms of geographical, human and financial resources meant their continued operation always seemed fragile in a competitive tourism sector. The recent creation of area-based private industry groupings, set up broadly as destination marketing organizations, such as Destination Loch Ness or Aviemore and Cairngorms Destination Management Ltd appear to fill a similar niche to TMPs and may also suffer from similar challenges of scale. From the above list it is clear that the organizational framework is complex with overlapping spheres of concern and accountability.

Scottish Government reports on tourism and debates in the Scottish Parliament devoted to tourism highlight some of the political background to tourism organization, in particular, the balance of public and private sector and the role of DMOs (Scottish Parliament 2007, 2008). One comment noted that the weight of opinion supported the restructuring:

> From our analysis of the written and oral evidence received, the Committee did not detect a groundswell of opinion towards further legislative changes for the tourism industry in Scotland. In particularly, calls for the repeal of recent legislative changes such as the Tourist Boards (Scotland) Act 2006, which in part wound up VisitScotland's 14 area tourist boards were not paramount.
>
> (Scottish Parliament 2008: 37)

While another note refers to the growth of DMOs:

> Some witnesses feel that these legislative changes have, at the very least, been the driver or the catalyst behind the more recent phenomena of the establishment of destination management/marketing organizations and/ or city convention/marketing bureaux. In short, the feeling that the national tourism board no longer supports the marketing of localities within Scotland as much as in the past through the then area tourist boards has meant the private sector and/or local public sector bodies (e.g. local authorities) have seen the need to step into the gap.
>
> (Ibid.: 37).

The views of VS towards DMOs seems, at best, lukewarm:

> In its evidence to the Committee, VisitScotland set out its views on the recent growth in DMOs. These could broadly be summarized as qualified support. VisitScotland did agree that it would support marketing by DMOs where this complements a clear emphasis on managing product delivery to the highest standards and where this fits with VisitScotland's own national and local marketing strategies.
>
> (Ibid.: 38)

However, VS did make it clear that direct duplication of tourism promotions at local level would not be supported:

> The national tourism body indicated it did not support destination marketing organisations, whose sole purpose is the promotion of an area. In its view, these types of body are too often focused solely on selling an area without necessarily having the supporting, consistent management of the quality of experience.
>
> (Ibid.: 38)

The conclusion to the debate placed the issue of DMOs within the context of the future relationship between the public and private sector in tourism and ended with a minor rebuke to VS regarding their communications with the private sector:

> The Committee believes that there has already been sufficient public sector restructuring in tourism and that a period of stability is needed now. However, we do understand the desire to ensure that local knowledge within the industry is not lost to any national initiative and that local partnerships designed to improve the tourism product and infrastructure and to promote a destination are not unnecessarily blocked by a too centralized approach. We suggest that the recent move to localized marketing partnerships such as destination marketing organizations (DMOs) is symptomatic of a need for VisitScotland to improve its industry engagement.
>
> (Ibid.: 38)

## Aviemore and Cairngorms Management Organization

The Aviemore and the Cairngorms DMO illustrates some issues related to a rural DMO. This mountain area has been a centre for outdoor recreation for decades but in organizational terms has not been without its troubles. Some would say that conflict has characterized the region for much of the latter half of the twentieth century, primarily based on land use differences between development and conservation interests. Well-documented disputes, from Lurcher's Gully in the early 1980s to the Funicular Railway in the 1990s, typify tourism-related disagreements in the Cairngorm Mountain area. Further down the glen, the rise and fall, and rise again, of the Aviemore resort has been a focal point for political and private sector conflict often related to the nature and volume of tourism development desired. A number of organizational mechanisms have been tested in the area (including TMPs), involving numerous public, private and voluntary organizations. The lack of an overarching authority seemed to exacerbate the problems with the Cairngorms Massif split between three local authorities. The establishment of the Cairngorms National Park (CNPA) in 2003 brought much-needed cohesion to the organization and management of the area with innovations such as the award of the European Charter for Sustainable Tourism demonstrating progress. However, the performance of the tourism sector, particularly in Aviemore, still seemed to lag behind international comparators, in spite of redevelopment and re-branding as the Macdonald Aviemore Highland Resort. So the advent of DMOs gave a group of local businesses the opportunity to reposition the area as one of Scotland's leading year-round short-break destinations, which ultimately led to the formation of ABSC Marketing Ltd in 2004, involving private businesses and public agencies including the Local Enterprise Company, the Highland Council and CNPA.

ABSC Marketing Ltd commissioned a benchmark report which investigated the success of other mountain destinations which was published in 2005 as *Cairngorm Vision: Shaping a World Class Mountain Tourist Destination in the Highlands of Scotland* (Stevens and Associates 2005). The report benchmarked Aviemore and the Cairngorms against 15 other mountain resorts and found that most Mountain Destinations that outperformed Aviemore and the Cairngorms had DMOs which were not only marketing the destination, but were also driving product development in line with the destination vision and taking full responsibility for the visitor experience within the Destination (ibid.). The report also identified the need for a clear understanding of the physical extent of their destination and that this should be shaped by three factors: (1) it should be coherent and understandable for visitors; (2) it should be cohesive and make sense from a local perspective; and (3) it should be competent in delivering an integrated visitor experience.

ABSC Marketing Ltd became a DMO in September 2006 with three-year sponsorship from the Carnegie UK Trust, and a clear vision and strategy. The work of the DMO had a clear set of activities to undertake on behalf of the destination, including: market research; creating a vision and strategy for the destination; creating a commercial income stream – self-sustaining within a three-year period; and working with participating businesses, communities and public sector stakeholders to develop the destination and vision.

Experience from the benchmarked destinations indicated that success appears to be built on applying a simple business approach to running a destination. For example, destinations should: have a clear mission statement with an agreed tourism vision; leadership and coordination by a strong destination management organization; a destination-wide commitment to quality and a clear customer focus; and innovation in product development, events and marketing, including an ability to work differently, take risks and form fresh partnerships/alliances. None of this is particularly radical for a marketing organization although ideas would need modification for a multi-partner destination. The report describes core activities:

The role of the DMO is to provide leadership, coordinate activities, service the needs of visitors, represent the interests of the community and market the destination. While the structure of these organizations varies according to local conditions, DMOs exist in each of the 15 case studies referred to earlier.

(Ibid.: 6)

The Aviemore and Cairngorm DMO started well but the scope of their objectives might be viewed as over-ambitious, in particular in relation to funding. Initial optimism in the first years has been tinged with disappointment as some core funding organizations have withdrawn and progress has not been as swift as expected. Core, underlying challenges for the destination remain, not least of which is the unreliable nature of snow cover, the core resource for a winter sports mountain resort. All 15 other benchmarked destinations had reliable snow cover to sustain several months of snow sports business. In spite of recent returns of colder winters, the reliability of snow places any reliant business on an unsustainable footing, witnessed by financial difficulties for Cairngorm Mountain Ltd in 2008. The lack of funds to support the DMO means it is a small operation that spends much of its efforts attempting to secure income streams and must restrict its activities to basic tourism promotions. Goodwill remains throughout local public agencies and most private businesses but this scale of operation must call into question the hyped expectations of this level of DMO. Contrast this with the urban DMOs in British cities that have a critical mass of tax revenues to support sophisticated destination marketing and establishment of an expensive DMS to assist in this. One must question the efficacy of encouraging small independent DMOs in rural areas that lie outside the established national tourism strategy, that may have a strong product and brand identity but lack the critical mass of human or financial resources to draw on. They may be enthusiastic and innovative but time will tell whether they are sustainable.

## Conclusion

In summary, post-devolution government in Scotland saw the need for changes in the political management of tourism and undertook a number of strategic reviews of tourism (Scottish Executive 2000; 2002; 2006). As part of these major reviews they took the decision to restructure not only the STB but also the ATB structure and merge all ATBs (city and country tourism bureaus) into one organization. In April 2005, led by VisitScotland, the core tourism structure became a single, country-wide comprehensive organization, managing all 120 Tourist Information Centres in Scotland, with 14 regional offices and its own offices in London, Edinburgh and Inverness. It is now probably the world's first fully integrated tourist board, providing a single contact point for all tourists and tourism businesses (Hay 2007).

However, the restructuring of tourism support structures within Scotland has been less than harmonious, in particular related to the reorganization of the ATB network with greater control from VisitScotland at the centre. There will always be tensions between national, regional and local organizations and there is evidence to suggest that Scotland has some way to go in the evolution of tourism support structures. The welcome growth in prominence of the private sector has been more than matched by the strengthening powers and confidence of the leading cities in Scotland, notably Edinburgh and Glasgow. Their autonomy in promoting their cities as places not only to visit but also to work, live, study and invest cannot be over-ruled by VisitScotland. Their brands and identity as destinations are arguably more cohesive and as strong as, if not stronger than, Scotland as a whole. New hybrid organizations have emerged in 2009 to lead the cities, for example, Destination Edinburgh Marketing Alliance, that explore new working mechanisms and challenge 'top-down' national tourism strategies. The concern over public sources of funds for tourism development is another long-standing issue that has yet to be resolved. Heated debates over options for national and local tourism taxes continue without a clear way forward emerging.

There have also been a number of independent Destination Management Organizations (DMO) formed, acting independently of VisitScotland and the reorganized tourism network. Ironically these have been encouraged and supported by VisitScotland's public sector partners, the economic development agencies, Scottish Enterprise and Highlands and Islands Enterprise, through its promotion of a DMO toolkit. SE have identified six key destinations suitable for DMO treatment, Edinburgh, Glasgow, St Andrews, Perthshire, Deeside, LL&T National Park and HIE have two main DMOs, Aviemore & Cairngorm and Loch Ness. This is further evidence of the anomaly of separating tourism development from tourism promotion roles and illustrates the type of mixed message emanating from government agencies. The small scale of some of these emergent rural DMOs calls into question their viability, however, they are popular in their local areas and do fill a vacuum in post-tourism reorganization and give a channel to independent local thinking and autonomy, always prominent in Scottish culture. Tourism organizational structures continue to evolve and, although the current situation may not be neat and tidy, it perhaps reflects the increased voice of private sector companies and local views, which is surely not a bad thing and something to be encouraged as a key goal of devolution.

## Lessons to be learned

The strategic reviews of tourism in Scotland have on the whole been a positive step forward but there is still a need for rationalization of public sector functions in tourism and a need for clarification of structures and hierarchies between national, regional and local level tourism organization. The current growth of local DMOs may irritate VisitScotland but they do reflect local desires for individual representation in tourism promotions and, in a mature country, should be viewed as a further level of devolved decision-making. Any plan requires a level of flexibility and local level autonomy.

There also remains concern, particularly within the private sector, about remaining duplication of effort, wasted resources, the plethora of initiatives and the increasing 'mission creep' whereby certain bodies are now acting in a fashion beyond that originally intended. For example, the separation of related functions such as inward investment, quality/product improvement and marketing is not viewed as a good example of joined-up thinking or integrated operations (Herbert 2009). There have already been several changes in public sector structures and a genuine effort to pass leadership to the private sector. This must continue so that the industry itself takes a lead role in shaping the vision for tourism and overseeing its implementation.

However, there have always been overlapping initiatives operated by different public bodies in Scotland and this is likely to continue as long as the quango system of arm's-length governance remains. The point here is that duplication and confusion have arguably been diminishing since devolution.

The initial enthusiasm for DMOs should be tempered with a realization that DMOs are not a panacea and that the scale and nature of their operation vary enormously. It is normal for different policy and planning methods to apply at different scales, from national to regional to local. A national DMO has power and resources to hand outwith the imagination of a rural region, as do urban centres such as Edinburgh and Glasgow compared to small rural DMOs like Aviemore or Deeside. It is naïve and misleading to expect the same models to apply. Therefore, it would be useful to clarify this distinction and devise appropriate visions, resourcing and operating mechanisms specific to rural DMOs.

## References

Agarwal, S. (2002) 'Restructuring seaside tourism: the resort life cycle', *Annals of Tourism Research* 29(1): 25–55.

Baloglu, S. and McClearly, K. W. (1999) 'A model of destination image formation', *Annals of Tourism Research* 26(4): 868–97.

Baum, T. (2005) 'Revisiting the TALC: is there an off-ramp?' in R. Butler *The Tourism Area Life Cycle*, vol. 2 *Conceptual and Theoretical Issues*. London: Routledge, pp. 219–30.

Blain, C., Levy, S. E. and Ritchie, J. R. B. (2005) 'Destination branding: insights and practices from destination management organizations', *Journal of Travel Research* 43(4): 328–38.

Brey, E. T., Morrison, A. M. and Mills, J. E. (2007) 'An examination of destination resort research', *Current Issues in Tourism* 10(5): 415–42.

Buhalis, D. (2000) 'Marketing the competitive destination of the future', *Tourism Management* 21(1): 97–116.

Butler, R. W. (1980) 'The concept of a tourist area cycle of evolution: implications for management of resources', *Canadian Geographer* 24: 5–12.

—— (2005) 'The future and the TALC', in R. Butler, *The Tourism Area Life Cycle*, vol. 2 *Conceptual and Theoretical Issues*. London: Routledge, pp. 281–90.

Caldwell, Niall and Freire, Joao R.(2004) 'The differences between branding a country, a region and a city: applying the Brand Box Model', *Journal of Brand Management* 12(1): 50.

Choy, D. (1992) 'Life cycle models for Pacific Island destinations', *Journal of Travel Research* 30(3): 6–31.

Communications Group plc (2005) *The Power of Destinations*. London: Buckingham Gate.

Dewer, J. (2007) *Tourism in Scotland : Subject Profile*, SPICe Briefing 07/34. Edinburgh: The Scottish Parliament.

Durie, A. J., Yeoman, I. S. and McMahon-Beatie, U. (2005) 'How the history of Scotland creates a sense of place', *Place Branding* 2(1): 43–52.

Enright, M. J. and Newton, J (2004) 'Tourism destination competitiveness: a quantitative approach', *Tourism Management* 25: 777–88.

Frew, A. and O'Connor, P. (1999) 'Destination marketing system strategies in Scotland and Ireland: an approach to assessment', *Information Technology and Tourism* 2(1): 3–13.

Gale, T. and Botterill, D. (2005) 'A realist agenda for tourist studies, or why destination areas really rise and fall in popularity', *Tourist Studies* 5(2) 151–74.

Gallarza, M. G., Gil, I. and Calderón, H. (2002) 'Destination image: towards a conceptual framework', *Annals of Tourism Research* 29(1): 56–78.

Go, F. and Govers, R. (2000) 'Integrated quality management for tourist destinations: a European perspective on achieving competitiveness', *Tourism Management* 21: 79–88.

Gunn, C. A. (1994) *Tourism Planning*, 3rd edn. London: Taylor and Francis.

Hall, C. M. (2000) *Tourism Planning: Politics, Processes and Relationships*. Englewood Cliffs, NJ: Prentice Hall.

Hay, B. (2007) 'Lessons for the future: the history and development of the Scottish Tourist Board', in V.T.C. Middleton *British Tourism: The Remarkable Story of Growth*. London: Butterworth-Heinemann.

Herbert, I. (2009) *Tourism Framework for Change: Scottish Tourism: Making a Step Change*. Review and Recommendations from the Scottish Tourism Forum; Edinburgh: Scottish Tourism Forum.

Ioannides, D. (1992) 'Tourism development agents: the Cypriot resort cycle', *Annals of Tourism Research* 19(4): 711–31.

Johnson, G. and Scholes, K. (2002) *Exploring Corporate Strategy: Text and Cases*. London: Prentice Hall.

Lagiewski, R. M. (2006) 'The application of the TALC model: a literature survey', in R.W. Butler (ed.) *The Tourism Area Life Cycle*, vol. 1, *Applications and Modifications*. Clevedon: Channel View, pp. 27–50.

McCrone, D., Morris, A. and Kelly, R. (1995) *Scotland the Brand: The Making of Scottish Heritage*. Edinburgh: Edinburgh University Press.

MacLellan, R. and Smith, R. (1998) *Tourism in Scotland*. London: International Thomson Business Press.

Mottiar, Z. and Tucker, H. (2007) 'Webs of power: multiple ownership in tourism destinations', *Current Issues in Tourism* 10(4): 279–95.

Prideaux, B. (2000) 'The resort development spectrum; a new approach to modelling resort development', *Tourism Management* 21: 225–40.

Ritchie, J. R. B. and Crouch, G. I. (2003) *The Competitive Destination: A Sustainable Tourism Perspective*. Wallingford: CABI.

Sainaghi, R. (2006) 'From contents to processes: versus a dynamic destination management model (DDMM)', *Tourism Management* 27(5): 1053–63.

Scottish Executive (2000) *A New Strategy for Scottish Tourism*. Edinburgh: The Stationery Office.

—— (2002) *Tourism Framework for Action 2002: 2005*. Edinburgh: The Stationery Office.

—— (2006) *Scottish Tourism: the Next Decade – A Tourism Framework for Change*. Edinburgh: The Stationery Office.

Scottish Parliament (2007) *Official Report on the First Parliamentary Debate on Tourism under the New SNP Administration, 29th November 2007*. Edinburgh: Scottish Parliamentary Corporate Body Publications.

—— (2008) *Economy, Energy and Tourism Committee 6th Report, 2008 (session3) Growing Pains – Can We Achieve 50% Growth in Tourist Revenue by 2015?* Edinburgh: Scottish Parliamentary Corporate Body Publications.

Stevens and Associates (2005) 'Benchmarking report on mountain destinations for Aviemore, Badenoch, Strathspey and Cairngorm', cited in *Cairngorm Vision: Shaping a World Class Mountain Tourist Destination in the Highlands of Scotland'*, Executive Summary for Inverness, Nairn, Badenoch and Strathspey Enterprise, July, 2005.

Urry, J. (2002) *The Tourist Gaze*, 2nd edn. London: Sage.

World Tourism Organization (2004) *WTO Survey of Destination Management Organisations Report 2004*. Madrid: WTO.

Yeoman, I. S., Durie, A. J., McMahon-Beatie, U. and Palmer, A. (2005) 'Capturing the essence of a brand from its history: The case of Scottish tourism marketing', *Brand Management* 13(2): 134–47.

**Pilgrimage and tourism in Bosnia-Herzegovina and Palestine**
Reporting from two of the
European Commission's TEMPUS
projects

*Tom Selwyn*

## Introduction

This chapter considers the cases of two substantial education and development projects, one in Bosnia-Herzegovina (BiH) and one in Palestine, concerned with the role of pilgrimage, tourism, and the cultural industries (PCTI) in the economic, social, and political development of the rural and urban areas of the two countries. Both projects were part of the European Commission's (EC) TEMPUS Programme. I directed the projects while Jonathan Karkut managed them, assisted in the Palestinian case by Les Roberts.

Consideration of the two projects opens up particularly illuminating insights into developments in a part of rural Europe just beyond the borders of the EU. The countryside of both BiH and Palestine forms a central part of the tourism offer of both countries. Moreover in both cases it is important to understand that the towns and cities of BiH and Palestine (Sarajevo, Banja-Luka, Mostar, for example in the former case; Jerusalem, Bethlehem, Nablus, and Hebron, for example, in the latter case) are part of a mosaic of urban and rural landscapes that are inextricably bound together and interdependent for residents and tourists alike.

The TEMPUS Programme as a whole involves work in the higher educational, civil society, and government sectors of countries within and outside the European Union (EU). The term used by EC officials to describe the organizational philosophy underpinning programmes such as TEMPUS is 'decentralized co-operation'. This refers to forms of work that are carried out below the level of the state by actors and institutions that are given a certain amount of operational flexibility in the management of their own projects. Consortia made up of representatives of member state and partner country universities and the other civil society institutions oversee all TEMPUS projects. One aim of what follows is critically to assess the role of such university-led projects in relation both to the particular cases discussed here and also more generally (cf. also Selwyn and Karkut 2007).

The chapter is divided into three parts. The first section describes the general aims, objectives, and methodologies of the TEMPUS Programme as articulated by the EC; the particular aims of the projects under review here; and the politico-geographic contexts within which they operated. At the core of the two projects described was the delivery of Master's degree courses in PCTI to a carefully selected cohort of mid-career professionals (25 in the BiH case, 10 in the Palestinian case) by local and European university staff. Part of the effort of the TEMPUS Programme as a whole is to encourage such university work to be embedded not only within universities but also in civil institutions and appropriate local, national, and international government departments and agencies, including the EC itself. The emphasis is upon building the capacities of institutions in partner countries to enable them more potently to engage in public/private policy/planning formulation and initiatives in the fields in question so that these may develop and expand to the benefit of all.

The second part of the chapter begins by describing the course curricula of the two projects and then describes the MA dissertations written by the project participants which, taken together, constitute the state of the art of the sectors in both countries, providing the strategic bases for generating increased activity in the field. Risking repetition, let us emphasize that tourism itself is routinely spoken of as the largest industry in the world. As far as BiH and Palestine are concerned, there is no doubt that the benefits to be gained from a strengthened PTCI sector in terms of employment, socio-economic well-being, and regional development would be very substantial indeed.

With the above comments in mind, the third and final part of the chapter offers a critical assessment of the two projects and the TEMPUS Programme as a whole.

## The TEMPUS Programme: general and particular aims

### General aims and objectives

The TEMPUS Programme is an attempt to move universities to the front line of development processes in transitional and border lands to the European Union. At its inception in the early 1990s, TEMPUS (the Trans-European Mobility Programme for University Studies) was directed towards Eastern Europe and those states that were at the time on the way to becoming members of the EU. For a brief period in the early 2000s, the programme was limited in scope to the Balkan countries before opening up again to encompass the North African states of the southern Mediterranean, the Occupied Palestinian Territories and Israel.

As noted above, TEMPUS projects are aimed primarily at the level below and/or beyond the state, namely at civil society institutions from, *inter alia*, non-governmental organizations (NGOs) to chambers of commerce to municipalities to private companies to regional organizations and to the universities that take leading roles in all cases. Projects are convened and directed by a staff member of the university leading the project and managed by a consortium of representatives from the project's partner institutions.

The Programme as a whole involves projects from across the broad spectrum of subjects taught in university departments including those within faculties of science, humanities, and social science. Calls to prospective consortia to apply for funding are routinely issued by the EC following the identification by partner countries of priority areas. In the present cases the educational authorities in both BiH and Palestine indicated in the late 1990s/early 2000s that the PCTI sector was a national priority.

There are two types of project within the TEMPUS Programme. The first consists of curriculum development (CD) in a given field. The aim of CD projects is to assist universities in partner countries to achieve parity in terms of curricula content, coverage, and organization with those of sister universities in EU universities. The second consists of TEMPUS Institution Building (TIB) projects. As already noted above, the declared aim of TIB projects is to embed university work within processes of institutional development. In the particular cases discussed here, although the BiH project was formally a TIB one (the first of its kind in south-east Europe) and the Palestinian project a CD one, there was a considerable measure of institution building involved in both projects.

### The projects in BiH and Palestine

The responsibility for the management of TEMPUS projects lies with consortia composed of members representing the projects' institutional partners. In the BiH case, the project consortium consisted of representatives from the Universities of Sarajevo and Banja-Luka in BiH, the University of Bologna in Italy, the Development Planning Unit of University College London, and London Metropolitan University, together with the Organization of Security and Co-operation in Europe (OSCE), the BiH Chamber of Commerce, two private tour operators (one from BiH and one from the UK), and a local NGO in Sarajevo concerned with urban issues. The Palestinian consortium consisted of representatives from the Universities of Bethlehem (Palestine), Joensuu (Finland), and London Metropolitan University as well as from Bethlehem's Centre for Cultural Heritage Preservation (CCHP). Both projects developed good relationships with the governments of the two countries. The Minister of Tourism was a member of the Palestinian project's consortium. In the BiH case there were Ministries of Tourism from the two halves of the country, the predominantly Serb *Republika Srpska* (*the RS*) and the predominantly Bosniak/Muslim and Croat Catholic *Federation of Bosnia-Herzegovina* (*the Federation*). The government of each entity possesses considerable power, leaving the whole country of BiH with a few select portfolios, including Foreign Affairs.

Both projects developed extensive networks of civil society organizations and institutions as well as ministries and departments within and beyond the partner countries. Both projects were also fortunate in having teachers and experts from various parts of the world including Malta, France, the Netherlands, and Australia who contributed in various ways to their work. All of this demonstrates one important advantage of de-centralized co-operation over state-run development, namely the heightened capacity of project teams to co-operate with others on a regional basis (clearly necessary in any tourism or pilgrimage context especially in regions such as the Balkans or the Middle East).

The aims of both projects were to develop cadres of experts capable of carrying forward institution building and development in the PTCI sector, to compose strategic plans for the field, paying particular attention to institutional structures and processes capable of dealing with the new tourism at the level of state and region, to influence policy-makers from municipalities to government departments and all points in between, and to disseminate the products of the work to as wide an audience as possible.

### Contexts: fragmented landscapes in BiH and Palestine

Our Bosnian TEMPUS project began in 2001, six years after the initialling of the Dayton Peace Agreement that brought the three-and-a-half-year-long Bosnian war to an end. This is not the place to analyse the agreement in any detail: there is a wealth of expert and scholarly commentary on that (Chandler 1999; Glenny 1999; Ignatieff 1993, for example) but we might risk three generalizations. The first is that Dayton contained much that seems rhetorically and intellectually admirable and reflective of, to use Ignatieff's expression, the 'western conscience' at its best. The Agreement deals with the complex interrelations between military and regional stabilization, inter-entity boundaries, elections, constitutional affairs, human rights and refugee return, institution building, and (in Annex 8) the setting up of a Commission to preserve national monuments. As Chandler observes (1999: 43), the effort of the Dayton peace-makers was 'to democratise Bosnia and to reconstruct the society'. The second is simply to note and emphasize the fact that 'national heritage' and its conservation were specifically placed within the rest of the political and military architecture on which the agreement was based.

But the third (and central) point is that Dayton set up political arrangements, namely the construction of two semi-autonomous 'entity' administrations (the RS and the Federation) and by doing so effectively rewarded those who had fought the war on the grounds of the primacy of ethnic rather than national identification. Thus, despite the attempts to lay down the means to achieve a national democratic framework, the political and constitutional facts on the ground established by Dayton left a situation in which there was (and remains) a Muslim/Croat entity (with a Croat population looking towards Croatia), on the one hand, and a Serb entity on the other, each with separate parliaments and ethnically determined political parties to match. Dayton did little to challenge the baleful soubriquet that Bosnia consists of a country of two entities and three peoples. Bosnia after Dayton has a fragmented look about it.

The fragmented features of contemporary Bosnia have a familiar ring when we come to the landscapes of Palestine sitting as this occupied territory does within a region consisting of an established state (Israel), a state (Palestine) that does not yet exist except in the rhetoric of those international spokespersons who speak in terms of a 'road map', 'two state solutions', and other phrases of this kind. It is not the intention of the present chapter to discuss the political structures and processes in the region – except insofar as they bear directly upon the PTCI sector. However, we may observe one obvious feature of the political landscape between the River Jordan and the Mediterranean that does indeed bear directly on the project discussed here, namely that the region is framed by two competing discourses. The first is built on the rhetorical (it is always more difficult to hold this view in relation to any known actual evidence on the ground) primacy of an ethnocratic view of the world. The line of argument here seeks to persuade us that boundaries between state and ethnic group coincide and that it is some way natural, necessary, and/or desirable for them so to do. The second stems from the search to find ways of advancing co-operative, democratic, and cosmopolitan theories and practices within and beyond the region. Whatever the future holds, however, it remains clear that the PTCI sector in Palestine – as in Israel, Bosnia-Herzegovina and all other states in the world, needs to work across frontiers – as in practice it always has done. Walls, barriers, checkpoints, road blocks, and all the other paraphernalia of occupation and fetishization of ethno state boundaries are all enemies of pilgrimage and tourism.

## The two projects

### The MA courses in BiH and Palestine

While each of the MA degree courses in BiH and Palestine were anchored to the particular histories and circumstances of the respective countries, there were common foundations to both courses. In both cases, therefore, we based the teaching modules (9 in the BiH case, 6 in the Palestinian case – each of 8/9 days length and taught in university departments in the countries of the participating states, namely BiH itself, Italy, and the UK in the BiH case, Palestine, Finland, and the UK in the Palestinian case) upon six principal topics.

The first topic consisted of the histories, systems, and structures of the PTCI sector in the relevant country. The second reviewed work on pilgrimage, tourism, and the cultural industries produced by social scientists insofar as these had a bearing on the circumstances of the two countries. The aim here was to trace the relations and connections between PTCI, society, and development. The third topic was the nature of the capital upon which tourism, pilgrimage, and the cultural industries are based. Clearly, the two main capital assets of the sector are the natural and cultural resources of the country. As far as the natural environment is concerned, the land and landscapes, together with the flora and fauna they contain, are leading priorities in any tourism policy. As far as cultural assets are concerned, these need to encompass the widest imaginable scope: from buildings (religious and secular) to art forms and productions to intangible culture of all kinds to food (and the agricultural bases for food production), together with all the administrative and organizational structures supporting these and other aspects of the cultural offer, including the role of museums. The fourth topic covered the whole range of subjects concerned with tourist motivations, marketing, and associated questions of imagery and the messages these imply. The fifth considered the sectors in their *regional* contexts. The idea (articulated simply by the then future foreign minister of BiH in terms of the necessity for each independent state of the former Yugoslavia to have regional markets) of a tourism and/or pilgrimage industry exclusive to a single state is far-fetched generally, let alone in regions such as the Balkans and/or Holy Land. The final topic was policy and planning in the sector.

Apart from the making of appropriate institutional networks, and the composition of strategic plans, we placed considerable emphasis on the presentation and dissemination of the work which we presented at, *inter alia*, the British House of Lords, Lambeth Palace, relevant universities and embassies, the European Parliament, and at the first international conference on pilgrimage, tourism, and the cultural industries at the University of Bethlehem.

So much, then, for the organization and teaching of the topics in the two MA courses. We may now come to the most important products of the two projects: the dissertations written by the participants.

### Review of dissertations by Bosnian and Palestinian project participants

The economic development of pilgrimage, tourism, and the cultural industries takes place within a discursive space framed by cultural histories, natural and cultural capital, identity, and policy. This is the reason for structuring the account here in these terms. Each dissertation was based on primary ethnographic research. Taken together, the collection constitutes the foundations of the PTCI strategy in both countries.

There is one further preliminary central point to be made. This links back to the general aims and objectives of the EC's TEMPUS Programme as a whole that we discussed earlier. At risk of repetition, therefore, the purpose of TEMPUS both generally and specifically is to contribute to the economic and social development and enhanced well-being of the partner countries, and to encourage ways in which they can reach the 'level playing field' that membership of the EU promises. In addition to presenting the theses in the four categories indicated above, we will add a fifth category of PTCI and development.

*Histories*

One of the Palestinian theses examined the work of a medium-sized local tour operator, the Alternative Tourism Group (ATG) – particularly in relation to its organization of tours for foreign university students, diplomats, and backpackers – and its production and use of the best overall historical tourist guidebook we have of the country, namely *Palestine and the Palestinians* (Giroud *et al.* 2005). Starting with a view of Palestine as the source of the three Abrahamic religions, the book covers the tragedies of the Palestinian *naqba*, the uprooting of villages and the creation of refugees in 1948, the place of Palestine in the various cultural regions it straddles, including the Arab and Muslim worlds, Europe and the Christian worlds, as well as the Jewish, Muslim, and Christian populations in Israel. As the ATG's guidebook tells us, in co-operation with appropriate Israeli partners, the group organizes tours in Palestine and Israel along with 'encounters with Palestinians and Israelis' and 'interfaith meetings with Muslim, Christian, and Jewish personalities'. The first time I personally visited one of the illegal Jewish settlements on the West Bank I did so with the ATG who at that time had a good working relationship with a rabbi in a settlement near Bethlehem.

A second largely historical thesis was by a graduate from Banja-Luka, the main city of the *Republika Srpska*, the Serbian 'entity' in BiH. Here the aim was to compose a national curriculum to train Bosnian tour guides and to start up a tour guiding school in two locations, Sarajevo in the Federation and Banja-Luka in the RS. The school was to be founded on the history of religious and cultural pluralism within which contemporary BiH was a part. Less than a decade after a bloody civil war in which eternal primacies of ethnic histories, identities, and boundaries were being trumpeted from all corners of the country, the thesis contained a quiet but determined proposal to set up a practical cultural tourist-related institution not only to address head on the ethnocratic ideologies that had underwritten the war but also to engage staff and students in co-ordinated co-operation across entity boundaries, thus making a seminal contribution to national and regional peace processes. Additionally, such a proposal as this *precisely* fulfilled the exhortations of the TEMPUS Programme to find ways of fitting private and public sector initiatives together and so enhance socio-economic development.

*Cultural and natural capital*

One Bosnian dissertation examined how the formerly thriving Muslim pilgrimage centre of Ajvatovica might be revived as a complement to the success of the Catholic pilgrimage site of Medjugorje. The enhancement of this site would generate additional tourists to Bosnia in the shape of Islamic travellers from such countries and regions as Iran, Indonesia and Malaysia, who would then make their way to Sarajevo and other Bosnian towns and cities, thus substantially increasing tourist numbers to the country's towns and cities. To advance the idea and make it into a practical concern would involve co-operation of the local municipality, the national authorities, as well as private investors from, for example, Malaysia. Indeed groups of potential investors from that country and other Islamic countries from the Far East did routinely visit BiH around the time that this dissertation was written, but unfortunately met with bureaucratic blockages that made proposals such as this fall by the wayside.

A second Bosnian thesis looked at the future potential of the former National and University Library in Sarajevo as a potential centre for local and tourist activity. Before the war this was one of the great libraries of the world – housing a unique collection of books and manuscripts in many languages including Arabic and Hebrew and being a potent symbol of Bosnia's Bosniak, Croatian, Serbian, Jewish, Latin, Western European, Persian, Turkish, and Austrian cosmopolitan identity. The description by the Bosnian author Jasna Samic was quoted of how in the Ottoman period some Bosniak (a Slav language) literature was written in Turkish, Arabic and Persian, using many Bosniak words and how the particular (poetic) genre of *Alhamijado* literature was written in Bosniak, by Bosnian Muslims using Arabic script and by Bosnian Jews using Hebrew script. The *Vijecnica* building, in which the Library was housed, was also the first building to be bombed in the siege of Sarajevo. The incendiary bombs fired from the hills surrounding the capital destroyed the majority of priceless manuscripts, books, and archives. Thus was destroyed one of the greatest testaments not only to the cosmopolitan heritage of BiH and the region, but also to Europe and the Middle East, and to the common histories and literatures of Christianity, Islam and Judaism. The thesis argued that the restoration of the library would enable it to become, once again, a cultural focus in Sarajevo, thus adding a very significant dimension to the tourism offer of BiH.

Another Palestinian dissertation shifted the focus to rural tourism, and examined the modalities of attracting and managing independent visitors to Batir, a village a few kilometres from Bethlehem. Apart from being a very beautiful village, with natural springs and pools, and agricultural terraces originating from (at least) Roman times, and good vantage points for bird watching, Batir has a lively and effective local council and civil society. The convincing argument was made that the village could support and derive benefit from a particular type of tourist (and the market is undoubtedly there to be tapped) interested in Palestinian culture and nature. It could also be the ideal location for a state-of-the-art museum concerned with Palestinian rural culture. The thesis argued strongly for a new rural tourism to be initiated in the country in which 'hiking, biking, cultural trails, horse/donkey riding, the visiting of archaeological sites, the eating of local food' could be encouraged. The author is, however, careful to observe that such types of tourism have the potential to harm rural communities unless carefully organized and planned. As she writes, 'There is a need for public and private partnerships to develop and manage tourism in rural areas. The local community has to feel it has "ownership" of the industry in order to accept and support tourism activities on its land.'

Finally, a Bosnian thesis took up the theme of rural tourism and examined the role in the country's tourism of natural parks. The argument was advanced that this subject is central to Bosnian tourism for three main reasons. The first is that the Bosnian countryside could and should be one of the jewels in the crown of the tourism, with its uniquely beautiful mountains and rivers. But the second is that for the countryside (outside the well-known ski and other resorts) to be used for tourism there needs to be careful consideration given to practical logistic matters such as the provision of appropriate transport facilities, accommodation, and guides. Third, despite its unique value as a tourist resource – principally for backpackers, walkers and hikers, bird watchers, those interested in historic bridges over rivers, and so on – it is also uniquely vulnerable to property speculation (see below). To ensure the containment of such property speculation within the boundaries of carefully thought through tourism policy (which would, for example, ensure that prime real estate was not simply 'cherry picked' by investors looking for easy profits), the thesis argued that the overall management of the countryside needed to be done within a framework of careful protective planning.

## The imagining and imaging of identity

Several theses addressed aspects of tourism relating to questions of imagining and imaging identity. One Palestinian thesis traced the historical presentation in the West of images of Palestine since the early nineteenth century to the present. The sweep of the study took us from orientalist paintings, the subjects of a recent exhibition in London's Tate Gallery, to contemporary images in Western media that routinely link Palestinian images with conflict. The thesis examined the relationships between images of Palestine/Palestinians, views about the country held by the outside world, the ways that images can change perceptions, and how all these considerations are central to tourism strategy. The central thrust of the thesis was to address the issue of how images of Palestine and Palestinians could be changed for the benefit not only of the tourism industry but also of the country more generally.

A second dissertation in this group by a Bosnian graduate examined the possible roles of traditional Islamic imagery in the design of contemporary tourism material. The author argued for design to be adopted as a tourism tool in order to improve the quality of the tourism offer in the country through the production of artefacts (some of which could find their way into souvenirs) designed and made in the context of university-led venture in co-operation with Sarajevo High School of Applied Arts. The author also drew attention to the links made during the course of one of the TEMPUS MA modules to the Italian town of Faenza, home of some of the finest ceramic producers in Europe, arguing convincingly that what we see in this town is an abundance of creative relationships between artists, craftsmen, museums, traders, schools (closely involved with the famous ceramics museum) and tourists. The writer argued that if the BiH cultural industries sector could follow the lead of Faenza, then there would be every opportunity for the country to experience a benign coalition between economic development and cultural creativity.

*Policy*

A Palestinian thesis in this group spoke of the need for the establishment of a Palestinian Tourism Board. The argument here was that this institution would have the capacity to bring coherence to Palestinian tourism strategy by introducing the dynamism of the private sector into planning without losing the containing organizational structures of the public sector in the shape of the Ministry of Tourism. A Bosnian dissertation mirrored very similar concerns and was concerned with administrative arrangements needed to organize the cultural industries sector at the level of state rather than the existing fractured landscape of 'two "entities" and "three peoples"', two and a half governments in the same country. A Palestinian thesis took up these and other issues by constructing a publicly available website (www.visitpalestine.ps) covering both necessary practical information needed by the traveller as well as comprehensive lists and reviews of Palestinian cultural life and cultural events, enabling in the process the independent traveller to navigate his/her way around a field that tends to be dominated by large tour operators.

Another Palestinian thesis examined the possibilities and modalities for the town of Beit Jala, close neighbour to Bethlehem, to take a leading role in introducing tourism to the municipality. Here the role of the Palestinian diaspora, especially in Chile and Latin America, was examined in the light of its importance to the future economy and society of the town. The writer, a practising architect, and advisor to the Municipality of Beit Jala, drew our attention to the importance to the residents of the municipal park, the music academy, the new library, and other such developments, stressing the links between domestic and foreign leisure and tourism.

## Tourism and development

All the dissertations were concerned in one way or another with the role of the PTCI sector in the economic development of the two countries involved in the TEMPUS programme. We may use four theses that have not yet been discussed to make particular points and to make some summary points.

Two Bosnian theses considered the relation between the PTCI sector and financial capital. One looked at ideas for micro-credit arrangements in BiH enabling small and medium-sized enterprises to find the financial capital to start businesses, while another examined the close but very complex relationships between the Bosnian tourism industry and donor agencies, some of which are associated with the large number of foreign governments involved in Bosnian economic regeneration. As in Palestine, the pivotal role of international agencies such as the UNDP, UNESCO, and the EC were examined.

A third (Palestinian) thesis in the group brought us back to our home territory of Bethlehem and overlaps with a recently published book chapter by two Palestinian TEMPUS graduates (Sansour and Zoughbi 2010). The thesis addressed the complex relationships between the elements of the private and public sectors and effectively demonstrated that urban planning for cultural tourism, especially in a city such as Bethlehem, poised as it is between traditional and post-modern forms of production and consumption, cannot rely exclusively or even primarily on private sector developers.

## Summary

The value of the theses, considered collectively, is that they combined considerations of the governance of tourism and heritage, with a realistic and detailed appreciation of what constitutes cultural and environmental capital. They also mined the past for inspiration about the possibilities for future initiatives in the field and followed this up into the field of education. While all of them explicitly and implicitly spoke about the uses of their work for strategies of economic development, all approached this subject with an awareness of the social and cultural context under which such development should proceed. Bosnian and Palestinian villages and small towns, and the rural areas around them need a kind of governance that is sensitively shaped to their particular economic and social needs.

## Lessons learned from the two TEMPUS projects

Moving towards some conclusions we may, using the particular eyeglass of our two TEMPUS projects, look out across the contemporary landscapes of

BiH and Palestine and reflect on what they look like now. Here, the tone is more negative than positive, although there are traces of the latter if we look hard enough.

Starting with Bosnia, the most recent report by the International Crisis Group (ICG) (2009) reports a 40 per cent unemployment that is inevitably accompanied by heightened nationalist/ethnic rhetoric. The former High Representative, Lord Paddy Ashdown, has recently written gloomily about the country sliding backwards into conditions comparable to those of pre-war days. As far as our own sector is concerned, there is still no overall national tourism legislation, governance, or nationally adopted tourism strategy that places a premium on achieving these. The result is straightforward enough. The door remains wide open for a type of frontier capitalism that pays scant attention to the demands of the Bosnian environment, society, or culture. Thus, for example, at an investment conference at the Bosnian Embassy in London, the star attraction was a proposal for a multi-million Euro development, in the shape of the usual mix of villas, hotels, and golf courses, to be placed on the site of an abandoned village in the mountains overlooking Dubrovnik. This was presented in such a way as to attract private investment from external investors including members of the UK's Bosnian diaspora as well as banks specializing in reconstruction and development. While the larger hotels in Sarajevo and Mostar have recently been added to the portfolios of property investment houses, the Sarajevo library remains empty and unused. Religious competition seems increasingly to dominate Mostar: a huge Christian cross overlooks the city from the neighbouring mountain and the recent addition to the city's Catholic cathedral of a spire of literally fantastic height, has inevitably stimulated a rise in the volume of the *muezzin* from the mosques on the east of the River Neretva. Despite the powerful cosmopolitan symbolism of the Bridge, Mostar itself remains as divided as it became during the war, very few Muslims displaced by the war into the city's eastern quarters finding their way back to their former places of residence in the west. Perhaps the dance of death is back again.

As for Palestine, and bearing in mind that a prime asset of the Palestinian tourism industry lies in the beauty of the West Bank hills, streams, flora and fauna – precisely the kind of natural capital asset that our project focused upon – we may follow Raja Shehadeh's (2008) observations in his recent prize-winning book, *Palestinian Walks*: 'The hills (on which I started walking as a child) were like one large nature reserve with all the unspoiled beauty and freedom unique to such areas.' Now, however, the region is promoted to would-be settlers, many from the USA, in terms of views of landscapes that are 'dotted by green olive orchards, enjoying a pastoral calm'. But, as the Israeli architects Rafi Segal and Eyal Weizman (2003) have observed:

That which renders the landscape 'biblical' – its traditional inhabitants, cultivation in terraces, olive orchards, stone building, and the presence of livestock – is produced by Palestinians whom the Jewish settlers came to replace: the very people who cultivate the 'green olive orchards' and render the landscape biblical are themselves excluded from the panorama. The Palestinians are there to produce the scenery and then disappear.

Whatever else the settlements have done, they have radically diminished the value of Palestinian natural heritage and capital. It hardly needs repeating here that in the case of one of the actual capital assets, water, 80 per cent of the West Bank's water supplies are used by Israelis on both sides of the Green Line. And as for the heritage leaked by the settlements into the Palestinian countryside, readers of the UK's *Independent* newspaper will recall the article by its young and courageous Jewish correspondent on the anniversary of Israel's 60th anniversary. Counterpart to Shahadeh in being the winner of the 2008 Orwell prize for journalism, Hari (2008) described one of the actual and symbolic features of this inheritance in terms of the pungent smell of untreated sewage flowing from the settlements into the Palestinian fields and reservoirs after heavy rain.

Looking then at the conflict-scarred landscapes of BiH and Palestine from our experiences, reflections, and discussions of our TEMPUS work, the view is, on the face of things, depressing. In the Bosnian case, two weak governments in one country make for even weaker political potency at regional, provincial, and municipal levels – mostly true also of Palestine. Frontier capitalism and the mobilization of ethno-religious symbols denoting ethno-religious separation at the level of the state in BiH and the region of Palestine/Israel thrive in the face of worthy symbolic tokens such as the Mostar Bridge. On the positive side there is a growth in tourist numbers in both countries. The role of operators such as ATG in identifying and successfully managing new forms of independent tourism, such as justice tourism, in Palestine may be linked with a rising market in Europe for a kind of tourism that promises to penetrate the walls of media- and travel advisory-generated mythologies about Palestine and Palestinians, Bosnia and Bosnians.

It seems clear that the work of the TEMPUS graduates make substantial contributions in the drafting of a co-operative theoretical and practical future for tourism in both regions. Our graduates speak of a fundamentally Mediterranean culture of open borders and free flows across them of goods and people. For BiH and Palestine, not to mention the peoples and states of the wider regions, the beneficial economic consequences of such openness would be immense. At the level of institutional Europe (including the EC), however, there seems very little evidence that its policy-makers are listening to those on the ground (including our TEMPUS graduates) with anything like the attention they could and should. Nor is it at all clear, despite the inspiring rhetorical declarations, that European universities and their colleagues in partner countries, are being given places at any of the policy-making tables that they might legitimately expect from the indications seemingly offered them in the Programmes' terms of reference. It feels as if we are left with donor conferences and investment seminars with less than convincing senses of direction.

## References

Chandler, D. C. (1999) *Bosnia: Faking Democracy after Dayton*. London: Pluto.

Giroud, S., Scheller-Doyle, C. and ATG staff (2005) *Palestine and Palestinians: A Guidebook*. Beit Sahour: Alternative Tourism Group.

Glenny, M. (1999) *The Balkans 1804–1999: Nationalism, War and the Great Powers*. London: Granta.

Hari, J. (2008) 'Israel is suppressing a secret it must face', *The Independent*, 28 April.

Ignatieff, M. (1993) *Blood and Belonging: Journeys into the New Nationalism*. London: Chatto and Windus.

Sansour, C. and Zoughbi, C. (2010) 'Contested politics of the Mediterranean: Star Street and the struggle for development in Bethlehem', in M. Kousis, D. Clark and T. Selwyn (eds) *Contested Mediterranean Spaces: Essays in Honour of Charles Tilly*. New York: Berghahn.

Segal, R. and Weizman, E. (2003) 'The mountain: principles of building in heights', in R. Segal and E. Weizman (eds) *A Civilian Occupation: The Politics of Israeli Architecture*. London: Verso.

Selwyn, T. and Karkut, J. (2007) 'The politics of institution building and European co-operations: reflections on an EC TEMPUS project on tourism and culture in Bosnia-Herzegovina', in P. Burns and M. Novelli (eds) *Tourism and Politics: Global Frameworks and Local Realities*. Amsterdam: Elsevier.

Shehadeh, R. (2008) *Palestinian Walks: Notes on a Vanishing Landscape*. London: Profile Books.

## Websites

www.atg.ps
www.visitpalestine.ps

# 10 Views on the scale and types of tourism development in the rural periphery

## The case of Gozo

*Samantha Chaperon and Bill Bramwell*

## Introduction

There are many published studies about residents' attitudes to tourism, but few that focus specifically on residents' views about the scale and types of tourism development in their area (Harrill 2004; Hernandez *et al.* 1996; Mason and Cheyne 2000). This is a pity as policy-makers would find it useful to understand local people's preferences for the volume of tourists and amount of development, notably about whether they want the development of large-scale mass tourism or else smaller-scale tourism (Pearce *et al.* 1996). Views can also be sought on the tourist types to be attracted, and on the tourist infrastructure that they consider acceptable. Such information can assist policy-makers to make better development and marketing decisions and to integrate tourism within overall sustainable development strategies. Residents' views on these issues seem to be a necessary research focus for development strategies using community-based tourism (Scheyvens 2002; Sofield 2003). More studies of these aspects of residents' views will also help to provide critical perspectives on how people perceive and experience tourism development, and on how they respond to its implications. Such 'emic' concerns can help to establish a more humanistic and critical appreciation of sustainable tourism development (Walle 1997).

Information on local attitudes to such aspects of tourism development is useful for all types of destination areas. It may be of particular value in peripheral rural areas – that is rural areas that are geographically remote from major population and economic centres – because their tourism industry may be relatively less developed, and thus the information can inform policies before it becomes more difficult to change the direction and character of development. It may also be especially helpful in these locations as the tourism industry there may be one of relatively few development options, and this can affect people's priorities for tourism growth. Thus, residents in peripheral regions might broadly accept mass tourism for its economic returns, even if they also consider that it entails environmental deterioration and an erosion of community life. They may feel they have few alternatives for much-needed economic development as they are distant from thriving economic centres (Wanhill and Buhalis 1999). Alternatively, local people in the periphery may also resist such changes brought by mass tourism. They may reject it because they do not want fundamental alterations to their community and environment, or because they prefer small-scale development, especially if it appeals to special interest tourists whom they may hope will spend more and dislike substantial local change (Nash and Martin 2003). Of course, in practice, many people's reactions may be more complex, ambiguous and even contradictory than is suggested by these extremes.

It is useful to understand views about tourism in peripheral rural areas that are held by people living there, and also opinions on the same issues held by externally-based decision-makers that affect development there (Blackman *et al.* 2004). These decision-makers may include commercial investors, developers, hotel operators, politicians and government agencies. They may be based in external metropolitan cities across the globe, or else in relatively nearby centres that have concentrations of economic, political or institutional resources (Nash and Martin 2003; Weaver 1998). Often significant administrative and commercial centres are found geographically relatively near to the rural periphery, and decisions made there can alter development in the peripheral region.

Views held about tourism development in a peripheral rural area may be almost the same between people living in the area and related decision-makers based in external 'cores', or there may be marked differences. The extent to which these views coincide or differ can affect whether or not tourism in the rural periphery promotes sustainable development. Actors in external cores may see peripheral rural areas mainly as places where short-term financial or economic returns on capital investment can be maximized. Indeed, much tourism research has focused on core–periphery relationships that are economically exploitative, with the relationships often interpreted using insights from dependency theory (Britton 1982; Mosedale 2006; Telfer 2002). There may be at least some actors in external cores, however, who resist large-scale development in peripheral rural areas, perhaps because of their interest in environmental issues. External actors concerned to protect peripheral regions may include government staff with territorial responsibilities for those regions, such as through their conservation and planning responsibilities, and also members of non-government environmental pressure groups.

This chapter examines views about the scale and types of tourism development in one peripheral rural area: the small, largely rural island of Gozo in Southern Europe. This theme is important, and may be particularly so for Gozo as its tourism industry is very significant but still relatively small-scale, and thus there are more options still available for the future scale and characteristics of its tourism development (Bramwell 2003, 2006, 2007). Views about these issues are examined for residents and tourism-related actors on rural Gozo and also for tourism-related actors based on the nearby and influential external core, the island of Malta. There is an assessment of similarities and differences in these attitudes, with this being important as both local and external actors can affect peripheral tourism development. Malta is the main island of the Maltese nation state – which is made up of the inhabited islands of Malta, Gozo and Comino – and it is relatively dominant in terms of population size, commercial activity and national government. Very many political and planning decisions affecting Gozo's development are made by government and ministries based on Malta (Boissevain 1979).

## Case study and methodology

Gozo has a tiny land area of only 67km², while the main island of Malta has an area of 246km². These two small islands – together with Comino – make up the Republic of Malta. Figure 10.1 shows Gozo and the main island separated by the physical barrier of a roughly 5km-wide, sea channel. The Republic of Malta is on Europe's southern periphery, so that Gozo is on the periphery of Europe's periphery.

Gozo has a mainly rural character, with agriculture accounting for about 60 per cent of its land area (MEPA 2002). It retains this character despite having quite a high population density, with its small settlements being surrounded by cultivated terraces that climb up to meet scrubby slopes and hilltops. The island's small size and double insularity contribute to its limited economic opportunities, with tourism being the second most important employment sector after public sector jobs (Government of Malta 2004). Its economic weakness is seen over the period 1999–2003 when its GDP per capita declined from 73.2 per cent to 69.3 per cent of that of the main island (Government of Malta 2004; MEPA 2006). The Republic of Malta's total population is only a little over 400,000, while Gozo has a population of around 30,000, making up only 8 per cent of the total (Government of Malta 2004, 2006).

Many tourists come to Gozo for its rural and coastal scenery, attractive and small scale settlements, slow pace and tranquil atmosphere, traditional ways of life and rich cultural resources, and its many heritage attractions. Some tourists are attracted specifically by the good quality diving sites around its coast. Gozo's tourism industry suffers because international visitors predominantly arrive at the main island's international airport, and if they go to Gozo they have to travel overland to the west and then take a ferry. Although it is visited by around 582,000 tourists annually, about 85 per cent are day visitors – often on organized trips – from the main island of Malta, with their contribution per head to Gozo's economy being relatively modest (Briguglio 1994; MTA 2005; Stevens and Associates 2000). It has been estimated that only 25 per cent of total spending on day excursions to Gozo directly benefits the Gozitan economy (Stevens and Associates 2000).

Most investment in Gozo's tourism-related industry – in accommodation,

*Figure 10.1* The Maltese Islands.

attractions, restaurants and shops – comes from the Gozitans themselves. Despite the Gozitan's entrepreneurial leadership on the island, many decisions by public agencies and civil society organizations affecting its tourism development are made on the main island. The Maltese Government and all its ministries, except the Ministry for Gozo, are based in Malta. Importantly, land-use planning decisions affecting Gozo's tourism are made by the Malta Environment and Planning Authority, which has its offices on Malta. In relation to tourism policy, the Malta Tourism Authority is also Malta-based and it has considerable influence over Gozo's tourism through its tourism marketing and strategy, and its licensing powers for hotel development. The Gozo Tourist Association is locally-based, however, and it offers advice to the Malta Tourism Authority and lobbies on behalf of the island's tourism interests. Further, many environmental non-governmental organizations that have opposed larger tourism schemes on the island are Malta-based. In all, as well as being geographically peripheral, Gozo is also peripheral to Malta in terms of much tourism-related policy-making.

Various sources were used to explore people's views about the scale and types of tourism development on the island between 1999 and 2005. First, in-depth interviews with questions on these themes were carried out between March and May 2005. These interviews were with 23 residents and also with 12 selected tourism-related actors on Gozo, and for the main island of Malta there were 12 interviews with selected Malta-based tourism-related actors. For the main island of Malta, the interviewees included representatives from the Malta Tourism Authority, the Ministry for Tourism and Culture, the tourism-related private sector, and actors involved in environmental protection. Ideally, both residents as well as tourism-related actors on the main island would have been interviewed, but Gozo was the focus of the larger study from which the chapter's findings are drawn, and it was decided just to examine the views of tourism-related actors on the main island as they were considered likely to have most direct influence on Gozo's tourism development. Thus comparisons are between the views of both residents and tourism-related actors interviewed on Gozo and of tourism-related actors only who were interviewed on Malta. It is important to remember this distinction when considering the results. A second important source was Maltese newspapers over the period from 1999, notably two daily newspapers, the *Times of Malta* and the *Malta Independent*. These included highly detailed news items, commentaries and letters on local issues, events and policies, with tourism frequently being discussed. A third type of source was policy documents produced by organizations such as the European Union, the Malta Tourism Authority, the Malta Environment and Planning Authority, the Gozo Chamber of Commerce and the Gozo Tourist Authority.

## Views on tourism development in the rural periphery

### Commonly held views about Gozo's tourism development

Many views expressed in the interviews about Gozo's tourism development by Gozitan residents and tourism-related actors were shared by the tourism-related actors on the main island. One widely held opinion, for example, was that Gozo could attract many more tourists, and that this would benefit its economy. A Malta Tourist Authority (MTA) representative believed that Gozo as a tourist destination could be: 'at the forefront of the Maltese islands . . . The potential is definitely there.' Tourism's economic importance for this marginal island was emphasized by many. Another MTA employee suggested that 'tourism in Gozo is a way forward in my opinion. In my opinion it is the main commercial economic activity. Tourism affects the entire population, and in terms of growth, potentially, I still maintain that tourism is the key.' A Gozo Tourist Authority representative also contended that 'Our economy depends totally on tourism, we don't have any manufacturing industry . . . there are no exports, so the only foreign income is to come from this service industry, that's all.'

Some people on both islands felt that Gozo's tourism potential had in part been frustrated by government inactivity, including its insufficient promotion as a separate destination. One Gozitan respondent asserted that: 'I honestly believe that Gozo could be a real paradise if only the politicians would open their eyes and take a good look around; I mean, Gozo has potential, but it just is not happening.'

Respondents from both islands also indicated that Gozo gained insufficient rewards from the many day visitors crossing over from Malta (Lockhart and Ashton 1990). These day visitors were sometimes depicted as not being 'real' tourists, largely because much of their spending was retained by Maltese tour operators that organized their trips. A Malta-based respondent noted how: 'There's a lot of mass tourists that go there [to Gozo] for a day, and those day-trippers hardly generate anything for the economy of Gozo.' Interviewees on both islands suggested that Gozo would benefit from focusing more on attracting overnight tourists. It was also often suggested by people in both places that Gozo should attract more tourists in winter in order to reduce the problem of seasonality. One Gozitan respondent commented that at the 'end of October Gozo just shuts down, it's like someone put an iron curtain across the channel'. It was suggested that the seasonal difficulties here were even greater than on its sister island: 'If Malta gets nine good months, we might get six'. Here the island suffers from a limited winter ferry service from Malta, and no service at all when sea conditions are rough.

Interviewees on both islands indicated that Gozo's supply of tourist accommodation far exceeded the tourist demand. No doubt this was a response to the island's low tourist accommodation occupancy, at only 34 per cent (Stevens and Associates 2000). According to a Gozitan church representative, 'The tourists usually come here just for one day for a few hours, and then they go [back] to Malta. The hotels here in Gozo don't have the opportunity to have tourists staying here for several nights.' A Malta Tourism Authority employee also noted how 'There was a time when there was quite a bit of development in accommodation: new hotels were being built. Now, because supply is exceeding demand in terms of accommodation, there is a problem with some hotels closing.' There was a general presumption on both islands that Gozo must attract more overnight tourists so as to raise hotel occupancies and bring wider economic benefits.

Opinions among the respondents about Gozo's potential as a tourist destination were generally very positive. This often reflected a sense of pride in Gozo's 'special' character, and a feeling the island has potential for greater success as a tourist destination. Respondents frequently admired the island's distinctive character and more traditional features, these sometimes being identified as key strengths for future tourism growth. A regular theme was that tourism development should be on a smaller scale than in Malta. One person commented: 'In my opinion this type of development should be very small', and 'The development should reflect the island, the smallness of the island. We say that small is beautiful, so I think Gozo does not fall within the parameters of the development of Malta.'

The island's heritage and culture were identified by many as appealing to tourists. Some highlighted the draw of the Ggantija Temple at Xewkija, believed to be the world's oldest free-standing structure. A Gozo Tourist Association spokesperson commented how:

> In Gozo we have the oldest free-standing temple. They make a lot of fuss about the Pyramids, they make a lot of fuss about Stonehenge, but we have Ggantija that is seven thousand years old. It's a jewel, and we are not optimizing on this temple.

Interviewees on both islands also singled out the appeal of Gozo's traditional way of life – as seen in the many village festivals or 'festas' – and which in turn is often influenced by the local strength of Catholic religious adherence. According to a Gozitan Mayor, 'certain tourists come also for our traditions and culture . . . And most of the tourists come to see the local festas, and come to see our local traditional food.' Respondents on both islands also identified Gozo's landscape, environment and relatively undeveloped character as important strengths in attracting tourists. The coastal underwater natural resources were also seen as appealing for diving tourists.

There were also more complex, alternative views concerning Gozo's tourism strengths, expressed by both Gozitan and main island respondents. A few, for example, made more sceptical comments about the island's potential to attract larger numbers of overnight stay tourists. Some too seemed to recognize that pride in Gozo's special character and relatively undeveloped environment could foster unrealistic expectations about its competitive position as a tourist destination. A Gozitan noted: 'Okay, let them [tourists] come over for history, but in one day you can tour the island for its history . . . Ggantija is unique, but there aren't enough [historical sites] for people to come over for a week.' Similarly, a prominent Maltese politician argued for greater realism around Gozo's potential for further growth in both dive tourism and heritage tourism:

> Gozo boasts some lovely diving sites, but there are far more impressive ones a few hours away in the Red Sea . . . [A] niche that is under-developed is Gozo's history and archaeology, which are truly remarkable, but realistically they must face stiff competition not just from nearby destinations such as Rome and Madrid, but even from Malta itself.
>
> (Fenech 2005)

Another shared perspective was that people quite often made direct comparisons between Gozo and Malta in relation to their respective levels of development, extent of the built-up area, and building heights. Gozo was widely depicted as less developed than Malta and with a much more rural feel, and several respondents saw this as a positive advantage for tourism. One industry spokesperson proudly commented how 'We sincerely believe that Gozo has special things to offer, which Malta has not because it lost them through the over-development.' Schembri (1994: 50) also asserts that Gozo's 'main attraction lies in its rural character, typical of the Maltese Islands before the advent of mass tourism'. Respondents on both islands contended that Malta had made mistakes in allowing the present scale of development, and that there should be efforts to prevent Gozo from repeating those errors and becoming a 'mini-Malta'. According to a main island respondent, 'One of the reasons why tourists like Gozo is because Gozo is still relatively unspoilt when compared to Malta, and not just in terms of building and development, but also in terms of living style.' The Chairman of Alternattiva Demokratica – the Green Party – further claimed: 'There will be no mystique and no value added if Gozo is allowed to become a smaller, poorer and uglier clone of Malta' (Vassallo 2003). Some on both islands stated that Gozo could learn from Malta's mistakes, and that it should be promoted as a comparatively less developed and more tranquil and rural destination.

Associated with this preference for Gozo remaining less developed, some respondents in both locations felt it should seek to attract 'niche' tourist markets. A Ministry for Tourism and Culture representative suggested it should encourage niche markets, for which Malta is less suited: 'Certainly in Gozo there is the possibility of having a different type of product. Smaller scale, less mass market, more focused on specific niches . . . Gozo has the possibility of developing the types of product which in Malta are not always possible.' This opinion accords with the conclusion of many academic researchers that peripheral destinations potentially have a comparative advantage in attracting niche markets (Hall 2006; Nash and Martin 2003). People often wanted specialist markets that are provided by the island's environmental and natural resources, such as tourists interested in walking, cycling and diving. For instance, a Malta Environment and Planning Authority representative acknowledged that, 'Diving is definitely more popular in Gozo than in Malta because of the diving sites, they have an advantage there compared to Malta.' Some interviewees on both islands felt that special interest tourists would be more suitable for Gozo than the large numbers and mass tourism found on the main island.

### More distinct perspectives about Gozo's tourism development

Although very many views about Gozo's tourism were shared between respondents on the two islands, Gozo's residents and tourism-related actors expressed some opinions more frequently. While people in both places acknowledged that Gozo has more tourist accommodation than the visitor numbers justify, some Gozitans in particular still wanted additional accommodation provision, appearing to believe this could stimulate demand. A Gozitan hotel receptionist commented: 'I don't think that there are enough hotels . . . not at the moment. As an island there are only a few hotels, and they are not as big as the ones in Malta.' Also, while many agreed that niche tourism is more suitable for Gozo, some Gozitans wanted to attract all types of niche tourists, one even suggesting that: 'Everybody is welcome as long as they have a great time.' The desire of some on Gozo for more tourist facilities and for diverse niche tourist types reflected their strong sense of urgency to improve the island's struggling economy.

The Gozitan respondents often recognized the island's potential in terms of its rural character, felt there had been mistakes in the sister island's tourism development, and generally wanted small-scale tourism development; yet they still sometimes also appeared to want to replicate features of Malta's tourism development. There was perhaps a sense of envy about Malta's tourism success, and at times this meant they could forget how the main island's development had involved significant environmental and social costs. When discussing specific plans for large-scale, tourism-related developments on Gozo, for example, many Gozitan respondents were in favour of them. They mostly favoured, for instance, a proposed 18-hole golf course to be located in an area partly designated as a Natura 2000 site by the European Union, a designation indicating strict conservation measures. A Gozo Tourism Association representative, who supported the golf development, argued that 'Anyone who loves Gozo and who loves tourism would be for a golf course.' Many Gozitans also supported a proposed large-scale marina and tourist accommodation complex on the island's east coast, with one asserting that 'Gozo is lacking from such development, and I think [that is why] the tourists are not coming along, it's one of the problems.' Although there were some complaints that the original plans may have been too large-scale, most Gozitans who were interviewed supported a scaled-down version of the development. The interviews suggest that, despite Gozitans accepting that small-scale development is more suitable for the island's size, they were still quite often attracted by larger-scale tourism developments, perhaps because they had seen such schemes bring economic benefits to Malta.

While very many views were shared between respondents on the two islands, some opinions were also expressed more by the tourism-related actors on the main island. Some respondents from the larger island, for instance, expressed concerns that the Gozitans did not fully appreciate the special characteristics of their island and the considerable tourism potential of those features. Gozitans were sometimes thought to focus too much on short-term economic benefits, rather than on tourism's longer-term health and the island's overall well-being. At times, respondents from the main island expressed a rather protective attitude towards Gozo's future tourism development. Thus, an influential Maltese actor involved in planning and environmental issues argued that 'What they [Gozitans] don't understand is that once Gozo becomes like Malta, then nobody wants to come here.' Similarly, a Malta Tourism Authority official commented that the Gozitans 'only tend to see the glittering lights from across the channel – the nice things – without realizing how much Malta has lost and how much it has affected the quality of life in Malta'. Another suggested that Gozitans tend to see Malta as a benchmark for Gozo to aspire to: 'and in many respects [Gozo] would like to equate itself with Malta in terms of accessibility, in terms of facilities, [and] in terms of development, without realizing that it is different'. The Malta Tourism Authority staff member feared that Gozitans would not make the best decisions for their own tourism industry, and that if 'left to their own devices they would emulate Malta. They would literally emulate Malta . . . they would go for the "full monty", which would be damaging'.

## Potential tensions around the differing views

Despite the numerous shared views about Gozo's tourism development between internal respondents (both residents and tourism-related actors on Gozo) and external respondents (the tourism-related actors only on the main island), there were differences in perspectives and potentially these could lead to tensions. This seems to apply to the question as to whether Gozo should remain less changed or else develop quite rapidly. The main island tourism-related respondents generally believed that for the sister island to retain its special character and tourist appeal it would be advantageous for it to remain relatively unchanged. One such respondent, who was active in environmental and planning issues, argued that Gozo should retain its rural and relaxed feel, because 'In today's world, where everything is fast – all the electronics – it's nice to be out in the real countryside.' Another Malta-based tourism actor argued that:

> One of the reasons why tourists like Gozo is because Gozo is still relatively unspoilt when compared to Malta; and it's not just in terms of building and development, but also in terms of living style. It's not the fast-tracked movements as in Malta, it's more the laid-back style.

Views were relatively more mixed among Gozo's residents and tourism-related actors about whether the island should remain unchanged. Around half suggested that in order to attract more tourists it would be beneficial for Gozo to remain relatively unchanged, but a roughly similar proportion also indicated that it needs to develop, so it can progress and modernize. Thus, a Gozitan school teacher suggested that the island is 'different; if it becomes like everywhere else, then it's not Gozo any more, and tourists won't come. We want tourists to come and see what it is like now.' By contrast, another local person argued that 'You can't keep a place unchanged in modern days.' At times it was contended that it was unfair to keep their island less developed, and that they should be allowed to modernize to the same extent as Malta.

Some Gozitan respondents accused people on Malta of wanting to keep the island unchanged so that they can use it as their own holiday haven. One complained:

> Well, the Maltese . . . want to leave it [Gozo] as it is; that's the charm of Gozo, with all our potholes. Because if we don't have potholes in our roads everybody will be driving fast; on Gozo it's good to have a slow car in front of you! . . . [The people on Malta want] to keep it as it is, less modernized.

Some people suggested it was unreasonable for residents of the larger island to want Gozo's development held back. One main island respondent noted that 'they accuse us – and they are right – that we want to keep Gozo backward – underdeveloped – because that's our playground. Gozo is our playground, and we want it to be less developed than Malta.' It seems there were some differences in view between the respondents on the two islands about whether Gozo should remain relatively unchanged, notably for the purposes of attracting tourists, including for the purpose of retaining its appeal for domestic (Maltese) tourists.

Several Gozitan respondents suggested that the island's most important tourist market was domestic tourists from the larger island. In fact, many people living on the main island visit their sister island several times a year, including during the off-peak months; and they are considered to be 'high spenders' who substantially benefit local tourism businesses and the island's economy. A Gozitan property developer claimed that 'If you talk to the people who are involved in the industry, they say the Maltese are the best tourists for us because they really spend. You know, they come for a week and they spend a lot of money.' Many locals were aware of their economic importance, but some gave the impression that they would really rather not be so dependent on them. According to a Malta Tourism Authority representative:

> Gozo has come to recognize the importance of the Maltese market because I think . . . it *is* the biggest touristic market for them – larger than the British, larger than the Germans. But they do not like the Maltese because the Maltese are not the best tourists in terms of noise . . . They need their money, but if they could do without them, they would . . . They depend on them, but some do misbehave.

One factor here was that the Gozitans did not always appreciate how the Maltese sometimes behave towards them when they visit, feeling that they do not always show them appropriate respect and that 'they regard the Gozitans as a class inferior to their own' (Boissevain 1979: 86–7). Thus, at times, there was evidence of some unease and even antagonism between the respondents interviewed on these two neighbouring islands.

## Conclusion

This study of the peripheral and largely rural island of Gozo explored attitudes to the scale and types of tourism among local residents and tourism-related actors on the island. It also assessed views about the same issues for Gozo among tourism-related actors on the neighbouring main island of Malta, with this considered valuable as many development decisions affecting Gozo are made in this external 'core'.

It might seem plausible that tourism-related actors on the main island would favour a substantial economic exploitation of Gozo's tourism. But the evidence here suggests this often was not the case, with many main island tourism actors voicing concerns to protect Gozo's distinctive features and environmental qualities. One reason for this was that they felt tourists were attracted to the island specifically because it was less developed. Another probable factor was that many of them regularly visited the sister island in their leisure time, partly for a change from the busy and highly urbanized main island. Some tourism-related respondents on the main island even suggested that they were more concerned about protecting Gozo from over-development than were some Gozitans. And, because of their considerable concerns about the weakness of Gozo's economy, some Gozitans were relatively enthusiastic about large-scale tourism development proposals, and such developments could be very damaging. Yet attitudes to Gozo's tourism among the main island tourism-related actors might have focused more on economic development if they had owned tourism businesses on Gozo – but it was shown that most of Gozo's tourism businesses were owned by Gozitans. In this context, and for comparative purposes, it would be interesting to examine views about tourism development in a similar core–periphery situation where tourism-related actors in the nearby external 'core' did have substantial business interests in the peripheral region.

Some of the main island tourism-related actors interviewed for the chapter were government staff or politicians, and all of the main island respondents were interested in the public policies for Gozo. Gozitans have considerable political influence on the islands' government because their total electoral vote is sufficient for the two main political parties to win or lose in national elections, with national elections often won by just a few thousand votes (Cini 2002; Mitchell 2002). This means the national government is anxious to please the Gozitan electorate, and with many Gozitans being anxious to boost jobs on the island, this may help to explain why in recent years both main political parties have appeared to favour some of

Gozo's proposed large-scale tourism development projects. Both political parties, for instance, have supported the principle of developing a golf course on Gozo (Bramwell 2007). Thus, the practical actions of tourism-related actors on the main island might be more pro-development than is indicated by the views expressed in the interviews.

It is notable that there were so many shared views among the respondents about the scale and types of tourism considered suitable for the peripheral island of Gozo. Many argued that the island should attract more tourists, seasonality ought to be reduced, and that the island's special qualities should be used as its key tourism draw. These distinctive qualities included its land-scapes, environment, heritage and culture. Many also saw the generally smaller scale of the island's tourism development and urbanization as a posi-tive feature, with several respondents anxious for Gozo to learn lessons from the main island's overdevelopment. These opinions meant that many respondents favoured Gozo attempting to attract 'niche' or special interest tourist markets. While there were many shared views, there was some evidence too that certain views were expressed more often by residents and tourism-related actors on Gozo, and others were held more often by tourism-related actors on the main island.

Future research in the case study area could helpfully extend the survey sample to also include residents living on the main island. This would provide a broader basis for the study of attitudes on both islands to the scale and types of tourism development on Gozo.

## Lessons to be learned

Two lessons or implications can be taken from this study of Gozo. First, it indicates that sustainable tourism development requires consultation with residents and other actor groups, including those engaged in tourism-related activities. This potentially means that people's preferences for tourism devel-opment in the region where they live or have business interests can be reflected in policy decisions. The present study was a response to the shortage of previous research on local views about the preferred specific scale and types of tourism development, with information on those views being highly relevant to inform policy-making in destinations. Such research can be particularly valuable for peripheral rural areas as here the tourist industry can be a mainstay of the local economy, yet the industry may be at a scale where the rejection of mass tourism is still a realistic option.

Second, the chapter reviewed information for one peripheral destination about similarities in views, differences in views, and also the related poten-tial tensions, about the scale and types of tourism development. It has shown that these views, and the issues they raise, are important but also complex and sometimes also contradictory. Such information can help in making better tourism development and marketing decisions and in integrating tourism preferences into overall sustainable development strategies. There is scope for more research that explores such views and related issues, both in the Maltese islands and elsewhere.

## References

Blackman, A., Foster, F., Hyvonen, T., Kuilboer, A. and Moscardo, G. (2004) 'Factors contributing to successful tourism development in peripheral regions', *Journal of Tourism Studies* 15(1): 59–70.

Boissevain, J. (1979) 'The impact of tourism on a dependent island: Gozo, Malta', *Annals of Tourism Research* 6: 77–90.

Bramwell, B. (2003) 'Maltese responses to tourism', *Annals of Tourism Research* 30(3): 581–605.

—— (2006) 'Actors, power and discourses of growth limits', *Annals of Tourism Research* 33(4): 957–78.

—— (2007) 'Complexity, interdisciplinarity and growth management: the case of Maltese resort tourism', in S. Agarwal and G. Shaw (eds) *Managing Coastal Tourism Resorts: A Global Perspective*. Clevedon: Channel View, pp. 73–89.

Briguglio, L. (1994) *Tourism in Gozo: Policies, Prospects and Problems*. Malta: University of Malta and Foundation for International Studies.

Britton, S. G. (1982) 'The political economy of tourism in the Third World', *Annals of Tourism Research* 9: 331–58.

Cini, M. (2002) 'A divided nation: polarization and the two-party system in Malta', *Southern European Society and Politics* 7: 6–23.

Fenech, E. (2005) 'The branding of Gozo', *The Malta Independent*, 21 August.

Government of Malta (2004) *Malta: Single Programming Document 2004–2006*. Malta: Government Press.

—— (2006) *National Strategic Referencing Framework 2007–2013: Draft Document for Consultation*. Malta: Government Press.

Hall, C. M. (2006) 'North-South perspectives on tourism, regional development and peripheral areas', in D. R. Muller and B. Jansson (eds) *Tourism in Peripheries: Perspectives from the Far North and South*. Wallingford: CABI, pp. 19–38.

Harrill, R. (2004) 'Residents' attitudes toward tourism development: a literature review with implications for tourism planning', *Journal of Planning Literature* 18(3): 251–66.

Hernandez, S. A., Cohen, J. and Garcia, H. L. (1996) 'Residents' attitudes towards an instant resort enclave', *Annals of Tourism Research* 23(4): 755–79.

Lockhart, D. G. and Ashton, S. E. (1990) 'Domestic tourism and leisure in Malta', *Hyphen* 6(3): 117–24.

Mason, P. and Cheyne, J. (2000) 'Residents' attitudes to proposed tourism development', *Annals of Tourism Research* 27(2): 391–411.

MEPA (2002) *Draft Gozo and Comino Local Plan*. Malta: Malta Environment and Planning Authority.

—— (2006) *Gozo and Comino Local Plan*. Malta: Malta Environment and Planning Authority.

Mitchell, J. (2002) *Ambivalent Europeans: Ritual, Memory and the Public Sphere in Malta*. London: Routledge.

Mosedale, J. (2006) 'Tourism commodity chains: market entry and its effects on St. Lucia', *Current Issues in Tourism* 9(4): 436–58.

MTA (2005) *Tourist Segments Report*. Malta: Malta Tourism Authority, Strategic Planning and Research Division.

Nash, R. and Martin, A. (2003) 'Tourism in peripheral areas: the challenges for Northeast Scotland', *International Journal of Tourism Research* 5(3): 161–81.

Pearce, P. L., Moscardo, G. and Ross, G. F. (1996) *Tourism Community Relationships*. Oxford: Elsevier.

Schembri, P. (1994) 'The environmental impact of tourism in Gozo', in L. Briguglio (ed.) *Tourism in Gozo: Policies, Prospects and Problems*. Msida: University of Malta and Foundation for International Studies, pp. 50–6.

Scheyvens, R. (2002) *Tourism for Communities: Empowering Communities*. Harlow: Prentice Hall.

Sofield, T. H. B. (2003) *Empowerment for Sustainable Tourism Development*. London: Pergamon.

Stevens and Associates (2000) *Gozo Tourism: Review and Framework for Future Development*. Malta: Gozo Tourism Association.

Telfer, D. J. (2002) 'The evolution of tourism and development theory', in R. Sharpley and D. J. Telfer (eds) *Tourism and Development: Concepts and Issues*. Clevedon: Channel View, pp. 35–78.

Vassallo, H. (2003) 'NUTS about Gozo', *Times of Malta*, 16 February.

Walle, A. H. (1997) 'Quantitative versus qualitative tourism research', *Annals of Tourism Research*, 24(3): 524–36.

Wanhill, S. and Buhalis, D. (1999) 'Introduction: challenges for tourism in peripheral areas', *International Journal of Tourism Research* 1(5): 295–7.

Weaver, D. B. (1998) 'Peripheries of the periphery: tourism in Tobago and Barbuda', *Annals of Tourism Research* 25(2): 292–313.

# Part III
# The local community and development

# 11 Approaches towards the development of sustainable recreational fishing

## A case study from the Nemunas Delta, Lithuania

*Ausrine Armaitiené, Eleri Jones and Ramunas Povilanskas*

## Introduction

In the past few decades, a global shift in rural employment towards non-commodity sectors has been evidenced in various societies throughout the world (Bouma *et al.* 1998; Bryden and Bollman 2000; Lanjouw and Lanjouw 2001). This shift is particularly dramatic in rural coastal communities, many of which face economic decline as a result of depletion of fish stocks and/or reduced incentives for maintaining commercial fishing (Armaitiené *et al.* 2006; Breber *et al.* 2008). The attitudes of coastal communities in relation to future alternatives for commercial fishing pose serious questions to researchers. Some appreciate tourism development, recreational fishing in particular, as a major vehicle for maintaining the economic viability of coastal communities (Hale 2001; Murphy 2003); others fear that tourism development might put off economic diversification, including the complete replacement of the commercial fishing industry (Inbakaran and Jackson 2005).

In some countries the shift from commercial fishing to recreational fishing has been successful, e.g. in Germany in 2002 the economic benefits associated with recreational fishing were estimated at over €6.4 billion per year with about 52,000 employees directly or indirectly dependent on the expenditure from recreational fishing although not all of this revenue was gained by coastal communities (Arlinghaus 2004). However, the economic benefits associated with recreational fishing are distributed quite evenly in Germany and other countries of the Baltic Sea Region, as later studies have shown (Povilanskas 2008). The prospect of lucrative recreational fishing services poses a dilemma for the coastal rural communities of Lithuania: whether they should continue to rely on the commercial exploitation of declining fish stocks or shift to the provision of recreational fishing services.

This chapter aims to highlight some of the controversies related to this shift and to discuss preconditions for the development of sustainable recreational fishing in the Nemunas Delta which is part of the Curonian Lagoon region in Lithuania (Figure 11.1). The chapter develops a case study of the Nemunas Delta focusing on the sustainability of recreational fishing in the area. It adopts a mixed methodology involving quantitative and qualitative methods to explore the sustainability of recreational fishing tourism at the community level in the Nemunas Delta and the conflict between socioeconomic development and the environment. The quantitative part of the study involved a survey of tourism quality. The qualitative part involved interviews with key stakeholders, including relevant officials and local interest groups, and interrogation of Lithuanian government statistics, reports and policy documents. The study benchmarks recreational fishing services in the northern part of the Nemunas Delta against those provided in

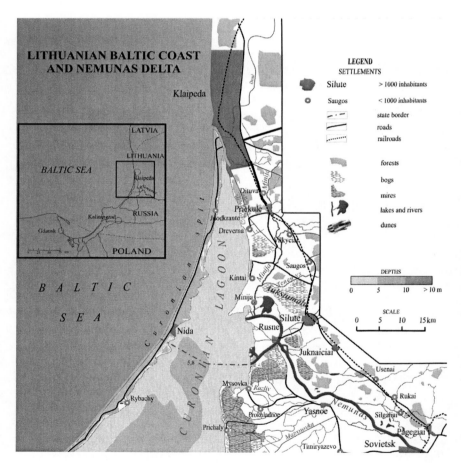

*Figure 11.1* Map of the Nemunas Delta, Lithuania.

the northern part of the Vistula Delta which is recognized as a high performing area in terms of its processes and the services delivered.

## The study area

The non-tidal Curonian Lagoon located on the southeast rim of the Baltic Sea is the largest coastal lagoon in Europe (Breber *et al.* 2008). The lagoon together with the adjacent region forms the south-east Baltic coastal accumulative plain (Povilanskas 2004) and covers a total area of approximately 4000 km². The northern part of the region belongs to Lithuania, whilst the southern part is in the Kaliningrad Oblast, an exclave of the Russian Federation. The major part of the east coast of the lagoon is, or has historically been, part of the Nemunas Delta, which stretches about 70 km inland (Gudelis 1998) and is also divided between Lithuania and Russia. The delta is covered by a dense maze of more than 60 rivers, rivulets and oxbow lakes. After the spring thaw, for several weeks, a large part of the delta is usually flooded and water submersion often persists until June creating favourable conditions for migratory waterfowl. The Nemunas Delta is a wetland of international importance (a Ramsar site) for nature conservation due to high concentrations of waterfowl (Povilanskas *et al.* 2002). The Nemunas Delta Regional Park covers the Lithuanian part of the delta.

The Curonian Lagoon region traditionally was famous as a major destination for recreational fishermen. Considering the numbers of tourists visiting the Curonian Lagoon, and particularly the Nemunas Delta, recreational fishermen constitute a significant part (approximately 50 per cent). The main game fish species, which are available in the Curonian Lagoon, the deltaic branches, tributaries of Nemunas and the oxbow lakes, include salmon, sea trout, trout, pike, pike-perch, perch, smelt, tench, white bream, vimba, eel, sheatfish and burbot (Švagždys 2006).

Ice-fishing is a very special and popular leisure activity, which is practised all over the Curonian Lagoon and throughout the whole winter season, as long as weather conditions allow walking on the ice. A phenomenon of particular interest is the upstream migration of smelt in winter and early spring which attracts thousands of recreational fishermen. This 'secondary' wave of tourists gives the major low-season share of income to local hospitality service enterprises in the region: small hotels, tourist farms and inns, which position themselves for the provision of basic services.

## Case study methodology

The case study of the Nemunas Delta regarding the sustainable rural and fishing tourism development was developed through the first-hand experiences of staff from the Department of Recreation and Tourism at Klaipėda University. Since 1997, scholars from the Department have investigated social and economic changes in the Lithuanian coastal rural areas following the collapse of the Soviet Union and the centrally-planned economic system. This study is a continuation of a previous study on rural tourism development in the coastal areas of Lithuania (Armaitienė *et al.* 2006).

The issues of interest have been explored through a combination of quantitative and qualitative research methods. The quantitative survey used for this study applied a dichotomized type of multiple regression analysis with dummy variables of attributes and dimensions of tourism quality (Fuchs and Weiermair 2004). A total satisfaction measure with the recreational fishing in the Nemunas Delta was used as the dependent variable and dummy variables for each of the following attributes and dimensions were used as independent variables: (1) catches; (2) accommodation; (3) catering; (4) fishing guide service; (5) sauna; (6) fish cleaning, cooking and smoking facilities; (7) fishing conditions from the boat; (8) fishing conditions from the shore; (9) nature and environment; (10) issuance system of the fishing licences; (11) grocery services; (12) information on fishing regulations; and (13) access and parking conditions.

The qualitative part of the case study of the Nemunas Delta regarding the development of recreational fishing tourism followed a similar methodology to the former study of the sustainable rural tourism development in the Lithuanian coastal rural areas (Armaitienė *et al.* 2006). Through interviews with key stakeholders, including relevant officials and local interest groups, and interrogation of Lithuanian government tourism statistics and a range of reports and policy documents, the study explores the sustainability of recreational fishing tourism in the Nemunas Delta at the local community level, and the conflict between the social and economic development, on the one hand, and environmental issues, on the other.

Additionally, a comprehensive benchmarking study was carried out which aimed to compare the current situation in the provision of the recreational fishing services in the northern part of the Nemunas Delta (Nemunas Delta Regional Park) with the northern part of the Vistula Delta (Elbląg Żuławy, Poland). We have adapted the approach developed by Bhutta and Huq (1999) and interpreted the benchmarking study as a complex exercise of comparison of the surveyed territory with a better performing territory in terms of processes and functionality (*functional process benchmarking*) of the delivered services.

## Results

### Dramatic societal shift

In the communist era (1945–89), four fishing co-operatives shared commercial fishing in the Lithuanian part of the Curonian Lagoon. Besides fishing, people were employed in dairy and duck-farming. Fishing quotas, milk and poultry production plans were determined centrally, and the local economy was fully dependent on cheap fuel and low-cost manual labour. The central government financed land reclamation, maintenance of dykes and polders in the Nemunas Delta, and restocking of fish in the Curonian Lagoon (Roepstorff and Povilanskas 1995).

After the collapse of the Soviet Union, most local agro-industrial activities proved to be economically unviable and soon collapsed as energy prices increased dramatically in 1991. Economic reforms of the 1990s caused the decline of commercial fishing in the Curonian Lagoon and dissolution of the co-operatives. Dairy cattle breeding and milk production have dwindled mostly to subsistence farming on small-scale individual farms. Economic reforms radically changed the fishing organization in the Curonian Lagoon. Nowadays, approximately 100 small private fishing enterprises have licences to fish (Breber *et al.* 2008). As a result, the proper control of landed catches becomes difficult which results in substantial but uncontrolled landing of fish (up to 60 per cent of the fish yield). Unemployment and emigration from the area soared and the remaining locals – mostly people in their forties and fifties – had to meet new life challenges without possessing proper knowledge and skills.

In this situation, rural tourism development was perceived as a cure-all by many local communities around the Curonian Lagoon (Armaitienė *et al.* 2006). The incentives of local municipalities to promote rural tourism development included alleviation of tax on provision of rural tourism services for local farmsteads for the first five years, allocation of matching funds to European Union grants for the construction of public tourism facilities, education and training of local tourism service providers (Povilanskas 2008).

In 2000, the first steps to facilitate the provision of rural tourism services on selected pilot farmsteads were taken by the Department of Recreation and Tourism at Klaipėda University on Rusnė Island in the Nemunas Delta. These efforts proved to be a real success and the number of farmsteads providing rural tourism services doubled each year from just two in 2000 to 28 in 2004, catering for demand from the growing number of visitors from the large cities of Lithuania (Armaitienė *et al.* 2006). Notably, these visitors are attracted mainly by the aforementioned excellent all-year-round recreational fishing conditions (Vaitekūnas *et al.* 2001).

*Gaps in the recreational fishing services in the Nemunas Delta*
*compared to the Vistula Delta*

The benchmarking study revealed major gaps in the provision of the recreation fishing services in the Nemunas Delta when compared with the Vistula Delta – much higher prices combined with much lower quality of the services were a major setback to the competitiveness of the recreational fishing service providers in the Nemunas Delta combined with extremely poor marketing skills and means.

We have identified five main reasons for the backwardness of the

Nemunas Delta as a recreational fishing tourism destination compared to the Vistula Delta:

1   *Experience.* Rural tourism development in Poland started 10 years earlier than in Lithuania. According to Marciszewska (2006: 129):

> Rural tourism, agri-tourism and active tourism in particular were seen to be important in assisting restructuring through the consolidation of economic back-linkages and stimulating value-added quality produce. Although tourism had existed in Polish rural areas since the nineteenth century, its development was considerably accelerated during the 1990s as a result of the introduction of a market economy and the restructuring of the Polish agricultural sector.

Experts in rural tourism, particularly those working in the regional chambers of agriculture and tourism, deliver regular and competent consultancy to the recreational fishing service providers.

2   *The different backgrounds of the recreational fishing service providers.* In the Nemunas Delta, the majority of the small-scale rural and fishing tourism service providers are former employees of the dissolved large-scale fishing co-operatives. They lack the traditions and skills of private entrepreneurship. Meanwhile, in the Vistula Delta, the majority of the small-scale rural and fishing tourism service providers enjoy a long record of small-scale private entrepreneurship and higher social and economic standards. According to the results of the recent comprehensive survey of the social and economic situation in the rural areas of Poland (Bański 2008), the communities in the northern part of the Vistula Delta (Elbląg Żuławy) enjoy higher than average scores of such social and economic indices including: the share of the population connected to the sewerage system; the number of non-governmental organizations; the number of economic entities in the private sector; trends of changes in population number; the average amount of investment expenditures in farms incurring investment costs; overall prevalence of positive changes.

3   *Specialization.* Although most of the rural tourism farms in the Vistula Delta are family-owned, in many cases, marketing, boating, fishing guides and ancillary services are delegated to the professional experts in these fields.

4   *External support.* Rural communities in Poland enjoy greater financial support from the European Union and tax incentives from the state than Lithuanian ones. This support helps to maintain lower prices of the rural hospitality services in Poland than in Lithuania.

5   *Fierce domestic competition.* Due to the vicinity of the Mazury Lake District, the recreational fishing service providers in the Vistula Delta have to keep prices as low as possible and pursue a flexible pricing policy. The price for accommodation at an angler's lodge on a high-

season weekend might treble compared to the price for accommodation in the low season. Armaitienė and Povilanskas (2009) showed that the lucrativeness of the bed-and-breakfast business is directly related to the prevailing external conditions, the stagnation or development conditions, and the capacity and willingness of the local community to meet the challenges.

### Nemunas Delta as a recreational fishing destination: competitiveness indices

By applying the 'penalty–reward' method (Fuchs and Weiermair 2004), we have identified the basic factors which establish a market entry threshold for the Nemunas Delta as a recreation fishing tourism destination: catches, fishing conditions from the shore, nature and environment, information on fishing regulations and a sauna. These attributes and dimensions must be delivered at a satisfactory level, although an increase in their performance does not, however, lead to an increase in tourist satisfaction.

Performance factors, which are directly connected to the explicit needs and desires of the recreational fishermen in the Nemunas Delta, include catering and grocery services. The available network of catering establishments and grocery shops in the Nemunas Delta is small and does not meet the needs of the recreational fishermen, particularly in the summer and low seasons. Therefore, an increase in supply of catering places and grocery shops in the Nemunas Delta would have a direct positive impact on its competitiveness as a recreational fishing tourism destination (see Figure 11.2).

Figure 11.2 shows the 'Penalty and reward' indices for tourist satisfaction in relation to key attributes and dimensions of the Nemunas Delta as a recreational fishing tourism destination. The attributes and dimensions used as independent variables are: (1) catches; (2) accommodation; (3) catering; (4) fishing guide service; (5) a sauna; (6) fish cleaning, cooking and smoking facilities; (7) fishing conditions from the boat; (8) fishing conditions from the shore; (9) nature and environment; (10) issuance system of the fishing licences; (11) grocery services; (12) information on fishing regulations; and (13) access and parking conditions.

Finally, excitement factors, which are not expected by the recreational fishermen visiting the Nemunas Delta but surprise them positively include: good accommodation, fish cleaning, cooking and smoking facilities, access and parking conditions. The availability of decent and inexpensive accommodation facilities (anglers lodges) with the opportunity to leave a car safely while fishing, and to take a shower, dry wet clothes, clean, cook and/or smoke the catch after the fishing could significantly improve the competitiveness of the Nemunas Delta as a recreational fishing tourism destination both on the domestic and on the inbound tourism market.

Remarkably, neither the issuance system of the fishing licences, nor the fishing guide service or fishing conditions from the boat had any significant

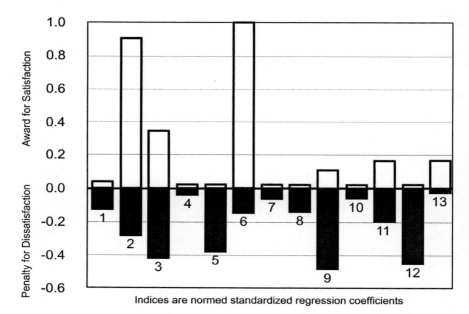

*Figure 11.2* Penalty and reward indices for tourist satisfaction.

impact on the overall satisfaction of the recreational fishermen visiting the Nemunas Delta.

## Discussion

The study revealed that the most important obstacles regarding the sustainable development of the Nemunas Delta as a recreational fishing tourism destination are: lack of professional skills of recreational fishing service providers, low quality, scarcity and high prices of accommodation, catering and other services, low motivation of the personnel and ignorance of the needs of the middle and upper-end recreational fishing tourism market, as well as mismanagement of the fish stock and fishing regulations. Excitement factors, which are not expected by the recreational fishermen visiting the delta but surprised them positively, include: good accommodation, fish cleaning, cooking and smoking facilities, access and parking conditions. The issuance system of the fishing licences, the fishing guide services and fishing conditions from the boat did not have any significant impact on the overall satisfaction of the recreational fishermen visiting the Nemunas Delta.

Therefore, we doubt if the current active efforts of nature conservationists pursuing the fast and complete abolition of commercial fishing in the Nemunas Delta and the Curonian Lagoon are sustainable in social and economic terms. Successful conversion of small-scale commercial fishermen into recreational fishing tourism service providers is impossible without their proper motivation and changes in their inherent psychological abilities, combined with professional training and sufficient initial external funding. The key to success, and to the long-term sustainability of the coastal rural communities and ecosystems of the Nemunas Delta, in our opinion, lies in strengthening local collaboration and joint marketing efforts, developing the right mix of proper high-quality services and amenities for recreational fishing tourism, including adequate quality lodging for anglers, catering and shopping facilities. The success of such approaches is confirmed by several case studies from distant but similar rural and fishing tourism destinations such as Ireland (Cawley *et al.* 2002) and Illinois (Wilson *et al.* 2001).

The economy of coastal communities in the Nemunas Delta must rely on the synergy between nature conservation and the provision of recreational fishing tourism services, environmental farming and low-intensity commercial fishing (Armaitienė *et al.* 2004, 2006; Breber *et al.* 2008; Brown and Schafft 2002; Paquette and Domon 2003; Stockdale *et al.* 2000). The solution to this problem might lie in the gradual shift of the European Common Agricultural Policy towards an increasing support for environmentally-friendly farming and fishing, diversification of rural development and maintenance of biological diversity (Donald *et al.* 2002).

We argue that the challenge is to encourage local people to regard the environment as a resource for sustainable economic development and to enhance their motivation for, and professional skills in, the provision of sustainable high-quality recreational fishing services. It would be a much safer guarantee for the sustainable use of the fish stock and other valuable natural resources if they were conserved for their yield in natural products, and biodiversity protection policies were applied, through a combination of both top-down regulations and local knowledge (Breber 1995; Breber *et al.* 2008; Bridgewater 2002; Doremus 2003; Hurni 2000; Shogren *et al.* 2003; Wallace and Russell 2004). It is critically important to pursue the 'think global, act local' perspective in both the development of tourism and care for the ecosystems (Teo 2002).

More European Union funds should be allocated to develop a proper mix of tourism products and package them in an attractive way to give tourists the opportunity to experience various rural leisure activities and nature amenities (Richards and Hall 2002). Such a comprehensive approach could indeed lead to the development of sustainable recreational fishing in the Nemunas Delta.

## Conclusion and lessons to be learned

The sustainable use of the recreational fish resources is a key precondition for sustainable fish stock management in the Nemunas Delta and the Curonian Lagoon. Appropriate measures would combine the rapidly increasing economic interests of the recreational fishermen in the Nemunas

Delta with the necessity of protecting endangered fish species. The key means of achieving this would be to deliver an appropriate number of well-paid jobs which would be sustainable in the face of declining demand for commercial fishing services.

In shifting from commercial fishing to recreational fishing, it is critically important that there is an understanding of the factors which make a recreational fishing destination competitive. These factors can be categorized as basic factors, performance factors and excitement factors. In terms of the Nemunas Delta, the basic factors establishing a threshold for market entry as a recreational fishing destination included: catches; fishing conditions from the shore; nature and environment; information on fishing regulations; a sauna, and delivery at a satisfactory level. Performance factors, which are directly connected to the explicit needs and desires of recreational fishermen, include catering and grocery services. Excitement factors, which are not expected by the recreational fishermen but surprised them positively included: good accommodation, fish cleaning, cooking and smoking facilities, access and parking conditions. Clearly, then, the issues which need to be addressed in the Nemunas Delta to enhance its competitiveness as a recreational fishing destination are increasing the provision of catering and grocery services and the availability of decent and inexpensive anglers' lodges offering safe parking and facilities for showering, drying wet clothes and cleaning, cooking and/or smoking the catch.

A shift from commercial to recreational fishing requires a different skill set and must be recognized in public sector support strategies. Operating as an employee in a large-scale business is very different from operating a small-scale recreational fishing enterprise. Marketing in particular is an issue which needs to be addressed appropriately and has the potential for public sector support ensuring that professional standards are met. Financial interventions must facilitate the enhancement of the quality of accommodation available to recreational fishermen and enable recreational fishing providers to match the prices offered in competitor destinations. The introduction of flexible pricing policies to match demand is essential.

The role of the public sector in coordinating the development of the Nemunas Delta as a recreational fishing destination cannot be underestimated. It must help to address skills gaps and strengthen local collaboration and joint marketing efforts, developing the right mix of proper high-quality services and amenities for recreational fishing tourism, including the provision of adequate quality accommodation, catering and shopping facilities. It must ensure that the area is able to offer an appropriate mix of products and services to meet customer needs while achieving a holistic approach to the management of the declining fish stocks. European Union funding must be used strategically to promote these endeavours. Striking a balance between nature conservation and a mix of economic development activities, including recreational fishing, will be the key to sustainable economic development in the Nemunas Delta.

# References

Arlinghaus, R. (2004) 'Angelfischerei in Deutschland – eine soziale und ökono-mische Analyse', in *Berichte des IGB*, 18, Berlin: IGB.

Armaitienė, A. and Povilanskas, R. (2009) 'Sustainable dune tourism on the Curonian spit: management principles', in A. Armaitienė, and R. Povilanskas (eds), *Perspectives of Seaside Tourism: Challenges for Science and Business. International Conference Proceedings*. Klaipeda University, pp. 59–62.

Armaitienė, A., Povilanskas, R. and Jones, E. (2006) 'Lithuania: sustainable rural tourism development in the Baltic coastal region', in D. Hall, B. Marciszewska and M. Smith (eds) *Tourism in the New Europe: The Challenges and Opportunities of EU Enlargement*. Wallingford: CABI, pp. 183–95.

Armaitienė, A., Raišutienė, J., Popa, L. and Poruncia, A. (2004) 'Comparative aspects of cultural sustainability for tourism development in European coastal wetlands', in D. Green (ed.) *Delivering Sustainable Coasts: Connecting Science and Policy – 7th International Multi-Disciplinary Symposium on Coastal Zone Research, Management and Planning, Aberdeen, September 2004*. Cambridge: Cambridge Publications Ltd, 2, pp. 678–9.

Bański, J. (2008) *Wiejskie obszary sukcesu gospodarczego*. Studia Obszarów Wiejskich, 14, IGiPZ PAN, Warsaw: PTG.

Bhutta, K. S. and Huq, F. (1999) 'Benchmarking – best practices: an integrated approach', *Benchmarking: An International Journal* 6(3): 176–209.

Bouma, J., Varallyay, G. and Batjes, N. H. (1998) 'Principal land use changes antici-pated in Europe', *Agriculture, Ecosystems & Environment* 67: 103–19.

Breber, P. (1995) 'The situation of lagoons in Italy today', *Journal of Coastal Conservation* 1: 173–5.

Breber, P., Povilanskas, R. and Armaitienė, A. (2008) 'Recent evolution of fishery and land reclamation in Curonian and Lesina lagoons', *Hydrobiologia* 611: 105–14.

Bridgewater, P. B. (2002) 'Biosphere reserves: special places for people and nature', *Environmental Science & Policy* 5: 9–12.

Brown, L. D. and Schafft, K. A. (2002) 'Population deconcentration in Hungary during the post-socialist transformation', *Journal of Rural Studies* 18: 233–44.

Bryden, J. and Bollman, R. (2000) 'Rural employment in industrialized countries', *Agricultural Economics* 22: 185–97.

Cawley, M., Gaffey, S. and Gillmor, D. A. (2002) 'Localization and global reach in rural tourism: Irish evidence', *Tourist Studies* 2(1): 63–86.

Donald, P. F., Pisano, G., Rayment M. D. and Pain, D. J. (2002) 'The Common Agricultural Policy, EU enlargement and the conservation of Europe's farmland birds', *Agriculture, Ecosystems & Environment* 89: 167–82.

Doremus, H. (2003) 'A policy portfolio approach to biodiversity protection on private lands', *Environmental Science & Policy* 6: 217–32.

Fuchs, M. and Weiermair, K. (2004) 'Destination benchmarking: an indicator-system's potential for exploring guest satisfaction', *Journal of Travel Research* 42: 212.

Gudelis, V. (1998) *Lietuvos pajūris ir jjūris*. Vilnius: Academia.

Hale, A. (2001) 'Representing the Cornish: contesting heritage interpretation in Cornwall', *Tourist Studies* 1(2): 185–96.

Hurni, H. (2000) 'Assessing sustainable land management (SLM)', *Agriculture, Ecosystems & Environment* 81: 83–92.

Inbakaran, R. and Jackson, M. (2005) 'Marketing regional tourism: how better to target and address community attitudes to tourism', *Journal of Vacation Marketing* 11(4): 323–39.

Lanjouw, J. O. and Lanjouw, P. (2001) 'The rural non-farm sector: Issues and evidence from developing countries', *Agricultural Economics* 26: 1–23.

Marciszewska, B. (2006) 'Tourism in Poland: changes in policy, management and education', in D. Hall, B. Marciszewska and M. Smith (eds) *Tourism in the New Europe: The Challenges and Opportunities of EU Enlargement*. Wallingford: CABI, pp. 127–38.

Murphy, A. E. (2003) 'Illustrating the utility of a modified gap analysis as a regional tourism planning tool: case study of potential Japanese and German travelers to the Cowichan Region', *Journal of Travel Research* 41: 400–9.

Paquette, S. and Domon, S. (2003) 'Changing ruralities, changing landscapes: exploring social recomposition using a multiscale approach', *Journal of Rural Studies* 19: 425–44.

Povilanskas, R. (2004) *Landscape Management on the Curonian Spit: A Cross-border Perspective*. Klaipėda: EUCC.

—— (2008) *Nemuno deltos regioninio parko rekreacinės žvejybos programa*. Klaipėda: EUCC.

Povilanskas, R., Purvinas, M. and Urbis, A. (2002) *Minija ir Karklė: Pamario paveldo kaimai ir jų aplinka*. Klaipėda: EUCC.

Richards, G. and Hall, D. (2002) *Tourism and Sustainable Community Development*. London: Routledge.

Roepstorff, A. and Povilanskas, R. (1995) 'On the concepts of nature protection and sustainable use of natural resources: a case study from the Curonian lagoon', in V. Gudelis, R. Povilanskas and A. Roepstorff (eds) *Coastal Conservation and Management in the Baltic Region: Proceedings of the EUCC-WWF Conference, 3–7 May, 1994, Rīga – Klaipeda – Kaliningrad*. Klaipėda: University Publishers, pp. 223–32.

Shogren, J. F., Parkhurst, G. M. and Settle, C. (2003) 'Integrating economics and ecology to protect nature on private lands: models, methods and mindsets', *Environmental Science & Policy* 6: 233–42.

Stockdale, A., Findlay A. and Short, D. (2000) 'The repopulation of rural Scotland: Opportunity and threat', *Journal of Rural Studies* 16: 243–57.

Švagždys, A. (2006) 'Condition and opportunities of recreational fishing in the Lower Nemunas River and the Curonian Lagoon', *Žuvininkystė Lietuvoje* 6: 195–206.

Teo, P. (2002) 'Striking a balance for sustainable tourism: implications of the discourse on globalisation', *Journal of Sustainable Tourism* 10(6): 459–74.

Vaitekūnas, S., Armaitienė, A. and Povilanskas, R. (2001) 'Social and geographical strengths and weaknesses of tourism development in the Curonian Lagoon region', *Tiltai* 1(14): 51–8.

Wallace, G. and Russell, A. (2004) 'Eco-cultural tourism as a means for the sustainable development of culturally marginal and environmentally sensitive regions', *Tourist Studies* 4(3): 235–54.

Wilson, S., Fesenmaier, D. R., Fesenmaier, J. and Van Es, J. C. (2001) 'Factors for success in rural tourism development', *Journal of Travel Research* 40: 132–8.

# 12 From obsolescent fish farm to developing ecotourism destination

## The Aranyponty ('Golden Carp') fishponds complex in rural Hungary

*David Watkins*

## Introduction

This chapter examines the history of a medium-sized family firm in rural Hungary. It tracks the changes in strategy that have turned it from a near-derelict and bankrupt fish farm in the aftermath of Communism to a highly innovative fishery around which have been built a series of related businesses that together comprise a successful ecotourism destination. The business reflects not only Hungary's transition from Communism to European Union (EU) membership, but at the same time reasserts and reinterprets far older farming and cultural traditions in a modern way. The firm now employs around 80 people in fish farming, raising spawn for sale to other farms, and fish processing. The firm exports much of its production, mainly to Germany and Austria, but including as far away as the UK.

However, the associated businesses which have been stimulated by the fishery and its natural environment are now of equal interest – and perhaps of greater future potential. Since the family took over the ownership of the farm a heritage museum has been developed using original artefacts to display the development of inland fish-farming since early modern times. This formed the nucleus of a complex which now includes a restaurant, hotel and spa. The restaurant features local products – particularly the fish. The buildings are constructed as exemplars of eco-friendly production and low-carbon maintenance. For example, heat pumps are used to tap a geothermal source and the owners are now also examining micro-hydro generation. An increasing market for this part of the business is foreign naturalists (particularly bird-watchers) and sport fishermen. However, to cater for a more local market, festivals are organized throughout the year when local people come to catch fish which then are cooked in the open air to the accompaniment of traditional folk entertainment.

One of the business drivers pushing the diversification is paradoxically the increased costs of operating the farm itself in a Ramsar/Natura 2000 site, where the 'stewardship' function is estimated by the Lévai family to have increased costs by up to 50 per cent. Producers in protected areas often see expansion into tourism services as an obvious move. However, it is not always easy to achieve success. At Aranyponty there has been considerable investment in diversification, with more people now employed on that side of the business than with fish. Yet the original business still forms the rock on which the enterprise is built, not just conceptually but in terms of income streams.

## Origin and development of the fisheries

The tradition of inland fish production in fishponds, particularly of carp, goes way back to the Middle Ages in Central and Eastern Europe, and nowhere more so than in Hungary. These agro-fishery practices did not die out under Communism – indeed, much valuable research work was undertaken at that time and Hungarian advisors helped other countries to establish fisheries of their own. However, that era did see a sustained lack of investment in Hungary's national infrastructure, including that in fishponds.

There has been fishing along the valley of the Sárvíz River since humans first came to Hungary, and fishponds have been in existence here for more than a century. At that time the present site was part of an estate owned by an important Hungarian landowner, Count Zichy, some of whose family lived in what is now the Fisheries Museum. However, the story of the present incarnation of the Aranyponty and the Rétszilas Fishponds Nature Reserve goes back to 1989, when the predecessor of today's company – the Association of Small Aranyponty Fish Farmers – was formed by Ferenc Lévai Snr. This was the first private sector fish farming enterprise anywhere in Hungary.

The new company's initial business areas were domestic and international fish trading, consultancy and the growing of spawn. A head office was set up at Százhalombatta, with the trading activities carried out from a business park in Gödöllő. It had instant credibility, even in the difficult time of transition, because of the reputation that Ferenc Lévai Snr had already established.

Ferenc Lévai Snr was born in 1950. In 1972, he joined the TEHAG Warm Water Fish Hatchery at Százhalombatta, where he was central to the major developments that took place in modern farm fishing techniques in Hungary at that time. By the time he left in 1988, he had risen to the post of Assistant Director of the facility. His expertise was internationally recognized, and he often worked abroad in a consultancy role, establishing new hatcheries in Greece, Sudan, Iraq and – particularly – in Algeria, where he set up a national fresh water fishing system from scratch.

Under Communism, the fishponds were operated by the Mezőfalva Agricultural Combine. After the transition, the first private firm to try farming the fishponds soon went into liquidation. In 1993, the Lévai family took over the lease. A year later, the operation was privatized in an open auction. The Lévais by then thought they knew the potential of the ponds and bid considerably more for the freeholds – 40 million Florints, about €150,000 – than any of their competitors, taking on substantial loans at interest rates of 30 per cent per annum to do so. Many thought them mad to pay this much, and even given their superior, 'insider' knowledge, it was still a substantial risk.[1] Under Communism, investment had been neglected. The ponds were overgrown. All the buildings had been stripped out. It took five or six years of hard work and infrastructure investment to put the fishponds back into efficient production. The bank loan taken out to purchase the fishponds in 1994 has now been repaid in full, though the company continues to service a planned level of debt.

The firm now owns about 1000 hectares of fishponds, but the main activity remains at the Örspuszta-Rétszilas Fishponds, which comprise some 760 hectares. This is also the centre for research and experimentation, as well as for the diversification into a range of related tourism/eco-tourism activities.

A wide range of fish farming activities is carried out on the basis of polyculture, with carp, Chinese schemer, bighead carp, grass carp, pike, catfish, pike-perch (zander) and tench being the main types of fish produced, as well as ornamentals. There is also a deliberate emphasis on the breeding of fish indigenous to the Carpathian Basin, for example: tench, yellow crucian carp, bream, golden orfe, perch and asp.

## Present structure and operations

The business is still headed by Ferenc Lévai Snr and is 95 per cent family-owned with just one other shareholder. Within the family, Ferenc Snr controls 50 per cent of shares, with the remainder divided between Ferenc Jnr and his sister.

Although now a success in the 'free-market' economy, Ferenc Snr's approach was conditioned by working for 19 years in the state sector where there was never any prospect of additional reward for extra effort or hours worked. Because of this he came to believe that the intrinsic worth of any job was the main reward, an attitude that he transferred into the monetized economy. 'Success,' he says, 'is when I feel good inside my skin. The best gift is to do what you love to do.' However, this should not be taken as a sign of business naivety; Ferenc Snr can be far-sighted and aware of cost trends. He began investing in alternative energy sources in 1990 – as much as a defensive measure as for ecological reasons – when he foresaw energy prices would rise. The first such investment was to use heat pumps to tap a geothermal source. He has subsequently expanded the use of heat pumps and is now also looking at micro-hydro generation. Ideally he would like the business to be completely independent of external energy suppliers for reasons of both cost reduction and energy security.

Ferenc Jnr came of age during the transition and so was always subject to a wider range of influences than his father. He studied business and economics in the US in 1993–94, and again in 1996–98, and only later obtained a second diploma in fishery management in Hungary. On his return from the States he worked in local government and in the development of industrial parks, only joining his father's firm in 1999. Although he felt it was 'always his destiny' to work with fish, and to do so within the context of the family business, he was not necessarily enthusiastic to do so at first and still speaks about the personal compromises that need to be made in a family firm. Although now central to the business, he still seems keener than his father on maintaining outside interests, such as his consuming hobby of motor sports, where he is a leading rally driver nationally and is known as a very competitive driver.

The business is currently undergoing something of a reorganization, with a recognition that it is no longer possible or desirable for everything to be run directly by Ferenc Snr. Ferenc Jnr says: 'The key strategic decisions are still in my father's hands, but day-to-day operations will change. Now we often do what is easiest, cheapest or fastest, but these don't necessarily make the most business sense. We need better cooperation between the different areas of operation.' Recently, responsibility for the three main areas of the business has been allocated to different family members. Ferenc Jnr concentrates on running the technical side of things, ensuring that equipment, machinery and facilities are kept in working order, while his sister is taking charge of tourism development. However, Ferenc Snr is only 60 and shows little sign so far of wanting to withdraw from the business

There are three principal elements to the business: fish farming, sports fishing and tourism. Farmed fish production and the associated activities still account for around 80 per cent of turnover, with sport fishing accounting for about 10 per cent (as does tourism). However, the balance is expected to change over a 10-year time horizon if current expectations are met. Fish farming will stay much the same in volume terms, although moving to products with a higher added value, while sport fishing is expected to be stable or perhaps grow just a little. The main growth is expected in tourism, which could account for 30–40 per cent of total income in 10 years time. However, people visit Aranyponty for many reasons and to achieve this may require the identification and pursuit of particular niches. Aranyponty currently employs a total of 70 people, including those at satellite locations as far away as Hortobágy. No area of the business is making a loss, but Ferenc Jnr recognizes the need for more careful analysis to determine how significant the profits are in relation to the time and effort invested in generating them. More people are employed on the tourism side of the business than in the fishery sector, even though the profits generated by the latter are far greater. Although there is no formal plan, the general strategy is clear and the hope is that the tourism side will eventually prove as profitable.

Labour supply is a challenge throughout the fishery sector; and in the Hungarian economy in general, with a shortage of unskilled/manual labour. The business busses in workers from up to 15km away. The Lévais have learned the hard way that unless they do so, employees don't bother to come in or arrive late. The going rate for employees in the business is typically €1.5 per hour. Pay rates for men and women are equal, with women perceived as being more reliable than men. The labour problem became more severe when the authorities clamped down on illegal migrant workers (especially from Romania and Ukraine), but the recent eastward expansion of the EU may reverse the trend. Unsurprisingly, Aranyponty is looking at mechanization and automating production wherever possible. In particular, it aims to take the physical labour out of tasks in order to recruit more women. These labour issues are another business driver towards the expansion into tourism rather than continuing to grow the fisheries side of the group.

Hungary's relatively recent accession to the EU increased regulation and to that extent has made running the business more complex.[2] But to set against this there are benefits such as access to some new kinds of grant aid.

## The core fisheries businesses

Aranyponty's principal business is not furnishing fish for the table but rather the supply of live fish for stocking sport-fishing lakes. This accounts for 70 per cent of its fishery production, with the balance going into the human food chain. The sport-fishing market breaks down as follows: 70–75 per cent common carp, 5 per cent carnivorous species (pike, pike-perch, catfish), with the remainder being grass carp and silver carp. The general aim is to provide fish-ponds in Hungary and wholesalers with a wide stock of fish, including plant-eaters, predators and 'accessory' fish such as crucian carp and miniature catfish. The export market is concerned primarily with predators, spawn, and materials for use in the organic breeding of fish. Fish are transported in twelve specially adapted lorries, some of which are equipped with liquid oxygen systems, thus enabling the firm to offer delivery of live fish throughout most of Europe all year round, regardless of external temperatures.

The fish production side of the business is now well established and stable, with both volumes and prices the same for several years now. In fact, for the Lévais it is *too* stable! Particularly in the market for table fish there seems to be a perception in the marketplace that carp is not a 'modern' fish like the ubiquitous salmon and the recently fashionable sea bass; indeed, some analysts feel that demand will actually decline. Fish production for the table has been stagnant in Hungary for some years now. Freshwater fish consumption is relatively low on a national scale, except for the traditional consumption of carp at Christmas. It is seen not only as an old-fashioned foodstuff but an inconvenient one owing to its boniness. Average Hungarian fish consumption is only 3kg per person per year compared with the Western European average of 24kg per person per year. Although 2–3 per cent of the meals consumed in Hungary contain fish, only 1.5 per cent of those eaten by the indigenous population do so.

## Prospects for developing the core business

This situation has led to a number of innovations, including an attempt to move to organic production, driven by a search for both higher quality and higher margins; adding value by de-boning; and a hunt for new species which might be farmed successfully for the first time.

The movement towards organic production has been the fastest growing branch of agriculture all over Europe. Inland fisheries are no exception, and the firm has been at the forefront of developments, playing a leading role in the establishment of national standards for organic fish production. Technical procedures were codified and tested in 2001, and the final versions were submitted for international audit. Organic inspections under the new standards regime took place alongside the first conversions to organic production in 2002. Full transition of a pond to organic production takes two years. Reception in the marketplace was very favourable in terms of quality, but the Hungarian market for organics is not yet well enough developed to bear the price premium. While production costs are comparatively high (the organic feed is of a grade suitable for human consumption and is therefore very costly), the retail premium for organic products is comparatively low and the market (principally exports to Austria and Germany) is small. Organic fish therefore currently represents only 2–3 per cent of the company's turnover from fish production. Preparation of fish for direct consumption is outsourced, but this is then sold under the Aranyponty brand.

The company is currently experimenting with the farming of pike. Pike are notorious predators, and this is one reason why no one has successfully farmed them before. If successful, this innovation would represent an important commercial breakthrough. Ferenc Lévai Snr also has ideas to experiment with new 'modern' fish products that are boneless and able to compete with the trend towards fast or convenience foods. He sees this as a defensive measure which will maintain the existing market but not necessarily expand it, except in niche areas such as hospital food.

## Conservation and ecotourism potential

The Rétszilas fish ponds are located in an area of special environmental interest. At the time the business was being established, the area was in the process of being designated a National Park under Hungarian law and as a Ramsar site under the intergovernmental Convention on Wetlands.[3] It was therefore clear from the outset that the company would have to operate and develop in an eco-conscious manner. This accorded with Ferenc Snr's values, but was by no means the driving force in developing the business. For this business, on this site, operating on sound ecological principles normally also makes good economic sense, and the founder is vocal in his identification of the conflicts that do occur. One EU-level issue that rankles with Ferenc Snr is the way in which agri-environmental payments are allocated.[4] At issue is the fact that Aranyponty, as a landowner at a Natura 2000 site, receives exactly the same agri-environment payment as a fish-farm owner at a non-Natura 2000 site although the costs of operation are likely to be higher. Ferenc Snr puts these at 20–40 per cent more. He perceives this to be a twofold problem. First, inland fisheries are weak and poorly co-ordinated nationally and internationally compared to marine fisheries. Second, wetlands businesses tend to be small and are poorly able to resist the agricultural and livestock lobbies which are dominated by large MNCs. Since the incentive system does not reward good stewardship, he feels too much is left to his own personal motivation and commitment – which other owner-managers may not share. Thus, because of the designations, Aranyponty cannot always drain out its ponds at the optimum time for fish farming since this may disrupt the life cycle of birds on the site. Although Aranyponty receives some Natura 2000 funds for on-site conservation work, these constraints represent a real cost to the firm.

Although there is a state monitoring system for water quality, Aranyponty has established its own laboratory and undertakes frequent testing. This facility is run by Ferenc Jnr's wife, Michelle, who is a microbiologist by training. Ferenc Jnr claims that the quality of water leaving the site is usually higher than that coming in and more generally believes that the company has a positive environmental impact. The management of the fishponds prevents them from silting up and becoming progressively vegetated, so that biodiversity would actually be *lower* without the natural operation of the business.

The area is very important for breeding water birds and for migrating geese and cranes – thousands of geese use the site in autumn. However, the natural endowment covers not just the ponds, fishery and birdlife, but also the production of reeds and willow twigs, and the rearing of indigenous farm animals. There are now 30 grey cattle, 50 racka sheep and 10 mangalica swine on site which graze on the grass-covered islands between the ponds. There are also water buffalo. This rich natural environment, and the protected area status designed to secure it, are used in promoting the site, but this is only beginning to be done in a targeted way. The tourist business attracted so far has only a small eco-tourism component in relation to the burgeoning market and the potential of the site on which the firm is located.

## Diversification into tourism

If the Lévais had rested on their laurels when the fish farming activity was securely in place, the business would have been successful, but little known outside its own locality.

However, in 1999, with the production infrastructure in place, the business began to diversify into tourism-related activities. As the story is now told, this was not a conscious decision: indeed, Ferenc Lévai Jnr describes his father as an instinctive manager but *not* a planner. In that year, through personal contacts, the Dutch government offered to part-finance the first (and indeed only) fishing museum in Hungary. This grant amounted to about 30 per cent of the one million Forint cost. It seems that at the time the motivation for establishing the museum was not tourism-related; it was rather a desire to record and celebrate the traditional way of life of the inland fishermen and their families at a time when this was fast disappearing. However, when the museum was completed, it was clear that this was also a tourism asset in its own right. At this point the fishing ponds were opened to a wider public than the serious sport anglers, who were previously the only people fishing them directly. A series of 'fairs' was established which included fishing competitions, entertainment, and food and drink. These are now held three times a year and attract approximately 2500 people each time. The most significant fair is that held on St Peter's Day. This now includes a 'Fish Olympics' in which various fish-related games are organized. Although the site could accommodate far more people, the main constraint is the lack of overnight rooms on site or in the vicinity. Consequently almost all participants are from those parts of Hungary where one can travel to and from the fisheries within the day. The business now plans to develop a number of low-priced cabins that families can rent with the aim of attracting visitors to stay for a longer period and increase the spend per head.

Foreign visitors are extremely rare, but no real attempt has been made so far to attract them either to the fairs – or for that matter for longer periods to explore the fishing and wildlife attractions. With one eye to this possibility, a spa or 'Wellness Centre' has recently been constructed in an attempt to further diversify the range of attractions on offer. The opening of the centre was delayed because of teething problems which the Lévais put down to the difficulty of obtaining good quality basic trade services such as plumbers and electricians in their locality. No real research on how to attract foreign visitors has been undertaken as yet, but there could be good potential for this, because some people have sought out the site without any real promotion beyond the locality. The fishponds site offers comfortable accommodation and good food with straightforward road links to Budapest airport. Foreign visitors, especially small groups of birdwatchers or other naturalists, artists, photographers, and those with an interest in Hungarian history, culture and music could be attracted to pay a premium price (by local standards) that would still be perceived by the client as representing good value for money (by international standards).

The popularity of the fairs has led to some local companies running 'family days' for their employees. Other firms visit the site to combine working conferences with fishing and other touristic pursuits in the afternoon. The existence of markets like this has led to the successive identification of further opportunities such as the development of the fish restaurant (which had started life as a staff restaurant and a place to entertain clients), conference meeting rooms, and the overnight accommodation mentioned above. Recently the facility has also become popular for wedding receptions, birthdays and other celebrations. Most people now visit as part of a group rather than as individuals.

So rather than a planned expansion into tourism, developments have taken place on an *ad hoc* basis as opportunities have arisen and further needs of existing customers have been identified. The owners describe this as 'gap filling': thus the predominance of day fishing led to the provision of cheap accommodation so people can fish for longer; the use of the Wellness Centre in the summer threw up the idea of making an artificial beach, and so on. The unifying principle seems to be keeping people on site for longer to increase the customers' spending. Future plans seem to confirm this: wine-tasting events; provision of bikes and trails; summer camp activities for the children, etc. Although other inland fishery establishments in Hungary have followed Aranyponty's lead into tourism and have some elements of the firm's marketing offer, the Lévais feel that they have several strengths which will keep them ahead: first mover advantage, which they reinforce through regular innovations such as those above; a more diverse range of services; and the unique quality of their surroundings.[5]

## The evolving strategy of Aranyponty

SMEs often do not have a formal planning approach to their development. Sometimes strategy develops as a less formal process, with a *post hoc* rationalization of what powerful individuals wanted to do anyway. Equally, successful entrepreneurs are oriented towards identifying and exploiting opportunities as they arise (the 'gap filling' that the Lévais describe as one key to their success). Entrepreneurship in the fish farming sector seems rarely studied in a formal way, although Kendree and Stucker (1983) is an interesting early exception and is also case-based.

Identifying and analysing strategy in SMEs are notoriously difficult. Whittington (1993) gives an appealing systematization of different models business strategists have proposed. He suggests strategic management insights can be classified into four main 'Schools': Classical, Evolutionary, Processual and Systemic.

Bhalla *et al.* (2009) and Basuki and Watkins (2005) suggest adding the Resource-Based View as a distinct 'School'. They also attempt to test out the validity of these 'Schools' – developed largely to analyse strategy within the context of large organizations – to smaller and family-based firms. In this, they claim some success, while also counselling that it is very difficult to interpret strategic behaviour retrospectively when examining *any* business cases, where a 'reading' of the situation may say more about the analyst's mental models than the firm's actual behaviour (Bhalla *et al.* 2005).

But however provisional it may be, it is instructive to attempt to use this framework – which embraces and structures almost all the 'classic' insights into to strategic management – to assess the development of the Aranyponty business from fishponds alone into the basis of a diversified group which sees most future potential in tourism rather than production and processing. In order to do so, we first need to examine in a little more detail what each of these 'Schools' actually means. The 'Classical School' sees the world as logical, with markets pre-eminent, and profit maximization as the only goal. Within this context it is possible to plan with some realistic prospect that it will be possible to follow the plan through to completion. This view is represented by the work of Chandler (1962), Ansoff (1965), and the earlier writings of Porter (1980). In direct contrast, the 'Evolutionary School' adopts an essentially Darwinian approach in which markets are all-powerful but unpredictable, strategy can only be short term, so any real planning is not only futile but wasteful of resources. This view is represented in the work of Hall and Hitch (1939), Alchian (1950) and Williamson (1975, 1991). The 'Processual School' goes beyond traditional economic rationality and contests profit maximization as the genuine target of firms, which it sees as having multiple objectives reflecting the goals of multiple stakeholders rather than just those of the owners. Behaviour tends to be satisficing rather than maximizing, and strategies 'emerge' rather than are planned. This view is associated with scholars such as Cyert and March (1963), Simon (1957, 1979), Pettigrew (1973) and Mintzberg (1973, 1978). The 'Systemic School' sees strategy as a manifestation of corporate culture. It encompasses planning, but sees the context – and therefore the goals – as not necessarily determined by a purely market perspective. This view is represented in the work of Marris (1964); Granovetter (1985); Swedberg *et al.* (1987). Finally, the Resource- Based View – which has been quite prominent in recent years – emphasizes strategic intent. It argues that firms can obtain a competitive advantage in the medium term through identifying and developing core competencies, and dynamically harmonizing these with market opportunities. This view is associated with Grant (1991), Hamel and Prahalad (1989, 1990), and the later work of Porter (1985).

When Ferenc Snr began his professional career, it was under the rigid state-planning system associated with Communism. Although philosophically this was diametrically opposite to the *über*-capitalistic world-view of the strategists from the classical school, in formal terms it was paradoxically equivalent in the sense of putting 'The Plan' at its heart. Ferenc Snr would have learned through his early experiences that delivery of the plan for the enterprise and business success was by no means an equivalent outcome. So it should come as no surprise that, since Hungary became part of a more marketized economy, the firm has never exhibited the explicit planning characteristics suggested by the classical school.

But nor does the extreme opposite perspective posited by the evolutionary theorists fit terribly well. Although in a general sense, extreme market uncertainty was certainly a factor in the immediate post-Communist period, Aranyponty had few effective competitors because of its unique geographical factor endowments (and recall that in less able hands even these had not guaranteed business success). Perhaps the framework suggested by the evolutionary theorists does not apply well to firms such as Aranyponty in niche markets where entry costs are high? Furthermore, there were clearly 'plans' in Ferenc Snr's mind in a generalized sense, although these were not always business directed in a traditional manner.

Consider next the Resource-Based View (RBV). It is a truism that any firm relies on its resources, and those at Aranyponty are certainly difficult to replicate, if not totally unique. However, the term 'resource' is used by RBV theorists in a more technical sense. It relates to the identification and development of unique competencies within the firm which are difficult to replicate and therefore generate sustained competitive advantage. In this sense, the key 'competencies' of the firm are wholly technical, deriving initially from Ferenc Snr's expertise in inland fish farming. The RBV would suggest that in a family firm, this competence should be maintained by sending Ferenc Jnr to learn about the most recent technical developments in fish farming and that the firm would remain focused on this business. Instead, Ferenc Snr sent his son to the USA to learn about modern business methods first and only later to study aquaculture. Moreover, it has been the physical resources of the firm – in particular those related to its location, which have driven business growth, particularly the diversification into tourism-related activity.

The view adopted by the 'Processual School' seems to fit the development of Aranyponty much more closely. Throughout, Ferenc Snr has had the multiple objectives one might expect to see and has not attempted to maximize short-run profit. In particular, environmental considerations were well to the fore long in advance of this becoming fashionable. He demonstrated classical satisficing behaviour in trying to live 'the good life' in a rural setting with his family rather than maximizing his income, for example, by developing his international consultancy opportunities. Overall, in less jargonistic terms, the company's development strategy under Ferenc Snr appears to have been: wait and see what happens and respond accordingly. This archetypal 'emergent' approach has served the business well throughout Ferenc Snr's tenure in control, although as Aranyponty approaches the key challenge of transition from one generation to another, even he is now applying business analysis in a more formal way. He has thus begun to adopt some of his son's vocabulary and now talks about the firm as 'needing to develop

*Table 12.1* Turnover by activity

| Activity | 1999 (%) | 2007 (%) | 2015 (%) |
|----------|----------|----------|----------|
| Farmed fish | 70 | 80 | 50 |
| Sport fishing | 30 | 10 | 10 |
| Tourism | 0 | 10 | 40 |

higher value-added products', such as organic fish. In terms of the Whittington framework, this seems to indicate an incipient change in behaviour to one which would be more readily acknowledged by adherents to the 'Systemic School'. Aranyponty is becoming more planning oriented, but this is firmly rooted in the evolved context, reflecting not just the culture of the locality, but the organizational culture which has developed within the firm itself. This is best demonstrated by the conscious decision to plan a shift in the balance between the different areas of the business, which took place around 2007. Table 12.1 shows the balance between the three main operating areas some eight years earlier, and the projections a similar period in advance.

These figures represent the targeted percentage share of income, with the fisheries business static in real terms and income growth seen as coming from tourism, at 40 per cent of a larger projected income.

## General lessons for SME development in rural areas

It is always dangerous to try generalizing from one very specific case study, but the experiences of Aranyponty do suggest a small number of general lessons.

The first has to do with out-region education. Aranyponty's founder very early on recognized that the general business skills available to the firm were weaker than the technical ones, which were – and remain – internationally competitive. He therefore sent his son to study not locally but in a location likely to maximize the introduction of new information and thought patterns. It was an added advantage that in so doing his son did not develop close competitive social networks within Hungary, which might have encouraged him to stay in, say, Budapest if he had studied there. In retrospect, this seems to have greatly strengthened the likelihood of a successful succession within the firm. This is a much more sophisticated approach than one sees usually in successful rural enterprises where the education and training task is often seen as ensuring succession by 'cloning' the founder.

The second has to do with labour supply. The local supply of willing male labour dried up well before the shift towards tourism and was a real constraint on growth. But it is clear that in comparison to heavier work in all weathers in a 'fishy' environment, many of the new jobs on the tourism side of the enterprise – although traditionally equally low paid – are more attractive, and more labour has become available. This seems to be as a result of greater participation in the labour market and is therefore 'real' growth rather than displaced activity.

Third, the move into tourism also, in the clichéd language of the SWOT analysis, turns the idyllic location from what was a 'weakness' for a fish farm into a 'strength' for a sustainable tourism destination. What was formerly a constraint in terms not just of constricted labour supply, but also access to industrial services and elevated logistics costs, now becomes a competitive advantage.

Finally, there is a lesson for advisors. Too often advisors come to the rural enterprise sector from a training or consulting background where the norms are to privilege the development of a detailed business plan to achieve financially driven goals around a single business focus: behaviour categorized as falling very much within the classical school of strategic thought above, let alone any of the more recent and sophisticated paradigms. Aranyponty, as the discussion above hopefully shows, does not wholly fit *any* of the kinds of model developed in the Anglo-Saxon world and in the context of much larger firms. Nevertheless, it has been internationally successful in aquaculture and seems set to repeat this success in tourism.

## Acknowledgements

The early part of this chapter draws heavily on material collected by the author and Tim Jones of DJEnvironmental, a UK-based consultancy, as part of an EU project entitled *Probioprise* (FP 6: 1.1.6.3/ 018356). This was an initiative of *Fauna and Flora International, European Bureau for Conservation Development* and *EFMD* (formerly *European Foundation for Management Development*) on behalf of DG Research which was intended to inform policy towards biodiversity-based entrepreneurship. The public summary report is available as Dickson *et al.* (2007).

## Notes

1  At this point the business environment *generally* was highly uncertain, with elements taken for granted in Western Europe, such as a stable tax regime and well-resourced business support agencies, in flux. For example, chambers of commerce initially had public law status on the German model, including obligatory membership introduced from 1994. In 1998, this obligation was removed, although around 60 per cent of firms remained members; chambers were also given additional powers from January 1 2004 in vocational training and other spheres to prepare for EU accession. Similarly, the balance between local and national taxation has changed over this period, which Ferenc Snr noted as having adverse effects. For a critical account of the state of SMEs in Hungary pre- and post-accession, see Tibor (2006).
2  See ibid.
3  The area was officially designated a nature reserve, part of the Duna-Ipoly National Park, in 1994.

4   While this may in practice be more to do with the Hungarian Government's allocation of the national envelope, the perception at the firm level is clearly that this is an EU issue.
5   The Lévais are well placed to judge. Another of their business activities is concerned with the technical side of maintaining the quality of other people's fisheries through their Aranyponty Club Lake Service.

## References

Alchian, A. A. (1950) 'Uncertainty, evolution and economic theory', *Journal of Political Economy* 58(3): 211–21.

Ansoff, I. (1965) *Corporate Strategy*. New York: McGraw-Hill.

Basuki, W. and Watkins, D. (2005) 'Gender and strategic choice in entrepreneurial ventures', paper presented at SMU EDGE Conference, Bridging the Gap: Entrepreneurship in Theory and Practice, Singapore Management University.

Bhalla, A., Henderson, S. and Watkins, D. (2005) 'The origins, lessons and definition of entrepreneurial achievement: a multi-paradigm perspective *via* the case method', in A. Fayolle, P. Kyrö and J. Ulijn (eds) *Entrepreneurship Research in Europe: Outcomes and Perspectives*. Cheltenham: Edward Elgar, pp. 150–73.

Bhalla, A., Lampel, J., Henderson, S. and Watkins, D. (2009) 'Exploring alternative strategic management paradigms in high-growth ethnic and non-ethnic family firms', *Small Business Economics* 32(1): 77–94.

Chandler, A. D. (1962) *Strategy and Structure*. Cambridge, MA: MIT Press.

Cyert, R. M. and March, J. G. (1963) *A Behavioural Theory of the Firm*. Englewood Cliffs, NJ: Prentice Hall.

Dickson, B., Watkins, D. and Foxall, J. (2007) *The Working Partnership: SMEs and Biodiversity*. Cambridge: Fauna and Flora International.

Granovetter, M. (1985) 'Economic action and social structure: the problem of embeddedness', *American Journal of Sociology* 91(3): 481–510.

Grant, R. M. (1991) 'The resource-based theory of competitive advantage: implications for strategy formulation', *California Management Review* 33(3): 114–35.

Hall, R. L. and Hitch, C. J. (1939) 'Price theory and business behaviour', *Oxford Economic Papers* 2: 12–45.

Hamel, G. and Prahalad, C. K. (1989) 'Strategic intent', *Harvard Business Review* 67(3): 63–76.

—— (1990) 'The core competence of the corporation', *Harvard Business Review*, 68(3): 79–91.

Kendree, J. M. S. and Stucker, J. C. (1983) 'Putting resources to work in aquaculture: the Georgetown story/entrepreneurs in the fish-farming business', *Business & Economic Review* (October): 23–9.

Marris, R. (1964) *The Economic Theory of the Managerial Capitalism*. London: Macmillan.

Mintzberg, H. (1973) 'Strategy making in three modes', *California Management Review* 16(2); 44–53.

—— (1978) 'Patterns in strategy formation', *Management Science* 24(9): 934–48.

Pettigrew, A. M. (1973) *The Politics of Organizational Decision-Making*. London: Tavistock.

Porter, M. (1980) *Competitive Strategy* New York: Free Press.

—— (1985) *Competitive Advantage*. New York: Free Press.

Simon, H. A. (1957) *Administrative Behaviour*. New York: Macmillan.

—— (1979) 'Rational decision-making in business organisations', *American Economic Review* 69(4): 493–513.

Swedberg, R., Himmerlstrand, W. and Brulin, G. (1987) 'The paradigm of economic eociology', *Theory and Society* 16(2): 169–213.

Tibor, Á. (2006) 'Small enterprises in Hungary and joining the European Union', in U. Fueglistaller, T. Volery and W. Weber (eds) *Rencontres de St-Gall 2006: Understanding the Regulatory Climate for Entrepreneurship and SMEs*. Wildhaus, Switzerland: Swiss Research Institute of Small Business and Entrepreneurship, University of St Gallen (KMU-HSG).

Whittington, R. (1993) *What is Strategy, and Does it Matter?* London: Routledge.

Williamson, O. E. (1975) *Markets and Hierarchies: Analysis and Antitrust Implications*. New York: Free Press.

—— (1991) 'Strategizing, economizing, and economic organization', *Strategic Management Journal* 12(Special Issue): 72–94.

# 13 From fishing industry to 'fish porn'

## Tourism transforming place

*Anniken Førde*

## Introduction

Tourism transforms places of the ordinary into the apparently spectacular and exotic. Tourism is a question of 'going places'; it takes place through encounters with distinct places and place images (Baerenholdt *et al.* 2004). Today there is an increasing interest in modelling place identities and images, especially within tourism. Constructing tourist places implies creating new images and narratives – new representations of place. As Burns and Novelli (2006) argue, there is a need for empirical studies of how culture and people are involved in the processes of tourism and production of place.

This chapter discusses tourism as a strategy for community development. Approaching tourism as complex processes, it presents perspectives on how tourism, culture and representations of place are interwoven. It further examines the transformation processes of Sørøya, a small coastal community in Northern Norway. Facing a crisis in the fishing industry, the community decided to pursue tourism. Through negotiations of practices, strategies and place identities, the local tourist enterprises created a common profile promoting the island as 'The land of the big fish'. Today fish tourism has become an important industry, mainly based on deep-sea, trophy fishing. The tourist material displays images of proud fishermen showing their catch. These images are filled with gendered symbolism. Profiling what local entrepreneurs call 'fish porn', the new representations of the community imply changing understanding of place. Analysing the strategies and networks of local tourism actors, and the images and narratives of Sørøya that are produced in local discourses, tourist brochures and websites, this chapter shows how place images and narratives are constructed and manifested within transformation processes of the community. The main argument is that tourism as a strategy of community development implies complex processes of negotiating social identities, and that turning the everyday into the exotic involves cultural reproduction of both change and maintenance.

## Tourism and community development

Tourism has become an important aspect of community development in many rural communities in Norway, as in other European countries. Facing a decline in traditional industries such as farming and fishing, rural communities are encouraged to incorporate new and complementary sources of income. And tourism is in many cases a major alternative to rural decline (McCabe and Marson 2006; Saxena *et al.* 2007). Many communities have defined tourism as a future core industry, seeing tourism as a means to increase their reputation and generate income and employment (Puijk 2001; Sletvold 1999).

As a consequence, current academic and policy debates advocate a more integrated and territorial approach to rural development. Tourism community relationships are seen as central to arguments of sustainable tourism, which is closely aligned to a concern with the well-being of communities (Pearce and Moscado 1999) and community participation (Cole 2006). Tourism and community development are interrelated through manifold relations and practices. This leads to a need to integrate tourism development into broader strategies for place-making. Butler (1999) defines integrated tourism planning and development as a process of introducing tourism into an area in a manner in which it mixes with existing elements in an appropriate way. He argues that this is crucial in respect of gaining acceptability, efficiency and harmony in tourism development. This is further elaborated by Saxena *et al.* (2007). They apply the term 'integrated rural tourism', defined as tourism explicitly linked to the economic, social, cultural, natural and human structures of the localities in which it takes place. This means that successful tourism development must be integrated with other local practices and processes. Tourism can be integrated into local economies in a complex manner, leading to both income benefits and developmental benefits for localities (Pearce and Moscado 1999). It is assumed that integrated tourism development can contribute to more diversification of tourism activities and increased outcome in the tourism industry, and contribute to viable communities. Saxena *et al.* (2007) argue that integrated rural tourism leads to more sustainable tourism because it creates powerful network connections between social, cultural, economic and environmental resources. But lack of knowledge about the nature of tourism often leads to the lack of such integration. There is little knowledge about the relationship between cultural and spatial development and the creation of tourist attractions and destinations, and how such elements are and should be integrated (Butler 1999; Saxena *et al.* 2007).

Such processes of integration involve a complexity of practices. Tourism is a product of and influence on people's history, cultures and lifestyles (Burns and Novelli 2006). As argued by Swain (1995) tourism development processes are signifiers of social change and embodiments of social practices. Women and men engage in tourism and community development through a multitude of tourism-related activities, where nature and culture are combined in new ways and new social identities are constructed. To gain knowledge of how to facilitate tourism development, and how tourism can contribute to develop viable communities, we need to explore the relation between the creation of attractions and destinations and the broader processes of community development. This includes the multitude of local and mobile practices involved in tourism activities, and processes of interaction between actors more or less integrated into tourism. It also implies studying how tourism development and the creation of destinations are integrated in the broader discourses of community development.

The complexity of tourism's social and economic relationship with the communities as performance and impact means that it should not be perceived as an integrated 'whole' (Burns and Novelli 2006). As pointed out by Woods (1993, cited in Burns and Novelli 2006), we must ask about the complex ways in which tourism enters and becomes part of already ongoing processes of symbolic meaning. As argued by Saxena *et al.* (2007), we must focus on the connectivity between different actors, activities and resources and the diversity of values related to tourism development. Before presenting the case of Sørøya, focusing on how tourism was integrated in processes of place-making, I will discuss perspectives on how tourism, culture and representations of place are interwoven.

## Tourist destinations: encountering the culture of others

It is largely recognized that tourism and culture are closely connected. Tourists experience destinations; their peoples and cultures. Performing tourism, people encounter the culture of others, and social identity becomes a commodity (Burns and Novelli 2006; Robinson and Smith 2006). At the same time, tourism becomes part of culture. Places emerge as tourist places through people performing tourism, and these performances include embodied and social practices (Baerenholdt *et al.* 2004). Tourism influences identities at destinations through changed practice, exposure to different values and ideas and interaction with the world around. Thus, as a set of social and cultural practices, tourism is both expression and experience of culture.

This makes tourism development complicated. Culture consists of a multitude of dynamic processes, encompassing the everyday, habitual practices of people. Localized culture and people's practices, which are of critical importance in shaping tourist experience, are difficult to manage. Tourists observe and encounter aspects of local culture in the form of representations and everyday practices. Yet crucial in shaping the tourists' experience of place, these everyday practices are easily overlooked in tourism development strategies (Robinson and Smith 2006).

As argued by Boissevain (1996), tourism implies contested culture. Contested as the private and local, backstage space sought after by tourists in their search for the authentic is violated by their presence. Cole (2006) points to the challenge of balancing modernization and socio-economic integration with cultural distinction. Tourism further implies contested cultures as it involves relations of power and identity. The promotion of culture legitimizes and normalizes parts of the totality of everyday cultural life. Representations freeze living forms and depict reality in incomplete ways. Culture becomes idealized in certain ways, and abstracted from ongoing social practice. But tourism takes place in a complex social milieu, with different actors bringing to the product different histories, culture and lifestyles. Social identities in a locality are not uniform. In the process of tourism development, some aspects of culture are privileged and others excluded (Robinson and Smith 2006). As Burns (2006) argues, representation of local culture is a political act.

Tourism implies processes of cultural exchange, change and reproduction. As Massey (1994) argues, globalization does not entail simply homogenization. It is rather a source of cultural vitalization and the reproduction of the uniqueness of places. Culture is dynamic, and all culture is continually changing. In tourism, processes of localization and globalization thus become inseparable, and the past and present become interwoven in processes of ongoing cultural reproduction. Though complex in nature and difficult to plan, parts of tourism development processes are characterized by intentional place-making strategies. As argued by Baerenholdt *et al.* (2004), destinations are produced images, partly shaped through policies as an element of community building. Destination development thus involves planned creation of representations (Sletvold 1999).

## Representations of place

It is widely recognized in tourism research that tourists visit places because of the image they hold. Tourist destinations are designed to project an appealing image. Images are offered to tourists as objects to consume. The processes of communicating places, attractions and destinations, influence both tourists' and locals' perception of place. Communicating tourist places at the same time reflects and contributes to the production and reproduction of culture and place identities. Tourism thus constantly (re)produces representations of place.

How destinations are experienced is largely a question of how they are communicated. As noted by Birds (2002), people make sense of places through shared narratives. And through the tales about place people are endowing the place with their cultural identity. Tales about place mark out spatial boundaries, they confirm the meaning of place and who belong in it. Tourism tales about place are created for a particular purpose. As Feifan Xie (2006) notes, the destinations need to offer icons of what tourists want to experience. The images created and communicated are therefore to some extent representations of what tourists seek. Place images result from stereotyping; they are partial and often either exaggerated or understated. But the modes and types of representations of tourist places are shifting, containing a multitude of voices (McCabe and Marson 2006). In the study of concrete processes of tourism development and destination organization, it is crucial to examine what kind of place images and identities that are created and made use of.

Massey (1994) states that there is no single sense of place: places, like people, don't have single, unique identities. Different people have different senses of and interests in place, based on, for instance, gender, age, class and ethnicity. These multiple identities, Massey argues, are sources of both richness and conflict. She further argues that communities consist of mobile networks and places rarely house single communities in the sense of coherent social groups. In a world where social relations are increasingly stretched out over space, and where any local place has multiple relations with the wider world, Massey argues for a global sense of the local. Rather than seeing places as areas with boundaries, she urges a progressive and outward-looking sense of place, which integrates in a positive way the global and the local. This implies that places must be understood as meeting places. The specificity of place thus derives from the fact that each place is the focus of a distinct mixture of local and mobile relations.

Massey's understanding of places as processes conceptualized in terms of the social interactions which they tie together presents challenging perspectives in the study of tourism and community relations. It implies that tourism development must be understood within its complex context of multiple practices, relations and networks, local as well as mobile. This does not deny the importance or uniqueness of place. The specificity of place is continuously reproduced, through a multitude of interactions. As argued by Salazar (2005, cited in Saxena *et al.* 2007), tourism can be seen as a process of continuous (re)interpretation and (re)negotiation of both internal and external elements that allows new forms of survival, opening up the cross-cultural production of local meanings, self-images, representations and modes of life.

## Sørøya in transition

Sørøya is an island situated on the harsh coast of Finnmark in North Norway. There are about a thousand inhabitants, mainly situated in the three fishing villages Hasvik, Breivikbotn and Sørvær. All three villages, which are part of the municipality of Hasvik, were founded on the fishing industry: filleting, salt fish and the prawn industry. In 2002, the three processing plants at the island were all closed down. More than a hundred people lost their jobs. Many left the island and the population declined from 1,200 in 2002 to 998 in 2008, and is steadily decreasing. Other industries as well were influenced by the collapse in the fishing industry. This was not least the case for the few tourist enterprises, which were based on visiting fishing boats and occupational travellers. They lost their customers over-night, and faced a critical situation.

The crises led to the search for a new normality at Sørøya. Everyone was affected by the bankruptcy in the fishing industry, and the situation was described as a collective depression. Hasvik was defined as a stagnating municipality with an urgent need to reform its industrial and economic structure. The municipality was given extraordinary allocations and a devel-opment company, HUT,[1] was formed to develop new job opportunities in the community. Since 2002, a variety of new activities and jobs have been created, comprising among others a knitting factory and an Arctic centre of slow food. Here have also been established new enterprises of fishing tourism, and a project of cooperation among the local tourism actors has resulted in the common profile of Sørøya as *The land of the big fish*. This has led to a considerable upswing in fishing tourism at the island. The tourism enterprises mainly promote trophy fishing, and attract deep-sea anglers from Norway and abroad. They are fully booked from March to September. HUT reports an incredible increase from 2,000 overnight stays in 2002 to 12,674 in 2007, occupational travellers not included.

The collapse of the fishing industry forced the community into a situation where they had no choice but to be open to new practices; which again imply new knowledge, new values and new tales of place. As the owner and director of the hotel, and one of the local women leading the tourism project puts it:

> We stated that we had no choice, we could either collect our keys in a bag and leave, or we had to find absolutely all guts and creativity we had and do something . . . We felt that here we were, all together, on the edge of the cliff, just millimetres from falling over. If we were to survive, we had to find something together.

In this situation, new relations, networks and alliances were created. Sitting 'on the edge of the same cliff' competing actors was brought together. As Saxena *et al.* (2007) argue, rural networks tend to be driven by needs or crises. And in these new relations, practices, values, self-images and repre-sentations are continuously negotiated.

The analyses of the transformation processes of turning Sørøya into a tourist destination are based on in-depth interviews with different actors participating in the process of rebuilding the community and creating and performing 'The land of the big fish'.[2] These are representatives from HUT, the political and administrative management of the municipality, tourism enterprises, voluntary associations and investors. It also comprises docu-ment analyses of tourism material, including websites, brochures and maga-zine articles. Such case studies offer an opportunity to grasp multiple relations, interests and mechanisms taking place between the many actors involved in tourism activities.

## Tourism development as place-making

The tourism development at Sørøya is a result of explicit place-making processes. After the collapse in the fishing industry, the local authorities in Hasvik arranged conferences where the inhabitants discussed and made strategies for the future. During the first period of rebuilding the community, the municipality stated that fishing would still be the main industry. The crisis in the fishing industry was followed by condemnation of fishing boats and sale of fish quotas. But Hasvik still remains a fishing community. Sørøya is known for its rich fish stocks and big fish. With about 60 coastal smacks and two minor fish plants, the fisheries employ about 20 per cent of the workforce. They further agreed on the need to find new modes of living. As stated by a former mayor: 'We will never return to the time when young girls filled the fish plants. Those days are gone . . . If we are to survive in the periphery we have to be creative'.

In the search for new strategies, tourism was seen as an industry with potential for growth and defined as the second most important industry. But there were few tourism enterprises at the island, and these were all on the edge of bankruptcy. A project was initiated, to investigate the possibilities for developing tourism and create a network of local tourism enterprises.

The tourism project was initiated and administered by HUT, the development company, and financed through the national allocations for economic restructuring. Through the project, all the tourism enterprises in the community were forced together. Two local women, representing different tourism enterprises, were employed to manage the project. Their story of the process that resulted in the 'The land of the big fish'[3] contains stories of support and close cooperation between commercial actors and municipal agents, but also of negotiations and confrontations. The project managers tell stories of battles to get competing actors to cooperate and to agree on the profile. They all had different perceptions of the island. They also had to fight to gain acceptance and support from regional authorities and financing institutions that doubted tourism development could succeed in such a 'marginal place', 'so far out in the sea'. And they had to overcome negative attitudes in their surroundings, from people sceptical of HUTs priorities and to the idea of Sørøya as a tourist destination. The project had a strong focus on local resources, and the project group had a strong social commitment to the community. The project group insisted on a community approach to business development: 'We don't work here, we live here. This is not just our job, it's our lives.'

Developing tourism is not just a question of creating profitable business, but of creating their future everyday life at the island. They insisted on identifying the qualities special for Sørøya, both natural (the special landscape with green mountains and steep rocks and the rich fishery) and cultural (like the qualities of a traditional fishing community, 'stubborn people' and the Sørøydagene with the fish festival). They also insisted on using and developing local competence. The former manager of HUT stresses their local knowledge, the possibility 'to put creative heads in the community together' in purposeful networks.

To become a tourist destination involves both embedded networks built on local knowledge and relations and a degree of disembeddedness to facilitate access to external markets (Saxena *et al.* 2007). In addition to a cooperation project comprising all the local tourism actors in Hasvik, new relations were created involving a range of actors within and outside the community; different community associations, local service institutions, investors, political institutions, public support systems, international sport fishing organizations and tour operators. In Massey's terms, this implies mobile networks and multiple relations (Massey 1994). The case study from Sørøya demonstrates the need to focus on the combination of mobile and territorial networks in order to grasp the complex processes of tourism development. The project managers explain their success as '1. The close cooperation of local actors and the common profiling, and 2. That the different actors have established their own networks out in the world.'

The tourism development at Sørøya is to a large extent integrated into complex processes of community development, with coordination both within the tourism industry and between tourism enterprises and other local actors. HUT has played a crucial role in the tourism development, implementing it in broader discourses of place-making. The somewhat hybrid organization of the development company, in between the municipality and private businesses, has enabled an unconventional management of the project combining public and private resources and competences. Such organizational hybrids can open up new channels for local participation and mobilization. But this does not imply harmonious integration without negotiations and confrontations. Local actors have different views of the tourism destination and different interests in the working process. As the community is multivoiced, so are the processes of integrating tourism development. Further, the mix of private and public roles in Hasvik has created strong political and personal conflicts. As pointed out above, processes of mobilization and inclusion in tourism development are also processes of exclusion (Burns 2006; Robinson and Smith 2006).

As Sletvold (1999) argues, community development and destination development are partly overlapping processes. Developing a destination implies community changes where tourism attractions are created, more or less integrated into broader processes of place making. By creating 'The land of the big fish', Sørøya was turned into a tourist destination.

## Negotiating the everyday into the exotic

The biggest fish in incredible numbers swim in the waters around Sørøya. Everybody will catch fish here – guaranteed! Welcome to Sørøya!

This is how Sørøya, 'The land of the big fish', promotes itself through the websites of Hasvik (www.hasvik.com). In the tourist brochures and the websites, slogans like '*Big fish guaranteed!*' and '*Record fish caught*' dominate. The island is presented as '*The deep sea angler's Mecca*'. The dominant pictures in the tourist material are proud fishermen with their catches; real big fishes – giant cods, wolfish, halibuts and large coalfish. The profile of 'The land of the big fish' is filled with gendered symbolism. The photos illustrating the tourist material show proud fishermen, posing with their trophies.

The tourism project managers call it 'fish porn'. It's an expression that came to their vocabulary during their first marketing campaigns. When they participated at international tourism fairs, showing films and photos of fishermen with rod-caught cods of about 40 kilos and halibuts of over one hundred kilos, sport fishermen visiting their stand got all exaggerated. One of the women said: 'I realized I fell into a pool. The men were all wet in their look. They said it was like porn. Fish porn. And it was a good expression.'

To agree on this profile has been a long process of negotiation. 'The land of the big fish' is a result of an explicit process of identifying and creating place images. Establishing the tourism project, the tourism actors sat down together to define the special qualities of Sørøya. They all report thorough discussions, with competing interests and interpretations. Asking themselves 'What do we have that other places don't have?', they finally agreed on deep sea fishing being the main attraction. But creating their first website they also wanted to present the great variety of qualities of the island; the white beaches, green hills, wildlife, midnight sun etc. Then a sport fisherman asked 'Where is the fish?' They had to remake it. As the project managers recounted:

> We had to ask: What do sport fishermen care about? They don't come to Sørøya to see nice beaches and green lawns. They care about fish, fish and fish. Big fish. Different fish. So that's what we did.

The strong profile on deep sea fishing is largely motivated by the reputation Sørøya has gained through the Sørøy deep sea fish festival. Established over 20 years ago, and reputed as it is for its tremendous catches, the festival is well known in sport fishing milieus in Norway and abroad. The festival has also made it acceptable in the community to see fish resources as a basis for experiences.

Sørøya is presented as an exotic destination 'on the fringe of the Arctic Ocean'. In addition to the giant fish, the profile encompass presentations of 'the rough and fascinating' life and nature at the island. While the summer months offer midnight sun, the winter months have no direct sunlight, and often bring storms and closed roads. The harsh conditions are turned into an advantage for tourists: 'We have a rugged and magnificent scenery with frequently shifting weather. This makes every deep sea fishing trip a unique experience' (www.hasvik.com).

The 'fish porn profile' constitutes new narratives of place. At the same time it is mainly based on existing and traditional resources, both natural and human, put together in new networks. Culture and nature, tradition and invention are connected in new ways. As the tourism project leaders explain, they sell the exotic and modern, but also 'the clichés of the typical fisherman, the small local community – all these typical things, right?' The presentation of 'the dream destination' for deep sea anglers also consist of 'active fishing communities'. Especially, Sørvær is presented as a 'traditional fishing village', 'an idyllic coastal village well known for its hospitality'. Following the links at the website of 'The land of the big fish', we find pictures and stories of the idyllic villages, the green island, the rough sea, the midnight sun, winter landscapes and colourful northern lights.

Deep-sea angling represents a 'modern' way of fishing which differs from the 'traditional' fishing of local fishermen. They use different equipment and fish for fun (Borch 2004). 'Fish porn', understood as producing and profiling fishing experiences, demands new interpretations, new knowledge and new networks. The tourist enterprises stress the importance of modern equipment: 'To attract sport fishermen you need speed-boats and top fishing equipment', But fishing at Sørøya is also described as a 'time travel to the good old days'. An article in the American magazine *Sport Fishing* claims that travelling to Sørøya is to travel back 100 years in time, to 'the ultimate fishing destination in an exotic cold-water setting', where you have elbow room and can fish without seeing other fishermen for days on end. The story of the ultimate sport fishing experiences contains detailed descriptions of modern equipment, but also blessings of the quietness, 'the breathtaking vistas', the tiny villages and 'the helpful and affable people' (Orlander 2006). This illustrates that even if the fish porn profile is a narrow representation of place, it also contains a variety of meanings, values and identities.

Most tourists at Sørøya come for the dream of the giant cod. They are Norwegians, Swedes, Dutch and Belgian sport fishermen, they lodge and either rent boats or go on trips with local skippers. The discourse of fish tourism in Norway is characterized by conflicts between conventional and sport fishing (Borch 2004). This conflict seems less important at Sørøya. The leader of Sørøya deep sea fishing club claims that it is quite absent. The first years of the fishing festival they met much scepticism from local fishermen, who found it ridiculous to fish with rods in the sea – they had more efficient equipment! But as the festival became established, the critical voices disappeared. The festival coordinators tell of local enthusiasm: 'The [local] fishermen thought it was great fun. Strangers came on board, flattering the fishermen and their boats . . . Their self-esteem grew enormously, they became proud of their village.'

Concentrated on trophy fishing, Sørøya to a large extent avoids the conflicts of quotas. The coordinator at HUT explains: 'The tourists coming here are the boys club . . . It is not facilitated for filling-the-freezer-tourism. Those coming here come by plane with their visa card in the pocket.' These kinds of tourists come and leave empty-handed. Foreign fish tourists in Norway are not allowed to bring more than 15 kilos of the catch when leaving the country. The owner of the biggest fish camp tells that half of his guests bring the allowed 15 kilos, the other half don't bother bringing the fish home. 'Their aim is to catch a huge halibut or a fat cod. Then they are pleased.' There seems to be agreement on the statement that this kind of fishing 'doesn't empty the sea'. This has facilitated the coexistence and collaboration with conventional fishermen. The fish camp owner reveals that local fishermen and sport fishers often come together in his pub, exchanging experiences and knowledge.

The transition processes of Sørøya contain economic, social and cultural change. New practices demand new knowledge and new ways of social organization. Established systems of meaning, interpretation and representation are being challenged. But the transition processes also contain cultural maintenance. As Macleod (2004) shows from his study of tourism in the Canary Islands, the transition from fishing to tourism reshapes social and cultural identities, with new identities being made and older ones, like the fishing village, being reconstructed and consumed as a marketed attraction. Through the development of tourism, culture and nature are connected in new ways, and traditions are connected to inventions. The traditional knowledge and skills of local fishermen are combined with new knowledge of sport fishing, experience production and marketing. New representations of Sørøya are being made. But these are to a large extent a continuation of traditional practices and identities.

The transition processes are driven by strong narrators pursuing new strategies and new narratives of place. But they also consist of resistance, of negotiation between competing values and strategies. As noted by Richter (2006), negotiating culture and coordinating development with a variety of stakeholders is not easy. Some are easily excluded. As Puijk (2001) shows from his study of tourism altering local culture in Northern Norway, this can result in division over conflicting social values. In tourism planning, some are ruled in, others ruled out (Cole 2006). The cultural narratives of tourist destinations are ambivalent, and multiple relationships mean multiple narratives. At Sørøya, they have managed to find new ways of exploiting the fishing resources and creating new narratives. The tourism development has involved a multitude of actors with different experiences and knowledge. These multiple roles and statuses have created extensive room for manoeuvre within the project. Combined with the shared experiences of the crises and need for new strategies, they have managed to construct new place images and integrate tourism development into the complex processes of rebuilding the community.

## Conclusion and lessons to be learned

What are the lessons to be learned from these complex processes of tourism development? The first lesson is that they always are just that: complex processes involving negotiations and competing interests, values and identities. Tourism development implies economic, social and cultural change and reproduction. These changes affect a range of relations and dynamics in the community. It implies new practices, new knowledge, new networks, new organizations, new systems of meaning and new representations. Second lesson, following Massey's perspective on place: transforming places does not imply that their qualities are deleted; it rather implies a continuous renewing of them. Places become multi-vocal in their identities. As Sletvold (1999) argues, destination development is a question of which voice to sing with in this cacophony.

The case of tourism development at Sørøya is very much a story of success. It is based on a neat process of defining a new future for the society, and inscribed in broader processes of place making. By creating 'The land of the big fish' they managed to turn the critical situation of the tourism industry into success in just a few years. There are many explanations for this success, and different actors have different stories to tell. There seems to be agreement on the close cooperation of local tourism actors and the common profiling as a major explanation. This is combined with extended local and mobile networks, comprised of a multitude of actors with different experiences and knowledge. Further, the strong focus on networking is stressed. Through the processes of rebuilding the community, HUT created meeting places and forced people together in deliberate networks. To make cooperation possible, they focused on tasks they could agree on. The tourism project started by cooperating on a brochure and a fair; they defined common things to be proud of. Even if the different actors had different interests and perspectives, they had some common narratives. They shared the experience of the crises. And they agreed on fishing being the girder of the society. After thorough negotiations they managed to agree on a common profile based on big fish being their greatest advantage and deep sea anglers their main clients. Following the 'fish porn line' all the way through, insisting on only fish in their brochures, they have managed to create a clear profile and find their niche in the tourism market.

But it is also a story of negotiation and conflicting social values. The transformation from fish industry to 'fish porn' implies new perceptions of place. Sørøya is presented as the exotic and exciting. New place images and social identities are created, representing just a part of local meaning systems. At the same time aspects of the 'traditional' are stressed. Sørøya also represents the authentic coastal community, time travel 'to the good old days'. In this way, the new representations of place contribute to maintaining the social identity as a fishing community: a fishing community with new practices, new knowledge, new networking relations and new narratives.

## Notes

1 HUT is an abbreviation for *Hasvik i utvikling*, which literally translates as *Hasvik in development* or *progress*. It was established as a project in 2002, and finished the end of 2008. The general aim was to replace the 110 jobs that were lost in the crisis in the fishing industry. HUT was owned by the municipality, but the majority of the board members represented private businesses. It was an administrative agency managing public allocations, but also a consulting company for local entrepreneurs.

2 The case study is part of the research project 'Innovative Communities – Community Entrepreneurship in a Rural Community Context', funded by the Norwegian Research Council and the county agricultural administration of the North Norwegian counties, and conducted by Nordland Research Institute and the University of Tromsø.

3 For a broader description and analysis of the entrepreneurial process of creating 'The land of the big fish', see Førde (2009).

## References

Baerenholdt, J. O., Haldrup, M., Larsen, J. and Urry, J. (2004) *Performing Tourist Places*. Aldershot: Ashgate.

Birds, E. (2002) 'It makes sense to us: cultural identity in local legend of place', *Journal of Contemporary Ethnography* 31(5): 519–47.

Boissevain, J. (1996) 'Introduction', in J. Boissevain (ed.) *Coping with Tourists: European Reactions to Mass Tourism*. Oxford: Berghahn Books, pp. 1–26.

Borch, T. (2004) 'Sustainable management of marine fishing tourism: Some Lessons from Norway', *Tourism in Marine Environments* 1(1): 49–57.

Burns, P. M. (2006) 'Social identities and cultural politics of tourism', in P. M. Burns and M. Novelli (eds) *Tourism and Social Identities: Global Frameworks and Local Realities*. Oxford: Elsevier.

Burns, P. M. and Novelli, M. (2006) 'Tourism and social identities: introduction', in P. M. Burns and M. Novelli (eds) *Tourism and Social Identities: Global Frameworks and Local Realities*. Oxford: Elsevier.

Butler, R. (1999) 'Problems and issues of integrating tourism development', in D. G. Pearce and R. Butler (eds) *Contemporary Issues in Tourism Development*. London: Routledge.

Cole, S. (2006) 'Cultural tourism, community participation and empowerment', in M. Smith and M. Robinson (eds) *Cultural Tourism in a Changing World: Politics, Participation and (Re)presentation*. Clevedon: Channel View.

Feifan Xie, P. (2006) 'The development of cultural iconography in festival tourism', in M. Smith and M. Robinson (eds) *Cultural Tourism in a Changing World: Politics, Participation and (Re)presentation*. Clevedon: Channel View.

Førde, A. (2009) 'Creating "the land of the big fish": a study of rural tourism innovation', in T. Nyseth and A. Viken (eds) *Place Reinventiion: Northern Perspectives*. Aldershot: Ashgate.

McCabe, S. and Marson, D. (2006) 'Tourists' constructions and consumption of space: place, modernity and meaning', in P. M. Burns and M. Novelli (eds), *Tourism and Social Identities: Global Frameworks and Local Realities*. Oxford: Elsevier.

Macleod, D. (2004) *Tourism, Globalisation and Cultural Change: An Island Community Perspective.* Cleveland: Channel View.

Massey, D. (1994) *Space, Place and Gender.* Minneapolis: University of Minnesota Press.

Orlander, D. (2006) 'Discover Norway's Arctic frontier: fish the U.S. northeast coast 100 years ago by travelling to Soroya island now', *Sportfishing Magazine* 21(4): 106–14.

Pearce, P. and Moscado, G. (1999) 'Tourism community analysis', in D. G. Pearce and R. W. Butler (eds) *Contemporary Issues in Tourism Development.* London: Routledge.

Puijk, R. (2001) 'Dealing with fish and tourists: A case study from Northern Norway', in J. Boissevain (ed.) *Coping with Tourists: European Reactions to Mass Tourism.* Providence, RI: Berghahn Books.

Richter, L. K. (2006) 'The politics of negotiating culture in tourism development', in P. M. Burns and M. Novelli (eds) *Tourism and Social Identities: Global Frameworks and Local Realities.* Oxford: Elsevier.

Robinson, M. and Smith. M. (2006) 'Politics, power and play: the shifting contexts of cultural tourism', in M. Smith and M. Robinson (eds) *Cultural Tourism in a Changing World: Politics, Participation and (Re)presentation.* Clevedon: Channel View.

Saxena, G., Clark, G., Oliver, T. and Ilbery, B. (2007) 'Conceptualizing integrated rural tourism', *Tourism Geographies* 9(4): 347–70.

Sletvold, O. (1999) 'Destinasjonsutvikling: stedsendring i turismens navn', in J. K. Steen Jacobsen and A. Viken (eds) *Turisme: Stedet i en bevegelig verden.* Oslo: Universitetsforlaget.

Swain, M. B. (1995) 'Gender in tourism', *Annals of Tourism Research* 22(2): 247–66.

# 14 Agritourism characteristics and contributions to destination and livelihood sustainability

## A case study from south-west Scotland

*Steven A. Gillespie*

### Introduction

Agritourism is not a new form of rural tourism. In some parts of Europe, such as Austria, farmers have been receiving visitors for over 100 years (Hummelbrunner and Miglbauer 1994) with a similarly long tradition in Germany and France (Dernoi 1983; Oppermann 1995). In fact, Nilsson (2002) suggests that agritourism is the oldest form of rural tourism with widespread development occurring after the Second World War. Agritourism is also clearly not a new focus for research (Dernoi 1983; Frater 1983), yet it continues to receive attention owing to its multifaceted roles as a rural tourism product, its contribution to sustainable rural livelihood strategies and diversification options addressing the declining fortunes of agricultural communities experiencing rural restructuring (Hara and Naipaul 2008; Haugen and Vik 2008; McGehee *et al.* 2007; Roberts 2002; Sharpley and Vass 2006; Shucksmith and Smith 1991; Sznajder *et al.* 2009; Tao and Wall 2009).

It has been recognized for some time that pluriactivity (in this context the generation of income from non-farming activities and sources either on or off the farm) seems to be growing (Bryden *et al.* 1993; Shucksmith *et al.* 1989). Some researchers have reported that as much as 77 per cent of Scottish farmers and spouses supplement farm income through alternative means (Slee *et al.* 2001). Among the various pathways open to farmers is 'the redeployment of farm resources (including human capital) into new non-agricultural products or services on the farm' (Ilbery and Bowler 1998: 71). This structural diversification pathway includes the provision of tourism facilities such as farm shops, visitor attractions and accommodation, although not confined to these (Blekesaune *et al.* 2008). However, the literature informs us that the most common form of agritourism is accommodation provision such as bed and breakfast (B&B), self-catering accommodation and caravan/campsites (Dernoi 1983; Nilsson 2002; Walford 2001).

Agritourism has been investigated in a variety of rural destinations including: Norway, Germany, North America, Australia, England and Wales (Denman 1994a; Hall 1995; Hara and Naipaul 2008; Ilbery and Bowler 1993; Ilbery *et al.* 1998; Morrison *et al.* 1996; Oppermann 1995; Weaver and Fennell 1997). However, there remain few studies from Scotland and how this form of rural tourism contributes to livelihood sustainability at the farm level. Slee (1998: 94) explains that the low level of farm and estate tourism in Scotland has resulted in enterprise owners and managers of these facilities often being considered 'bystanders' rather than 'stakeholders' in the tourism industry, although their contribution to the portfolio of rural tourism products may be significant. Indeed, it has been noted that agritourism in Scotland has been 'largely overlooked from the point of view of providing much needed regeneration in rural Scotland' (Gladstone and Morris 1998: 209). This chapter builds upon research by Gladstone and Morris (1998, 2000) in the tourist authority administrations of Ayrshire and Arran, Perthshire and Orkney through a case study of agritourism in Dumfries & Galloway, south-west Scotland.

## Characteristics and typology of agritourism

Reviewing the agritourism literature reveals a range of different terms used to explain similar, but sometimes distinct concepts (Phillip *et al.* 2009). Among these are agritourism, farm-based tourism, agro-tourism, farm tourism and rural tourism. It is generally recognized that the last of these, rural tourism, is a wider concept encompassing a variety of different forms of tourism and agritourism is merely one sub-sector (Nilsson 2002; Phillip *et al.* 2009). For the purposes of this chapter the term agritourism has been adopted to explain the phenomenon in Dumfries & Galloway.

The diversity of defining characteristics of agritourism offered in the literature has led Phillip *et al.* (2009) to propose a valuable typology in order to provide some clarity and initiate research consistency (Figure 14.1).

The typology builds upon the key characteristics of agritourism identified through the literature, including the status of the farm as either a working enterprise or ex-agricultural premises. In this case study of agritourism, all questionnaire respondents were located on 'working farms' engaged in varying modes of production such as: cattle and sheep (44.4 per cent), mixed farm (29.6 per cent), dairy (11.1 per cent), specialist beef (5.6 per cent), specialist sheep (5.6 per cent and other (3.7 per cent). Most respondents in this research operate conventional or traditional farms (70 per cent) with a high proportion managing land designated as Less Favoured Area (LFA) in recognition of the lower productivity and higher production costs of farming in upland environments. These farms are reported to be some of the lowest earning farm types in Scotland (Scottish Executive 2006). Other farm characteristics of the sample population are given elsewhere (Gillespie 2007).

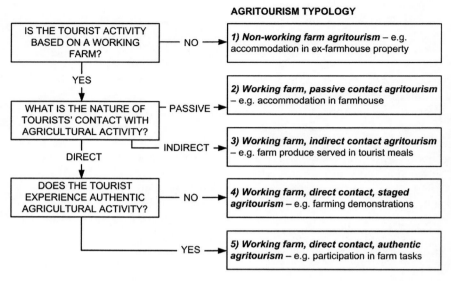

*Figure 14.1* A typology for defining agritourism.
Source: Phillip *et al.* 2009: 3.

Another defining characteristic of agritourism is the nature of interaction between guests and agricultural activity. Here a distinction is made on the basis of whether interactions are passive, indirect or direct (Phillip *et al.* 2009). Direct contact suggests agricultural activity is a feature of the tourism offering; not evident from the surveys or interviews conducted in Dumfries & Galloway. Some 92 per cent of agritourism operators in the current research stated that visitors do not engage in any farm duties. Liability fears, disruption to the working day and lack of guest knowledge were cited as reasons for discouraging direct contact. Under the typology offered by Phillip *et al.*, the majority of enterprises in Dumfries & Galloway fall within the category of 'working farm, passive contact agritourism'. However, five agritourism owners revealed consumers sometimes engaged in hands-on farm activities. One interviewee who operates a 121-hectare organic cattle and sheep farm with her husband describes how some guests have experienced authentic farming activities:

> At the moment we have a couple with four girls and the girls are aged 3, 5, 7 and 9, and one day last week we told them we were gathering sheep in so they came into the field and helped to gather the sheep in. The mother also helped to dowse the ewes. So actually, it was a subtle bit of education. It's quite nice and they like it, it works well.

Evident from these five enterprise owners was the fact that direct contact was spontaneous, unstaged, and dependent on the type of activity. A proportion of the respondents in this case study therefore fall under the fifth agritourism typology offered by Phillip *et al.* (2009) which constitutes 'working farm, direct contact, authentic agritourism'.

## Methods

This case study of agritourism in Dumfries & Galloway draws upon data collected by the author from 2003–7. The main methods were self-administered questionnaires and 13 semi-structured interviews with enterprise owners. Given that there is no single inventory of agritourism enterprises in Dumfries & Galloway (or Scotland as a whole), a sampling frame was created by scrutinizing a wide variety of publications (Farm Stay UK brochures; South of Scotland Organic Network; The Green Holiday Guide), websites (over 15 regional and national) and utilizing a 'snowballing technique' (Robson 2002; Scott 2000). Analysis of the sampling frame revealed the dominance of accommodation facilities and the decision was made to concentrate on operators of these enterprises.

A total of 110 agritourism accommodation enterprises were identified in the region. Self-administered questionnaires were sent on two occasions yielding response rates of 54.5 per cent and 49 per cent. Interviewees were drawn at random from the sampling frame.

## The study region

The term 'rural' is problematic (Halfacree 1995; Ilbery 1998) yet it is difficult to describe Dumfries & Galloway (Figure 14.2) in any other terms. Some 70 per cent of Dumfries & Galloway is under some form of agriculture with a further 25 per cent in forestry. Population density is 0.23 people per hectare; almost three times lower than the Scottish average. Employment is based on a number of key industries including agriculture and forestry, manufacturing, construction, tourism and public sector (Scottish Enterprise Dumfries & Galloway 2004; VisitScotland 2009).

The administrative centre of the region, and the largest town, is Dumfries with a population of around 32,000 (22 per cent of the region's population). There are a number of other settlements of significant size including the port of Stranraer in the west and Annan in the east (c.10,000). All other settlements have populations fewer than 4000. The region as a whole is suffering from population decline, with an out-migration of young people and in-migration of retirees. Future population decline is forecast to be in the region of −7.8 per cent by 2018, and is predicted to lead to a significant skills shortage in Dumfries & Galloway (Scottish Enterprise Dumfries & Galloway 2004).

Reflecting the upland topography of the region, agriculture is mainly based on cattle and sheep. Dumfries & Galloway is also home to a third of Scotland's dairy cattle. Similar to many other rural regions, agricultural

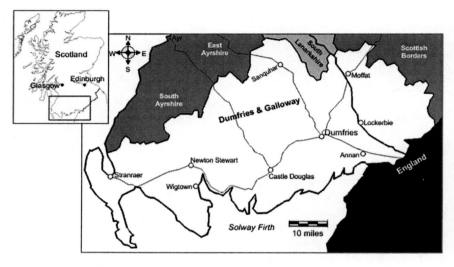

*Figure 14.2*  The location of Dumfries & Galloway, south-west Scotland.

communities are facing a number of problems. From 1983 to 2003, there has been a 40 per cent decrease in the number of regular agricultural workers in Dumfries & Galloway, a 25 per cent decrease in the number of seasonal and casual workers, and a 50 per cent increase in the number of spouses working (Scottish Enterprise Dumfries & Galloway 2004). Despite the overall decrease in agricultural employment, the region still currently provides employment for around 10 per cent of Scotland's agricultural workforce, although half of these are part-time or less (Scottish Executive 2006). Furthermore, at the national level, agricultural incomes have been falling dramatically since 1995 (Slee *et al.* 2001).

Dumfries & Galloway is dissected in the east by the M74, the main motorway between Scotland and England providing good access to key domestic tourism markets and within reasonable driving distance of large urban populations (two hours from the Central Belt of Scotland, three to four hours from Manchester, Liverpool, Leeds and Birmingham). Further west there are a number of key roads running across the region which are serviced with public transport. The region does not contain any airports although Prestwick near Ayr, Glasgow and Edinburgh are accessible within two hours. The Glasgow to London west coast railway line follows the M74, providing some access to the east of the region. There is also a rail link between Dumfries and Glasgow which follows the Nith Valley. The far west of the region also has a rail link between Stranraer and Glasgow; however, most of Dumfries & Galloway is not serviced by rail transportation. Subsequently, Dumfries & Galloway relies heavily on visitors with access to private transportation (79 per cent of domestic trips – VisitScotland 2009).

Tourism is fundamental to the Dumfries & Galloway economy, providing employment for 11.5 per cent of the workforce (excluding self-employed) and generating £125 million in 2008. Around 0.85 million tourist trips were taken to the region in 2008 (93 per cent UK domestic) (VisitScotland 2009). Although tourism is important for the region's economy, it remains one of the least visited regions of Scotland along with Angus, Fife and the neighbouring Scottish Borders.

## Type, number and bed-space availability of agritourism in Dumfries & Galloway

The 110 agritourism accommodation enterprises identified comprise a variety of different types as shown in Table 14.1. The most frequent form is self-catering followed by bed and breakfast (B&B). Several businesses incorporate a mixture of different types, mainly B&B and self-catering. Using a variety of different data sources (see Gillespie 2007), it is estimated that agritourism accommodation enterprises represent around 20 per cent of all rural accommodation businesses in the region, therefore, one could argue that these enterprise owners have a significant stake in the tourism system.

Although fewer in number, campsites tend to offer much higher bed-space/pitch potential as illustrated in Table 14.2. Agritourism B&Bs in the study region conform to findings elsewhere in the UK, Canada and Sweden, suggesting that six or fewer bed-spaces are typical (Dernoi 1991a; Gössling and Mattsson 2002; Questions Answered Ltd 2004; Weaver and Fennell 1997).

In terms of self-catering agritourism, these findings suggest the presence of two units each sleeping six to seven people as fairly common, similar to north-west England (Questions Answered Ltd 2004). While small-scale enterprises are the norm, some self-catering enterprises in Dumfries & Galloway are of a substantial size. One interviewee has 16 letting properties (96 available bed-spaces) on his 101-hectare organic farm which is three times the size of the average number of bed-spaces available in hotels in Dumfries & Galloway.[1] The owner still farms the land and views himself as

*Table 14.1* Type and number of agritourism accommodation businesses in Dumfries & Galloway

| Accommodation type | Agritourism accommodation businesses |
| --- | --- |
| Bed & breakfast/guesthouses | 35 |
| Self-catering accommodation | 60 |
| Campsite/caravan site | 5 |
| Mixture of accommodation | 10 |
| Total | 110 |

*Table 14.2*  Number of available bed-spaces/pitches, and proportion of
questionnaire respondents

| | Number of available bed-spaces/pitches[1] | | | | | | | |
| --- | --- | --- | --- | --- | --- | --- | --- | --- |
| | ≤ 6 | 7–12 | 13–18 | 19–24 | 25–30 | 31–36 | ≥37 | Mean |
| Self-catering only | 37% | 44% | 4% | 4% | 4% | 4% | 4% | 13.5 |
| Bed & breakfast only | 80% | 15% | 5% | – | – | – | – | 6.4 |
| Mixture of accommodation | 29% | 43% | 29% | – | – | – | – | 9.3 |
| Caravan/campsite only[2] | – | – | – | – | – | – | 100% | 50.0 |
| Combined total (N = 60) | 51% | 33% | 7% | 2% | 2% | 2% | 4% | 11.0 |

Notes
1 Percentages may not add up due to rounding.
2 Only one caravan/campsite business responded to the self-administered questionnaire, therefore a note of caution is applied.

a farmer first and foremost although concedes that his household income, at the time of interview, was entirely composed of tourism revenue.

Using data collected via questionnaires (sample = 60) and applying these to the total population (110), the average number of bed-spaces offered on working farms in Dumfries & Galloway is estimated at 1377. This amounts to around 9 per cent of available regional bed-space and strengthens the status of agritourism operators as significant stakeholders.

## Economic sustainability: employment and income

Research informs us that the main motive for diversification is economic (Ilbery and Bowler 1998; Marsden 1998). This is also the case in Dumfries & Galloway where 67 per cent of questionnaire respondents cited the need to 'generate additional income' as the main motive for starting the tourism enterprise (N = 54). This, however, was not the only reason suggested. 'Making use of redundant farm buildings' was the second most cited reason (46 per cent), a finding also evident from research in Orkney (Gladstone and Morris 2000). Several interviewees described how the decline in external labour had resulted in surplus buildings attached to the farm.

Several participants started the enterprise with help from government grant schemes (Farm Diversification Grant Scheme; Farm Business Development Scheme), however, 94 per cent claimed they only used their own capital. This finding replicates other studies from England and Wales where it was found that farmers often diversify regardless of state support (Edwards *et al.* 1994).

Potential time input and labour input into the tourism business in addition to existing available farm buildings and financial capital are important factors for farmers and spouses when deciding what form of accommodation to develop. One positive aspect of developing self-catering stems from the flexibility it provides visitors in light of changing uses of the countryside and activity-focused holidays (Cater and Smith 2003) although it is generally more expensive to develop and may not be an option for some cash-poor farmers.

One fundamental requirement of sustainable tourism and private business in general is the ability to generate income (Lane 1994). In Dumfries & Galloway, most agritourism accommodation enterprises appear to generate a relatively low proportion of household income from tourism (Table 14.3). This mirrors findings elsewhere in Europe and the UK where agritourism businesses were found to generate ≤ 10 per cent of total household income from tourism (Cavaco 1995; Hummelbrunner and Miglbauer 1994; Gössling and Mattsson 2002).

In terms of financial contribution, there is considerable variation across different forms of agritourism accommodation. It is interesting to find that operators with a mixture of accommodation types appear to generate more household income from tourism than any single form of accommodation. Perhaps this is the most economically sustainable strategy to adopt?

While the percentage of total household income from tourism is marginal in comparison to other sources of income, 76 per cent felt it had been a good financial decision and a similar proportion were personally satisfied with choosing this diversification pathway. In the majority of cases, agritourism does not transform the economic situation although 33 per cent of respondents in Dumfries & Galloway felt it had been crucial in the survival of the farm, with a further 37 per cent unsure if the farm would still be operating without tourism revenue. One B&B operator explains how the economic importance of the tourism enterprise has changed:

It used to be pocket money when we first started and now it is a big part of the income. We only have one room that sleeps up to five. Its full

*Table 14.3* Proportion of total household income from agritourism

| | Proportion of household income from agritourism | | | | | | |
|---|---|---|---|---|---|---|---|
| | <5 (%) | 5–10 (%) | 11–25 (%) | 26–50 (%) | 51–75 (%) | >75 (%) | N |
| Self-catering only | 31 | 25 | 19 | 19 | 6 | | 32 |
| Bed & breakfast only | 42 | 25 | | 33 | | | 12 |
| Mixture of accommodation | 33 | | 11 | | 33 | 22 | 9 |
| Caravan/campsite only | 100 | | | | | | 1 |
| All accommodation types | 35 | 20 | 13 | 19 | 9 | 4 | 54 |

most of the time now, but it's taken a few years to build up. It adds a lot to the farm income.

For around 13 per cent of respondents, the revenue from the agritourism enterprise is greater than the agricultural business, thus suggesting that income from agritourism is not always of marginal importance and can be essential in farm household survival.

Similar to research reported elsewhere in Europe (Hjalager 1996), the development of agritourism provides insignificant external opportunities outwith the farming family in Dumfries & Galloway (Table 14.4). Some 78 per cent of employees (including the owner) were found to be family members with the remainder recruited from the wider rural population. The majority of agritourism enterprises provide employment just for the owner, a smaller proportion provide work for two (9 per cent) and three people (4 per cent) although the jobs created typically involve cleaning duties on a part-time or informal basis. If such findings are indicative of agritourism accommodation provision across Dumfries & Galloway, then approximately 110 full-time jobs are supported, but this does not necessarily mean 110 full-time wages.

Despite generating relatively few external opportunities, agritourism can contribute to economic sustainability by creating self-employment opportunities in remote areas where few other prospects exist. In this respect it can be considered ecologically-sustainable accommodation according the criteria outlined by Moscardo *et al.* (1996). Overall, farm-based accommodation development is perhaps unlikely to transform the economic situation in Dumfries & Galloway although it can play a fundamental financial function at the household level.[2]

*Table 14.4* Agritourism accommodation employment in Dumfries & Galloway

| The enterprise owner<br>Additional workers | Farm-based accommodation employment | | | | |
|---|---|---|---|---|---|
| | 1 | 2 | 3 | 4 | N |
| Self-catering only | 50% | 41% | 6% | 3% | 32 |
| Bed & breakfast only | 75% | 17% | – | 8% | 12 |
| Mixture of accommodation[1] | 33% | 33% | 33% | – | 9 |
| Caravan/campsite only[2] | 100% | – | – | – | 1 |
| Combined total | 54% | 33% | 9% | 4% | 54 |

Notes
1  Percentages do not add up due to rounding.
2  Only one caravan/campsite business responded to the self-administered questionnaire, therefore a note of caution is applied.

## Environmental practices

Global warming and climate change are arguably the greatest challenge facing the future sustainability of tourism destinations, affecting almost all facets of the tourism system (Becken and Hay 2007; Hall and Higham 2005; Scott *et al.* 2008). The tourism industry's contribution to global anthropogenic $CO_2$ emissions (carbon dioxide) is thought to be in the region of 4.9 per cent, most of which is generated by transportation (Scott *et al.* 2008). However, accommodation is the second largest contributor responsible for 21 per cent of tourism's $CO_2$ emissions (ibid.). While the global tourism industry does not have any agreed greenhouse gas (GHG) mitigation targets, many governments have committed to reduce emissions at national levels under the United Nations Framework Convention on Climate Change.[3] Scotland has one of the most ambitious $CO_2$ reduction targets (42 per cent reduction target for 2020, 80 per cent target for 2050: baseline year 1990).[4] In order to achieve these targets, all industries in Scotland, including tourism, will need to manage operations in a much more environmentally sustainable way.

An in-depth analysis of the environmental performance/footprint of agritourism accommodation operators in Dumfries & Galloway is beyond the scope of this chapter, therefore the aim is simply to highlight some of the environmental practices which enterprise owners currently pursue. First, this section uses membership of the Green Tourism Business Scheme (GTBS) as an indicator of sustainable management within the agritourism accommodation sector.

The GTBS is an accreditation scheme developed in partnership with VisitScotland which encourages accommodation providers and other sectors of the tourism system to reduce negative environmental impacts by adopting a range of environmental management procedures. Although the GTBS is aimed primarily at increasing environmental sustainability, it also incorporates social and economic dimensions. With over 1400 members across the UK, it is the leading accreditation body for sustainable tourism.

The use of GTBS membership as an indicator for sustainable tourism in Scotland has been suggested by Blackstock *et al.* (2006). In Dumfries & Galloway as a whole, there are just 33 members, 12 of which are accommodation providers. Of these, four are agritourism providers. Despite being lauded as one of the best known environmental management schemes in Europe, it is apparent that the uptake of the GTBS is extremely low and this creates a significant challenge for enhancing the environmental sustainability of the tourism supply.

One interviewee used to be a member of the scheme but pulled out because she felt participation was not bringing any more customers and therefore she could not justify the cost of joining the GTBS. One of the barriers to joining the scheme, beyond financial commitment, is that GTBS members should also be accredited under VisitScotland's Quality Assurance scheme. This situation inevitably restricts potential new entrants to the GTBS given that 29 per cent of agritourism accommodation providers sampled were not members of VisitScotland's QA scheme.

One farmer made the valid point that 'You can be environmentally friendly and not be part of the scheme'. Consequently, the current research also asked agritourism accommodation providers to indicate if they pursued any of the environmental practices shown in Figure 14.3.

Despite revealing that just four agritourism providers are members of the GTBS, it is evident that many more engage in environmental practices. Therefore, this sub-sector of rural tourism is not as environmentally unsustainable as it might first appear. Of considerable note is the high level of engagement in recycling activities. Since agriculture is a voracious consumer of water, it is perhaps unsurprising that over one-third of respondents follow water conservation procedures. The elimination of non-organic chemicals probably reflects the finding that a similar percentage of enterprises are located on organic farms.

Pursuing environmental sustainability can be extremely difficult for small enterprises that lack the skills, knowledge and resources (Berry and Ladkin 1997). For some businesses, economic survival may be considered more important than sustainable tourism practices (Carlsen *et al.* 2001). Many farmers in Dumfries & Galloway who have diversified into tourism have contributed towards environmental sustainability without recognizing this achievement. For example, the renovation of redundant farm buildings for tourism purposes makes use of significant reserves of embodied energy and therefore contributes towards environmentally benign and sustainable rural development (Simpson and Brown Architects 2001).

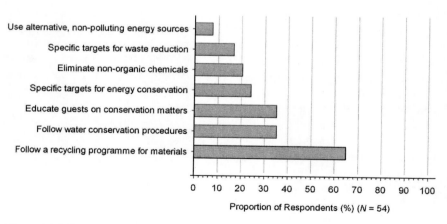

*Figure 14.3* Engagement in selected environmental practices.

## Social dimensions of agritourism

Lane (1994), among others, believes that sustainable rural tourism should sustain the culture and character of host communities. It is over-simplistic to suggest that there is a single culture in Dumfries & Galloway to sustain; nevertheless the region has historically been shaped by agriculture which carries with it an associated cultural identity (Crouch 1994). For many of the farming families surveyed, diversification into agritourism provides a relatively low, but important, source of income that allows them to sustain their cultural identity as farmers and consequently maintain the social fabric of farming communities (Roberts 2002). Even the 13 per cent of farming families in the sample, who generate most of their income from tourism and the one farmer who generates all of his income from tourism, continue to farm despite falling agricultural profits. This demonstrates that agricultural identity is important to agritourism accommodation providers and serves an important role in social status.

Agritourism accommodation provision in Dumfries & Galloway is primarily managed and owned by females (74 per cent), a finding which appears to be universal regardless of destination (Gladstone and Morris 2000; McGehee *et al.* 2007). A considerable proportion of agritourism operators in Dumfries & Galloway have been in the tourism business for a long time (26 per cent for more than 15 years) and the knowledge and experience accrued by these stakeholders make them a valuable asset to tourism planners aiming to position the region as a sustainable destination.

The high proportion of female agritourism owners can be viewed as addressing one social aspect of sustainable development and Agenda 21 – the empowerment of women and ownership of resources (United Nations 1992). While tourism in general is a major employer of women worldwide, there appears to be significant horizontal and vertical segregation of the labour market (Hemmati 1999). Horizontally, women and men are often given different roles – women being employed as waitresses, chambermaids, cleaners, travel agency sales persons, flight attendants,[5] whereas men are employed as barmen, construction workers, drivers, pilots, etc. Vertically, the typical 'gender pyramid' is also prevalent – lower levels and occupations with few career development prospects being dominated by women and key managerial positions being dominated by men (ibid.). Research in France has shown that gender is the driving force behind the development of farm tourism and this is related to women's fight for professional status within the farm and their desire to create new activities for which they are responsible (Girauld 1999).

Most of the interviewees indicated that the spouse (predominantly male) often has nothing to do with the operation of the tourism enterprise, preferring instead to concentrate efforts on agricultural production and in some cases other forms of pluriactivity. One interviewee, a dairy farmer, self-catering operator and part-time schoolteacher noted:

I look after the tourism side of things. Jim takes nothing to do with it. I don't even think he's been in the house. He sticks to the farming side of things. But I enjoy that, it is good for me.

This situation benefits this agritourism operator in a social capacity in as much as she enjoys having control over the business; she has a passion for educating guests about farming and the countryside, and considers her tourism business to be fundamental for the survival of the dairy farm. While the division of labour with regards to the operation of the tourism business appears fairly entrenched, most female interviewees divulged that they pursue agricultural work alongside their spouse. So although the tourism enterprise can empower women and therefore address issues of social sustainability and ownership of resources, it can also create gender inequality in terms of labour division. The dualistic role of female agritourism owners has long been recognized by other researchers (Dernoi 1991a; McIntosh and Campbell 2001). Only two of the agritourism providers interviewed in Dumfries & Galloway did not participate in some form of agricultural work.

An interesting finding is that proportionally fewer women in Dumfries & Galloway manage farm-based accommodation businesses that contribute to more than half of the total household income (8 per cent) in comparison to men (29 per cent). This might indicate that women are disempowered once the tourism enterprise is more economically sustainable than the farm business. Further research is required here.

Visitor satisfaction is often used as an indicator of sustainable tourism (Dymond 1997) yet little consideration is given to the contentment of the enterprise owners. It is argued here that satisfaction is a two-way process and operators need to gain some form of personal fulfilment from operating a tourism enterprise for it to be socially sustainable in the long term. Unsatisfied and negative tourism operators are more likely to provide a poor personal service which is unlikely to encourage repeat custom, therefore impacting on economic capability (Reisinger 1994).

Agritourism operators gain fulfilment in different ways; the most cited being 'satisfied customers' (44 per cent). Others point to the social function of 'meeting new people' (32 per cent) as particularly satisfying. Another way in which agritourism provision can contribute towards social sustainability is through contact and meeting new people, a motivation given by 9 per cent for starting the business. This social benefit reflects the isolated nature of farming which is often perceived to be a lonely profession associated with higher than normal suicide rates (Stark *et al.* 2006). Some 75 per cent of B&B owners and 53 per cent of self-catering providers have daily conversations with their guests.

Besides being personally satisfying to agritourism operators in Dumfries & Galloway, educating guests and the social contact between the host and visitor can 'pave the way for understanding and thereby diminish the risk of prejudices, conflicts, and tensions' (Nilsson 2002: 10). This is the basic premise of the 'contact hypothesis' described by Reisinger (1994) who suggests dissimilar views of diverse cultures can be reconciled through contact. Some enterprise owners revealed their intention to use their status as farmers to educate visitors on farming issues and primary production, and hopefully derive some economic benefits through direct selling of produce. Other interviewees enjoy educating visitors about the countryside, a service that visitors staying in other forms of rural accommodation are less likely to encounter. For some enterprise owners, contact with visitors provides an opportunity to dispel myths and attempt to install appreciation of agricultural production. Further research might attempt to determine whether educative agritourism changes the views and perhaps even the purchasing habits of visitors.

## Challenges of operating an agritourism business

It is essential to examine the challenging aspects of operating an agritourism accommodation business as this provides a depiction of the realities of the tourism agriculture juxtaposition. While almost one-fifth of questionnaire respondents suggested there were 'no difficult aspects' of operating an agritourism business, a number of enterprise owners did identify challenges (Table 14.5).

Conflicts are considered here to be those that are inherent difficulties of operating both a tourism and agricultural business, including the 'smell of slurry' and 'consumers seeing dead animals'. These challenges can be overcome by educating guests about the realities of farming. The peaking of agricultural and tourism activity at the same time represented a challenge for several participants. Encouraging visitation during periods when agricultural activity is less intensive and reducing visitation levels during peak agricultural periods may partly ameliorate this difficulty. Issues over health and safety and in particular liability represent another challenge for agritourism providers. This was the main reason why most farmers did not allow visitors to engage in farm duties.

The constant demands of tourists have been highlighted as an issue with regards to mass tourism but is seldom highlighted as an issue in rural tourism. Boissevain (1996: 9) writes: 'Without some respite from the constant demands of tourists, hosts become enervated and their behaviour towards tourists hostile'. However, there is no evidence presented here to suggest that agritourism accommodation providers are hostile to visitors: in fact, visitor satisfaction appears to be a top priority for enterprise owners.

Although only one enterprise owner mentioned 'skills' as a particular challenge, one quarter of all agritourism owners found the lack of tourism training problematic when starting, and 30 per cent found a general lack of guidance difficult. The greatest problem for most farmers was establishing how to market the tourism enterprise (59 per cent found this problematic).

*Table 14.5* Difficult aspects of operating an agritourism accommodation business

|  | *N times cited* |
| --- | --- |
| *Conflicts with agriculture* |  |
| Practical conflicts | 14 |
| Both businesses peaking at same time | 3 |
| Health & safety issues | 3 |
| *Time issues* |  |
| No free time | 6 |
| Too much work | 4 |
| Long hours | 2 |
| Extremely busy summers | 2 |
| Ties you down | 1 |
| *Customers* |  |
| Constant demands | 3 |
| Customers with a lack of respect for the countryside | 1 |
| Customers with limited knowledge about farms | 1 |
| Noise | 1 |
| Getting visitors we like | 1 |
| *Family commitments* |  |
| Balancing work and family | 4 |
| *Uncertainty* |  |
| Uncertainty of bookings | 1 |
| Knowing how much advertising is needed | 1 |
| Making money | 1 |
| *Support/help* |  |
| Finding people to help with tourism tasks | 2 |
| *Skills/training* |  |
| Need new skills | 1 |

These findings confirm that many agritourism enterprises have developed in an *ad hoc* manner (Gillespie 2007). The lack of use of organizations such as Scottish Enterprise and the local tourism body (VisitScotland Dumfries & Galloway) in planning the enterprise may represent stubbornness on the behalf of farmers, or could indicate that many diversifiers are unaware of the services that can help businesses achieve their capabilities.

## Conclusion and lessons to be learned

Utilizing qualitative and quantitative approaches, this chapter has provided some characteristics of agritourism in Dumfries & Galloway, south-west Scotland. This constitutes the first exploration of its kind in the region and contributes more generally to a better understanding of this rural sub-sector in Scotland and Europe. The research has probed a limited number of economic dimensions concluding that the proportion of household income derived from agritourism, in most cases, is low. Nevertheless, most enterprise owners acknowledge the importance of this income in sustaining livelihoods at the farm level. This reality needs to be acknowledged where farmers in other regions are considering diversification into tourism. It is also important to point out that agritourism development may not be appropriate or a sustainable option in all rural areas. Available capital, access to markets, landscape characteristics, availability of space or redundant buildings, type of agricultural production, regional saturation of facilities and propensity to tourism activity are just a few factors that need to be considered. Another economic dimension probed was the ability of agritourism to generate employment. It is evident that this form of rural tourism, possibly owing to its small-scale nature, provides few external employment opportunities. However, it can create self-employment opportunities in locations where few other opportunities exist.

This case study also uncovered several social dimensions of agritourism that factor into the sustainability of this form of rural tourism. The maintenance of agricultural identity, ability to meet (and educate) people from different cultures, reducing feelings of isolation, and empowerment of typically female spouses are just some of the social benefits discussed. Potential diversifiers would perhaps benefit from the knowledge that agritourism can have purpose beyond financial dimensions. That said, it should also be made explicit to those considering this diversification pathway that there are challenges to face including conflicts with agriculture and the demanding nature of tourists.

With regards to environmental performance, agritourism businesses, like other tourism enterprises, are likely to come under increasing scrutiny as governments attempt to reduce greenhouse gas (GHG) emissions. Participants engaged with a range of environmental practices and many agritourism owners have utilized embodied energy by recycling redundant farm buildings. As an indicator of environmental performance, membership of the GTBS is very low and more could be done to encourage environmental stewardship in the agritourism sector. The cost of joining such schemes together with strict quality assurance criteria appears to be significant barriers in this case study.

Clarke (1996: 25) has argued that agritourism of the future will profit if it 'strengthens its identity with the "environmentally responsible" position' and suggests agritourism should have an advantage over other types of tourism enterprises owing to its, predominately, small scale and integration within relatively unmodified environmentally attractive rural settings. There appears to have been little progress in terms of the environmental positioning of agritourism and more needs to be done to encourage both provision and utilization of sustainable tourism facilities.

## Notes

1    2002 figures. Number of hotels/motels bed-spaces in Dumfries & Galloway (2840) / (102) Number of hotel/motels in Dumfries & Galloway. Source: www.staruk.org.uk/default.asp?ID = 591&parentid = 512.
2    There are various other factors that can contribute to economic and livelihood sustainability which the author has examined in Dumfries & Galloway, but are beyond the scope of this chapter. These include business goals and strategy (Mitchell and Hall 2005), networking and promotion (Clarke 1996).
3    See http://unfccc.int/2860.php.
4    Climate Change (Scotland) Act 2009.
5    Globally, 90 per cent of the people in these occupations are women (Hemmati 1999).

## References

Becken, S. and Hay, J. E. (2007) *Tourism and Climate Change: Risks and Opportunities*. Clevedon: Channel View.

Berry, S. and Ladkin, A. (1997) 'Sustainable tourism: a regional perspective', *Tourism Management* 18(7): 433–40.

Blackstock, K., McCrum, G., Scott, A. and White, V. (2006) *A Framework for Developing Indicators of Sustainable Tourism*. The Macaulay Institute and The Cairngorms National Park Authority. Part of a SEERAD funded project on Sustainable Rural Development (RO203909).

Blekesaune, A., Brandth, B. and Haugen, M. S. (2008) 'Visiting a farm based tourist enterprise – who are the visitors and what is the future potential?', paper presented at the 17th Nordic Symposium in Tourism and Hospitality Research, 25–27 September.

Boissevain, J. (1996) 'Introduction', in J. Boissevain (ed.) *Coping with Tourists: European Reactions to Mass Tourism*. Oxford: Berghahn Books, pp. 1–26.

Bryden, J., Bell, C., Gilliat, J., Hawkins, E. and MacKinnon, N. (1993) *Farm Household Adjustment in Western Europe, 1986–92*. Brussels: Commission of the European Communities.

Carlsen, J., Getz, D. and Ali-Knight, J. (2001) 'The environmental attitudes and practices of family businesses in the rural tourism and hospitality sectors', *Journal of Sustainable Tourism* 9(4): 281–97.

Cater, C. and Smith, L. (2003) 'New country visions: adventurous bodies in rural tourism', in P. Cloke (ed.) *Country Visions*. Harlow: Pearson Education Limited, pp. 195–217.

Cavaco, C. (1995) 'Rural tourism: the creation of new tourist spaces', in A. Montanari and A. Williams (eds) *European Tourism: Regions, Spaces and Restructuring*. Chichester: John Wiley & Sons, pp. 129–49.

Clarke, J. (1996) 'Farm accommodation and the communication mix', *Tourism Management* 17(8): 611–20.

Crouch, D. (1994) 'Home escape and identity: rural cultures and sustainable tourism', *Journal of Sustainable Tourism* 2(1&2): 93–101.

Denman, R. (1994a) 'The farm tourism market', *Insights* 5: B49–64.

Dernoi, L. A. (1983) 'Farm tourism in Europe', *Tourism Management* 4: 155–66.

—— (1991a) 'Canadian country vacations: the farm and rural tourism in Canada', *Tourism Recreation Research* 16(1): 15–20.

—— (1991b) 'About rural and farm tourism', *Tourism Recreation Research* 16(1): 3–6.

Dymond, S. J. (1997) 'Indicators of sustainable tourism in New Zealand: a local government perspective', *Journal of Sustainable Tourism* 5(4): 279–93.

Edwards, A., Gasson, R., Haynes, J. and Hill, G. P. (1994) *Socio-Economic Evaluation of the Capital Grant Element of the Farm Diversification Grant Scheme*, FBU Occasional Paper No. 22. London: Wye College.

Frater, J. M. (1983) 'Farm tourism in England', *Tourism Management* 4: 167–79.

Gillespie, S. A. (2007) 'Sustainable rural tourism: the ecological attitudes of visitors and farm-based tourism in Dumfries & Galloway, South-West Scotland', unpublished PhD thesis, University of Glasgow.

Girauld, C. (1999) 'Misunderstanding between men and women in a farm activity', paper presented at the Rural Conference in Wageningen.

Gladstone, J. and Morris, A. (1998) 'The role of farm tourism in the regeneration of rural Scotland', in D. Hall and L. O'Hanlon (eds) *Rural Tourism Management: Sustainable Options*. Auchincruive: The Scottish Agricultural College, pp. 207–21.

—— (2000) 'Farm accommodation and agricultural heritage in Orkney', in F. Brown and D. Hall (eds) *Tourism in Peripheral Areas: Case Studies*. Clevedon: Channel View.

Gössling, S. and Mattsson, S. (2002) 'Farm tourism in Sweden: structure, growth, characteristics', *Scandinavian Journal of Hospitality and Tourism* 2(1): 17–30.

Halfacree, K. H. (1995) 'Talking about rurality: social representations of the rural as expressed by residents of six English parishes', *Journal of Rural Studies* 11(1): 1–20.

Hall, C. M. (1995) *Introduction to Tourism in Australia: Impacts, Planning and Development*, 2nd edn. Melbourne: Longman Cheshire.

Hall, C. M. and Higham, J. (eds) (2005) *Tourism, Recreation and Climate Change*. Clevedon: Channel View.

Hara, T. and Naipaul, S. (2008) 'Agritourism as a catalyst for improving the quality of the life in rural regions: a study from a developed country', *Journal of Quality Assurance In Hospitality & Tourism* 9(1): 1–33.

Haugen, M. S. and Vik, J. (2008) 'Farmers as entrepreneurs: the case of farm-based tourism', *International Journal of Entrepreneurship and Small Business* 6(3): 321–36.

Hemmati, M. (ed.) (1999) *Gender and Tourism: Women's Employment and Participation*. Report to the UN Commission on Sustainable Development, 7th Session, April 1999. London: UNED-UK.

Hjalager, A. (1996) 'Agricultural diversification into tourism: evidence of a European Community Development Programme', *Tourism Management* 17(2): 103–11.

Hummelbrunner, R and Miglbauer, R. (1994) 'Tourism promotion and potential in peripheral areas: the Austrian case', *Journal of Sustainable Tourism* 2(1&2): 41–50.

Ilbery, B. (1998) 'Dimensions of rural change', in B. Ilbery (ed.) *The Geography of Rural Change*. Harlow: Prentice Hall, pp. 1–10.

Ilbery, B. and Bowler, I. (1993) 'The Farm Diversification Grant Scheme: adoption and Non-adoption in England and Wales', *Environment and Planning C* 11: 161–70.

—— (1998) 'From agricultural productivism to post-productivism', in B. Ilbery (ed.) *The Geography of Rural Change*. Harlow: Prentice Hall, pp. 57–84.

Ilbery, B., Bowler, I., Clark, G., Crockett, A. and Shaw, A. (1998) 'Farm-based tourism as an alternative farm enterprise: a case study from the Northern Pennines, England', *Regional Studies* 32(4): 355–64.

Lane, B. (1994) 'Sustainable rural tourism strategies: a tool for development and conservation', *Journal of Sustainable Tourism* 2(1–2): 102–11.

McGehee, N. G., Kim, K. and Jennings, G. R. (2007) 'Gender and motivation for agri-tourism entrepreneurship', *Tourism Management* 28(1): 280–9.

McIntosh, A. and Campbell, T. (2001) 'Willing Workers on Organic Farms (WWOOF): a neglected aspect of farm tourism in New Zealand', *Journal of Sustainable Tourism* 9(2): 111–27.

Marsden, T. (1998) 'Economic perspectives', in B. Ilbery (ed.) *The Geography of Rural Change*. Harlow: Prentice Hall, pp. 13–30.

Mitchell, M. and Hall, D. (2005) 'Rural tourism as sustainable business: key themes', in D. Hall, I. Kirkpatrick and M. Mitchell (eds) *Rural Tourism and Sustainable Business*. Clevedon: Channel View, pp. 3–16.

Morrison, A. M., Pearce, P. L., Moscardo, G., Nadkarni, N. and O'Leary, J. T. (1996) 'Specialist accommodation: definition, markets served, and roles in tourism development', *Journal of Travel Research* 35(1): 18–26.

Moscardo, G., Morrison, A. M. and Pearce, P. L. (1996) 'Specialist accommodation and ecologically-sustainable tourism', *Journal of Sustainable Tourism* 4(1): 29–52.

Nilsson, P. A. (2002) 'Staying on farms: an ideological background', *Annals of Tourism Research* 29(1): 7–24.

Oppermann, M. (1995) 'Holidays on the farm: a case study of German hosts and guests', *Journal of Travel Research* 34(1): 63–7.

Orban, C. and Teckenberg, K. (1996) *Farm Tourism as a Substitute for Decline in Agro-based Economies: Case Studies in Wales*. Ostersund: Mid-Sweden University, Department of Tourism Studies.

Phillip, S., Hunter, C. and Blackstock, K. (2009) 'A typology for defining agritourism', *Tourism Management*, in press.

Questions Answered Ltd (2004) *North West Farm Tourism Initiative Evaluation: Baseline Study*.Available at: www.cumbriatourism.info (accessed 18 October 2005).

Reisinger, Y. (1994) 'Social contact between tourists and hosts of different cultural backgrounds', in A. V. Seaton *et al.* (eds) *Tourism: State of the Art*. Chichester: John Wiley & Sons, pp. 743–54.

Roberts, L. (2002) 'Farm tourism – its contribution to the economic sustainability of Europe's countryside', in R. Harris, P. Williams and T. Griffin (eds) *Sustainable Tourism: A Global Perspective*. Oxford: Elsevier Butterworth-Heinemann.

Robson, C. (2002) *Real World Research: A Resource for Social Scientists and Practitioner-researchers*, 2nd edn. Oxford: Blackwell.

Scott, D., Amelung, B., Becken, S., Ceron, J. P., Dubois, G., Gössling, S., Peeters, P. and Simpson, M. (2008) 'Climate change and tourism: responding to global challenges', paper presented to United Nations World Tourism Organization (UNWTO), United Nations Environment Programme (UNEP) and World Meteorological Organization (WMO), UNWTO, Madrid, Spain.

Scott, J. (2000) *Social Network Analysis: A Handbook*. London: Sage.

Scottish Enterprise Dumfries & Galloway (2004) *Economic Audit 2004: Statistics and Trends in Dumfries & Galloway's Economy*. Dumfries: SEDG and CogentSI.

Scottish Executive (2006) *Scottish Agricultural Census Summary Sheets by Geographic Area: June 2005*. Edinburgh: Scottish Executive.

Sharpley, R. and Vass, A. (2006) 'Tourism, farming and diversification: an attitudinal study', *Tourism Management* 27(5): 1040–52.

Shucksmith, D. M. and Smith, R. (1991) 'Farm household strategies and pluriactivity in Upland Scotland', *Journal of Agricultural Economics* 42(3): 340–53.

Shucksmith, D. M., Bryden, J., Rosenthall, P., Short, C. and Winter, D. M. (1989) 'Pluriactivity, farm structures and rural change', *Journal of Agricultural Economics* 40: 345–60.

Simpson and Brown Architects (2001) *The Conversion of Redundant Farm Steadings to Other Uses*. Report produced for the Scottish Executive Central Research Unit, Edinburgh.

Slee, B. (1998) 'Tourism and rural development in Scotland', in R. MacLellan and R. Smith (eds) *Tourism in Scotland*. Oxford: International Thomson Business Press, pp. 93–111.

Slee, B., Barnes, A., Thomson, K., Roberts, D. and Wright, I. (2001) *Agriculture's Contribution to Scottish Society, Economy and Environment: A Literature Review for the Scottish Executive Rural Affairs Department and CRU*. Aberdeen: University of Aberdeen Department of Agriculture & Forestry and Macaulay Land Use Research Institute.

Stark, C., Gibbs, D., Hopkins, P., Belbin, A., Hay, A. and Selvaraj, S. (2006) 'Suicide in farmers in Scotland', *Rural and Remote Health* 6(509): 1–9.

Sznajder, M., Przezborska, L. and Scrimgeour, F. (2009) *Agritourism*. Wallingford: CABI.

Tao, T. C. H. and Wall, G. (2009) 'Tourism as a sustainable livelihood strategy', *Tourism Management* 30(1): 90–8.

United Nations (1992) *Agenda 21: Earth Summit – The United Nations Programme of Action from Rio*. New York: The United Nations Department of Public Information.

VisitScotland (2009) *Tourism in Dumfries & Galloway 2008*. Available at: www.visitscotland.org/provisional_dumfries – galloway_2008.pdf (accessed 10 February 2010).

Walford, N. (2001) 'Patterns of development in tourist accommodation enterprises on farms in England and Wales', *Applied Geography* 21: 331–45.

Weaver, D. B. and Fennell, D. A. (1997) 'The vacation farm sector in Saskatchewan: a profile of operations', *Tourism Management* 18(6): 357–65.

# 15 Moorsbus

## Towards a holistic approach to rural bus services in the North York Moors National Park

*Lynton J. Bussell and William Suthers*

## Introduction

Increased tourism has resulted in transport problems around the world, none more so than in the UK National Parks where narrow country roads become easily congested. To address the problem, National Parks seek transport solutions to alleviate the environmental impact of visitors and in pursuit of other objectives. This chapter examines the reasons for introducing subsidized public transport, focusing on one particular park, the North York Moors National Park (NYM). Like many tourist areas, NYM suffers from traffic congestion that is linked to park visitor use of private cars. To persuade them to switch from their cars to public transport, the notion of Moorsbus was conceived.

In the early 1980s, a subsidized network of buses was introduced which operated throughout the peak tourist period. Since then the Moorsbus network has experienced significant growth and is now recognized as an example of best practice among the numerous schemes which run throughout UK National Parks. The objectives of schemes like Moorsbus are fourfold: (1) to improve social inclusion; (2) to reduce the environmental impact; (3) to maintain links between rural communities; and, (4) to help stimulate the rural economy. Although all four notions are considered, the NYM park authority focus on the first two objectives. This chapter explores a variety of approaches to investigate the effectiveness of Moorsbus which include a series of face-to-face interviews with NYM officers and representatives of North Yorkshire County Council (NYCC). A survey of local businesses was carried out via a postal questionnaire and follow-up telephone interviews. Finally, an ethnographic approach was adopted through participant observation in the NYM. The study raises a number of questions relating to the efficiency and effectiveness of the operation. More generally, it raises questions of the impact of initiatives such as the Moorsbus as a means of encouraging sustainable tourism within National Parks. In conclusion, a framework for assessing the rural bus systems in a more holistic manner is proposed.

## Background

The concept of the National Park was first raised by the poet William Wordsworth in 1810 with regard to the Lake District, when he published his *Guide to the Lakes* in which he expressed the opinion that the area should be: 'a kind a national property in which every man has a right and interest who has an eye to perceive and a heart to enjoy' (Lake District National Park Authority 2001: 1). However, it was in the USA that the establishment of the first National Park, Yellowstone, occurred in 1872, and it was to be more than half a century before the concept crossed back over the Atlantic.

The objective of the National Park was that the countryside should be protected from the threat posed by population growth as a consequence of rapid industrialization. In 1750, the UK population was 5.74 million; by 1800, this had increased to 10 million, by 1900, to over 30 million and in 1950, 56 million (Jefferies 2005). Since then, it has levelled off to the current figure of 60 million (ONS 2009). Hence, protecting the countryside became a pressing issue in the UK from the mid-nineteenth century following the Industrial Revolution a century earlier. This concern for the environment was enunciated by John Ruskin who was a contemporary of John Muir (the driving force behind the Yosemite National Park) and Wordsworth's successor as an advocate of Lake District preservation (Sarre *et al.* 1991). Eventually, this type of pressure led to the formation of four National Parks in England and Wales in 1951, following the Dower Report (NPEW 1945). There are now 15 National Parks in the UK and over 1000 worldwide.

In more recent years the expansion in car ownership has brought the countryside and National Parks within reach of both day trippers and commuters and with it increased threats to the environment. In the UK, over 90 per cent of visits to National Parks (Reeves 2006) and 57 per cent of day visits to the countryside are by car, while just 1 per cent are by bus or coach (Natural England 2007). As a consequence, National Parks have been facing pressure to promote alternative methods of access.

The NYM lies on the east coast of Northern England and covers an area of 1436 km² (554 square miles). It is quite a low-lying area of moorland with the highest point, Round Hill on Urra Moor, only 409m above sea level. The area is dotted with a number of small villages based on a traditional sheep farming, agricultural economy, although now an increasing proportion of employment is connected with the tourist industry. The resident population is around 25,000 which is boosted by 10 million visitor days per year. This means that on average half those in the park are visitors (NYMPA 2006).

Visitors to the NYM are often day trippers from the nearby urban conurbations: Teesside on the northern boundary; Humberside to the south east; and Leeds to the south west. Like tourist areas everywhere, over recent decades the NYM has experienced an increasing traffic problem. In response to the negative environmental impacts of traffic on the otherwise quiet countryside infrastructure, NYM has promoted Moorsbus, a subsidized bus network which attempts to persuade drivers to switch from their cars during the peak tourist times and hence reduce the carbon footprint of the park. It also aims to facilitate visits from less affluent groups residing in nearby urban conurbations. Although Moorsbus is one of the earliest subsidized transport networks in National Parks, it is far from unique as all face similar problems (see Table 15.1).

The aims of these services are the same: to encourage social inclusion; to preserve the environment; to connect local communities; and to enhance the local economy. Although some services operate all year round, service density is increased during the summer months from Easter to the end of September and most only operate during that period. The most comprehensive network is that of the NYM Moorsbus and hence it provides the ideal subject for further detailed investigation.

All the operations are subsidized and so there is an obligation on the part of park authorities to show that they provide value for money. Hence, it is important to assess the benefits which accrue from the service and weigh these against the costs of subsidizing the network. The NYM collect a great deal of data from users to analyse their effectiveness. This chapter adopts a more holistic assessment using data collected through: interviews; participant observation (Gillham 2000); a business survey; and the use of published data from a variety of sources including the NYM and the Lake District National Park Authority (LDNPA). The main focus is the impact of Moorsbus on the local economy and the environmental impact of service.

## The Moorsbus operation

Public transport access to National Parks has been provided for many years but took its present form following bus deregulation in 1986, which saw substantial change in the UK bus industry (Bussell and Suthers 1999; 2008). It is overseen by NYM who pay great attention to user comments, carrying out regular surveys on the buses. Moorsbus sits well with the NYM philosophy of a Greater National Park concept and is a key element in the NYM best value reports (NYMPA 2006; Reeves 2006). Moorsbus aims to be inclusive and tries to encourage those who live close to the NYM to use its facilities, especially those from nearby urban conurbations. However, participant observation suggests that such journeys would be arduous at best. For example, to catch the Moorsbus from Hartlepool or Hull, take a walk in the hills and return all in one day is almost impossible.

Moorsbus currently costs over £250,000 per year to operate, with recent tender costs being £260,694 which, along with a publicity budget of £18,000, amounts to a subsidy of £4.19 for each journey (CNP 2006). The main source of funds is NYCC supplemented by other national funding schemes. The level of subsidy raises an important policy issue as NYCC

*Table 15.1* Public transport provision in UK National Parks

| National Park | Bus service | Rail service |
| --- | --- | --- |
| Brecon Beacons | Beacons Bus (bikes) | Brecon Mountain Railway |
| The Broads | Anglian 711<br>Broads Hopper (cycles) | |
| Cairngorms | Heather Hopper | Strathspey Steam Railway |
| Dartmoor | Sunday Rover<br>Haytor Hopper<br>Freewheeler<br>Canoebus | Dartmoor Railway |
| Exmoor | Local buses only | West Somerset Railway |
| Lake District | Mountain Goa<br>Honister Rambler<br>Borrowdale Rambler | Lakeside and Haverthwaite<br>Ravenglass and Eskdale<br>Also, Lake Crusiers |
| Loch Lomond and the Trossachs | Trossachs Trundler | West Highland Line |
| New Forest | Bluestar Tour Bus | Brokenhurst-Lymington Branch |
| North York Moors | Moorsbus<br>Yorkshire Coastliner | North Yorkshire Moors Railway<br>Esk Valley Line |
| Northumberland | AD122 Hadrian's Wall Bus Kielder Bus<br>Postbus | |
| Peak District | Transpeak<br>PeakBus | Hope Valley Line<br>Peak Rail |
| Pembrokeshire Coast | Poppit Rocket<br>Celtic Coaster<br>Coastal Cruiser<br>Puffin Shuttle | |
| Snowdonia | Sherpa | Conway Valley Line<br>Ffestiniog Railway<br>Cambian Coast Line |
| South Downs | Downlander | |
| Yorkshire Dales | Dalesbus<br>Nidderdale Rambler<br>Ingleborough Pony<br>Fountains Abbey Shuttle<br>Malham Tarn Shuttle | Settle-Carlisle<br>Dales Rail |

Source: National Parks (2009).

subsidizes bus travel for five reasons, the lowest priority being tourism. Interviews with representatives of NYCC indicate they have a current maximum subsidy level of £7.50 and so Moorsbus is potentially one of the most expensive parts of their subsidized bus network. These costs are further complicated by the controversy of free UK wide bus travel for the over-60s which led to large numbers of Moorsbus users not even paying the £4 daily fare during 2008. The concession has subsequently been withdrawn for some tourist buses which will impact on Moorsbus. Hence, care will have to be exercised and these policy adjustments should be taken into account in any future user analysis.

Originally Moorsbus operated on Sundays and two days per week. This was subsequently extended to all days during the school summer holidays and it currently runs from Easter to the end of September with increased density during the school summer holiday period. Hence, any analysis of Moorsbus statistics should take into account such operational changes, although this is not straightforward as Table 15.2 shows.

It is clear from the figures in Table 15.2 that the number of passengers carried has grown steadily over the past 10 years. However, this is partly due to the increase in the number of operating days up to 2006. Of particular significance is the fall in the number of operating days over the past two years and the increase in passengers carried per day. This may suggest that the operation has been targeted more effectively over the past two years.

Before bus deregulation, West Yorkshire and United bus companies ran registered commercial services into the moors with NYM making a nominal contribution of £500 towards their marketing costs. In 1992, the basis on which contracts and timetables could be set was changed. Funding could be justified by social inclusion and subsidies became available to operators like Moorsbus. This applied particularly to Teesside and Humberside where car ownership was low but also applied to York and West Yorkshire. Hence, the service expanded progressively to achieve a range of strategic goals.

*Table 15.2* Moorsbus usage

| Year | Total passengers | Operating days | Passengers per day |
|------|------------------|----------------|--------------------|
| 1998 | 13,603 | 27 | 368 |
| 2001 | 28,235 | 64 | 441 |
| 2004 | 40,592 | 141 | 288 |
| 2006 | 60,856 | 173 | 352 |
| 2008 | 62,202 | 122 | 510 |

Source: NYMPA (2003; 2009).

Note
These figures must be considered with care as the structure of the service in terms of network density and frequency has changed continuously.

These focused primarily on persuading people to use the bus rather than their car so as to reduce congestion and, more recently, the carbon footprint of NYM. The routes were extended outside the park to encourage visits from areas with low car ownership and to target holidaymakers in Whitby. The latter group can now travel more easily into the park on steam trains following the extension of the North York Moors Railway. The management of NYM also have an obligation to support their local communities under the Access to the Countryside Act (1949). Moorsbus helps the conservation of these communities by supporting the social networks and economic needs of NYM villages. The Environment Act (1995) implied that local communities should be supported within expenditure limits. Hence, subsidies for Moorsbus can be justified on a wide and complex range of policy grounds.

Every five years NYM draw up a Management Plan which is supplemented by regular 'Best Value' audits. The operation of Moorsbus and public transport arrangements form a central theme of the plan. Furthermore, it highlights the issue of potential conflict in the optimal operation of the service when the interests of locals may be at odds with those of tourists (Dickinson and Robbins 2008). The bus may be seen as a lifeline for small local communities, which enables residents without cars to visit friends and relatives, transport children to school or provide OAPs with independence. An optimal service with these requirements will be at odds with the appropriate service network which focuses on the needs of tourists.

NYM are constantly reviewing the operation of the Moorbus with a view to implementing changes. However, it should be noted that the operation of the Moorsbus is often cited as an example of 'best practice' in relation to the operation of rural bus services (Transport 2000, 2001). Lumsden (2006: 761) elaborates further stating that the Moorbus is highlighted as the best practice example, 'where bespoke networks are planned as part of a holistic approach to sustainable tourism transport development and branded accordingly in collaboration with all stakeholders'.

## Measuring performance

For all subsidized bus operations of this nature, it is imperative that subsidy levels are justified. This leads to considerable data collection and analysis. Generally based on consumer satisfaction, some attempt is made to consider the impact on car journeys or car journeys saved. A recent study carried out by Guiver and Lumsden (2005), considered whether rural leisure bus services were doing the following: reducing car use; reducing social exclusion; and increasing economic activity due to spending by bus passengers. The study covered 18 areas of the country which operate leisure bus services (Guiver *et al.* 2007). However, the North Moors National Park did not participate in this survey, preferring to rely on their own survey methods.

The idea of using 'carrots' and 'sticks' to persuade or force passengers to use public transport was suggested by Bussell and Suthers (1999). Holding and Kreutner (1998) analysed such an approach in their study of Bayerischer-Wald, a National Park on the border of south-east Germany and the Czech Republic. Holding and Kreutner compare both 'carrot' and 'stick' transport strategies where one route was closed with visitors forced to 'park and ride' while another offered an optional park and ride service. In this instance, the 'stick' approach was clearly more successful. Visitors were happy to accept the switch to a bus so long as waiting times were minimized by a regular network operating to timetable. They appreciated the environmental benefits and were in favour of further road closures. In fact, the weather was a greater concern than the inconvenience of the bus. Locals were less favourably inclined to the road closures and of course as they can vote, hold greater sway with policy-making local politicians. There are clearly questions about whether the response would be the same in the UK where the only example of such a road closure in the Peak District National Park has met with a mixed response. It could be argued that the time has come for UK National Park authorities to be more ambitious, introduce more 'sticks' in the form of car park charges, road pricing and selective road closure. Certainly, rural transport problems are likely to increase in future so inaction is not an option.

Downward and Lumsden (2004) are similarly critical of the lack of progress in achieving a transport solution in National Parks. They highlight the dilemma in objectives of stimulating rural tourism for economic reasons and reducing traffic for environmental reasons. Three transport management tools are suggested: restriction ('sticks'); encouragement of environmentally friendly modes ('carrots'); and education measures. There are many examples of 'carrots' relating to Moorsbus from heavy subsidy to discount vouchers at park businesses. Authorities are more reluctant to introduce 'sticks', although NYM have recently introduced more car park charges, partly refundable against a Moorsbus ticket. Downward and Lumsden suggest that segments react differently to 'sticks': locals are not generally keen and local businesses feel that car visitors spend more and should, therefore, not be discouraged.

Guiver and Lumsden (2005) report that there are few comparisons of the spending by car users and bus users and that those which do exist give contradictory evidence. For example, in Shropshire, the average spending of bus users visiting a National Trust property exceeded that of car users, whilst in Borrowdale the car users spent an average of around £11 more than bus users. The results of a 2006 Survey (Guiver et al. 2007), showed that across the 18 areas considered, spending varied between £8.83 and £23.51 per person, with the largest expenditure being on food and drink. In some instances, spending by passengers without cars exceeded that of car users.

Downward and Lumsden's (2004) survey of visitors to the NYMs compared expenditure by car visitors and those arriving by bus. They found that car visitors spend significantly more, perhaps almost twice as much as bus visitors. The main item of expenditure, food, accounted for 34 per cent of total spend. Downward and Lumsden suggest that for a 'carrot and stick' strategy to become more acceptable to local businesses, bus operators must adjust their operations to encourage increased spending. They suggest that bus timetables should be adjusted to enable passengers to stay longer and that they should be directed towards local businesses. It could be argued that NYM authority addresses this issue by providing discount vouchers at local businesses for Moorsbus users. Participant observation also supported the view that bus users spend less as opportunities to eat and shop prove very limited during a full day in the NYM due to scheduling aspects of the service which were compounded by a timetabling error. However, in more recent literature there has been a shift in emphasis away from discussion of the efficacy of the traditional 'sticks and carrots approach' towards an understanding of the attitude of those visitors who might shift modes under certain circumstances (Dickinson *et al.* 2004; Guiver *et al.* 2007). Anable (2005), for example, suggests a typology of visitors with varying potential to switch from car to less environmentally damaging modes of travel and differences in the type of trigger that would encourage such a change.

Lumsden (2006), reporting on the views of transport planners designing bus routes, identified two core groups: 'Activity Seekers' who use the bus mainly to avoid taking one or two cars in order to complete a linear walk; 'Sightseers' who prefer not to use the car to avoid car parking costs or driving in an unfamiliar area. A further more loosely based grouping identified by Lumsden is those using the services to visit friends and relatives or to visit local inns/shops and those travelling for nostalgia reasons or as transport enthusiasts. The challenge to transport planners is to make the bus network a more attractive option to car owners in these two identified groupings. NYM have begun to publish a range of short guides of walks which can be completed by using Moorsbus and have introduced the Heritage Bus, a vintage bus, based at Goathland. The Heritage Bus has proved very popular and there are plans to expand this type of service although unfortunately it does little to meet environmental objectives due to high carbon emissions.

## Moorsbus and the local economy

As mentioned above, NYM have attempted to direct passengers towards local businesses by advertising special discounts at various establishments on the routes. These are advertised in the Moorsbus literature and on the tickets. It is interesting to consider the impact of this strategy on these 'frontline businesses'. Twenty businesses feature on the Moorsbus literature and these were surveyed by Bussell and Suthers (2008). All businesses were sent a postal questionnaire which was followed up with a telephone call to those who did not respond. Seventeen businesses replied and ten agreed to further in-depth interviews. Some results from the questionnaire are summarized in Table 15.3.

*Table 15.3* Impact of Moorsbus on business

|  | (%) |
| --- | --- |
| Records of Moorsbus customers | 53 |
| Moorsbus leads to increase in customers | 24 |
| Moorsbus leads to increase in profits | 18 |
| Moorsbus is good for the local community | 77 |

Source: Bussell and Suthers (2008).

Only just over half of the businesses responding kept records of those customers using vouchers. One respondent stated, 'There are so few, it's not worth recording',

However, most respondents were able to give an opinion on whether the link with Moorsbus was leading to an increase in customers or profits. The general results are not encouraging with less than a quarter of respondents experiencing an increase in either customers or profits. One respondent summed up the problem as follows: 'Most people who use the Moorsbus are walkers who come to appreciate the beauty of the moors and enjoy the countryside – not necessarily to spend money',

Clearly, such comments support the findings of previous studies in the NYM such as Downward and Lumsden (2004) and participant observation (Bussell and Suthers 2008). Although, as highlighted above, nationally the evidence is by no means conclusive in terms of rural bus users in general (Guiver and Lumsden 2005).

It was also a concern that a majority of businesses felt that customer numbers from Moorsbus had declined in the last five years. As we have shown earlier in Table 15.2, this is not the case according to official statistics but it could be that fewer customers are making use of the discount vouchers. Although this was only a small survey of a few 'frontline businesses', it provides a gloomy picture from businesses who would expect to feel the greatest impact from Moorsbus. However, despite little support for the view that businesses directly benefited from the operation of the Moorsbus, business respondents did overwhelmingly express the view that the Moorsbus benefits the local community and the area in general. Respondents were asked to list the perceived general benefits of the Moorsbus to the area and the local community. Table 15.4 summarizes the factors most frequently mentioned by the business respondents.

Table 15.4 shows that the most important perceived benefit of Moorsbus was that it provided affordable transport for both local people and tourists. All the business respondents agreed that the service provided excellent value for money at £4.00 for a day ticket. To quote one of the respondents on this issue, 'Local people and visitors gain benefits from this network of transport by the availability and quality of the service . . . it is also good value for money'.

*Table 15.4* Benefits of Moorsbus

| Factors mentioned | Number of responses | (%) |
|---|---|---|
| Provides affordable transport | 7 | 41 |
| Improves access to countryside | 5 | 29 |
| Reduces congestion | 4 | 24 |
| Improves the environment | 3 | 18 |
| Provides an appreciation of nature | 1 | 6 |

Source: Bussell and Suthers (2008).

A number of our respondents also mentioned that Moorsbus provides access to the countryside for those without cars and for low income groups, which meets an objective of the NYM outlined above. Business respondents were also aware of the environmental benefits of the operation of the Moorsbus. This response is poignantly summed up in the following quote: 'A reduction in car use can only be beneficial to the North York Moors and local population and environmentally', Another respondent added, 'During the daffodil season in Farndale it [the Moorsbus] helps to relieve congestion on narrow roads up the valley',

A further area of research carried out by Bussell and Suthers (2009), on behalf of the NYM, involves the impact of the operation of the Moorsbus on the environment. In the past, calculations have been carried out to show the number of car miles saved by the operation of the Moorsbus and this data was used to demonstrate the reduction in the carbon footprint. For example, the Park Authority estimate that Moorsbus has reduced car trips in the National Park by in excess of a million since its inception in 1994, and that 45 per cent of their passengers came from households with a car (Transport 2000; 2001). The Park Authority calculates the savings in terms of carbon dioxide emissions, which amounted to 562 tonnes in 2008 (NYMPA 2009). Bussell and Suthers (2009) used information on the Moorsbus fleet along with published data on the carbon dioxide emissions from rural buses to estimate the carbon footprint of Moorsbus in the same period at 328 tonnes. The calculations were corroborated by telephone interviews with bus operators. This benchmark confirms the positive environmental impact of Moorsbus in terms of carbon emissions as well as congestion. It should, however, be noted that changes in engine design and a reliance on carbon alone as a proxy for pollution, may mean that environmental benchmarks such as this need reassessing in the near future.

### Conclusion and lessons to be learned

NYM carry out extensive user surveys which show that users are satisfied with the service and also show that there has been a significant increase in users of the service, with a saving of 1,670,000 car miles in the National

Park during 2008. Nevertheless the cost is high. A subsidy level in excess of £4 per journey has meant that the service is under pressure, from NYCC in particular, to operate more efficiently and reduce subsidy levels. These surveys also show that the service is most widely used by the 'greying' middle classes rather than widening the horizons of working-class families from the nearby urban conurbations, a view confirmed by participant observation and supported by Guiver and Lumsden (2005). It is therefore a challenge to the Moorsbus marketing team to engage more successfully with families and young people.

Although the service commands a great deal of support from local residents, this is not translated into economic benefits as perceived by local business. However, it should be noted that even though local businesses do not recognize any great direct financial benefit, they do generally support the service and see wider general advantages in terms of social inclusion and environmental gains. The service is currently under review to ensure that the benefits can be maximized and costs minimized. Recent studies (Bussell and Suthers 2008; Guiver *et al.* 2007) suggest a need for a more holistic view of the network that would clearly demonstrate Moorsbus' contribution towards sustainable tourism which in turn would assist the achievement of sustainable communities within the NYM.

The type of framework envisaged would combine the bus user surveys currently carried out to assess satisfaction; the monitoring of social inclusion objectives; and an accurate view of spending within the Park. More accurate data on spending will assist the calculation of the multiplier effect within the NYM by both bus and car users (Weaver and Lawton 2002). The Park Authority are also planning to carry out non-user surveys to discover ways of persuading car users to switch to the bus network ('Carrots') and to assess their views on measures designed to increase the relative cost of car use through car park charges or road pricing ('Sticks') (Steiner and Bristow 2000). However, other important measurements are the reduction in emissions which would support an environmental case and a regular business survey to monitor the economic impact of the service.

Other ideas which have emerged from surveys such as those by Bussell and Suthers (2008) and Guiver and Lumsden (2005) could be introduced quickly and with relatively little expense were: the need to introduce capacity for earlier arrivals and later departures; extended stops at popular places on the route to allow bus travellers to make more use of local facilities before carrying on their journey; improved signage and on-board information at key stops to make visitors more aware of the amenities; and a general improvement in the reliability of the service and information provided. The review is also considering the introduction of 'real-time information' at key stops and perhaps on the buses, leaflets linking the bus network to popular local walks and more integration with other modes of local transport.

Perhaps the most obvious lesson when dealing with the environmental problems of transport is that ultimately there is no definitive solution. Although one lesson learned from this study is that there is always scope for improvement when attempting to promote sustainable transport policies in places such as National Parks. After over twenty years operation with Moorsbus seen as an example of best practice, the Park Authority and its partners now recognize that they should adopt a more holistic approach to the operation of Moorsbus, taking account of all the stakeholders involved. In the absence of such an approach, stakeholder conflicts arise which threaten the long-term viability of this type of venture. A further lesson is that in addition to targeting users and obtaining their views, attention should also be paid to non-users who may potentially be attracted to the service. The views of non-users may enable customization leading to increased usage by: younger people; ethnic groups; working-class groups from urban centres; and car users. Ultimately the success of Moorsbus and similar operations should be judged on the extent to which they meet four objectives: environmental, economic, social inclusion and community benefits, and the degree to which this enables justification of their subsidy.

## References

Anable, J. (2005) '"Complacent car addicts" or "aspiring environmentalists"? Identifying travel behaviour segments using attitude theory', *Transport Policy* 12: 65–78.

Bussell, L. J. and Suthers, W. (1999) 'On the buses? Bus deregulation on Teesside, 10 years down the road', *Northern Economic Review* 28(Winter): 35–52.

—— (2008) 'The impact of the North York Moors National Park on local businesses', *Northern Economic Review* 38(Spring): 103–11.

—— (2009) 'Moorsbus Emissions', unpublished report to North York Moors National Park Authority.

CNP (2006) *Sustainable Recreation Transport: National Park Authority Activity on the Ground*. London: CNATIONAL PARK.

Dickinson, J. E. and Robbins, D. (2008) 'Representations of tourism transport problems in a rural destination', *Tourism Management* 29: 1110–21.

Dickinson, J. E., Calver, S., Watters, K. and Wilkes, K. (2004) 'Journeys to heritage attractions in the UK: a case study of National Trust property visitors in the South West', *Journal of Transport Geography* 12: 103–13.

Downward, P. and Lumsden, L. (2004) 'Tourism transport and visitor spending: a study in the North York Moors National Park, UK', *Journal of Transport Research* 42(May): 415–20.

Gillham, B. (2000) *Case Study Research Methods*. London: Continuum.

Guiver, J. and Lumsden, L. (2005) *Tourism on Board: Report of Survey of Buses in Tourist Areas*. Preston: Institute of Transport and Tourism. University of Central Lancashire.

Guiver, J., Lumsden, L., Weston, R. and Ferguson, M. (2007) 'Do buses help meet tourism objectives? The contribution and potential of scheduled buses in rural destination areas', *Transport Policy* 14: 275–82.

Holding, D. M. and Kreutner, M. (1998) 'Achieving a balance between "carrots" and "sticks" for traffic in National Parks: the Bayerischer Wald project', *Transport Policy* 5: 175–83.

Jefferies, J. (2005) 'The UK population: past, present and future', in *Focus on People and Migration*, London: HMSO.

Lake District National Park Authority (2001) *A National Park for 50 Years: A National Treasure Forever*. Outcome of Symposium, Royal Geographical Society, November.

Lumsden, L. M. (2006) 'Factors affecting the design of tourism bus services', *Annals of Tourism Research* 33(3): 748–66.

National Parks (2009) *Home Page*. Available at: www.nationalparks.gov.uk.

Natural England (2007) 'England tourism day visits 2005', in *England Leisure Visits Survey*, London: Visit Britain.

NPEW (National Parks in England and Wales) (1945) *Dower Report*, Cmnd 6628. London: HMSO.

NYM (North York Moors Park Authority) (2003) *State of the Park Report 2003*. Helmsley: NYM.

—— (2006) *State of the Park Report 2006*, Helmsley: NYM.

—— (2009) *Moorsbus Review 2009*, Item 11, June, Helmsley: NYM.

ONS (Office of National Statistics) (2009) *Population Trends 136*, Summer. London: HMSO.

Reeves, R. (2006) *Tracking Traffic*. London: CNATIONAL PARK.

Sarre, P., Smith, P. and Morris, E. (1991) *One World for One Earth*. London: Earthscan/OU.

Steiner, T. J. and Bristow, A. L. (2000) 'Road pricing in National Parks: a case study in the Yorkshire Dales National Park', *Transport Policy* 7: 93–103.

Transport 2000 (2001) *Tourism Without Traffic: A Good Practice Guide*. London: Transport 2000 Trust.

Weaver, D. and Lawton, L. (2002) *Tourism Management*. Queensland: John Wiley and Sons Australia Ltd.

# 16 Cultural tourism clusters
## Experiences from Ireland

*Breda McCarthy*

## Introduction

The very concept of cultural tourism suggests that there is a symbiotic relationship between the arts and tourism, and that opportunities for cluster development abound. In fact, relationships between artists and travelers have existed for centuries. The concept of 'cultural tourism' is said to date from the beginning of the seventeenth century when an educated, wealthy elite undertook the Grand Tour (Towner 1984). However, it is only recently that governments have begun to recognize the value of supporting cooperative activity between tourism and the arts. This chapter presents a case study of a cultural tourism cluster in the south-west of Ireland. The research illustrates some of the opportunities and problems that small communities encounter in their attempts to develop cultural tourism. Conclusions are drawn regarding the potential of clustering to support, or hinder, the achievement of arts and tourism policy objectives. The author concludes that cultural tourism clusters are valuable, but they are not the panacea to local economic development that public policy-makers suggest they are.

## Cultural tourism

Cultural tourism, as a sub-discipline of tourism, is attracting increasing interest in the social sciences (Gibson and Connell 2003; Ivanovic 2009; Richards 1994; Urry 1990). According to the World Tourism Organization (2004), cultural tourism involves an immersion in, and the enjoyment of, the lifestyle of the local people, the local area and its identity and character. It encompasses the performing arts, festivals and events, visits to sites and monuments, study tours and pilgrimage travel. Tourism bodies see culture as a means to secure a unique advantage in a competitive marketplace (Getz 1991; Zeppel and Hall 1991). Around the world, state bodies have funded heritage trails, produced festival and events guides and disseminated information on ancestry (Getz 1991; Richards 1994; Zeppel and Hall, 1991). Visits to the country of one's ancestors is associated with both the consumer's history and sense of place and represents a merging of the real and imagined (Herbert 1999).

Music has become part of a branding and destination marketing strategy. Music has the power to transform certain places, as a result of the images and associations with place which are captured in lyrics and in the connections generated between artists and bands or the whole music 'scene' (Gibson and Connell 2003). As regards Ireland, the growth in the Irish diaspora created a new audience for music and dance (Kearns and Taylor 2003); the music appeals not only to large immigrant communities, but to the world market (Smith 2001). The increasing pace of life and commercialization of societies is used to explain the growing interest in traditional music (Kneafsey 2002). Music and dance are signifiers of national myths and stereotypes and shape tourists' expectations (Nicholls 2000; Strachan and Leonard 2004).

According to Hughes (2002), tourism supplies extra audiences for the arts, so tourist boards actively foster relationships with art managers through publications, seminars and best-practice case studies. For those who produce arts events, tourism can be a means of supporting and developing regional arts (Mackellar 2006; Paleo and Wijnberg 2006). Cultural tourists, like any other, require food, accommodation and transportation. Museums and art galleries are expected to meet the needs of visitors by providing visitor information sites, parking, tea rooms and other services. It is axiomatic that retailing, art and culture are part of the overall tourism industry. Governments tend to support entrepreneurial activity in the arts such as the start-up of an arts and craft enterprise, packaged tours, and so forth. However, the literature suggests that the drawing power of the arts is easily overestimated. According to Hughes (2002), the performing arts are important in drawing tourists to a destination, but there are other reasons for travelling to a destination such as the weather, scenery or heritage.

The consumption of culture remains a highly discretionary activity in economic terms and one that is purchased only after more basic needs have been met (Bull 1995). Cultural tourists are regarded favourably as they are affluent, well educated, broadly travelled and in more mature age groupings (Holcomb 1999; Michael 2007a). Cultural tourists come to a destination in search of authenticity and meaningful experiences (Urry 1990). They often seek to participate in experiences related to a particular hobby or recreational interest (Hall and Weiler 1992). For arts organizations, and indeed many other organizations, the capacity to 'produce pleasure' is a dimension of the user's experience (Campbell 1989). Hedonic consumption, which plays an important role in the performing arts, relates to the 'multi-sensory, fantasy and emotive aspects of one's experience with products' (Hirschman and Holbrook 1982: 92). Traditionally, arts organizations have been producer-led or arts-centred (Lampel *et al.* 2000) but there is increasing evidence that arts organizations are adopting a more customer or audience-driven focus and attempting to meet tourist demand (Kennelly 2005).

## The cluster concept and its relevance to tourism destinations

Cluster theory is strongly associated with Michael E. Porter (1990). Porter (1990; 1998), drawing on the work of Alfred Marshall (1890), developed his diamond model which provides a broad framework for the analysis of successful regions. He argues that four factors interact and produce a cluster, which are: a firm's strategy, industry structure and rivalry; factor conditions; demand conditions, and related and supporting industries. Two other factors, chance and government lie outside the diamond model, but influence the business environment in important ways. A key feature of Porter's cluster concept is that location is a significant explanation of competitive advantage and is something that competitors outside the cluster are unable to imitate. Porter (1998: 78) states:

> Critical masses – one place – of unusual competitive success in partic-
> ular fields . . . clusters are geographic concentrations of interconnected
> companies and institutions in a particular field. Clusters encompass an
> array of linked industries and other entities important to competition.

Successful clusters are characterized by access to skilled labour and high quality suppliers; supportive institutions and improved access to specialized training and information; exposure to sophisticated buyers at a local level; innovation through visibility and proximity; lower risk of business failure and higher rates of new business formations (Malmberg and Maskell, 2002; Porter 1990; Rosson 2003).

## The cluster concept and tourism

Despite the substantial literature on clusters (see Lindequist and Power 2002 for a review), its merits and shortcomings (Martin and Sunley 2003), research into the existence of cultural tourism clusters is sparse. Scholars have long noted the tendency for musicians and artists to cluster together (Braunerhjelm 2005; Florida and Mellander 2008; Rosenfeld 2004). Scholars highlight the importance of a creative milieu (Florida 2002) and the potential for in-migrants to develop enterprises and foster the translocation of capabilities. Clustering of cultural activities tends to be associated with cities with the result that cluster formation in non-urban areas has been neglected. Michael (2003: 136), in a paper on tourism micro-clusters in rural Australia, notes that: 'the Porterian approach has been demonstrated in macro-regional analyses, but little has been done to apply these concepts in small regional environments'. He argues that clustering helps create economic and social opportunity in small communities. Irish cluster studies have been undertaken into the software, dairy processing and music sectors

(Clancy *et al.* 2001) but the focus has been on national rather than on regional clusters of competitive performance. Jackson and Murphy (2002: 38) note that 'the cluster concept's applicability to tourism destinations would appear to be particularly germane', given that tourism involves the combination of complementary services. Therefore, the potential for policy applications remains constrained by the absence of any understanding of clustering in the context of cultural tourism. This lacuna in the literature provides a rationale for this study.

As regards the broader tourism field, Porter (1990) used the California wine cluster and Las Vegas gambling cluster as examples in his treatise. There is a small, but growing literature in tourism which addresses the implications of clusters for enhancing tourism growth. The predominant focus has been on wine clusters (Getz and Brown 2006; Hall 2005) but scholars have explored micro-clusters based around antiques (Michael 2007a), healthy lifestyle tourism (Novelli *et al.* 2006), culture (Brown and Geddes 2007), music (Gibson 2002; Gibson and Connell 2003), sun-and-surf tourism (Lafferty and van Fossen 2005), ski tourism (Nordin 2003), and book tourism (Seaton 1999). In an interesting study of Bryon Bay, Australia, Gibson (2002) found that a local university played a central role in music tourism by providing specialized programs, training and infrastructure (i.e. recording facilities and performance venues). In another study on cultural tourism in Cape Breton, the author concluded that the 'inherently local' attributes of physical beauty, friendly people, vibrant culture, helped establish the destination as a tourism cluster (Brown and Geddes 2007).

Table 16.1 outlines the key characteristics of clusters which are further explored in the data findings section. This research is guided by the study of Jackson and Murphy (2002) which analysed tourism destinations in Australia within the framework of Porter's cluster model.

*Table 16.1* Characteristics of clusters

Attract needed services and infrastructure to a region

Generate demand for firms with similar and related capabilities

Require both cooperation and competition

Underpinned by networks and based on social values that foster trust, encourage reciprocity and sustained collaboration

Community culture with supportive public policies, at national and local level

Institutional involvement, associations and organisations providing training, education, information, research and technical support

Private sector leadership and innovation

Source: Rosenfeld (2004), Jackson and Murphy (2002).

## Research objectives, methods and cluster identification

The aim of this chapter is to explore the factors that lead to successful clustering in regional parts of Ireland and to assess the impacts that arise from co-location of complementary firms or actors.

The main research method was the exploratory case study analysis that attempts to determine the existence and impact of clustering on cultural tourism development. A total of 40 semi-structured, in-depth interviews were conducted with policy-makers and practitioners. Since cultural tourism is multifaceted, festivals and interpretative centres were included in the sample. The aim was to engage with local voices as well as the representatives of the main agencies active in tourism and the arts. The interviews were usually conducted face-to-face, although in a few cases, upon request, the interview was conducted over the telephone. Given the local nature of the activity, a tape recorder was not used as it was felt that respondents might feel uncomfortable with a tape recorder or reluctant to commit their words to tape. Participant observation was also undertaken over the five-month research period (May to September 2007). This generated field notes containing the author's personal experience of festivals, events and interpretative centres. A review of policy documents, newspaper articles, websites and promotional literature was also undertaken.

Researchers grappling with the cluster concept are invariably faced with inadequate data and information – usually provided in the form of standard industry classifications – and must interpret it, or reorganize it, in order to identify a cluster (Porter 1990). A decision was taken to focus on two case study regions: peninsular Kerry and County Clare. Based on preliminary research and interviews with experts, these areas seemed to have a distinctive cultural tourism environment with the potential to influence competitive performance.

## Profile of clusters

South Kerry is a prime tourist destination and visitors are attracted by the combination of natural beauty and cultural heritage (ranging from country houses, castles, towers, crosses, monastic remains and museums). Dingle town is reputed to be a haven of traditional music and 'trad sessions' in public houses are an important source of night-time entertainment. A regional airport (Kerry International Airport) has facilitated growth in tourism. The area has a history of in-migration and many well-known visual artists, writers and film-makers live in the area and they evoke the tranquillity and beauty of the area in their work.

The cluster in County Clare is more narrowly focused on the traditional arts, notably, Irish music, song, dance and story-telling. The tourism authority has consistently deployed music to attract backpackers, domestic travellers and international tourists. The region's natural attractions include the Burren (a Special Area of Conservation) and the Cliffs of Moher, an iconic attraction which attracts about a million visitors each year.

## Research findings

### *Attract needed services and infrastructure to a region*

In both South Kerry and Clare, government funding of interpretative centres has increased the scope of heritage resources in these areas.

### *Generate demand for firms with similar and related capabilities*

Related firms include coach tourism, transport, accommodation, local foods, indigenous arts and crafts, website designers, publicans and tour operators, who are independent of the subsidized arts sector, yet part of the local cultural tourism economy. The responsiveness of local industry to tourist demand can be shown in the attempts made to package music into for-profit workshops, hosting of traditional music nights in the local pub, and provision of all-inclusive, cultural holidays that attract long-distance visitors.

### *Require both cooperation and competition*

Cluster participants may compete with other members in their field or support other cluster members by sharing resources. The tourism destinations studied show signs of informal cooperation, such as business referrals, to formal cooperation such as alliances and regional branding initiatives. There are examples of alliances where complementary products are joined together. For instance, the existence of a golf course in a small village had consequential benefits for an art gallery. An enterprising B&B owner marketed their accommodation service with a visit to the nearby World Heritage Site. An agri-tourism venture worked with another to develop a one-day sight-seeing tour.

Tourism operators in small villages are competing against externally-owned, large hotels and coach tour operators, and they are looking for ways to capture greater tourist revenue. The *Kerry GeoPark brand* was driven out of economic necessity and the belief that the arts, heritage and culture have the potential to attract the independent traveller, increase bed-nights, extend visitor length of stay and counteract leakage. Cooperation has led to significant outputs, such as a website, a promotional DVD, provision of training to enhance management capabilities. Local cafés, restaurants and accommodation providers are encouraged to sell locally grown foodstuffs. The rural B&B owners now have a viable hill-walking and cultural tourism package to offer visitors.

Arts-tourism cooperation was evident in the form of an *Open Arts Trail* which was designed to give the visitor a chance to meet the artist who creates and sells the product. Other examples of cooperation are the establishment of a *Cooperative Art Gallery* (the artist essentially cuts out the middle-man), production of local *Arts and Crafts Guides* for the tourist market, the establishment of a conference and *Forum for the Traditional Arts* in county Clare. In this cluster, the local tourist office was also used as a festival office, so shared infrastructure was a benefit in this cluster. Festival organizers had a relationship with local tourist offices is terms of presenting leaflets and advising officials of what was happening over the course of the festival

### Underpinned by networks and based on social values that foster trust, reciprocity and sustained collaboration

There were several examples of networking activity which were outlined in the previous section. This activity resulted in joint marketing, knowledge transfer, training and regional branding. Different ideologies were evident among stakeholders, which has the potential to undermine trust. Attitudes towards arts-tourism networks were generally positive, but some respondents had concerns about the repositioning of traditional music as a tourist spectacle. One respondent remarked that traditional music sessions have an informal and spontaneous nature which could be eroded by tourism and she doubted whether musicians would capture a share of tourism expenditure. Traditional music is not defined in terms of 'professional' or 'amateur' and most musicians are either unable, or do not seek, to make a living out of music. Another example of conflicting ideology comes from the heritage sector. The Office of Public Works (OPW) that oversees heritage sites does not have a marketing remit: its mission is to conserve and preserve, and its agenda is largely separate from tourism.

### Community culture with supportive public policies, at national and local level

Festivals are endemic in the clusters. They typify many festivals around Ireland: they celebrate local traditions, are community-driven and stimulate the local economy. The people who organize the events are doing so in an unpaid capacity and are juggling full-time jobs, yet leadership stability is evident (the same people run these festivals year after year). With funding from the local County Council, seminars on event management have been organized at a local level.

The Local County Council and the Arts, Heritage and Tourism officers act as conduits for information. Attempts are being made to gather specialized information at a local level, i.e. a database of musicians in County Clare, a Visitor Satisfaction Survey; dissemination of information on preservation issues surrounding local heritage sites. Local festival and events guides are designed to build awareness of musical activity and meet the needs of short-stay tourists who would otherwise have to depend on word-of-mouth information. According to the Regional Development Manager, the ultimate aim is 'to make Clare the leading County for quality, all year-round cultural events and festivals'.

The cluster in Kerry, like most Irish-speaking areas, has a tradition of working closely with the development body, Údarás na Gaeltachta.[1] Údarás na Gaeltachta (2005) includes all facets of cultural tourism in its strategic plan, such as language-based enterprise, hill-walking, archaeology courses, painting, making pottery, playing an instrument, learning about literary traditions and traditional life on the Islands. A new branding strategy and website 'GaelSaoire' (Holidays in the Gaeltacht) was developed in the mid-1990s. According to the regional manager, their approach to cultural tourism is to develop 'the marketing, the softer aspects, the capacity-building or training or destination profiling'. The regional manager sees opportunities to market the uniqueness of the area; to package festivals, bring different service providers together and sell the 'totality of the holiday experience'.

### *Institutional involvement, organizations providing training, education, information, research and technical support*

Cultural associations play an important role in keeping traditions alive and setting standards. These include *Comhaltas Ceoltóirí Éireann*[2] who provides music training to young children and adults. Furthermore, their international branch network is used to market traditional festivals. Other associations include the *World Music Centre*, University of Limerick, which is the source of guest speakers and performers for local festivals. *Diseart*, is an educational institute in Dingle, and together with its Director, it plays a central role in cultural tourism by hosting arts festivals, providing advice to local writers and poets and infrastructure for local exhibitions and festivals. *AOIFE* (Association of Irish Festivals and Events) was established to promote best practice and the sharing of experience among a growing network of festival organizers. A local training facility, an *Adult Education Centre*, developed Summer Leisure courses aimed at the tourist market. This project was shaped and orchestrated by the manager. The establishment of a new school, *Oidhreach an Chláir* (Clare College for Traditional Studies, www.oac.ie) is another example of dynamism in the sector. It emerged out of the success of a traditional music festival, the Willie Clancy Summer School, in Clare. Rural development bodies, whose ethos is one of help and support for people living in remote, disadvantaged and peripheral regions, play a role in the cluster. For example the *South Kerry Development Partnership* (SKDP), supports start-ups and work opportunities that are art-related.

*Entrepreneurship and innovation*

Some pioneering cultural tourism initiatives were made by individuals. Private sector projects include *Cill Rialaig* – the rescue and redevelopment of a pre-famine village as a retreat for artists – and there are plans to develop a related World Museum of Contemporary Art. Another ambitious initiative came from the small village of Sneem where local economic necessity has led to the creation of the *GeoPark* brand. The local community were concerned about leakage and that the gains from tourism were flowing outwards. European GeoPark status is being sought. However, gaining the support of the community, the development of business skills and competence are ongoing priorities. World Heritage Site Status is being sought for the *Blasket Islands*.

Cultural vibrancy is shown by the emergence of new festivals, with some being held in the shoulder period of the season in order to improve the seasonality of tourism within the area. Innovation takes on many different forms in the context of cultural tourism – births of new festivals or events, new artistic partnerships and the fusion of different musical traditions. The festival organizers sought to draw on, and showcase, local cultural and heritage resources in its festival programme. For example, a replica famine ship was used to launch one arts festival. Festival organizers included hillwalking in their arts programme. Festivals drew on local talent – local poets, writers, craftspeople, musicians – as well as international talent.

## Discussion

The cultural tourism cluster consists of a rather confused and eclectic range of organizations, people and activities. It is a temporal cluster, since it is more visible and more active in summer, the peak tourist season; it is a small, local, community-driven cluster but one that has links to global musical networks. Key features of this study's cluster are: government involvement, sophisticated demand and entrepreneurship, with regional branding being a key outcome (see Figure 16.1). Figure 16.2 identifies the key elements of the Porter (1998) diamond model and adapts the model to reflect the cultural tourism clustering process.

This study lends support to Porter's (1998) thesis that sophisticated, local demand is a key feature of clusters. In the context of this study, traditional music shapes tourist demand. Anchor events succeed in drawing both a sophisticated, as well as a less sophisticated, market to the region: the dedicated musicians and casual visitors who are not in a position to judge quality. The sophisticated nature of demand is important because it helps shape the image of the destination and spawn demand for cultural tourism – illustrated in the organized pub sessions, fee-paying concerts and packaged tours. The state has supported the development of the cluster by its focus on image-building and in anchoring this vision in practical networking events

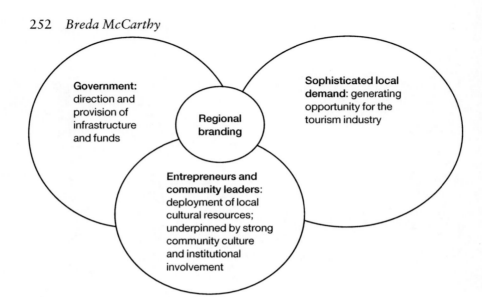

*Figure 16.1* State-dependent cultural tourism cluster.

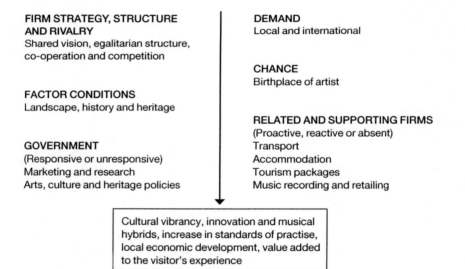

*Figure 16.2* Cultural tourism cluster formation: influential factors.

and provision of arts and heritage infrastructure. The importance of festivals in drawing tourists is well known in the literature (Gibson and Connell 2003; Quinn 2006).

Clusters are underpinned by strong social relationships, networks and a sense of common purpose (Porter 1998). According to Porter (ibid.: 225), networks are the 'social glue that binds clusters together, contributing to the value creation process'. The work of Putnam (1994) on social capital is highly relevant given that festival organizers play a role in strengthening social networks and rejuvenating rural communities. The literature suggests that different ideologies can undermine trust in networks. Artists are hesitant about entering the marketplace and concerned that they may lose control over the quality of their work. Their mission is not explicitly commercial and tensions stem from the artists' creative principles (Brokensha and Guldberg 1992). Another useful viewpoint is provided by Baerenholdt and Haldrup (2006) who emphasize the mobile, global, dispersed nature of networks that underpin cultural tourism. Scholars emphasize the complex nature of interactions and connections in some clusters which can be simultaneously close to home and extending around the world, thus producing local 'buzz' and tapping into global pipelines (Bathelt *et al.* 2004). The importance of local and non-local contacts certainly seems clear from the data collected in this study. Drawing on local musicians helps festival organizers retain support, but they also tap into non-local networks for a pool of talent.

The literature on clusters shows that one of the characteristics of a cluster is the existence of related and supported industries, a 'pooled market' of specialized workers, local suppliers and service providers (Birkinshaw and Hood 2000). The study supports this to a certain extent: the music tourism cluster in Clare led to some demand for specialized inputs such as musical instruments, specialist retailing and recording. However, Ireland's weakness in the downstream stages of the music industry's value chain, i.e. publishing, printing, marketing and distribution, has been noted (Music Board of Ireland 2002). Therefore the impact of music on the Irish economy is not as significant as it could be in terms of turnover, employment and exports.

The concept of 'diagonal clustering' (Michael 2003; 2007b) refers to the co-location of complementary producers (accommodation, activities, transport, etc.) which adds value to the tourism experience. There is some evidence that local conditions, local infrastructure and resources support entrepreneurial activity. Festival organizers draw on local history, myths and legends in their festival programming. Local tour operators are attempting to capitalize on the musical/cultural resources in the area. However, the ad-hoc and informal nature of traditional music activity does limit the development of structured, holiday packages aimed at overseas visitors. In the music field, the emphasis is on the development of social and musical networks as opposed to the creation of business opportunities.

Porter provides a compelling case in defence of rivalry and minimal, direct state involvement in business. Yet, one can argue that cultural tourism is a special case since it is a state-dependent, diverse and highly fragmented sector. For instance, heritage sites are often dependent on public subsidy (Cooke 2006). The history of Irish tourism shows heavy reliance on EU funds (Hurley *et al.* 1994). Business researchers are devoting more attention to different forms of clusters (Markusen 1996). Markusen's concept of the 'state-anchored district' based on a hub-and-spoke design is interesting. The cluster profiled here is not driven primarily by the state; rather it looks something like the triple helix model, based on the relationship between university-industry-government (Etzkowitz and Leydesdorff 2000).

## Cultural cluster development: lessons to be learned

Policy-makers and communities need to be aware of the limits to clustering and the barriers faced by cluster participants. This study suggests that arts and craftspeople are willing to engage with tourism, but musicians seem to have some difficulties with music-tourism packaging and organizers of music festivals do not always see themselves as being part of the tourism industry. While music stimulates growth in tourist demand, and as a corollary, gives rise to new business opportunities, the informal, ad-hoc nature of traditional music and tensions that exist between cultural and commercial perspectives may serve to limit local development.

Many lessons can be learned from this cluster study. The entrepreneurial nature of the community, combined with a close working relationship with local government, is what makes clustering initiatives work. An important characteristic for cluster development is shared vision, shared understanding of what cultural tourism is and how it can contribute to the local economy. The role of the policy-maker in cluster-based economic development is to provide leadership, enhance linkages and relax any impediments or constraints to enterprise development. This study was useful in diagnosing strengths and weaknesses and indicated where improvements may be made. The cultural sector is highly fragmented; tourism policy, heritage policy and arts policy have largely separate agendas and priorities, so it is a difficult sector to manage and coordinate. One recommendation is the appointment of tourism cluster officer, the preparation of cluster strategic plans and cluster funding projects. A cluster approach represents a shift away from funding an individual firm to a cluster – a group of festivals and service providers.

Another lesson for policy-makers is that appropriate data needs to be gathered. The benefits of cultural tourism are often covert and intangible, such as quality of the visitor's experience. This study found that quantitative data was limited or unavailable at local level. Without data, it is impossible to measure the benefits of cultural tourism and easy to overstate or understate its economic benefits. There is a need to track attendance figures at local level: visitor expenditure during festivals, accommodation occupancy rates, employment concentration in cultural sectors, wage rates, in-migration, new business formation, new festivals, and so forth. Such data provides a stronger case for support of the arts, culture and tourism.

# Conclusion

It is part of conventional wisdom that the arts and tourism are linked and enjoy a mutually beneficial relationship (Hughes 2002). This chapter has revealed that Porter's (1990; 1998) cluster concept is a relevant paradigm through which to study cultural tourism. Rural and regional parts of Ireland have a distinct musical and cultural identity that has have helped foster cultural tourism. The clusters enjoy advantages which include sophisticated local demand; growth in arts infrastructure; presence of networks; emergence of related and supporting firms; strong community culture; institutional involvement and private sector leadership. There seems to be little doubt that cultural tourism gives rise to social and business opportunities in small communities.

# Acknowledgements

This study was sponsored by Fáilte Ireland under the Fáilte Ireland Fellowship Scheme 2006/7.

# Notes

1  This state organization promotes the socio-economic development of the islands and Irish-speaking areas in Ireland and it provides 'hard' support in the form of grant-aid and equity but also 'soft' support such as marketing, training and brand-building, in order to develop the tourism economy.
2  Comhaltas Ceoltóirí Éireann, founded in 1951, established numerous branches for music education in Ireland. As a result, expert tuition in dance and music was available to all. It is also known for hosting the *feis cheoil* or music festival. The Fleadh Cheoil na hÉireann (the All-Ireland Fleadh) is the culmination of several county and regional competitions (Fleming 2004).

# References

Baerenholdt, J. and Haldrup, M. (2006) 'Mobile networks and place-making in cultural tourism: staging Viking ships and rock music in Roskilde', *European Urban and Regional Studies* 13(3): 209–24.

Bathelt, H. A., Malmberg, A. and Maskell, A. P. (2004) 'Clusters and knowledge: local buzz, global pipelines and the process of knowledge creation', *Progress in Human Geography* 28(1): 31–56.

Birkinshaw, J. and Hood, N. (2000) 'Characteristics of foreign subsidiaries in industry clusters', *Journal of International Business Studies* 31(1): 141–54.

Braunerhjelm, P. (2005) 'Madonna and the music miracle: the genesis and evolution of a globally competitive cluster', Working Paper No. 29, Stockholm: Centre of Excellence for Science and Innovation Studies (CESIS), The Royal Institute of Technology.

Brokensha, P. and Guldberg, H. (1992) *Cultural Tourism in Australia*. Canberra: Department of Arts, Sports and the Environment and Territories.

Brown, K. G. and Geddes, R. (2007) 'Resorts, culture, and music: the Cape Breton tourism cluster', *Tourism Economics* 13(1): 129–41.

Bull, A. (1995) *The Economics of Travel and Tourism*. Melbourne: Longmans.

Campbell, C. (1989) *The Romantic Ethic and the Spirit of Modern Consumerism*. London: Blackwell.

Clancy, P., O'Malley, G., O'Connell, L. and Van Egeraat, C. (2001) 'Industry clusters in Ireland: an application of Porter's model of national competitive advantage to three sectors', *European Planning Review* 9(1): 7–28.

Cooke, P. (2006) 'Building a partnership model to manage Irish heritage: a policy tools analysis', *Irish Journal of Management* 27(2): 75–97.

Etzkowitz, H. and Leydesdorff, L. (2000) 'The dynamics of innovation: from National Systems and Mode 2 to a triple helix of university-industry-government relations', *Research Policy* 29(2): 109–23.

Fleming, R. (2004) 'Resisting cultural standardization: Comhaltas Ceoltóirí Éireann and the revitalization of traditional music in Ireland', *Journal of Folklore Research* 41(2/3): 227–57.

Florida, R. (2002) *The Rise of the Creative Class – And How It's Transforming Work, Leisure, Community, and Everyday Life*. New York: Basic Books.

Florida, R. and Mellander, C. (2008) 'Music clusters: a preliminary analysis', Working Paper, Toronto: Martin Prosperity Institute, Joseph L. Rotman School of Management, University of Toronto.

Getz, D. (1991). *Festivals, Special Events and Tourism*. New York: Van Nostrand Reinhold.

Getz, D. and Brown, G. (2006) 'Benchmarking wine tourism development: the case of the Okanagan Valley, British Columbia, Canada', *International Journal of Wine Marketing* 18(2): 78–97.

Gibson, C. (2002) 'Migration, music and social relations on the NSW Far North Coast', *Transformations* 2: 1–15.

Gibson, C. and Connell, J. (2003) *On the Road Again: Music and Tourism*. Clevedon: Channel View.

Hall, C. M. (2005) 'Rural wine and food tourism cluster network development', in D. Hill, I. Kirkpatrick and M. Mitchell (eds) *Rural Tourism and Sustainable Business*. Clevedon: Channel View, pp. 149–64.

Hall, C. M. and Weiler, B. (1992) 'Introduction: what's special about special interest tourism?', in B. Weiler and C. M. Hall (eds), *Special Interest Tourism*. London: Belhaven Press, pp. 1–15.

Herbert, D. T. (1999) 'Artistic and literary places in France as tourist attractions', *Tourism Management* 17(2): 77–85.

Hirsch, P. (2000) 'Cultural industries revisited', *Organisation Science* 11(3): 356–61.

Hirschman, E. C. and Holbrook, M. B. (1982) 'The experiential aspects of consumption: consumer fantasies, feelings and fun', *Journal of Consumer Research* 9(2): 132–40.

Hughes, H. (2002) 'Culture and tourism: a framework for further analysis', *Managing Leisure*,7(3): 164–75.

Hurley, A., Archer, B. and Fletcher, J. (1994) 'The economic impact of European Community grants for tourism in the Republic of Ireland', *Tourism Management* 15(3): 203–11.

Holcomb, B. (1999) 'Marketing cities for tourism', in D. Judd and S. Fainstein (eds) *The Tourist City*. New Haven, CT: Yale University Press, pp. 54–70.

Ivanovic, M. (2009) *Cultural Tourism*. Johannesburg: Juta and Company Limited.

Jackson, J. and Murphy, P. (2002) 'Tourism destinations as clusters: analytical experiences from the New World', *Tourism and Hospitality Research* 4(1): 36–52.

Kearns, T. and Taylor, B. (2003) *A Touchstone for the Tradition: The Willie Clancy Summer School*. Dingle: Brandon Publications.

Kennelly, K. (2005) 'Arts tourism', unpublished MBA thesis, Dublin Institute of Technology.

Kneafsey, M. (2002) 'Cultural geographies in practice: sessions and gigs: tourism and traditional music in North Mayo, Ireland', *Cultural Geographics* 9(3): 354–8.

Lafferty, G. and van Fossen, A. (2005) 'The role of clusters in preventing tourism decline: a conceptual and empirical examination', *International Journal of Services Technology and Management* 6(2): 142–52.

Lampel, J., Lant, T. and Shamsie, J. (2000) 'Balancing act: learning from organizing practices in cultural industries', *Organisation Science* 11(3): 263–9.

Lindequist, P. and Power, D. (2002) 'Putting Porter into practice? Practices of regional cluster building: evidence from Sweden', *European Planning Studies* 10(6): 685–704.

Mackellar, J. (2006) 'Conventions, festivals and tourism: exploring the network that binds', *Journal of Convention and Event Tourism* 8(2): 45–56.

Malmberg, A. and Maskell, P. (2002) 'The elusive concept of localization economies: towards a knowledge-based theory of spatial clustering', *Environment and Planning* 34(3): 429–49.

Markusen, A. (1996) 'Sticky places in slippery space: a typology of industrial districts', *Economic Geography* 72(3): 293–313.

Marshall, A. (1890). *Principles of Economics*. London: Macmillan.

Martin, R. and Sunley, P. (2003) 'Deconstructing clusters: chaotic concept or policy panacea?' *Journal of Economic Geography* 3(1): 5–35.

Michael, E. (2003) 'Tourism micro-clusters', *Tourism Economics* 9(2): 133–45.

—— (2007a) 'Micro-clusters: antiques, retailing and business practice', in E. Michael (ed.) *Micro-Clusters and Networks: The Growth of Tourism*. Oxford: Elsevier, pp. 63–78.

—— (2007b) 'Development and cluster theory' in E. Michael (ed.) *Micro-Clusters and Networks: The Growth of Tourism*. Oxford: Elsevier, pp. 21–32.

Music Board of Ireland (2002) *The Economic Significance of the Irish Music Industry*. Dublin: Music Board of Ireland.

Nicholls, J. (2000). 'Introduction', in J. Nicholls and S. J. Owens (eds) *A Babel of Bottles: Drink, Drinkers and Drinking Places in Literature*. Sheffield: Sheffield Academic Press, pp. 9–20.

Nordin, S. (2003) 'Tourism clustering and innovation: paths to economic growth and development', Working Paper, European Tourism Research, Oestersund: Mid-Sweden University.

Novelli, M., Schmitz, B. and Spencer, T. (2006) 'Networks, clusters and innovation in tourism: a UK experience', *Tourism Management* 27(6): 1141–52.

Paleo, I. O. and Wijnberg, N. M. (2006) 'Classification of popular music festivals: a typology of festivals and an inquiry into their role in the construction of music genres', *International Journal of Arts Management* 8(2): 50–81.

Porter, M. E. (1990) *The Competitive Advantage of Nations*. London: Macmillan.

—— (1998) 'Clusters and the new economics of competition', *Harvard Business Review* 76(6): 77–90.

Putnam, R. (1994) *Making Democracy Work: Civic Traditions in Modern Italy*. Princeton, NJ: Princetown University Press.

Quinn, B. (2006) 'Problematising festival tourism:arts festivals and sustainable development in Ireland', *Journal of Sustainable Tourism* 14(3): 288–306.

Richards, G. (1994) *Cultural Tourism in Europe*. Wallingford: CABI.

Rosenfeld, S. (2004) 'Art and design as competitive advantage: a creative enterprise cluster in Western United States', *European Planning Studies* 12(6): 891–905.

Rosson, P. (2003) 'Clusters and innovation in biotechnology', paper presented at the 19th Industrial Marketing and Purchasing Conference. Lugano, Switzerland, 4–6 September 2003.

Seaton, A. V. (1999) 'Book towns as tourism developments in peripheral areas', *International Journal of Tourism Research* 1(5): 389–94.

Smith, S. (2001) 'Irish traditional music in a modern world', *New Hibernia Review* 5(2): 111–25.

Strachan, R. and Leonard, M. (2004) 'A musical national: protection, investment and branding in the Irish music industry', *Irish Studies Review* 12(1): 39–49.

Towner, J. (1984) 'The Grand Tour: sources and a methodology for an historical study of tourism', *Tourism Management* 5(3): 215–22.

Údarás na Gaeltachta (2005) *Strategic Development Plan 2005–10*. Dublin: Údarás na Gaeltachta.

Urry, J. (1990) *The Tourist Gaze*. London: Sage.

World Tourism Organization (2004) *Technical Seminar on Cultural Tourism and Poverty Alleviation*. Siem Reap, Cambodia: 41st Meeting of the WTO Commission for East Asia and the Pacific.

Zeppel, H. and Hall, C. M. (1991) 'Selling art and history: cultural heritage and tourism', *The Journal of Tourism Studies* 2(1): 29–44.

# Conclusion

*Donald V. L. Macleod*

## Introduction

Striving for sustainable tourism in rural Europe is of major importance for numerous reasons which include the impact of tourism on the natural environment, the economy, local and national culture, and society. Diverse approaches towards tourism development have been and continue to be taken by individuals, grass-roots organizations, local community leaders and small businesses, as well as supra-national organizations, nation-state organizations, regional councils, and multinational corporations. This book covers a wide spectrum of places and people involved in sustainable tourism and its development. It deals with contemporary examples as well as issues which are often seen as increasingly vital, partly due to the nature of tourism as an industry with its rapid growth and multiple impacts, and partly due to the wider, external circumstances relating to economies, political problems and global preoccupations including climate change, energy sources, food supplies and latterly, credit supply and employment. Very few things, if any, in the world of tourism happen in isolation and the repercussions of tourism activity are felt at greater distances the more interconnected the world becomes. As a consequence of the above, this book with its focus on rural Europe is of relevance to other continents and to non-rural settings, including cities. Thus, some models, examples and themes explored in the chapters here, while being absolutely pertinent to the specified examples, could also be conceivably used to consider different situations elsewhere; the experience of cities in Asia, for example.

## State-driven versus local community development

This book has been organized in a way which aims to reflect the rough division between types of approaches to development known as 'top-down' (the state and development) and 'bottom-up' (the local community and development) also referred to as 'grass-roots' development. Inevitably case studies have been chosen to comply with this division, but it becomes apparent on examination and consideration that the division is not always clear-cut, and that there are more often than not instances where both the local community and the state are involved in development (Telfer and Sharpley 2008). This relationship may develop over time according to the scale of the project, or the level of urgency from the perspective of local community-led initiatives. In Part II, dealing with the state-driven projects, it is often reported that planners should engage with the community, at least soliciting their views on tourism development, if not including their 'local knowledge' and where possible employing their skills as workers. The cases examined in Part III are relatively small in scale, but nevertheless crucial to the communities involved, and illustrate that such communities are often in need of financial and perhaps professional support from state organizations.

## General themes emerging

The following themes have recurred in chapters throughout the volume and they are worthwhile mentioning and emphasizing specifically as they have general application for many regions where tourism development is taking place, and these will help to give an insight into the current state of tourism development in rural Europe.

- *The uniqueness of the destination*: The importance of the destination having unique or distinctive qualities is emphasized in numerous chapters. This quality of uniqueness is an asset that needs to be protected, for example, by EU policies as discussed by Leslie in Chapter 3. A unique aspect can be developed through work on heritage at the tourist destination as argued by Koutsoukos and Brookes (Chapter 6). Such is the value of uniqueness that authorities need to be aware that pressure from increasing visitor numbers may threaten the asset if it is based on the natural environment or is a fragile part of the cultural built heritage as Hall notes in Chapter 5 with his examples from the Baltic States.
- *The identity of the destination*: There is a close relationship between the uniqueness and the identity of a destination. Hall, in Chapter 5, notes that good management enhances and gives meaning to the identity of a region. Førde (Chapter 13) argues that change can lead to multi-vocal identities. Moreover, Koutsoukos and Brooks in Chapter 6 draw attention to the fact that people shape the identities of places. In his examination of development in Bosnia-Herzegovina and Palestine, Selwyn (Chapter 9) observed that cultural identity, related to personal identity, is a primary motivation for pilgrimage and tourism. Personal identity associated with cultural practices and linked to regional identity emerged as an important part of being a farmer in Scotland as examined by Gillespie in Chapter 14. This further suggests the common link between regional identity and the resident population.
- *Planning and policy at the destination*: Lessons from the Baltic, as argued by Hall in Chapter 5, show that there needs to be a strong policy

for tourism which integrates with other relevant management plans. Koutsoukos and Brookes (Chapter 6) suggest there is a need for planning and policies to deal with the UK coastal tourism. In Lithuania, planning is lacking and urgently needed for a host of problems as Armaitienė, Jones and Povilanskas observe in Chapter 11. Policymakers should be leaders, in the opinion of McCarthy (Chapter 16). MacLellan (Chapter 8) in his assessment of DMOs in Scotland, notes the importance of providing leadership in the region for tourism management and marketing. Overall, the chapters indicate a general need for planning at the destination, a point which is made by Selwyn (Chapter 9) when referring to the lack of a national form of legislation or strategy in Bosnia-Herzegovina.

- *Linkages at the destination*: Links within the destination community are seen as important for its development by Førde in Chapter 13, they are also important in terms of connections between the rural community and the city as Hall (Chapter 5) points out in his study of peripheral attractions and their relations with nearby cities in the Baltic States. McCarthy in Chapter 16 suggests that policy-makers need to be proactive in enhancing links for development. Hall, Hultman and Gössling in Chapter 2 indicate the importance of links for rural development using the concept 'social capital' to describe positive links creating working networks.

- *Different points of view*: Local points of view are highly relevant and need to be ascertained and included in decisions concerning tourism. In Chapter 1, Butler suggests that people are not always in favour of tourism development in their region; and Macleod (Chapter 7) believes that local viewpoints should be embraced when planning for tourism development. Bussell and Suthers (Chapter 15) suggest that even the viewpoints of non-customers need to be understood in order to possibly expand and enhance service offerings to include them in future operations. In Ireland, McCarthy (Chapter 16) found that a shared vision and understanding were needed for successful cultural tourism. However, it should be appreciated that there are often multiple views on development held by different individuals in the smallest of communities as mentioned by Macleod in Chapter 7. Such varied views need to be fed into marketing decisions and tourism development plans, according to Førde (Chapter 13). These multiple views are important to ascertain and include in decisions concerning tourism, and should be embraced in tourism planning for development as argued by Chaperon and Bramwell in Chapter 10. However, McCarthy (Chapter 16) suggests that a shared vision and understanding are needed for successful cultural tourism.

- *The complexity of tourism issues*: As noted above, local views are often multiple and conflicting, even in small rural communities. Butler, in Chapter 1, shows how tourism is diversifying in terms of activity and impact in rural areas, and he illustrates the complexity of economic impact brought about by second homes and the trend for ex-tourists to retire in destinations. The *ad hoc* nature of the growth of some businesses and service involvement also adds to the unpredictability on the ground as enterprises grow, demonstrated by Watkins in Chapter 12. Furthermore, there is a complex mix of tourism types in even the smallest destinations as Macleod (Chapter 7) demonstrates. Tourism development is a complex process involving negotiation, competition, different values and identities as Førde explains in Chapter 13. Chaperon and Bramwell (Chapter 10) also emphasize the variety of views, contradictions and complexity of factors in decision-making. Moreover, the broader political, social and cultural environment, including ethnicity, adds an additional layer of complexity in some situations as exemplified in Selwyn's chapter on Bosnia-Herzegovina and Palestine (Chapter 9).

- *A holistic approach to rural development*: A holistic approach which includes various aspects of society and culture is advocated by Macleod (Chapter 7) regarding the involvement of tourism as an industry in development plans and as part of broader regional development. According to McCarthy (Chapter 16), the involvement of the local community should be promoted in destination development. Armaitienė, Jones and Povilanskas (Chapter 11) argue that tourism development should be perceived as impacting on many aspects of the community. All stakeholders should be involved in decision-making, as Bussell and Suthers suggest in Chapter 15. Hall, Hultman and Gössling (Chapter 2) use the concept of mobility to help explain the interconnected relationship between urban and rural groupings and emphasize the need to embed tourism as a development tool into broader issues relating to service provision and the role of the state.

## The rural dimension

The above themes have recurred in chapters in this volume, and it is suggested that they are relevant to rural regions beyond Europe and probably to some urban regions undergoing tourism development. There are, moreover, distinctive features of rural regions which are highly relevant for sustainable tourism development and these include the following: problems associated with being peripheral, including access; the lack of economic diversification; demographic weaknesses regarding the working population such as a lack of appropriate workers, an ageing population and the corresponding need for social support; in many cases a distinctive cultural tradition based on a primary industry; and the vulnerability of the natural environment to physical threats including pollution, disease and disaster. These features are mentioned in the above chapters, and give tourism in rural areas a distinctly critical role because of the inherently sensitive aspects of the rural scenario. Equally, rural regions will be sensitive to events beyond the control of managers and others because of the global and external nature of these phenomena. The next section examines such events.

## Broader issues

As mentioned in the Introduction to this chapter, interconnectedness is a feature of tourism as a phenomenon, and improving links and connections is part of successful sustainable tourism development. Consequently, it is necessary to be aware of and react to, where possible, events occurring beyond the boundary or outside the control of the destination; this includes those phenomena termed 'external' forces or impacts (Mason 2003: 172) and it is worthwhile considering the degree to which those involved in the development of tourism destinations should be aware of them. Globalization has led to a massive increase of linkages and exchange throughout the world, involving travel, economic exchange; the flow of goods, ideas, people and information (see Waters 1995). The economic downturn in 2008, including the 'credit crunch' limitation on credit accessibility, is an example of a global catastrophe impacting tourism in many ways, such as limiting international tourist numbers, increasing some domestic tourism and creating cash-flow problems for businesses. Rural destinations may be particularly prone to suffer when national economies go into recession as their relative dependency on tourism is high, and the lack of alternative employment or source of revenue exposes their vulnerability.

In a similar vein to economic sensitivity, rural destinations will be vulnerable to climate change, another external factor which recurs as a theme in this book. With temperatures rising together with coastal water levels, food supplies and water supplies changing, the natural environment is threatened as a major attraction: coastal resorts may become submerged (the Maldives); coral reefs destroyed through changing water temperatures and acidification; communities are flooded due to increased and erratic rainfall (the English Lake District); and increased temperatures lead to hazards such as forest fires (the Canary Islands) and biodiversity loss. Rural destinations must be informed and aware of change to the climate and its potential repercussions.

These massive issues of globalization and climate change can only be dealt with by people through their behaviour and management of the situation. And this is where the topic of tourism development becomes particularly interesting because it represents human activity at its most frenetic and explicit, as well as the fact that the industry is extremely sensitive to change. Many of those characteristics of humanity which are most universally recognizable and possibly lamentable are displayed in the arena of tourism: self-interest, pleasure-seeking, fashion-led, cynical, intractable and unpredictable behaviour. As a result, tourism needs to be managed intelligently, sensitively and with abundant forethought. Policy and planning measures have been discussed in this book and the need for adequate management to achieve sustainable tourism development has been a regular feature of discussion. The drive to deal with common experiences related to problems such as pressures on carrying capacity, pollution, and issues concerning renewable energy supplies, recycling, as well as preparation for unknown occurrences including disease and terrorism, demands that well-educated and experienced professionals are required. This professional staff will also need to be capable of engaging with a variety of different stakeholder groups, and able to grasp the situation from a holistic perspective. As such, those educating and training staff need to include and recognize these demands and design courses accordingly.

## The cultural context of sustainable development

It is worth considering the cultural context in which sustainable tourism development takes place. By cultural context is meant the cultural and social environment including values, morals, beliefs, political influences, and ideas – all of which underpin behaviour (Lewis 1985). Clearly there is a diversity of interests and attitudes involved in decisions regarding tourism development as witnessed in the chapters above, and there may also be divergences between planners and groups at the destination where tourism is experienced. However, within Europe, it is likely that there are broad sets of cultural practices and perspectives which contrast with other groupings of people, in other continents or countries, such as Saudi Arabia or Burma, for example. These differences will relate partly to religious and political outlooks, and they will, moreover, impact on attitudes regarding tourism and its development, as well as approaches to sustainability (Swarbrooke 1999: 344–5).

Furthermore, there are ideas and concerns in general global currency which could persuade people to reduce or change their travel habits and stay in accommodation that is ecologically sustainable. These general trends in thinking, often related to practical reality such as economics or environmental conservation, help shape behaviour and influence the individual tourist and the policy-makers. We can see how the cultural context has shaped behaviour in the case studies above where European Union policy and the national governments' drive towards sustainable development, and distinctive local community behaviour also influence matters.

In an increasingly globalized world, where ideas circulate rapidly and the market for tourism becomes more competitive, the concept of sustainability has become ubiquitous; it is one of the major paradigms and preoccupations of the twenty-first century. However, the interpretation of sustainability, and the practical implementation of development differ widely and are subject to the cultural context (Richards and Hall 2000: 297). This collection gives an insight into a part of the world, Europe, which is important and influential for the tourism industry and the communities impacted by tourism, and as such offers us a crucial view of sustainable tourism development, one which is regionally focused, but which has relevance for the rest of the world.

## References

Lewis, I. M. (1985) *Social Anthropology in Perspective: The Relevance of Social Anthropology*, 2nd edn. Cambridge: Cambridge University Press.

Mason, P. (2003) *Tourism Impacts, Planning and Management*. Oxford: Elsevier.

Richards, G. and Hall, D. (2000) 'Conclusion', in G. Richards and D. Hall (eds) *Tourism and Sustainable Community Development*. London: Routledge, pp. 297–306.

Swarbrooke, J. (1999) *Sustainable Tourism Management*. Wallingford: CABI.

Telfer, D. J. and Sharpley, R. (2008) *Tourism and Development in the Developing World*. London: Routledge.

Waters, M. (1995) *Globalization*. London: Routledge.

# Index

| DATE DUE | RETURNED |
|---|---|
|  |  |
|  |  |
|  |  |
|  |  |
|  |  |
|  |  |
|  |  |
|  |  |
|  |  |
|  |  |
|  |  |
|  |  |
|  |  |
|  |  |